German Vocabulary

HANDBOOK

Joy Saunders

German Vocabulary Handbook

The Author:
Joy Saunders is an experienced teacher, schools inspector and educational consultant.

The Series Editor:
Christopher Wightwick is a former UK representative on the Council of Europe Modern Languages Project and principal Inspector of Modern Languages for England.

Other titles in the Berlitz Language Handbook Series:

French Grammar Handbook
German Grammar Handbook
Spanish Grammar Handbook
Italian Grammar Handbook
French Verb Handbook
German Verb Handbook
Spanish Verb Handbook
Italian Verb Handbook

French Vocabulary Handbook
German Vocabulary Handbook
Spanish Vocabulary Handbook

Copyright © 1994 Joy Saunders

Published by Berlitz Publishing Co., Ltd.,
Peterley Road, Oxford OX4 2TX

1st printing 1994

Printed in England by Clays, St Ives plc

CONTENTS

How to use this Handbook

C   *Appendices*

D   *Subject index*

How to use this Handbook

This Handbook is a carefully ordered work of reference covering all areas of German vocabulary and phrasing. It is based on the thesaurus structure of the Council of Europe's Threshold Level, expanded to include other major topics, especially in the fields of business, information technology and education. Unlike a dictionary, it brings together words and phrases in related groups. It also illustrates their usage with contextualized example sentences, often in dialogue form. This enables learners and users of the language to:

- refresh and expand their general knowledge of vocabulary;
- organize systematically revision for public examinations, using the word-groups to test their knowledge from German to English and *vice versa*;
- extend their knowledge of authentically German ways of saying things by studying the example sentences;
- support their speaking and writing on a given topic, when the logical arrangement of the sections will often prompt new ideas as well as supplying the means of expressing them.

THE STRUCTURE OF THE HANDBOOK

After the List of Contents, the Handbook is divided into four parts:

A Introduction: Word formation in German

A concise account of the ways in which German creates compound words and phrases in order to express more complex ideas. (For a more extensive treatment of this topic, see the Berlitz *German Grammar Handbook*.)

B The Topic Vocabularies

98 Vocabularies, grouped under 27 major areas of experience. Many Vocabularies are divided into a number of sections, so that words and phrases are gathered together into closely related groups. Almost all sections contain example sentences showing the vocabulary in use. Wherever it makes sense to do so, these sentences are linked together to form short narratives or dialogues which help to fix them in the memory.

C The Appendices

Lists of specific terms such as the names of countries or musical instruments. These would simply clutter up the main Vocabularies, but they are linked to them by clear cross-references. Each Appendix is numbered according to the Vocabulary to which it most closely relates.

D The Subject Index

An alphabetical index of topics and themes, enabling you to locate quickly the area you are interested in.

LOCATING THE RIGHT SECTION

The Handbook can be approached in two main ways.
• If you are not sure which topic will be best suited to your needs, start with the *List of Contents* on page iii. This will give you a general picture of the areas covered. You can then browse through the sections until you find the one you want.

• Alternatively, if you have a specific topic in mind, look it up in the *Subject Index* at the end of the book. This will take you directly to the relevant Vocabulary or Appendix. To help you find what you are looking for, topics are often listed more than once, under different headings. Within most sections there are cross-references to other, related areas.

A
INTRODUCTION

Word formation in German

One of the great strengths of German is its ability to combine or modify words so as to express new meanings. A knowledge of how this is done helps the learner to understand new language and to build up a wide vocabulary.

1 Nouns

> Berlitz *German Grammar Handbook* ch.19g

1a Many nouns are formed from the stem of strong verbs, using:

(a) the stem of the infinitive: **der Fall** 'fall', **der Schlaf** 'sleep';

(b) dropping the **-n** of the infinitive: **die Bitte** 'request' **die Hilfe** 'help', **die Lüge** 'lie';

(c) the simple past: **der Griff** 'grip', **der Klang** 'sounds';

(d) another vowel, often **-u-**: **der Schuß** 'shot', **der Fluß** 'river'.

Sometimes the connection is not very easy to see, but it is worth noting the link: **ankommen - die Ankunft** 'arrival', **ziehen - der Zug** 'train', 'draught', **gehen - der Gang** 'corridor', 'gait'.

1b Forming nouns with suffixes

Nouns are often formed by adding suffixes to other words. Note that suffixes may cause the preceding vowel to take an Umlaut, particularly if the suffix has a short **i** in it.

(i) Diminutives (with Umlaut):

-chen	**das Kätzchen**	kitten
-lein	**das Entlein**	duck

(ii) Other suffixes

-e	**die Größe** 'size', **die Ferne** 'distance'
-ei	**die Metzgerei** 'butcher's shop', **die Angeberei** 'boasting'
-er, ler	**der Bäcker** 'baker', **der Sportler** 'sportsman'
-ie	**die Harmonie** 'harmony', **die Philosophie** 'philosophy'
-in	*(female form)* **die Ärztin** 'woman doctor', **die Sportlerin** 'sportswoman'

-nis	die **Finsternis** 'darkness', **das Verhältnis** 'relationship'
-schaft	die **Eigenschaft** 'quality', **die Gesellschaft** 'society'
-sal	das **Schicksal** 'fate'
-tum	der **Reichtum** 'wealth', **das Christentum** 'Christianity'
-ung	die **Hoffnung** 'hope', **die Begegnung** 'meeting'
-heit, -(ig)keit	die **Schönheit** 'beauty', **die Tapferkeit** 'bravery', **die Tätigkeit** 'activity'

1c   Nouns formed with prefixes

Erz-	der **Erzbischof** 'archbishop'
Miß-	das **Mißverständnis** 'misunderstanding'
Un-	das **Unglück** 'misfortune'
Ur-	der **Urgroßvater** 'greatgrandfather', **der Urwald** 'primeval forest'

1d   Compound nouns

➤   Berlitz *German Grammar Handbook* 3b

Many nouns are formed by combining two or more words. With very few exceptions, they take the gender of the final part.

noun + noun	das **Rathaus** 'town hall'
noun + **s** + noun	die **Landungsbrücke** 'landing stage'
noun + **(e)n** + noun	das **Studentenheim** 'student hostel'
adjective + noun	das **Schwarzbrot** 'black bread'
verb stem + noun	das **Schlafzimmer** 'bedroom'
particle + noun	die **Umwelt** 'environment', **das Abteil** 'compartment' (but **der Teil** 'part')

1e   Adjectival nouns

➤   Berlitz *German Grammar Handbook* 24d

Many adjectives and present and past participles can be used as nouns. They start with a capital letter, but otherwise behave just like adjectives:

der Deutsche 'the German', **der Verletzte** 'the injured man',
die Fremde 'the stranger' (female);
ein Beamter 'official' (male), **eine Auszubildende** 'trainee' (female);
Deutsche, 'Germans';
etwas Interessantes 'something interesting'.

3

1f   *Verbal nouns*

The infinitive is often used as a noun, usually with a meaning similar to the English form in '-ing': **das Parken** 'parking', **das Schreiben** 'writing'.

2   *Genders & plurals*

➤ Berlitz *German Grammar Handbook* 20, 21

The gender and plural of a noun should be learned at the same time as the word.

The gender of nouns is shown in the word list by giving the definite article: **der** (masculine), **die** (feminine) or **das** (neuter). The article is given with most noun entries.

2a   There are four common plural endings: **-e**, **-er**, **-(e)n**, **-s**, but some words take no plural ending. Words with a stem vowel in **a**, **o**, or **u**, and no ending or **-e** in the plural, sometimes have an Umlaut on the stem vowel. Those with a plural in **-er** always take an Umlaut. The plural form is given with every noun entry.

2b   Other case endings are not shown, so remember to add:

(i) **-s** to the genitive singular of masculine and neuter nouns, eg **des Arms**;

(ii) **-(e)n** to the dative plural of all nouns not ending in **-n** or **-s**, eg **den Häusern**.

2c   *Weak masculine nouns*

➤ Berlitz *German Grammar Handbook* 22g(i)

A few nouns, usually ending in **-e** in the nominative singular, add **-n** or **-en** in every other case of the singular and in the plural: **der Junge, den Jungen, des Jungen, dem Jungen, die Jungen** etc.

Note that:

(i) many of these nouns refer to people or animals;

(ii) a large number of foreign nouns ending in **-and, -ant, -arch, -at, -ent, -ist, -krat, -loge** and **-nom** are also weak: **der Student, den Studenten; der Demokrat, den Demokraten;**

(iii) **Herr** takes **-n** in the singular and **-en** in the plural: **den Herrn, die Herren**;

d) a few masculine nouns ending in **-e** add **-n** in every case and also **-s** in the genitive singular: **der Gedanke, des Gedankens**; others include: **der Glaube, der Wille**. One neuter noun **das Herz** follows this pattern but has no ending in the accusative singular.

2d *Useful short cuts*

(i) many masculine nouns add **-e** or **⁼e: der Stuhl**, pl **Stühle**

(ii) many feminine nouns add **-(e)n**: **die Frau**, pl **Frauen**

(iii) many neuter nouns, mostly one-syllable, add **⁼er**: **das Haus**, pl **Häuser**.

(iv) masculine and neuter nouns ending in **-el**, **-en** or **-er** add no ending (other than the dative plural **-n** after **-el** and **-er**), but may take an Umlaut: **der Garten**, *pl* **Gärten**.

Some suffixes always take the same plural ending and are almost always linked to a particular gender:

Feminine:

(i) add **-en**: words ending in **-anz**, **-ei**, **-enz**, **-heit**, **-ie**, **-ik**, **-ion**, **-keit**, **-schaft**, **-tät**, **-ung**, **-ur**;

(ii) add **-nen**: words ending in **-in**.

Masculine:

(i) add no plural ending: words ending in **-ler**, **-ner**, **-er** (words formed from verbs);

(ii) add **-e**: words ending in **-an**, **-än**, **-är**, **-eur**, **-ich**, **-ig**, **-ling**, stressed **-or**;

(iii) add **-en**: words ending in **-and**, **-ant**, **-ent**, **-et**, **-graph**, **-ist**, **-krat**, **-loge**, **-nom**, unstressed **-or**;

(iv) words with the ending **-ismus** change it to **-ismen**.

Neuter:

(i) add no plural ending: words ending in **-chen**, **-lein**, **-sel**, **-tel**;

(ii) add **⁼er**: words ending in **-tum**;

(iii) add **-e**: words ending in **-at**, **-ett**, **-il**, **-ment**;

(iv) words with the ending **-um**: change **-um** to **-en** or **-a**.

3 Adjectives

3a Forming adjectives with suffixes

> Berlitz *German Grammar Handbook* 24

-bar '-able, -ible'

wunderbar	wonderful	**sichtbar**	visible

-en, -ern 'made of'

golden	golden	**hölzern**	wooden

-haft 'like a'

fehlerhaft	deficient	**vorteilhaft**	advantageous

-ig '-y'

staubig	dusty	**gütig**	kind

-isch '-ish',

identisch	identical	**kindisch**	childish

-lich '-ly, -able, -ish'

täglich	daily	**möglich**	possible
gelblich	yellowish		

-los '-less'

hilflos	helpless	**namenlos**	nameless
arbeitslos	unemployed		

-mäßig 'according to'

planmäßig	according to plan	**verhältnismäßig**	relatively

-sam 'having the quality of'

grausam	cruel	**ratsam**	advisable

-voll 'full'

sorgenvoll	anxious	**anspruchsvoll**	demanding
liebevoll	loving		

3b Adjectives formed with prefixes

The prefixes **un-** and **miß-** are used in the same way as with nouns:

unglücklich	unhappy	**mißverstanden**	misunderstood

3c Compound adjectives

Adjectives, like nouns, can be formed of two or more words. Only the last part adds endings:

blutarm	anaemic
wasserdicht	watertight
schwarzweiß	black and white

4 Formation of verbs

4a Verbs are often formed from nouns as below:

-(e)n (often with Umlaut) **der Trost - trösten** 'comfort', **der Gruß - grüßen** 'greet'

-ieren (common with new verbs) **marschieren** 'march', **konkurrieren** 'compete'

4b Verb families formed with prefixes and verbal particles.

German uses prefixes and particles to extend the meaning of basic verbs. For any one verb there may be an immense range of compound verbs, and of nouns and adjectives formed from these compounds. It is worth studying these word families to enlarge your vocabulary, e.g.:

er fällt	he falls	**er fällt hin**	he falls down
er überfällt	he attacks	**es verfällt**	it decays
der Fall	the fall		

Sometimes compounds develop figurative meanings or meanings only loosely linked with each other or the basic verb:

der Fall	case	**der Zufall**	chance
die Abfälle pl	rubbish	**es fällt ihm ein**	it occurs to him

These prefixes are always attached to the verb stem:

be-, emp-, ent-, er-, ge-, hinter-, miß-, ver-, zer-.

Particles are always placed in the final part of the sentence and are therefore often separated from the verb stem, e.g.:

particles from prepositions: **ab, an, aus, ein, mit, nach, vor, zu;**

compound particles: **hinunter, vorbei, durcheinander, davon;**

particles from other verbs, adverbs, adjectives or nouns: **stehen, spazieren, statt, fern.**

The following can be used either as prefixes or as particles:

durch-, über-, um-, unter-, wider-, wieder-.

For a fuller treatment of how the meaning of verbs can be modified or changed by the use of prefixes and particles, ▶Berlitz *German Grammar Handbook* 4e(iii) and 16e, and the Berlitz *German Verb Handbook*.

5   English cognates

German is rich in words which have a similar origin to English, or have been borrowed from English or other languages. Understanding can often be greatly helped by referring to the English.

5a   The following categories of words should be noted:

(i) identical spelling and meaning: **die Hand, der Computer**

(ii) similar spelling, and identical meaning; note some common consonant changes:

offen	open	**helfen**	help
der Pfeffer	pepper	**das Pfund**	pound
lassen	let	**essen**	eat
sitzen	sit	**das Herz**	heart
gut	good	**tun**	do
dies	this	**der Bruder**	brother
machen	make	**suchen**	seek
kommen	to come	**der Keller**	cellar
leben	live	**lieben**	love
der Schnee	snow	**schlafen**	sleep
der Tag	day	**der Weg**	way

(iii) similar or identical spelling but a different meaning:

Lust haben	to want (to do something), but not in the sexual sense
aktuell	present, modern
das Gymnasium	grammar school

(iv) loan translations from English or Latin stems:

der Buchmacher	bookmaker
das Mitleid	compassion
der Einfluß	influence

5b

Sometimes a word derived from an English or common international source exists alongside a word of German origin: **der Hörfunk, das Radio; der Fernsprecher, das Telefon; der Mittelpunkt, das Zentrum.** With recent introductions, particularly those relating to technology, the English/international form is usually preferred, especially in speech.

Conventions used in this Handbook

(i) Noun plurals

The plural of almost every word is indicated in brackets (except for adjectival nouns, where the plural depends on the presence of the article ►Berlitz *German Grammar Handbook* 24d):

Entry	*plural*
Arm(e)	**Arme**
Hand(¨e)	**Hände**
Haus(¨er)	**Häuser**
Garage(n)	**Garagen**
Auto(s)	**Autos**
Wagen(-)	**Wagen**
Garten(¨)	**Gärten**
Fluß (¨sse)	**Flüsse**
Zentrum (-en)	**Zentren**
Praktikum (-a)	**Praktika**
Ministerium (-ien)	**Ministerien**

For some nouns the plural is shown in full in the bracket:

Firma   **(Firmen)**

(ii) Feminine forms

Feminine forms ending in **-in** are not given in full. They are freely formed, and where they are in normal use they are indicated after the masculine form by **[-in]**:
der Lehrer(-) [-in] = **der Lehrer**, pl **die Lehrer** male teacher, **die Lehrerin**, pl **die Lehrerinnen** female teacher.
Masculine nouns ending in **-e**, drop this before adding **-in**:
der Zeuge, die Zeugin.

(iii) Cases

The cases taken by a preposition or verb are only indicated where there might be confusion.

(iv) Verbs

Verbs are given in the first or occasionally the third person in the word lists, so that the particle is always placed after the stem.
To avoid confusion, the particle is marked with an asterix, eg: **ich komme an*** 'I arrive'. To check the verb in the Berlitz *German Verb*

Handbook or a dictionary you need to find the infinitive, which will start with the particle, eg **ankommen**.

Where a verb is shown in the third person singular and there is a vowel change, the infinitive, without the particle, is shown in brackets: **es gibt** *(geben)*.

Abbreviations

acc	accusative
adj	adjective
adj/n	adjectival noun (plurals in **-e** or **-en**)
adv	adverb
conj	conjunction
dat	dative
etw.	**etwas**
fam	familiar form
gen	genitive
inf	infinitive
invar	invariable
jdn.	**jemanden** (accusative)
jdm.	**jemandem** (dative)
n	noun
pl	plural
pol	polite form
pop	popular form
sing	singular
sth	something
wk	weak masculine noun

Symbols

-	no ending: **Wagen(-)** = plural **Wagen**.
( )	plural ending or a part of a word which is optional: **ich (ver)traue**.
( )	the infinitive, where the third person singular entry shows a vowel change: **es gibt** *(geben)*
*	the particle is separable: **ich komme an***, infinitive **ankommen**.
/	a) alternatives in adjective endings: **dieser/e/es = dieser, diese, dieses**, **mein/e/-** = **mein, meine, mein** b) alternative word: **erst als/wenn** = **erst als** or **erst wenn**.
,	an alternative translation.
➤	a cross-reference to a Vocabulary or chapter.

B

VOCABULARY TOPICS

Functional words

Personal pronouns

	Nom	Acc	Gen	Dat
I	ich	mich	meiner	mir
you (fam)	du	dich	deiner	dir
he, it	er	ihn	seiner	ihm
she, it	sie	sie	ihrer	ihr
it	es	es	seiner	ihm
we	wir	uns	unser	uns
you (fam pl)	ihr	euch	euer	euch
you (pol)	Sie	Sie	Ihrer	Ihnen
they	sie	sie	ihrer	ihnen
one	man	einen	seiner	einem

Reflexive pronouns

	Acc	Dat
myself	mich	mir
yourself (fam)	dich	dir
himself	sich	sich
herself	sich	sich
itself	sich	sich
ourselves	uns	uns
yourselves (fam)	euch	euch
yourself/ves (pol)	sich	sich
themselves	sich	sich
oneself	sich	sich
each other	sich	sich

Interrogative pronouns

	Nom	Acc	Gen	Dat
who?	wer	wen	wessen	wem

which one? **welcher/e/es**
what? **was**

what sort of? *(sing)* **was für einer/e/es?**
what sort of? *(pl)* **was für welche?**

Relative pronouns who, that, which:

	Masc	Fem	Neut	Plur
Nom	der	die	das	die
Acc	den	die	das	die
Gen	dessen	der	dessen	deren
Dat	dem	der	dem	denen

what you say is true **das, was du sagst, stimmt**

Demonstrative pronouns

Demonstrative adjective/pronoun *this, this one, that one* :

	Masc	Fem	Neut	Plur
Nom	dieser	diese	dieses	diese
Acc	diesen	diese	dieses	diese
Gen	dieses	dieser	dieses	dieser
Dat	diesem	dieser	diesem	diesen

this **dies** *(invar)*
this **dieser/e/es**
this **der/die/das** *(stressed)*
this one **der/die/das** *(declined like relative pronoun)*
this one **dieser/e/es**
these (ones) **diese**
that **das (hier)** *(invar)*
that **jener/e/es**
those (ones) **jene**
that one **der/die/das, derjenige/diejenige/dasjenige** *(both parts decline)*
the one, which **der(jenige), der**
the same one **derselbe, dieselbe, dasselbe** *(both parts decline)*
the red one **der/die/das Rote**

such a one   **solch/so einer**
ones like that   **solche**

Indefinite pronouns

anybody   **irgend einer**
both (people)   **beide**
both (things)   **beides**
each one   **jeder/e/es**
everyone   **jeder/e/es**
everything   **alles**
everyone   **alle**
one   **einer/e/es**
one like that   **so einer**
one which   **einer, der**
none, not any   **keiner/e/es**
nobody   **keiner**
no-one   **niemand, keiner/e/es**
not a single one   **kein einziger**
nothing   **nichts** *(invar)*
a lot   **vieles**
quite a lot   **manches**
not much   **weniges**
someone/body   **jemand**
something   **etwas** *(invar)*
something else   **etwas anderes**
something good   **etwas Gutes**
some things   **einiges**

Stressed pronouns

it's me   **ich bin es, ich bin's**
it's us   **wir sind es, wir sind's etc**
it's he who   **er ist derjenige, der**
it's she who   **sie ist diejenige, die etc**

*Possessive pronouns (declining like **dieser**)*

mine   **meiner/e/es**
yours *(fam)*   **deiner/e/es**
his   **seiner/e/es**
hers   **ihrer/e/es**
its   **seiner/e/es**
ours   **unserer/e/es**
yours *(fam)*   **eu(e)rer/e/es**
yours *(pol)*   **Ihrer/e/es**
theirs   **ihrer/e/es**
ones   **seiner/e/es**

this is mine   **das hier ist meiner/meine/mein(e)s**
mine is better   **meiner/meine/meines ist besser**

*Possessive adjectives (declined like **ein**)*

my   **mein/e/-**
your *fam*   **dein/e/-**
his/its   **sein/e/-**
her/its   **ihr/e**
its   **sein/e/-**
our   **unser/e/-**
your *fam*   **euer/eu(e)re/euer**
your *pol*   **Ihr/e/-**
their   **ihr/e/-**
one's   **sein/e/-**

Determiners

DEFINITE ARTICLE *the*

	Masc	Fem	Neut	Plur
Nom	der	die	das	die
Acc	den	die	das	die
Gen	des	der	des	der
Dat	dem	der	dem	den

INDEFINITE ARTICLE *a(n)*, **kein** *not any*

	Masc	Fem	Neut	Plur
Nom	ein	eine	ein	keine
Acc	einen	eine	ein	keine
Gen	eines	einer	eines	keiner
Dat	einem	einer	einem	keinen

DEMONSTRATIVES

this, that   **der/die/das**
this   **dieser/e/es**
that   **jener/e/es**
that   **derjenige/diejenige/ dasjenige**
the same   **derselbe, dieselbe, dasselbe**
such a   **solcher/e/es, solch ein/e/-**

*Indefinite determiners, (declined like **ein** or **dieser**)*

a few   **wenige**
a couple/few   **ein paar** *(invar)*
a little   **ein bißchen, ein wenig** *(invar)*

all (of them) **alle**
all kinds of **allerlei, allerhand** *(invar)*
all sorts of **vielerlei** *(invar)*
all the same **einerlei** *(invar)*
any **irgendein/e/-**
any **irgendwelcher/e/es**
both **beide**
both (of them) **die beiden**
each **jeder/e (der beiden)**
every **jeder/e/es**
every child **alle Kinder**
many **viele**
many a **mancher/e/es, manch ein/e/-**
no **kein/e/-**
not any **kein/e/-**
several **mehrere**
some (of them) **einige**
two kinds of **zweierlei, usw.** *(invar)*

Question forms

how many **wieviele?**
how **wie?**
how much **wieviel?**
how many **wieviele?**
what **was?**
what kind of **was für ein/e/-?**
when **wann?**
where **wo?, wohin?, woher?**
which (one) **welcher/e/es?**
who **wer?**
whom **wen?**
to whom **wem?**
whose **wessen?**
why **warum?**

Logical relations

CO-ORDINATING CONJUNCTIONS
as well as **sowie**
or **oder**
and **und**
both ... and **sowohl ... als/wie**
but **aber**
either ... or **entweder ... oder**
for (because) **denn**
neither ... nor **weder ... noch**

not only ... but also **nicht (nur) ... sondern (auch)**
or alternatively **beziehungsweise**

SUBORDINATING CONJUNCTIONS
although **obgleich**
as **wie, da**
before **bevor, ehe**
after **nachdem**
especially as **zumal**
although **obwohl**
even though **trotzdem**
in case, if **falls**
unless **es sei denn, (daß)**
whenever **wenn**
as if **als ob**
as soon as **sobald**
as long as **solange**
as well as **sowohl**
as (since) **da**
as soon as **sobald**
because **weil**
even though **auch wenn**
if **wenn, ob**
in order that **damit**
not until **erst als/wenn**
provided that **wenn nur**
since *(time)* **seit(dem)**
since *(as)* **da**
so that **so daß, damit**
that **daß**
unless **wenn nicht**
until **bis**
when **als, wenn, wann**
whether **ob**
while/whereas **während**

(in order) to **um ... zu** +inf
instead of (doing) **(an)statt ... zu** +inf
without (doing) **ohne ... zu** +inf
apart from (doing) **außer ... zu** +inf

Adverbial expressions

about **etwa, ungefähr**
admittedly **allerdings**
again **wieder**
allegedly **angeblich**
almost **fast, beinahe**

also **auch**
by chance **zufällig**
certainly **bestimmt, doch**
entirely **ganz**
equally **gleich**
exactly **genau**
extremely **äußerst, höchst**
for that reason **darum, deshalb**
hardly **kaum**
hopefully **hoffentlich**
however **aber, jedoch**
in fact **zwar, tatsächlich**
in those days **damals**
just **eben, mal**
(like) **gern**
merely **bloß**
naturally **natürlich**
naturally **selbstverständlich**
no longer **nicht mehr**
not at all **keineswegs**
not at all **gar nicht**
not either **auch nicht**
not even **nicht einmal**
not **nicht**
only **nur, erst**
perhaps **vielleicht**
possibly **möglicherweise**
probably **wohl, wahrscheinlich**
quite **ganz**
rather **lieber**
really **ja, recht**
relatively **verhältnismäßig**
so **so**
then **denn, dann**
therefore, consequently **deshalb**
to be sure **zwar**
too **auch**
totally **durchaus**
very **sehr**

Prepositions

WITH ACCUSATIVE
against **gegen**
along **entlang**
at about **gegen**
by *(time)* **schon um, bis**

for **für**
round **um**
through **durch**
until **bis**
without **ohne**

WITH DATIVE
according to **nach**
after **nach**
ago **vor**
along **an ... entlang**
at the house of **bei**
beside **außer**
except for **außer**
from **von**
opposite **gegenüber**
out of **aus**
since (time) **seit**
to **zu, nach**
towards **nach, entgegen**
with **mit**

WITH DATIVE OR ACCUSATIVE
across **über**
apart from **neben**
at **an**
behind **hinter**
between **zwischen**
in **in**
in front of **vor**
next to **neben**
on **auf**
over **über**
to **an**
under **unter**

WITH GENITIVE
above **oberhalb**
because of **wegen**
below **unterhalb**
during **während**
in spite of **trotz**
inside **innerhalb**
instead of **anstatt**
not far from **unweit**
on both sides of **beiderseits**
outside **außerhalb**
this side of **diesseits**

② Where? – position & movement

2a Position

about   **ungefähr, circa**
above   **über** +acc/dat
 above *(adv)* **oben, nach oben**
across   **über** +acc/dat
 across there   **da drüben**
after   **nach** +dat
against   **gegen** +acc
ahead *(adv)* **vorne, nach vorne**
ahead of   **vor** +acc/dat
along   **entlang** +acc, **an** +dat
among   **unter** +acc/dat
anywhere   **irgendwo**
around *(adv)* **umher/herum**
 around in the garden   **im Garten umher**
as far as   **bis zu** +dat
at   **an** +acc/dat
 at home   **zu Hause**
 at school   **in der Schule**
 at work   **bei der Arbeit**
back   **die hintere Seite(n)**
 at the back *(adv)* **hinten**
 at the back of   **hinter** +acc/dat
 to the back   **nach hinten**
backwards   **rückwärts, nach hinten**
before   **vor** +acc/dat
 before *(adv)* **vorher**
behind   **hinter** +acc/dat
 behind *(adv)* **hinten**
below   **unter** +acc/dat
 below   **unterhalb** +gen
 below *(adv)* **unten, (nach) unten**
beside   **neben** +acc/dat
between   **zwischen** +acc/dat
beyond   **jenseits** +gen
bottom   **der Grund, der Boden, der Fuß**
 at the bottom (of)   **unten (in**

 +dat)
centre/center   **die Mitte(n), das Zentrum (-en)**
 in the centre/center   **in der Mitte, mitten in** +acc/dat
direction   **die Richtung(en)**
 in the direction of Bonn   **Richtung Bonn**
distance   **die Entfernung(en)**
 in the distance   **in der Ferne**
distant   **fern**
down   **hinab, hinunter** +acc
 down there   **dort unten**
 downstairs   **(nach) unten**
edge   **der Rand(̈-er)**
 at the edge   **am Rande**
end   **das Ende(n)**
 I end   **ich beende**
 at the end   **am Schluß**
everywhere   **überall**
far   **weit, fern**
 far away (from)   **weit weg/entfernt (von** +dat)
first   **erst**
 first (of all)   **zuerst**
 I am first   **ich komme als Erste(r)**
for   **für** +acc
forward(s)   **vorwärts**
from   **von** +dat
front   **der vordere Teil(e)**
 at the front   **vorn(e)**
 I am in front   **ich stehe an der Spitze**
 in front of   **vor** +acc/dat
 to the front   **nach vorn**
here   **hier**
 here and there   **hie und da**
in   **in** +acc/dat
 in there   **da drinnen**

inside *(adv)* **drinnen**
   inside **innerhalb** +gen
into **in** +acc
last *(adj)* **der/die/das letzte**
   last of all **der/die/das allerletzte**
   last of all *(adv)* **zu allerletzt**
   I am last **ich stehe hinten**
left *(adj)* **der/die/das linke**
   the left **die linke Seite**
   on the left **links**
   to the left **nach links**
middle **die Mitte(n)**
   in the middle (of) **mitten (in** +acc/dat)
I move **ich bewege mich**
movement **die Bewegung(en)**
near **neben** +acc/dat
near(by) **in der Nähe, nebenbei**
neighbourhood/neigborhood **die Nachbarschaft**
   in the neighbourhood/ neigborhood of **in der Nähe von** +dat
next *(adj)* **der/die/das nächste**
   next *(adv)* **daneben, zunächst, dann**
   next to **neben** +acc/dat, **dicht bei** +dat
nowhere **nirgendwo**
on **auf** +acc/dat
onto **auf** +acc
opposite **gegenüber** +dat
out of **aus** +dat
   out there **dort draußen**
outside *(adv)* **draußen**
   outside **außerhalb** +gen

over **über** +acc/dat
   over there **dort drüben**
   over where **da drüben, wo**
past **an** +dat **vorbei**
right *(adj)* **der/die/das rechte**
   the right **die rechte Seite**
   on the right **rechts**
   to the right **nach rechts**
round/around **um** +acc
   round/around the tree **um den Baum herum**
side **die Seite(n)**
   at the side **an der Seite**
   at both sides of **beiderseits** +gen/**von** +dat
I am situated **ich befinde mich**
somewhere **irgendwo**
there **dort, da**
   there, where **dort, wo**
to **zu** +dat, **an** +acc, **nach** +dat
top **die Spitze(n)**
   top *(of mountain)* **der Gipfel(-)**
   at the top **oben auf der Spitze/dem Gipfel**
   on top *(adv)* **oben**
   to the top **nach oben**
towards **nach** +dat, **auf** +acc, **zu** +dat
under **unter** +acc/dat
up **hinauf** +acc
   up here/there **hier/dort oben**
upstairs *(adv)* **(nach) oben**
where? **wo?**
where from? **woher?**
where to? **wohin?**
with **mit** +dat

We are going to London.	**Wir fahren nach London.**
He is going to work.	**Er geht zur Arbeit.**
We fly to the States.	**Wir fliegen in die USA.**
He walked to the front.	**Er ging nach vorne.**
She goes to school everyday.	**Sie geht jeden Tag in die Schule.**
He went to the door.	**Er ging an die Tür.**
I am going home.	**Ich fahre nach Hause.**

2b Directions & location

Directions

atlas **der Atlas(se/Atlanten)**
compass **der Kompaß (-sse)**
on the corner **an der Ecke**
east **der Osten**
   east *(adj)* **Ost-, östlich**
   in the east **im Osten**
   to the east **nach Osten**
   east of **östlich von**
first left **die erste links**
first right **die erste rechts**
floor **die Etage(n)**
   on the first floor **in der ersten Etage**
the furthest *(adj)* **der/die/das weitentfernteste**
at the junction **an der Kreuzung**
Keep left **Links halten!**
Keep right **Rechts halten!**
latitude **die Breite(n)**
location **die Lage(n), die Positionsbestimmung(en)**
longitude **die Länge(n)**

map **die Karte(n)**
2 miles from here **2 Meilen von hier**
the nearest *(adj)* **die nahegelegendste/nächste**
north **der Norden**
   north *(adj)* **Nord-, nördlich**
   in the north **im Norden**
   to the north **nach Norden**
northeast **der Nordosten**
   northeast *(adj)* **nordöstlich**
northnortheast **der Nordnordosten**
northwest **der Nordwesten**
northnorthwest **der Nordnordwesten**
point of the compass **die Himmelsrichtung(en)**
second right **die zweite rechts**
south **der Süden**
   south *(adj)* **Süd-, südlich**
   in the south **im Süden**
   to the south **nach Süden**

The distance from there to Bonn is about 100 kilometres/kilometers. Look on the map. You go north(wards). | **Die Entfernung von dort nach Bonn beträgt circa 100 Kilometer. Sehen Sie auf der Karte. Man geht nach Norden.**

To the south of the wood you can see the church spire. | **Südlich vom Wald erblickt man den Kirchturm.**

– Are you lost? – I am looking for the tourist office. Is there a bank nearby? | **– Haben Sie sich verlaufen/verfahren? – Ich suche das Touristenbüro. Gibt es hier in der Nähe eine Bank?**

Do you know your way in the town centre/center? | **Kennen Sie sich in der Stadtmitte aus?**

Can you find your way? | **Können Sie sich zurechtfinden?**

southeast **der Südosten**
southsoutheast **der Südsüdosten**
southwest **der Südwesten**
southsouthwest **der Südsüdwesten**
straight ahead **gerade (da)vor, geradeaus**
third left **die dritte links**
this way **hier entlang**
west **der Westen**
    west *(adj)* **West-, westlich**
    in the west **im Westen**
    to the west **nach Westen**

Location & existence

I am **ich bin**

there is **es gibt *(geben)*** +acc
there isn't (any) **es gibt *(geben)* keinen/-e/-**
I become **ich werde**
I have got/I have **ich habe, ich besitze**
I exist **ich existiere, ich bestehe**
existence **die Existenz, das Dasein**
I possess **ich besitze**
possession **der Besitz** *(no pl)*, **das Besitztum(-̈er)**
present **anwesend**
    I am present **ich bin da/ zugegen**
    I am present at **ich bin bei** +dat

Some contracted forms

at the **an das → ans**	in the **in dem → im**
at/by the **an dem → am**	into the **in das → ins**
by the **bei dem → beim**	onto the **auf das → aus**
from the **von dem → vom**	to the **zu der → zur**
	to the **zu dem → zum**

The river is not far away - about 1 km from our house.

Der Fluß ist nicht weit weg/entfernt - ungefähr einen Kilometer von unserem Hause.

Opposite the houses is the church and nearby are the shops/stores.

Den Häusern gegenüber befindet sich die Kirche und dicht daneben sind die Geschäfte.

– Who's that? – It's me.

– Wer ist da? – Ich bin es/bin's.

– How many children are present?
– There are 25. Five of them are at home.

– Wieviele Kinder sind zugegen?
– Es sind 25. Fünf von ihnen sind zu Hause.

Is there any cake? Are there still any biscuits/cookies?

Gibt's Kuchen? Sind noch Plätzchen da?

I have been to London. I was at a concert.

Ich war in London. Ich war bei einem Konzert/Ich bin ins Konzert gegangen.

➤ MOVEMENT 2c; UNITS OF LENGTH 4a

2c Movement

I arrive   **ich komme an***
I bring   **ich bringe (mit*)**
by car   **mit dem Auto**
I carry   **ich trage**
I climb *(intr)*   **ich steige, ich klettere**
  I climb *(tr)*   **ich besteige**
I come   **ich komme**
  I come along too   **ich komme mit***
I creep   **ich krieche**
I drive   **ich fahre**
  I drive on the right   **ich fahre rechts**
I fall   **ich falle, ich stürze**
  I fall down   **ich falle um***
I follow   **ich folge** +dat
I go   **ich gehe**
  I go along too   **ich gehe mit***
  I go for a walk   **ich gehe spazieren***
I go (by vehicle)   **ich fahre**
I hike   **ich wandere**
I hurry   **ich eile**
  I hurry up   **ich beeile mich**
I jump   **ich springe**
I leave   **ich fahre ab***
  I leave sth   **ich verlasse etw.**
I march   **ich marschiere**
I move   **ich bewege mich**
on foot   **zu Fuß**

I pass   **ich gehe an** +dat **vorbei**
  I pass *(in car)*   **ich überhole**
I pull   **ich ziehe**
I push   **ich stoße**
I put (flat)   **ich lege**
  I put (into)   **ich tue, ich stecke**
  I put (onto)   **ich setze**
  I put (upright)   **ich stelle**
I ride   **ich fahre**
  I ride *(a horse)*   **ich reite**
I run   **ich laufe**
  I run away   **ich laufe weg***
I rush   **ich stürze (mich)**
I sit up   **ich setze mich gerade**
I slip   **ich rutsche aus***
I stand   **ich stehe**
  I stand still   **ich bleibe stehen***
I step/come/go   **ich trete**
I stop   **ich halte, ich bleibe stehen***
straight   **gerade**
  straight ahead   **geradeaus**
I stroll   **ich schlendere, ich bummele**
I take   **ich nehme, ich bringe**
I turn   **ich biege (ein*)**
  I turn left   **ich biege nach links**
  I turn off   **ich biege ab***
  I turn round   **ich drehe mich um***
  I turn to so   **ich wende mich an** +acc

I am going by car but some of us will go on foot. John is going by bike.

Ich fahre mit dem Auto, aber einige von uns werden zu Fuß gehen. John fährt mit dem Rad.

I will take you as far as the river. Then you must get out and walk.

Ich bringe Sie bis zum Fluß. Dann müssen Sie aussteigen und zu Fuß gehen.

We go down the hill, along the river, and then turn left towards the woods.

Wir gehen den Berg hinunter, am Fluß entlang und biegen dann nach links ab, auf den Wald zu.

walk   der Gang(-̈e), der
        Spaziergang(-̈e)
I walk   **ich gehe**
I wander   **ich wandere**
way   der Weg(e)

Here & there

Come here!   **Komm her!***
I go there   **ich gehe hin***
I rush there   **ich stürze hin***
I travel there   **ich fahre hin***

In & out

Come in!   **Herein!**
I come in   **ich komme herein***
I come here   **ich komme (hier)her***
I come out   **ich komme heraus***
I go in   **ich gehe hinein***
I go into the house   **ich gehe in
        das Haus (hinein)***
I go into the room   **ich betrete das
        Zimmer**
I come in (to the room)   **ich trete
        ein***
I get in   **ich steige ein***
I get out *(of vehicle)*   **ich steige
        aus***
Get out!   **Raus!**
I go out   **ich gehe hinaus***
Go out!   **Gehen Sie hinaus*!**
I go out of the room   **ich gehe aus
        dem Zimmer (hinaus*)**
I go out (on an outing)   **ich gehe**

aus*
I get out (of vehicle)   **ich steige
        aus***

Up & down

I climb the mountain   **ich besteige
        den Berg**
I climb up the mountain   **ich
        klettere auf den Berg (hinauf*)**
I climb the stairs   **ich steige die
        Treppe hinauf***
I climb the wall   **ich steige auf die
        Mauer**
I come down   **ich komme
        herunter***
I come up   **ich komme herauf***
I fall down   **ich falle/stürze hin***
I get up   **ich stehe auf***
I go down the path   **ich gehe den
        Weg hinab*/hinunter***
I go up   **ich gehe hinauf***
I lie down   **ich lege mich hin**
Stand up!   **Stehen Sie auf*!**
Do sit down!   **Setzen Sie sich hin*!**

Round

I go round the town   **ich gehe um
        die Stadt (herum*)**
I run round in the garden   **ich laufe
        im Garten umher***
I run around   **ich laufe
        umher/herum***

– Where are you going? – To
town. Are you coming? – No, I am
going to my mother's.
– Which direction is that?
– I take the first road on the left,
then straight ahead up to the
market place, then I turn right.

– **Wo gehen Sie hin? – In die
Stadt. Kommen Sie mit? – Nein,
ich gehe zu meiner Mutter.
– In welcher Richtung liegt das?
– Ich nehme die erste Straße
links, dann geradeaus bis zum
Marktplatz, dann biege ich nach
rechts ab.**

Note use of **hin** (movement away from the speaker) and **her** (movement
towards the speaker) to make compound verbs expressing movement.

When? – expressions of time

3a Past, present & future

about **gegen** +acc
after **nach** +dat
  after *(conj)* **nachdem**
  afterwards **nachher, danach, hinterher**
again **nochmals, wieder**
  again and again **immer wieder**
ago **her** *(adv)*, **vor** +dat *(prep)*
  a short time ago **vor kurzem**
already **schon**
always **immer**
anniversary **der Jahrestag(e), der Hochzeitstag(e)**
annual **jährlich**
annually **jedes Jahr, jährlich**
as long as *(conj)* **solange**
as soon as *(conj)* **sobald**
at once **sofort, gerade, gleich**
before *(adj)* **vor** +acc/dat
  before *(conj)* **bevor, ehe**
  before, beforehand **vorher, davor**
I begin **ich beginne, ich fange an***
  it begins **es geht los***
beginning **der Anfang(¨e)**
birthday **der Geburtstag(e)**
brief *(adj)* **kurz**
briefly **vorübergehend**
by (next month) **bis (nächsten Monat)**
calendar **der Kalender(-)**
centenary **der hunderste Geburtstag(e)**
century **das Jahrhundert(e)**
  in the twentieth century **im zwanzigsten Jahrhundert**
continuous(ly) **dauernd, ständig**
daily **täglich**
date **das Datum (-en)**
  date **der Termin(e)**

dawn **der Tagesanbruch(¨e)**
  at dawn **bei Tagesanbruch**
day **der Tag(e)**
  by day **bei Tag**
  every day **jeden Tag**
decade **das Jahrzehnt(e)**
delay **die Verspätung(en)**
  delayed **verspätet**
during **während** +dat/gen
early **früh**
  I am early **ich bin früh dran**
  I am early **ich komme zu früh**
end **das Ende(n)**
  I end (sth) **ich mache etw. fertig**
  it ends **es endet, es ist aus**
ever **je**
every **jeder/-e/-es**
  every time **jedesmal**
  every day **jeden Tag**
exactly **genau, punkt**
fast **schnell**
  my watch is fast **meine Uhr geht vor***
finally **schließlich**
I finish (reading) **ich (lese) zu Ende**
first *(adj)* **der/die/das erste**
  at first **zuerst**
firstly **erstens**
for **seit** +dat, **für** +acc, **auf** +acc
for a day *(duration)* **einen Tag (lang)**
  (past continuous/progressive) **seit einem Tag**
  (future) **auf/für einen Tag**
for good/ever **auf immer**
formerly **früher***
fortnight/two weeks **vierzehn Tage**
frequent **häufig**
frequently **häufig, öfters**

from **von** +dat
   as from (today) **ab (heute)**
   from now on **von nun an, von jetzt ab**
I go on (reading) **ich (lese) weiter**
half **die Hälfte(n)**
   half *(adj)* **der/die/das halbe**
   one and a half **anderthalb, eineinhalb** *(invar)*
   two and a half **zweieinhalb** *(invar)*
it happens **es ereignet sich**
holiday/vacation **der Feiertag(e)**
I hurry up **ich beeile mich, ich mache schnell**
   hurry **die Eile**
   I am in a hurry **ich habe es eilig**
instant **der Moment(e)**
just **gerade**
   just now **gerade jetzt**
last *(final) (adj)* **der/die/das letzte**
   last night **gestern in der Nacht**
   last *(previous) (adj)* **der/die/das vorige/vergangene**
   it lasts a long time **es dauert lange**

last a short time **es dauert kurze Zeit**
late **spät**
   I am late **ich komme zu spät**
   lately **neulich**
   later (on) **später**
long **lang**
   long term **langfristig**
   in the long term **langfristig gesehen**
many **viele**
   many times **vielmals**
meanwhile **unterdessen**
   in the meanwhile **inzwischen**
middle **die Mitte(n)**
moment **der Augenblick(e)**
moment **der Moment(e)**
   at the moment **im Moment**
   at this moment **in diesem Augenblick**
   at this moment *(right now)* **zur Zeit**
   in a moment **in einem Augenblick**
month **der Monat(e)**
   monthly **monatlich, jeden Monat**
much **viel**

– Last Friday the train was late and you didn't get there till a quarter to/before three.
– Three at the latest, then. How long does your bus take?
– Half an hour.
– If I'm late, you can have a coffee till I get there.

– I don't want to spend all afternoon drinking coffee.

– You're sometimes late too.
– Only in winter or in bad weather.

– **Letzten Freitag hatte der Zug Verspätung, und du bist erst um Viertel vor drei angekommen.**
– **Also drei Uhr spätestens. Wie lange dauert die Busfahrt?**
– **Eine halbe Stunde.**
– **Wenn ich zu spät komme, kannst du einen Kaffee trinken, bis ich da bin.**
– **Ich will den ganzen Nachmittag nicht beim Kaffeetrinken verbringen.**
– **Du kommst auch mal zu spät.**
– **Nur im Winter oder bei schlechtem Wetter.**

never **nie**
next *(adj)* **nächst-, kommend-, folgend-**
next *(adv)* **dann**
not till/until **erst (um)**
not before **erst**
not always **nicht immer**
now **jetzt**
now *(next)* **nun**
nowadays **heutzutage**
occasionally **zufällig**
it occurs **es ereignet sich**
often **oft**
on and off **ab und zu**
once **einmal, mal**
once upon a time **einmal**
once in a while **ab und zu**
once a day **einmal am Tag**
one day (when) **eines Tages (als/wo)**
only **nur**
only when **erst als/wenn**
past **die Vergangenheit**
past **nach** +dat
per (day) **pro (Tag)**
present **die Gegenwart**
present *(adj)* **gegenwärtig**
presently **bald**
at present **zur Zeit**

previous(ly) **früher**
prompt **pünktlich**
promptly (at two) **punkt (zwei Uhr)**
rare(ly) **selten**
recent **neu**
recently **kürzlich, neulich**
regular(ly) **regelmäßig**
I remain **ich bleibe**
right away **sofort**
Saint's day **der Namenstag(e)**
school term/semester **das Trimester(-), das Semester(-)**
season **die Jahreszeite(n)**
seldom **selten**
several **mehrere**
several times **mehrmals**
short **kurz**
short term **kurzfristig**
in the short term **kurzfristig gesehen**
shortly **in kurzem**
since *(conj)* **seit** +dat
slow **langsam**
my watch is slow **meine Uhr geht nach**
some **einige**
sometime **irgendwann**
sometimes **manchmal**

– When do you go on holiday/vacation?
– Next month. In three weeks we'll be in Spain. I've never been before. We are spending a long time there, all June. Finally we go to Portugal for a week.

– I've been there before; that was a long time ago. The flight only lasts a short time. Last time we got there three hours late.

– **Wann fahren Sie in Urlaub?**

– **Nächsten Monat. In drei Wochen werden wir in Spanien sein. Ich war noch nie da. Wir bleiben lange da, den ganzen Juni. Zum Schluß fahren wir auf eine Woche nach Portugal.**
– **Ich war mal da, das war schon lange her. Der Flug dauert nur kurze Zeit. Das letztemal sind wir mit drei Stunden Verspätung angekommen.**

soon **bald**
   sooner or later **früher oder**
   später
   the sooner the better **je eher**
   desto besser
I stay **ich bleibe**
still **noch**
I stop (doing) **ich höre auf* (zu ...**
   tun)
suddenly **plötzlich, auf einmal**
sunrise **der Sonnenaufgang(-̈e)**
   at sunrise **bei Sonnenaufgang**
sunset **der Sonnenuntergang(-̈e)**
   at sunset **bei**
   Sonnenuntergang
I take (an hour) **ich brauche (eine**
   Stunde)
   it takes (an hour) **es dauert**
   (eine Stunde)
then *(next)* **dann**
   then *(at that time)* **da, damals,**
   dann
thousand years **das**
   Jahrtausend(e)
till **bis** +acc
time *(in general)* **die Zeit(en)**
time *(occasion)* **das Mal(e)**
   at any time **jederzeit**
   at other times **zu anderen**
   Zeiten
at the same time **gleichzeitig**
from time to time **von Zeit zu**
Zeit
for a long time **lange, lange**
Zeit
in good time **rechtzeitig**
a long time ago **längst**
the whole time **immer, die**
ganze Zeit
time zone **die Zeitzone(n)**
twice **zweimal**
until **bis** +acc
   until **bis zu** +dat
usually **meistens**
I wait **ich warte auf** +acc
week **die Woche(n)**
   this week **diese Woche**
   weekly **jede Woche**
   weekday **der Werktag(e), der**
   Wochentag(e)
   weekend **das Wochenende(n)**
when **wann, wenn, als**
whenever **wenn**
while *(conj)* **während**
year **das Jahr(e)**
   yearly **jährlich, jedes Jahr**
yet **schon**
   not yet **noch nicht**

– Anyway, I'll call you as soon as we get there.

– **Ich werde dich sowieso anrufen, sobald wir ankommen.**

– Hello Peter, John Brown here/speaking. I have been working on the project for a few days. We must meet sometime, what about the first of March?

– **Hello Peter, hier John Brown. Ich arbeite seit einigen Tagen an dem Projekt. Wir müssen uns unbedingt mal treffen, wie wäre es mit dem ersten März?**

– Perhaps it would be better to meet another time. I'll call next week.

– **Vielleicht wäre es besser, uns ein anderes Mal zu treffen. Ich rufe nächste Woche an.**

3b Time, days & date

Time of day

a.m. **vormittags**
morning **der Morgen(-), der Vormittag(e)**
  in the morning **morgen früh**
  in the mornings **vormittags**
  early in the morning **frühmorgens**
  this morning **heute morgen**
noon **der Mittag(e)**
at noon **zu Mittag**
afternoon **der Nachmittag(e)**
  in the afternoon **am Nachmittag**
  in the afternoons **nachmittags**
  this afternoon **heute nachmittag**
p.m. **nachmittags**
evening **der Abend(e)**
  in the evening **am Abend**
  in the evenings **abends**
  this evening **heute abend**
night **die Nacht(-̈e)**
  at night **nachts**
midnight **die Mitternacht(-̈e)**
  at midnight **um Mitternacht**
today **heute**
  today week **heute in einer Woche**
tomorrow **morgen**
  tomorrow morning **morgen früh**
  tomorrow afternoon **morgen nachmittag**
  tomorrow evening **morgen abend**
  the day after tomorrow **übermorgen**
tonight **heute abend/nacht**
yesterday **gestern**
  yesterday afternoon **gestern nachmittag**
  yesterday morning **gestern vormittag**
  yesterday evening **gestern abend**
the day before yesterday **vorgestern**

Telling the time

second **die Sekunde(n)**
minute **die Minute(n)**
hour **die Stunde (n)**
  half an hour **die halbe Stunde(n)**
  in an hour's time **in einer Stunde**
  hourly **jede Stunde**
quarter **das Viertel(-)**
  quarter of an hour **die Viertelstunde(n)**
  three quarters of an hour **drei Viertelstunden**
  quarter past/after (two) **Viertel nach (zwei)**
  quarter to/of (two) **Viertel vor (zwei)**
half past (two) **halb (drei)**
17:45 **siebzehn Uhr fünfundvierzig**
five past/after six **fünf nach sechs**
five to/of six **fünf vor sechs**
twenty five to/of six **fünfundzwanzig (Minuten) vor sechs**
twenty five to/of six **fünf nach halb sechs**
twenty five past/after five **fünfundzwanzig (Minuten) nach fünf**
twenty five past/after five **fünf vor halb sechs**
two a.m. **zwei Uhr nachts**
eight a.m. **acht Uhr vormittags**
two p.m. **zwei Uhr nachmittags**
eight pm **acht Uhr abends**
12:00 noon **zwölf Uhr mittags**
12:00 midnight **zwölf Uhr nachts**

The day of the week

Monday **der Montag(e)**
Tuesday **der Dienstag(e)**
Wednesday **der Mittwoch(e)**
Thursday **der Donnerstag(e)**
Friday **der Freitag(e)**
Saturday **der Samstag(e),**
    Sonnabend(e)
Sunday **der Sonntag(e)**

The month

January **der Januar(e)**
February **der Februar(e)**
March **der März(e)**
April **der April(-)**
May **der Mai(e)**
June **der Juni(s)**
July **der Juli(s)**
August **der August(e)**
September **der September(-)**
October **der Oktober(-)**
November **der November(-)**
December **der Dezember(-)**

The season

spring **der Frühling(e)**
summer **der Sommer(-)**
autumn/fall **der Herbst(e)**

winter **der Winter(-)**

The date

last Friday **letzten Freitag**
on Tuesday **am Dienstag**
on Tuesdays **dienstags**
by Friday **bis Freitag**
the first of January **der erste**
    Januar
on the third of January **am dritten**
    Januar
in (the year) 2000 **2000, im Jahre**
    2000
1st January/January 1st, 1994 **den**
    ersten Januar 1994
1.1.1994 **1.1.1994**
at the end of 1999 **Ende 1999**
by the end of 1999 **bis Ende 1999**
at the beginning (of July) **Anfang**
    (Juli)
by the beginning (of July) **bis**
    Anfang (Juli)
in December **im Dezember**
in mid/the middle of January **Mitte**
    Januar
at the end of March **Ende März**
in spring **im Frühling**

– I am going shopping tomorrow morning.
– I'd prefer to go in the afternoon. I always have such a lot to do on Mondays.
– I'll see you on the first, at 14:30 hours.

– What time does the film/movie start this evening?
– At 19:00 hours.
– How long does it last?
– One and a half hours. It will be over by 20:30 hours.

– **Morgen früh gehe ich einkaufen.**
– **Ich würde lieber nachmittags gehen. Montags habe ich immer voll zu tun.**
– **Also bis zum ersten, um vierzehn Uhr dreißig.**

– **Wann beginnt der Film heute abend?**
– **Um neunzehn Uhr.**
– **Und wie lange dauert er?**
– **Anderthalb Stunden. Er ist bis zwanzig Uhr dreißig zu Ende.**

➤ NUMBERS 4c

How much? – expressions of quantity

4a Length and shape

angle	**der Winkel(-)**
area	**die Fläche(n)**
big	**groß**
centre/center	**die Mitte(n)**
concave	**konkav**
convex	**konvex**
curved	**gebogen**
deep	**tief**
degree	**der Grad** *(no pl)*
depth	**die Tiefe(n)**
diagonal	**schräg**
distance	**die Entfernung(en)**
I draw	**ich zeichne**
hectare	**das Hektar(e)**
height	**die Höhe(n)**
high	**hoch, hoh-**
horizontal	**waagerecht**
large	**breit**
length	**die Länge(n)**
line	**die Linie(n)**
long	**lang**
low	**niedrig**
it measures	**es beträgt**
narrow	**eng**
parallel	**parallel**
perpendicular	**senkrecht**

point	**der Punkt(e)**
room	**der Platz(¨e)**
round	**rund**
ruler	**das Lineal(e)**
shape	**die Form(en)**
short	**kurz**
size	**die Größe(n)**
small	**klein**
space	**der Raum(¨e)**
straight	**gerade**
tall	**groß, hoch**
thick	**dick**
thin	**dünn**
wide	**breit, weit**
width	**die Breite(n)**

Shapes

circle	**der Kreis(e)**
circular	**kreisförmig**
cube	**der Würfel(-)**
cubic	**Kubik-**
cylinder	**der Zylinder(-)**
pyramid	**die Pyramide(n)**
rectangle	**das Rechteck(e)**
rectangular	**rechteckig**
sphere	**die Kugel(n)**

You need a straight ruler and pencil.	**Sie brauchen ein gerades Lineal und einen Bleistift.**
Measure the space and then draw a plan.	**Messen Sie den Raum and machen Sie dann einen Entwurf.**
Don't make the lawn too wide.	**Machen Sie den Rasen nicht zu breit.**
Leave room for some vegetables.	**Lassen Sie Platz für das Gemüse.**
The distance from the house to the fence is 12 metres/meters.	**Die Entfernung vom Haus bis zum Zaun beträgt 12 Meter.**

spherical **kugelförmig**
square **das Quadrat(e)**
square **Quadrat-**
square **quadratisch, viereckig**
triangle **das Dreieck(e)**
triangular **dreieckig**

Units of length

centimetre/centimeter **der Zentimeter(-), cm**
foot **der Fuß** *(no pl)*
inch **der Zoll** *(no pl)*
kilometre/kilometer **der Kilometer(-), km**
metre/meter **der Meter(-), m**
mile **die Meile(n)**
millimetre/millimeter **der Millimeter(-), mm**
yard **das Yard(s)**

Expressions of quantity

about **etwa, ungefähr**
almost **fast, beinahe**
approximate **ungefähr**
approximately **circa**
as much as **soviel**
at least **mindestens**
capacity **der Inhalt(e)**
it contains **es enthält** *(enthalten)*
cubic capacity **das Fassungsvermögen(-)**

it decreases **es geht zurück***
difference **der Unterschied(e)**
empty **leer**
I empty **ich leere**
enough **genug**
it is enough **es reicht**
I fill **ich fülle**
full **voll**
full of **voll von** +dat, **voller** *(invar)*
I grow **ich wachse**
growth **das Wachstum** *(no pl)*
hardly **kaum**
increase **die Vergrößerung(en)**
it increases **es nimmt zu***, **es vermehrt sich**
little **wenig** *(invar)*, **klein**
a little **ein wenig, ein bißchen**
a lot (of) **viel**
I measure **ich messe**
measuring tape **das Bandmaß(e)**
more **mehr** *(invar)*
nearly **fast**
number **die Zahl(en)**
part **der Teil(e)**
quantity **die Menge(n)**
rarely **selten**
it suffices **es genügt**
sufficient **genügend**
too much **zu viel, zuviel**
volume **das Volumen**
whole **ganz**
whole **das Ganze**

The garden is not wide enough for a pool.

Der Garten ist nicht breit genug für ein Schwimmbecken.

– How high is the tree? – About 5 metres/meters.

– Wie groß ist der Baum? – Ungefähr 5 Meter.

The shed will be at an angle of about 40 degrees to the house.

Der Schuppen wird in einem Winkel von 40 Grad zum Haus stehen.

The area of our garden/yard is 100 square metres/meters.

Unser Garten mißt 100 Quadratmeter.

▶ MATHEMATICAL & GEOMETRICAL TERMS App.4d

4b Measuring

Expressions of volume

bag **die Tüte(n)**
bar **die Tafel(n)**
bottle **die Flasche(n)**
box **das Etui(s), die Dose(n)**
container **der Behälter(-)**
cup **die Tasse(n)**
gallon **die Gallone(n)**
glass **das Glas(⁻er)**
litre/liter **der/das Liter**
   centilitre/centileter **der/das Zentiliter**
   millilitre/milliliter **der/das Milliliter**
pack **die Packung(en)**
   packet **das Paket(e)**
   packet *(small)* **die Schachtel(n)**
pair **das Paar(e)**
piece **das Stück(e)**
   a piece of cake **ein Stück Kuchen**
pint **das Pint(s), das halbe Liter(-)**
portion **die Portion(en)**
pot **das Glas(⁻er)**
sack **der Sack(⁻e)**
tube **die Tube(n)**

– How many centilitres/centiliters are there in the bottle? – 75, but you can also get it in litre/liter bottles.

– How many cubic metres/meters of concrete do you need? – About two.

– Would you like a cup of tea? – No, I would prefer a glass of water.

– How much wood do you want? – Enough for the whole fence. I must not buy too much. Yes, that should be sufficient. Give me a bag of cement too.

– I need a little flour and a lot of sugar. Give me a piece of butter - half a packet will do. I will need several eggs.

– That's too little. We do need even more cakes. Make a bit more.

– Wieviel Zentiliter sind in der Flasche? – Fünfundsiebzig, aber man kann es auch in Literflaschen kaufen.

– Wieviel Kubikmeter Beton brauchen Sie? – Ungefähr zwei.

– Möchten Sie eine Tasse Tee? – Nein, ich möchte lieber ein Glas Wasser.

– Wieviel Holz brauchen Sie? – Genug für den ganzen Zaun. Ich darf nicht zuviel kaufen. Ja, das wird schon genügen. Geben Sie mir auch einen Sack Zement.

– Ich brauche ein wenig Mehl und viel Zucker. Gib mir ein Stück Butter - ein halbes Paket wird reichen. Ich brauche mehrere Eier.

– Das ist zu wenig. Wir brauchen noch mehr Kuchen. Mach ein bißchen mehr.

Temperature		*Weight and density*	
it boils	**es kocht**	dense	**dicht**
I chill	**ich kühle, ich stelle kalt**	density	**die Dichte(n)**
cold	**kalt**	gram	**das Gramm** *(no pl)*
cold	**die Kälte**	heavy	**schwer**
cool	**kühl**	kilo	**das Kilo(gramm)** *(no pl)*
I cool down	**ich kühle mich ab**	light	**leicht**
degree	**der Grad** *(no pl)*	mass	**die Masse(n)**
I freeze	**ich friere**	ounce	**die Unze(n)**
heat	**die Hitze**	pound (lb)	**das Pfund** *(no pl)*
I heat	**ich erhitze**	scales/balance	**die Waage(n)**
I heat *(the house)*	**ich heize**	ton(ne)	**die Tonne(n)**
hot	**heiß**	I weigh	**ich wiege**
temperature	**die Temperatur(en)**	weight	**das Gewicht(e)**
I warm (up)	**ich wärme auf***		
warmth	**die Wärme**		

It's so hot! What's the temperature? It must be nearly 30 degrees.	**Es ist so warm! Wie ist die Temperatur? Es muß fast 30 Grad sein.**
I am too hot. Have you chilled the wine?	**Mir ist zu warm. Haben Sie den Wein kaltgestellt?**
In winter it's cold here. We all freeze in this house and have to put the heating on in September.	**Im Winter ist es hier kalt. Wir frieren alle in diesem Haus und müssen schon im September heizen.**
When the temperature reaches zero we have to light two fires.	**Wenn die Temperatur bis null Grad fällt, müssen wir zwei Feuer anzünden.**
Can you heat some water? The vegetables are still frozen … The water is boiling now. Warm up the pizza in the oven.	**Kannst du Wasser heizen? Die Gemüse sind noch gefroren … Das Wasser kocht jetzt. Wärm die Pizza im Backofen auf.**
Can you weigh out the ingredients?	**Wollen Sie die Zutaten wiegen?**
How many grammes/grams of sugar do we need?	**Wieviel Gramm Zucker brauchen wir?**
I want a pound - that must be about 450 grammes/grams.	**Ich brauche ein Pfund - ungefähr 450 Gramm.**

➤ WEATHER 24d

4c Numbers

Cardinal numbers

zero	**null**
one	**eins, einer/e/-**
two	**zwei**
two *(telephone)*	**zwo**
three	**drei**
four	**vier**
five	**fünf**
six	**sechs**
seven	**sieben**
eight	**acht**
nine	**neun**
ten	**zehn**
eleven	**elf**
twelve	**zwölf**
thirteen	**dreizehn**
fourteen	**vierzehn**
fifteen	**fünfzehn**
sixteen	**sechzehn**
seventeen	**siebzehn**
eighteen	**achtzehn**
nineteen	**neunzehn**
twenty	**zwanzig**
twenty-one	**einundzwanzig**
twenty-two	**zweiundzwanzig**
twenty-nine	**neunundzwanzig**
thirty	**dreißig**
thirty-one	**einunddreißig**
forty	**vierzig**
fifty	**fünfzig**
sixty	**sechzig**
seventy	**siebzig**
eighty	**achtzig**
ninety	**neunzig**
a hundred	**hundert**
a hundred and one	**hunderteins**
two hundred	**zweihundert**
a thousand	**(ein)tausend**
two thousand	**zweitausend**
million	**eine Million**
two million	**zwei Millionen**
milliard/billion *(US)*	**die Milliarde(n)**

Ordinal numbers

first	**der/die/das erste**
second	**der/die/das zweite**
third	**der/die/das dritte**
fourth	**der/die/das vierte**
nineteenth	**der/die/das neunzehnte**
twentieth	**der/die/das zwanzigste**
twenty-first	**der/die/das einunzwanzigste**
hundredth	**der/die/das hundertste**

Nouns

zero	**die Null(en)**
one	**die Eins(en)**
unit	**der Einer(-)**
ten	**die Zehn, der Zehner(-)**
dozen	**das Dutzend(e)**
hundred	**das Hundert(e)**
hundreds of	**Hunderte von**
million	**die Million(en)**

Half of the house belongs to my brother. We divided it between us.

Die Hälfte des Hauses gehört meinem Bruder. Wir haben es geteilt.

– You cannot all have half a bar of chocolate. There is only enough for a quarter each.
– I don't want a quarter, I want a half.

– Ihr könnt nicht alle eine halbe Tafel Schokolade haben. Es reicht nur für ein Viertel jedem.
– Ich will kein Viertel haben, ich möchte die Hälfte.

Writing numerals

1,000 **1.000**
1,500 **1.500**
1,000,000 **1 000 000**
1st **1.**
2nd **2.**
1.56 **1,56 (eins Komma fünf sechs)**
.05 **0,05 (null Komma null fünf)**

Fractions

half **die Hälfte(n)**
 a half **der/die/das halbe**
 one and a half **eineinhalb** *(invar)*

two and a half **zweieinhalb** *(invar)*
quarter **das Viertel(-)**
 a quarter **ein Viertel-**
 two and a quarter **zwei einviertel**
third **das Drittel(-)**
fifth **das Fünftel(-)**
five and five sixths **fünf fünf Sechstel**
tenth **das Zehntel(-)**
sixth **das Sechstel(-)**
hundredth **das Hundertstel(-)**

---

double the price **das Doppelte**
twice as much **das Doppelte**
second best **der/die/das zweitbeste**
third from last **der/die/das drittletzte**
fourfold **vierfach**
four times as much **das Vierfache**

1,800,265 **eine Million achthunderttausendzweihundertfünfundsechzig**
1995 **im Jahre neunzehnhundertfünfundneunzig**

telephone number 360542
 Telefon sechsunddreißig, null fünf, zwoundvierzig
dialling code 0482 **Vorwahl null vier acht zwo**

It was A1 **Es war eins A**
the 100 (bus) **der Hunderter**
the ten-mark note/ten Pfennig coin **der Zehner(-)**
The Big Four **die Vier**
We went in fours **Wir sind zu viert (vieren) gefahren**
We make a foursome **Wir haben einen Vierer**

Only a few people in their nineties can remember the twenties.

Nur wenige Leute in den Neunzigern erinnern sich an die zwanziger Jahre.

Paul has straight As.
I had a C in maths/math, he had an A.

Paul hat lauter Einsen (Einser). Ich habe eine Drei in Mathe geschrieben, er hatte eine Eins.

4d Calculations

addition **die Addition(en)**
  I add **ich addiere, rechne zusammen***
  plus **plus, und**
  two plus two **zwei und/plus zwei**
average **der Durchschnitt(e)**
  I average out **ich nehme den Durchschnitt**
  on average **im Durchschnitt**
I calculate **ich berechne**
  calculation **die Berechnung(en)**
  calculator **der Taschenrechner(-)**
correct **richtig**
I count **ich zähle**
data **die Daten** *(pl)*
  piece of data **das Datum (-a/-en)**
decimal **die Dezimalzahl(en)**
  decimal point **das Komma(s)**
diameter **der Durchmesser(-)**
digit **die Ziffer(n)**

two digit **zweistellig**
I double **ich verdopple**
division **die Division(en)**
  I divide by **ich teile durch** +acc
  six divided by two **sechs geteilt durch zwei**
it equals **es gleicht**
equation **das Gleichnis(se)**
it is equivalent to **ist gleich**
I estimate **ich schätze**
even **gerade**
figure **die Ziffer(n)**
graph **der Graph(en), die Grafik(en)**
is greater than **ist größer als**
is less than **ist kleiner als**
maximum **das Maximum(-a)**
  maximum **maximal, Maximal-**
  a maximum of **ein Maximum an** +dat
  up to a maximum of **bis zu maximal**
medium **die Mitte(n)**

An inch is the same as 2.54 cm, and there are twelve inches in a foot, 36 in a yard. A mile is 1760 yards. A kilometre/kilometer is 1000 metres.

What is 14 plus 8? It equals 22. Did you get the right result?

20 minus 5 is 15, 20 divided by 5 equals 4.

Work out 12 times 22. That is an easy sum.

2 to the power of 3 is 8. Three squared equals 9.

Ein Zoll ist gleich 2,54 Zentimeter, und es gibt 12 Zoll in einem Fuß, 36 in einem Yard. Eine Meile ist 1760 Yards. Ein Kilometer ist 1.000 Meter.

Was macht 14 und 8? 14 plus 8 (ist) gleich 22. Hast du das richtige Ergebnis?

20 weniger 5 gleich 15, 20 geteilt durch 5 gleich 4.

Rechnet 12 mal 22. Das ist eine leichte Aufgabe.

Zwei hoch drei macht 8. Drei hoch zwei macht neun.

medium **Mittel-, mittler-**	**100 zu 1**
minimum **das Minimum(-a)**	result **das Ergebnis(se)**
minimum **Mindest-**	similar **ähnlich**
minus **minus**	solution **die Lösung(en)**
mistake/error **der Fehler(-)**	I solve **ich löse**
multiplication **die**	square **die Quadratzahl(en)**
Multiplikation(en)	square root **die zweite Wurzel(n)**
I multiply **ich multipliziere**	three squared **drei hoch zwei,**
three times two **drei mal zwei**	**zum Quadrat**
negative **negativ**	statistic **die Statistik**
number **die Zahl(en)**	statistics **die Statistik(en)**
numeral **die Ziffer(n)**	statistical **statistisch**
odd **ungerade**	sum **die Rechenaufgabe(n)**
percent **das Prozent(en)**	subtraction **die Subtraktion(en)**
by 10% **um 10%**	I subtract **ich ziehe ab***
percentage **der**	symbol **das Symbol(e)**
Prozentsatz(¨e)	take away **weniger**
positive **positiv**	total **die Endsumme(n),**
power **die Potenz(en)**	**Gesamtzahl(en)**
to the power of **hoch**	in total **insgesamt**
to the fifth **hoch fünf**	I treble **ich verdreifache**
problem **die Aufgabe(n)**	triple **dreifach**
quantity **die Menge(n)**	I work out **ich rechne aus***
ratio **das Verhältnis(se)**	wrong **falsch**
a ratio of 100:1 **im Verhältnis**	

Two negatives make a positive.	**Zweimal minus gibt plus.**
You have made a mistake there.	**Da hast du einen Fehler gemacht.**
– I estimate that we have about 500 visitors a year.	**– Ich schätze, wir haben etwa 500 Gäste im Jahr.**
– What percentage of visitors are local? – 20% (percent).	**– Welcher Prozentsatz kommt aus der Gegend? – 20 Prozent.**
– Have you got any statistics about it?	**– Haben Sie eine Statistik darüber?**
A snail travels at an average speed of 0.04 miles per hour.	**Eine Schnecke bewegt sich mit einer Durchschnittsgeschwindigkeit von 0,06 Stundenkilometern.**
Can you do me a graph?	**Wollen Sie mir bitte eine Grafik zeichnen?**

➤ MATHEMATICAL TERMS App.4d

5 What sort of? – descriptions & judgements

5a Describing people

appearance **das Aussehen**
attractive **attraktiv**
average **mittel, mittelmäßig**
he is bald **er hat eine Glatze**
beard **der Bart(⁻e)**
bearded **bärtig**
beautiful **schön**
beauty **die Schönheit(en)**
blond **blond**
broad **breit**
build **der Körperbau** *(no pl)*
chic **schick**
clean-shaven **glattrasiert**
clumsy **ungeschickt**
complexion **die Gesichtsfarbe(n)**
curly **lockig**
dark **dunkel**
I describe **ich beschreibe**
description **die Beschreibung(en)**
different (from) **anders (als)**
elegant **elegant**
energy **die Energie(n)**
expression **der Gesichtsausdruck(⁻e)**
fat **dick**
feature **der Gesichtszug(⁻e)**
female/feminine **weiblich**
figure **die Figur(en)**

fit **fit**
I frown **ich runzele die Stirn**
glasses **die Brille**
good-looking **gutaussehend**
I grow **ich wachse**
hair **das Haar, die Haare**
hairstyle **die Frisur(en)**
handsome **gutaussehend**
heavy **schwer**
height **die Größe(n)**
homosexual **homosexuell**
large **breit, groß**
I laugh **ich lache**
laugh **das Lachen**
I am left-handed **ich bin Linkshänder [-in]**
light **leicht**
long-sighted **weitsichtig**
I look like **ich sehe aus* wie**
I look well **ich sehe gut aus***
male **männlich**
masculine **männlich**
moustache **der Schnurrbart(⁻e)**
neat **ordentlich**
neatness **die Sauberkeit**
obese **fettleibig**
overweight **übergewichtig, korpulent**

---

adolescence **die Pubertät**
adolescent **der/die Jugendliche** *(adj/n)*
age **das Alter**
elderly **ältlich, älter**
grown up **der/die Erwachsene** *(adj/n)*
grown up *(adj)* **erwachsen**
middle-aged **in den mittleren Jahren**

old **alt**
older/elder **älter**
teenager **der Teenager(-)**
young **jung**
young person **der/die Jugendliche** *(adj/n)*
young people **junge Leute**
youth **die Jugend**
youthful **jugendlich**

► PARTS OF THE BODY 5b, App.5b; HUMAN CHARACTER 6

part of body   **der Körperteil(e)**
paunch   **der Bauch(⁻e)**
physical   **körperlich**
plump   **fett, pummelig**
pretty   **hübsch**
red-haired   **rothaarig**
I am right-handed   **ich bin Rechtshänder [-in]**
I scowl   **ich sehe jdn. finster an***
sex/gender   **das Geschlecht(er)**
short   **kurz, klein**
short-sighted   **kurzsichtig**
similar (to)   **ähnlich** +dat
similarity   **die Ähnlichkeit(en)**
size   **die Größe(n)**
slim/slender   **schlank**
small   **klein**
I smile   **ich lächele**

smile   **das Lächeln**
spot   **der Pickel(-)**
spotty   **pickelig**
stocky   **stämmig**
strength   **die Kraft(⁻e)**
striking   **auffallend**
strong   **stark**
tall   **groß, lang**
thin   **mager, dünn**
tiny   **winzig**
trendy   **schick**
ugliness   **die Häßlichkeit**
ugly   **häßlich**
walk   **der Gang**
wavy   **gewellt**
I weigh   **ich wiege**
weight   **das Gewicht(e)**

– What a wonderful family photo! What's your uncle like? Can you describe him?

– He looks very like my father, but he wears glasses. And he's put on weight.

– Look, who's that tall fellow? – That's my brother, with the beard. He's mad on keeping fit.

– What a pretty girl! Is that your cousin? – Yes, she's blond with blue eyes. She's very slim, with a good figure and a beautiful smile.

– Little Ben has dark hair and is about 1 metre tall. He looks very well, but he's very thin. – Yes, he only weighs 16 kilos.

– **Was für ein schönes Familienfoto! Wie ist dein Onkel? Kannst du ihn beschreiben?**

– **Er sieht meinem Vater sehr ähnlich, aber er trägt eine Brille. Und er hat zugenommen.**

– **Guck mal, wer ist der lange Kerl da? – Das ist mein Bruder, der mit dem Bart. Er ist ein Trimm-Dich-Fanatiker.**

– **Was für ein hübsches Mädchen! Ist das deine Cousine? – Ja, sie ist blond mit blauen Augen. Sie ist sehr schlank, mit einer guten Figur und einem schönen Lächeln.**

– **Der kleine Ben hat dunkles Haar und ist ungefähr ein Meter groß. Er sieht sehr gesund aus, aber er ist sehr mager. – Ja, er wiegt nur 16 Kilo.**

➤ PHYSICAL STATE 11d

5b The senses

bitter **bitter**
bright **hell**
bright *(harsh)* **grell**
cold **kalt**
   cold **die Kälte**
colourful/colorful **bunt**
dark **dunkel**
darkness **das Dunkel, die Dunkelheit**
delicious **lecker**
disgusting **ekelhaft**
dull **matt**
ear **das Ohr(en)**
eye **das Auge(n)**
face **das Gesicht(er)**
I feel ... **ich fühle mich, mir ist ...**
   it feels **es fühlt sich an***
I feel very cold **Mir ist sehr kalt**
hand **die Hand(ᵉe)**
I hear **ich höre**
hot **warm, heiß**
light *(colour/color)* **hell**
I listen **ich höre** +dat **zu***
I look **ich blicke**

I look at sth **ich sehe etw. an***
loud **laut**
mouth **der Mund(ᵉer)**
noise **der Lärm** *(no pl)*, **das Geräusch(e)**
noisy **laut, lärmend**
nose **die Nase(n)**
odour/odor **der Geruch(ᵉe)**
opaque **trüb, undurchsichtig**
perfume **das Parfüm(s)**
perfumed **parfümiert**
quiet **ruhig**
rough **rauh**
salty **salzig**
I see **ich sehe**
sense **der Sinn(e)**
silence **die Stille**
silent **schweigend, still**
   I am silent **ich schweige**
smell **der Geruch(ᵉe)**
   I smell **ich rieche**
   it smells (of) **es riecht nach** +dat
   smelly **stinkend**

– What colour/color is your new coat? – Well, it's sort of red.
– Dark or light red? – It is more maroon.

– **Welche Farbe hat Ihr neuer Mantel?– Er ist rötlich.**
– **Dunkel oder hellrot. – Eher rötlichbraun.**

– What colour/color are you painting the living room?
– Pale blue-green.
The hall is brownish with a bright pattern in contrast. It matches the beige carpet well.

– **In welcher Farbe streichen Sie das Wohnzimmer an?**
– **Ein blaßes Blaugrün.**
Der Eingang ist bräunlich mit einem hellen Muster in Kontrast. Es paßt gut zum beigefarbenen Teppich.

The jam tastes of fruit but is very bitter.

Die Marmelade schmeckt nach Obst, aber sie ist sehr bitter.

soft *(sound)* **sanft, leise**
soft *(texture)* **weich**
sound **der Klang(⁼e), das Geräusch(e)**
it sounds **es klingt**
it sounds like **es hört sich an***
sour **sauer**
sticky **klebrig, schmutzig**
it is sticky **es klebt**
stomach **der Magen(-)**
sweet **süß**

taste **der Geschmack**
I taste **ich schmecke**
it tastes (of) **es schmeckt nach** +dat
tepid **lauwarm**
tooth **der Zahn(⁼e)**
I touch **ich berühre**
transparent **durchsichtig**
visible (in-) **sichtbar (un-)**
warm **warm**
warmth **die Wärme**

Colours/Colors

beige **beige** *(invar)*
black **schwarz**
blue **blau**
brown **braun**
brownish **bräunlich**
cream *(colour/color)* **die Creme**
cream *(adj)* **cremefarben**
gold **Gold-, golden**
green **grün**
grey/gray **grau**
maroon **rötlichbraun**
orange *(colour/color)* **das Orange**

orange *(adj)* **Orangen-, orangenfarbig**
pink **rosa** *(invar)* , **rosarot**
purple **violett**
red **rot**
scarlet **hochrot**
silver **Silber-, silbern**
turquoise *(colour/color)* **das Türkis**
turquoise *(adj)* **türkisfarben**
violet **lila** *(invar)*
white **weiß**
yellow **gelb**

– What's in that bag? It feels hard.

– Let me feel - It's a bottle. What's in it?

– I don't know. It looks like orange juice. I'll taste it … It's disgusting. It tastes of oranges but it's too sweet.

– Have you seen my new perfume?
– What does it look like?
– It's in a small, pink bottle

– **Was ist in der Tasche? Es fühlt sich hart an.**
– **Laß mich mal fühlen - es ist eine Flasche. Was ist denn da drinnen?**
– **Ich weiß nicht. Es sieht wie Orangensaft aus. Ich werde es probieren … Es ist ekelhaft. Es schmeckt nach Orangen, aber es ist zu süß.**

– **Hast mein neues Parfüm gesehen?**
– **Wie sieht es aus?**
– **Es ist in einer kleinen, rosa Flasche.**

NOTE: most colours/colors can be used as neuter nouns eg **das Blau**.

5c Describing things

big **groß**	flat **flach**
broad **breit**	flexible **flexibel**
broken **kaputt, gebrochen**	fresh **frisch**
appearance **die Erscheinung(en), das Aussehen**	full (of) **voll (von** +dat), **voller** *(invar)*
clean **sauber**	genuine/real **echt**
closed **zu, geschlossen**	hard **hart**
colour/color **die Farbe(n)**	hardness **die Härte**
colourful/colorful **bunt**	height **die Größe(n)**
coloured/colored **farbig**	high **hoch**
damp **feucht**	kind **die Art(en)**
deep **tief**	large **groß**
depth **die Tiefe(n)**	liquid **flüssig**
dirt **der Schmutz**	little **klein**
dirty **schmutzig**	long **lang**
dry **trocken**	it looks like **es sieht aus* wie**
empty **leer**	low **niedrig**
enormous **ungeheuer**	main **Haupt-**
fashionable **modisch**	material **der Stoff(e)**
fat **dick**	it matches **es passt zu** +dat
firm **fest**	matter **der Stoff(e)**

– What's that over there?	**– Was ist das da drüben?**
– That thing there? It's a new kind of bottle opener.	**– Das Dings da? Es ist eine neue Art Flaschenöffner.**
– Does it work?	**– Funktioniert er?**
–Yes indeed. It's the best there is.	**– Selbstverständlich. Er ist der beste, den es gibt.**
– I'm looking for something big to stand on.	**– Ich suche etwas Großes, worauf ich stehen kann.**
– Will anything do? – Well, it must be something solid.	**– Ist es egal, was? – Na, es muß etwas Solides sein.**
– What about this?	**– Wie wäre es mit dem da?**
– Is there nothing bigger?	**– Gibt es nichts Größeres?**
– Stand on the chair.	**– Stellen Sie sich auf den Stuhl.**
– It's too soft.	**– Er ist zu weich.**
– All the other chairs are too low.	**– All die anderen Stühle sind zu niedrig.**
The fridge/refrigerator is empty and the sink full of water.	**Der Kühlschrank ist leer und das Spülbecken voller Wasser. -**

moist **feucht**
mouldy/moldy **modrig**
narrow **eng**
natural **natürlich**
new **neu**
open **auf, offen**
painted **bemalt**
pale **blaß**
pattern **das Muster(-)**
plump **rundlich**
resistant **dicht**
rotten **morsch**
shade **der Farbton(-̈e)**
shallow **flach, seicht**
shiny **glänzend**
short **kurz**
shut **zu, geschlossen**
small **klein**
smooth **glatt**
soft *(texture)* **weich**
softness **die Weichheit**
solid **solid**

soluble **wasserlöslich**
sort **die Sorte(n)**
spot **der Punkt(-̈e)**
spotted **getupft**
stain **der Fleck(en)**
stained **fleckig**
stripe **der Streifen(-)**
striped **gestreift**
subsidiary **Neben-**
substance **die Substanz(en)**
synthetic **Kunst-, künstlich**
thick **dick**
thing **das Ding(e)**
thingummyjig **das Dings, das Dingsbums**
tint **der Ton(-̈e)**
varied **variiert**
water-proof **wasserdicht, wasserfest**
wet **naß**
wide **weit, breit**
width **die Weite**

Ten questions

What's that thingummyjig? **Was ist das Dings da?**
What's it for? **Wozu dient es?**
What do you use it for? **Wozu dient es?**
Can you see it? **Kannst du es sehen?**
What's it like? **Wie ist es?**
What does it look like? **Wie sieht es aus?**
What does it sound like? **Wie klingt es?**
What does it smell of? **Wonach riecht es?**
What colour is it? **Welche Farbe hat es?**
What kind of thing is it? **Was für eine Sache ist das?**

– I am looking for a striped material, something to match my coat.
– This is a genuine natural material, soft and thick. That is a synthetic material, it feels smooth but the colours/colors are harsh.
– Have you something cheaper?

– **Ich suche einen gestreiften Stoff, der zu meinem Mantel paßt.**
– **Dies hier ist echte Naturfaser, weich und dicht. Das da ist Kunstfaser, es fühlt sich weich an, aber die Farben sind grell.**
– **Haben Sie etwas Billigeres?**

► MEASURING 4b; FUNCTIONAL WORDS 1

5d Evaluating things

abnormal **anormal**	I enjoy **ich genieße, es macht mir Spaß**
I adore **ich liebe sehr**	easy **leicht**
all right **okay**	essential (in-) **(un)wesentlich**
it is all right **es geht**	excellent **ausgezeichnet**
appalling **entsetzlich**	expensive **teuer**
bad **schlecht**	I fail **es ist mir nicht gelungen**
beautiful **schön**	failure **der Mißerfolg(e)**
better/best **besser, best-**	a total failure **eine totale Pleite**
cheap **billig**	false **falsch**
correct **richtig**	fine **schön**
it costs **es kostet**	good **gut**
delicious **köstlich**	good value **preiswert**
I detest **ich hasse**	great/terrific **großartig**
difficulty **die Schwierigkeit(en)**	I hate **ich hasse**
difficult/hard **schwer, schwierig**	high **hoch**
disgusting **ekelhaft**	important (un-) **(un)wichtig**
I dislike **ich mag nicht**	

– Would you like to try this wine? – Please. It is quite delicious.	**– Möchten Sie diesen Wein probieren? – Bitte. Er schmeckt ausgezeichnet.**
How do you like our neighbour's garden/neighbor's yard? We do not like it at all.	**Wie gefällt Ihnen der Nachbargarten? Wir mögen ihn gar nicht.**
The garden seat is only plastic anyway. We always buy the best! Our garden furniture is made of wood.	**Der Gartensitz ist sowieso nur aus Kunststoff. Wir kaufen immer das Beste! Unsere Gartenmöbel sind aus Holz.**
I fear he's not a very successful gardener. His vegetables are a complete failure.	**Leider ist er kein sehr erfolgreicher Gärtner. Sein Gemüse ist eine totale Pleite.**
I do like to keep the garden/yard tidy/neat. I always put everything away. People always say our garden/yard is the best in the road.	**Ich mag es, wenn der Garten schön ordentlich ist. Ich räume immer alles weg. Unser Garten soll der beste in der Straße sein.**

incorrect **falsch**
interesting (un-) **(un)interessant**
I like **ich mag, es gefällt mir**
mediocre **mittelmäßig**
necessary (un-) **(un)nötig**
normal **normal**
order **die Ordnung**
   in order **in Ordnung**
   out of order **außer Betrieb**
out of date **veraltet**
ordinary **normal**
pleasant **angenehm**
poor **arm**
practical (im-) **(un)praktisch**
I prefer **ich ziehe vor***
quality **die Qualität(en)**
   top quality **die beste Qualität**
   poor quality **die schlechte Qualität**

right **richtig**
strange **seltsam**
I succeed **es gelingt mir**
success **der Erfolg(e)**
successful **erfolgreich**
true **wahr, echt**
I try **ich versuche**
ugly **häßlich**
unpleasant **unangenehm**
unsuccessful **erfolglos**
I use **ich verwende, ich benutze**
use **der Gebrauch**
useful **praktisch**
well **gut**
worse/worst **schlimm/schlimmst-**
I would rather **ich möchte lieber**
wrong **falsch**

---

a bit **ein bißchen**
enough **genug**
extremely **äußerst**
fairly **ziemlich**
hardly ... at all **kaum**
litte **wenig** *(invar)*
   a little **ein wenig**
a lot **viel, eine Menge**
much (better) **viel (besser)**

not at all **gar nicht**
particularly **besonders**
quite **ganz**
rather **ziemlich**
really **wirklich**
so **so**
too (good) **zu (gut)**
very **sehr**

– Do you enjoy going to the cinema/movie theater? – Yes, I particularly enjoyed last week's film/movie.

– **Macht es Ihnen Spaß, ins Kino zu gehen/Gehen Sie gern ins Kino? – Ja, der Film von letzter Woche hat mir besonders gut gefallen.**

– Which dress would you like? The most beautiful dress is the one made of cotton.
– All the same I would rather have the other.

– **Welches Kleid möchtest du haben? Das schönste Kleid ist das aus Baumwolle.**
– **Trotzdem möchte ich lieber das andere nehmen.**

➤ EXPRESSING VIEWS 6d

5e Comparisons

Regular comparatives & superlatives

| small | **klein** | smallest (*adj*) | **der kleinste** |
| small | **kleiner** | smallest (*adv*) | **am kleinsten** |

Irregular comparatives and superlatives

big **groß, größer, größt-**
elderly **der/die/das ältere**
extremely **äußerst**
good **gut, besser, best-**
healthy **gesund, gesünder, gesündest-**
high **hoch, höher, höchst-**
  highly **höchst**
little **wenig, weniger, wenigst-**
  least of all **am wenigsten, am mindesten**

at least **wenigstens**
at the very least **mindestens**
much **viel, mehr, meist-**
  mostly **meistens**
near **nah, näher, nächst-**
soon **bald, eher, am ehesten**
willingly **gern, lieber, am liebsten**

NOTE: some common one-syllable adjectives take an Umlaut eg **stark, stärker, stärkst-** ➤ Berlitz *German Grammar Handbook*.

Have you seen our products? They are just as cheap as the competition.	**Haben Sie unsere neuesten Produkte gesehen? Sie sind genauso billig wie die Konkurrenz.**
We can not ask a higher price, as the greatest demand is for the cheaper product.	**Wir dürfen keinen höheren Preis verlangen, da der billigere Produkt am meisten gefragt ist.**
Look at the children! Peter, our eldest son, is now the tallest. He's best at football, too. That's what he enjoys best.	**Sehen Sie die Kinder an! Peter, unser ältester, ist jetzt der größte. Er spielt auch am besten Fußball. Das macht ihm am meisten Spaß.**
John is now fairly large, almost as tall as Peter, and he really is too fat. He prefers swimming. He behaves less well than his brother.	**John ist jetzt ziemlich groß, fast so groß wie Peter, und er ist wirklich zu dick. Er schwimmt am liebsten. Er benimmt sich weniger gut als sein Bruder.**

5f Materials

acrylic **das Acryl**	paper **das Papier(e)**
brick **das Backstein(e)**	plastic **der Kunststoff(e)**
camel-hair **das Kamelhaar**	polyester **der Polyester**
cashmere **die Kaschmirwolle**	pottery **die Keramik**
cement **das Zement**	satin **der Satin**
china **das Porzellan**	silk **die Seide**
concrete **das Beton**	silk *(adj)* **seiden**
corduroy **der Cord**	silver **das Silber**
cotton **die Baumwolle**	steel **der Stahl**
denim **der Jeansstoff**	steel *(adj)* **stählern**
felt **der Filz**	stone **der Stein(e)**
flannel **der Flanell**	stone *(adj)* **steinern**
gas **das Gas**	suede **das Wildleder**
glass **das Glas**	terylene **das Trevira, Diolen**
gold **das Gold**	towelling **das Frottee**
iron **das Eisen**	velvet **der Samt**
iron *(adj)* **eisern**	viscose **die Viskose**
lace **die Spitze**	wood **das Holz**
leather **das Leder**	wooden **hölzern**
leather *(adj)* **ledern**	wool **die Wolle**
linen **das Leinen**	woollen/woolen **wollen**
material **der Stoff(e)**	worsted **das Kammgarn**
metal **das Metall(e)**	
mineral **das Mineral(e/ien)**	
nylon **das Nylon**	
oil **das Öl(e)**	

NOTE: compound nouns are commonly used instead of adjectives, eg **das Backsteinhaus, der Wollpullover**.

Silk is softer than wool, but it costs a lot. Nylon is cheapest.	**Seide ist weicher als Wolle, aber es kostet eine Menge Geld. Nylon ist am billigsten.**
The colours/colors are brighter and I think the cut is better, although it is not as warm as the woollen/woolen dress.	**Die Farben sind heller, und meinetwegen ist der Schnitt besser, obwohl es nicht so warm wie das Wollkleid ist.**
– Did you succeed in finding something less expensive? – Yes, this coat is particularly good value. And it's better quality.	**– Ist es Ihnen gelungen, etwas weniger Teueres zu finden?** **– Ja, dieser Mantel ist besonders preiswert. Und er ist in der Qualität besser.**

➤ CLOTHES 9c; MINERALS, CHEMICAL ELEMENTS App.23b

The human mind & character

6a Human character

active **aktiv**
I adapt **ich passe mich an***
amusing **lustig**
I annoy **ich ärgere**
bad **schlecht**
bad-tempered **schlechtgelaunt**
I behave **ich benehme mich**
behaviour/behavior **das Benehmen**
I boast **ich gebe an***
calm **ruhig**
care **die Vorsicht**
careful **vorsichtig**
careless **nachlässig**
character **der Charakter(e)**
characteristic **die Eigenschaft(en)**
characteristic **charakteristisch**
charming **charmant, anmutig**
cheerful **lustig**
clever **begabt, klug**
confident **voller Selbstvertrauen**
discipline **die Disziplin**
dreadful **schrecklich**
evil **böse**
I forget **ich vergesse**
forgetful **vergeßlich**

friendly (un-) **(un)freundlich**
fussy **anspruchsvoll**
generous **großzügig**
I get on with **ich verstehe mich
gut mit** +dat
gifted **begabt**
good **gut**
good-tempered **gutgelaunt**
guilty **schuldig**
habit **die Gewohnheit(en)**
hard-working **fleißig**
help **die Hilfe**
I help **ich helfe**
helpful **hilfreich**
honest (dis-) **(un)ehrlich**
humour/humor **der Humor**
humorous **humorvoll**
immorality **die Unsittlichkeit, die
Unmoral**
innocent **unschuldig**
intelligence **die Intelligenz**
intelligent **intelligent**
kind (un-) **lieb, (un)freundlich**
kindness **die Liebenswürdigkeit**
lazy **faul**

Do you remember our neighbour/neighbor?	**Erinnern Sie sich an unseren Nachbarn?**
He is a lazy fellow, but very gifted.	**Er ist ein fauler Kerl, aber sehr begabt.**
He has a good sense of humour/humor but is always boasting.	**Er hat Humor, aber er gibt immer an.**
His wife is very pleasant and helpful.	**Seine Frau ist sehr lieb und hilfsbereit.**
The children are lively characters.	**Die Kinder sind sehr temperamentvoll.**
They never obey their mother.	**Sie gehorchen nie der Mutter.**

laziness **die Faulheit**
lively **temperamentvoll**
mad **verrückt**
manners **die Manieren**
mental(ly) **geistig**
moral (im-) **(un)moralisch**
morality **die Moralität**
morals **die Moral**
nervous **nervös, ängstlich**
nice **nett**
I obey **ich gehorche** +dat
optimistic **optimistisch**
patient (im-) **(un)geduldig**
personality **das Temperament(e)**
pessimistic **pessimistisch**
pleasant **lieb, angenehm**
polite (im-) **(un)höflich**
popular **beliebt**
quality **die Eigenschaft(en)**
reason **die Vernunft**
reasonable (un-) **(un)vernünftig**
respect **der Respekt**
respectful **respektvoll**
rude **unhöflich**
sad **traurig**
self-confidence **das Selbstvertrauen**
self-confident **selbstsicher**
self-esteem **die Selbstachtung**
sense **der Sinn(e)**
   (common) sense **der gesunde Menschenverstand**

good sense **die Vernunft**
sense of humour/humor **der Sinn für Humor**
sense of shame **das Schamgefühl**
sensible **vernünftig**
serious **ernst**
shy **schüchtern**
skill **die Fertigkeit(en)**
skilful **geschickt**
sociable (un-) **(un)freundlich, gesellig**
strange **eigenartig**
stupid **dumm**
stupidity **die Dummheit(en)**
suspicious **argwöhnisch**
sympathetic **sympatisch**
sympathy **das Mitgefühl, das Mitleid**
tactful/tactless **taktvoll**
tactless **taktlos**
talented **begabt**
temperament **das Temperament(e)**
temperamental **launenhaft**
I trust **ich traue** +dat
trusting **vertrauensvoll**
warm **warm**
well-known **bekannt**
wise **klug**
wit **der Witz(e)**
witty **geistreich**

The pupils here are hard-working and well-behaved.
We encourage self-confidence and discipline.
Bad behaviour/behavior and laziness are punished.

Don't be so suspicious. Please trust me.

Die Schüler hier sind fleißig und benehmen sich gut.
Wir fördern Selbstvertrauen und Disziplin.
Schlechtes Benehmen und Faulheit werden bestraft.

Seien Sie nicht so argwöhnisch. Bitte verlassen Sie sich auf mich.

➤ THOUGHT PROCESSES 6c; EXPRESSING VIEWS 6d

6b Feelings & emotions

I am afraid (of)   **ich habe Angst (vor +dat)**
I am amazed (at)   **ich staune (über +acc)**
amazement   **das Erstaunen**
I amuse   **ich amüsiere**
   I am amused by   **es amüsiert mich**
amusement   **das Vergnügen**
anger   **die Wut**
angry   **wütend**
I am annoyed (at/about)   **ich ärgere mich (über +acc)**
anxiety   **die Angst, Ängstlichkeit**
anxious   **ängstlich**
I approve (of)   **ich bewillige etw.**
I am ashamed (of)   **ich schäme mich (vor +dat)**
I am bored   **ich langweile mich**
boredom   **die Langeweile**
content (with)   **zufrieden (mit +dat)**
cross (with)   **böse (auf +acc)**
delighted (about)   **entzückt (über +acc)**
I dislike   **es gefällt mir nicht**
dissatisfaction   **die Unzufriedenheit(en)**
dissatisfied (with)   **unzufrieden (mit +dat)**
embarrassed (about)   **verlegen (wegen +gen)**
embarrassment   **die Verlegenheit(en)**
emotion   **das Gefühl(e)**
emotional(ly)   **emotional (emotionell)**
I enjoy ...   **... gefällt mir**
envy   **der Neid**
envious (of)   **neidisch (auf +acc)**
I feel   **ich fühle (mich)**
I forgive   **ich vergebe/verzeihe +dat**
forgiveness   **die Vergebung**
I am frightened (of)   **ich habe Angst (vor +dat)**
furious (about)   **wütend (über +acc)**
fussy   **pingelig**
grateful (to)   **dankbar (+dat)**
gratitude   **die Dankbarkeit**
happiness   **das Glück**
happy (about)   **glücklich (über**

I like our neighbour/neighbor a lot but worry about his wife. She cares for her old mother, who has not adapted to life in town. She is often in a bad temper and very fussy.	**Ich mag unseren Nachbarn sehr, aber seine Frau macht mir Sorgen. Sie sorgt für ihre alte Mutter, die sich dem Stadtleben nicht gut angepaßt hat. Sie ist oft schlechter Laune und ist sehr pingelig.**
The boss is in a bad mood. He is cross with his secretary. She is bored with the work and indifferent to his annoyance	**Der Geschäftsführer ist in schlechter Laune. Er ärgert sich über seine Sekretärin. Die Arbeit langweilt sie, und sein Ärger macht ihr nichts aus.**

+acc)
hate **der Haß**
I hate **ich hasse**
I have a grudge against him **ich bin ihm böse**
hope **die Hoffnung(en)**
I hope (for) **ich hoffe (auf** +acc)
I hope that **hoffentlich**
hopeful **hoffnungsvoll**
idealism **der Idealismus**
indifference **die Gleichgültigkeit**
indifferent (to) **gleichgültig (gegenüber** +dat)
I am indifferent **es macht mir nichts aus***
interest **das Interesse(n)**
I am interested (in) **ich interessiere mich (für** +acc)
jealous **eifersüchtig auf** +acc
jealousy **die Eifersucht**
joy **die Freude(n)**
joyful **freudig**
I like **ich mag**
love **die Liebe(n)**
I love **ich liebe**
miserable (about) **miserabel, unglücklich (über** +acc)
misery **das Elend**

mood **die Laune(n)**
in a good/bad mood **gut/schlecht gelaunt**
I prefer **ich ziehe vor***
I regret **ich bedauere**
satisfaction **die Zufriedenheit**
satisfied (with) **zufrieden (mit** +dat)
surprise **die Überraschung(en)**
I am surprised (at) **ich bin überrascht/erstaunt (über** +acc)
thankful **dankbar**
unhappy **unglücklich**
unhappiness **die Traurigkeit, die Trauer**
I am upset (about) **aufgeregt (wegen** +dat)
I wonder (at) **ich wundere mich (über** +acc)
I wonder if **ich bin gespannt, ob**
worried (about) **besorgt (wegen** +gen)
worry **die Sorge(n)**
I worry (about) **ich mache mir Sorgen (über** +acc)
it worries me **es beunruhigt mich**

– I am really ashamed of my behaviour/behavior. I was so upset and worried. Please forgive me.
– It really doesn't matter. I am thankful that you feel better.

– I am so glad you are not angry with me.
– Please don't worry about it any more.

I prefer sport. I am also interested in the cinema/movies.

– Ich schäme mich wirklich wegen meines Benehmens. Ich war so aufgeregt und ängstlich. Bitte verzeihen Sie mir.
– Es macht nichts/es ist schon gut. Es freut mich, daß es Ihnen jetzt besser geht.

– Ich freue mich, daß Sie mir nicht böse sind.
– Machen Sie sich keine Sorgen darüber.

Ich mag lieber Sport. Ich interessiere mich auch für das Kino.

6c Thought processes

advantage **der Vorteil(e)**
  disadvantage **der Nachteil(e)**
against **gegen** +acc
  I am against it **ich bin dagegen**
I analyze **ich analysiere**
analysis **die Analyse(n)**
I assume **ich nehme an***
assuming that ... **angenommen, daß ...**
I base **ich gründe**
basic **Grund-**
basically **im Grunde genommen**
basis **die Grundlage(n)**
belief **der Glaube(n) (gen -ns)**
I believe **ich glaube** +dat
  I believe in **ich glaube an** +acc
certainty **die Sicherheit(en)**
certain/sure **sicher**
I consider **ich überlege**
  I consider ... (to be) **ich halte ... (für** +acc)
consideration **der Faktor(en)**
  I take into consideration **ich berücksichtige**
  taking everything into

consideration **alles in allem**
context **der Zusammenhang(⁻e)**
on the contrary **im Gegenteil**
controversial **umstritten**
I decide **ich beschließe, ich entschließe mich**
decision **der Entschluß (⁻sse)**
I determine **ich stelle fest***
I disbelieve **ich glaube nicht**
I distinguish **ich unterscheide**
doubt **der Zweifel(-)**
I doubt **ich bezweifle, ich zweifle an** +dat
doubtful **zweifelhaft**
doubtless/without a doubt **ohne Zweifel**
exception **die Ausnahme(n)**
evidence **der Beweis(e)**
evidently **offensichtlich**
fact **die Tatsache(n)**
  in fact **in der Tat, tatsächlich**
false **falsch**
for **für** +acc
  I am for it **ich bin dafür**
I forbid **ich verbiete**

– I suggest we try to analyze the problem carefully.
– I hope we are not going to argue about it.
– What is your conclusion?

– From the beginning I would like to make our position clear. On the one hand we need to do more research. On the other hand we must cut the budget. In short, we can not afford it.

– **Ich schlage vor, wir versuchen die Frage genau zu analysieren.**
– **Hoffentlich werden wir uns nicht darüber streiten.**
– **Zu welchem Schluß sind Sie gekommen?**
– **Ich möchte unsere Lage von Anfang an klarmachen. Auf der einen Seite müssen wir mehr Forschung betreiben. Auf der anderen Seiten müssen wir das Etat kürzen. Kurz und gut, wir können es uns finanziell nicht leisten.**

hypothesis **die Hypothese(n)**
implication **die Bedeutung(en)**
interesting **interessant**
issue **die Frage(n)**
I judge **ich beurteile**
judgement **das Urteil(e)**
justice **die Gerechtigkeit**
I justify **ich rechtfertige**
I know **ich weiß**
knowledge **das Wissen, die
Kenntnis(se)**
logic **die Logik**
logical **logisch**
memory **das Gedächtnis(se)**
philosophy **die Philosophie(n)**
point of view **der Gesichtspunkt(e)**
I presume **ich nehme an***
principle **das Prinzip(ien), der
Grundsatz(-̈e)**
in/on principle **im/aus Prinzip**
problem **das Problem(e)**
proof **der Beweis(e)**
I prove **ich beweise**
I reason **ich denke durch***
I reason *(conclude)* **ich
schließe**
reason *(faculty)* **der Verstand**

I recognize **ich erkenne**
I reflect **ich denke nach***
relevant **relevant**
I remember **ich erinnere mich** +acc
right **richtig**
I am right **ich habe recht**
it is right **es stimmt**
I see **ich sehe**
I solve **ich löse**
solution **die Lösung(en)**
I suppose **ich vermute**
theoretical **theoretisch**
theory **die Theorie(n)**
in theory **theoretisch**
I think **ich denke, ich meine**
thought **der Gedanke(n)** (gen -ns)
true **wahr**
truth **die Wahrheit(en)**
I understand **ich verstehe**
understanding **das Verständnis**
valid (in-) **gültig (un-)**
view **die Ansicht**
in my view **in/nach meiner
Ansicht**
wrong **falsch**
I am wrong **ich habe unrecht**
it is wrong **es stimmt nicht**

– What do you think of the
speaker?
– In my opinion he did not consider
the basic problem. I would have
liked to ask more questions.

– In principle I agree with his
views. On the one hand he proved
the need for new housing. On the
other hand he discussed the
problems of finding a site.

– **Was halten Sie vom
Referenten?**
– **Meiner Meinung nach hat er
das Hauptproblem nicht in
Betracht gezogen. Ich hätte gern
noch einige Fragen gestellt.**
– **Im Prinzip bin ich mit seinen
Ansichten einverstanden. Auf
der einen Seite hat er den
Bedarf an neuen Häusern
festgestellt. Auf der anderen hat
er die Probleme diskutiert, wie
man ein Grundstück findet.**

6d Expressing views

I accept   **ich nehme an***
I agree (with)   **ich bin (mit +dat) einverstanden**
I agree   **ich stimme zu***
we agree (about)   **wir sind einig über** +acc
I answer   **ich beantworte**
answer   **die Antwort(en)**
I argue   **ich diskutiere, ich streite**
argument   **das Argument(e)**
I ask   **ich frage**
I ask (a question)   **ich stelle eine Frage**
I contradict   **ich widerspreche** +dat
I criticize   **ich kritisiere**
I define   **ich definiere**
definition   **die Definition(en)**
I deny   **ich leugne, ich bestreite**

I describe   **ich beschreibe**
description   **die Beschreibung(en)**
I disagree (with)   **ich bin (mit** +dat) **nicht einverstanden**
we disagree about   **wir streiten uns über** +dat
I discuss   **ich bespreche, ich diskutiere**
discussion   **die Diskussion(en)**
I maintain   **ich behaupte**
I mean   **ich meine**
opinion   **die Meinung(en)**
in my opinion   **meiner Meinung nach**
question   **die Frage(n)**
I question   **ich bezweifle**
a thorny question   **eine heikle Frage**

Let me quote my colleague. As is well known, these statements are contradictory. For example, we can not have total freedom of the press, and censorship.

Darf ich meinen Kollegen zitieren. Wie allgemein bekannt ist, widersprechen sich diese Behauptungen. Zum Beispiel, wir können nicht die totale Pressefreiheit und die Pressezensur haben.

– Can you justify that view? I believe that basically he will be for it.

– Können Sie diese Ansicht rechtfertigen? Ich meine, er wird im Grunde genommen dafür sein.

– In my opinion he is asking too much.

– Meiner Meinung nach verlangt er zu viel.

– I think you are wrong. – No, I know that I am right. Assuming that we can find the money, do you think the site is right?

– Ich glaube, das stimmt nicht.
– Nein, ich weiß, daß das stimmt. Nehmen wir an, daß wir das Geld finden. Meinen Sie, daß das Grundstück das Richtige ist?

– I consider it to be ideal.
– Ich halte es für ideal.

it is a question of **es handelt
sich um** +acc
I say **ich sage, ich meine**
I state **ich behaupte**
statement **die Behauptung(en)**
suggestion **der Vorschlag(ˉe)**
I suggest **ich schlage vor***
I summarize **ich fasse
zusammen***
summary **die
Zusammenfassung(en)**
I think (of/about) **ich denke
(an/über** +acc)
I think of **ich halte von** +dat
thought **der Gedanke**
I sum up **ich fasse zusammen***

Giving examples

as is known **wie bekannt**
etc./and so on **und so**
example **das Beispiel(e)**
for example **zum Beispiel**
I give an example **ich gebe ein
Beispiel**
i.e. **das heißt, d.h.**
namely **und zwar**
I quote **ich zitiere**
such as **wie zum Beispiel**

Comparing and contrasting

advantage **der Vorteil(e)**
I compare **ich vergleiche**
comparison **der Vergleich(e)**
in comparison with **im
Vergleich mit** +dat
I contrast **ich stelle** +dat
gegenüber*
it contrasts with **es unterscheidet
sich von** +dat
contrast **der Gegensatz(ˉe)**
in contrast **im Gegensatz zu**
+dat
I differ **ich unterscheide mich**
difference **der Unterschied(e)**
different **unterschiedlich**
different (from) *(adv)* **anders
als**
disadvantage **der Nachteil(e)**
dissimilar **verschieden**
I distinguish **ich unterscheide**
pros and cons **die Vor- und
Nachteile**
relatively **verhältnismäßig**
same **gleich, der/die/dasselbe**
similar **ähnlich**

---

beginning **der Anfang(ˉe)**
from the beginning **von Anfang
an**
I am brief **ich fasse mich kurz**
in brief **kurz**
I conclude **ich schließe**
conclusion **der Schluß (ˉsse)**
in conclusion **zum Schluß**
final **Schluß-**
finally **schließlich**
first **der/die/das erste**
firstly **erstens**
furthermore **weiter**
on the one hand **auf der einen
Seite**

on the other hand **auf der
anderen Seite**
initially **zu Anfang**
last **der/die/das letzte**
lastly **schließlich**
at last **endlich**
next **der/die/das nächste**
place **die Stelle(n)**
in the first place **an erster
Stelle**
in the second place **an
zweiter Stelle**
secondly **zweitens**
in short **kurz**
and so on **und so weiter, usw**

Arguing a point

admittedly **zwar**
all the same **trotzdem**
although **obgleich**
anyway **auf jeden Fall**
apart from **abgesehen von** +dat
as for … **was … betrifft**
as I see it **nach meiner Ansicht**
as well **auch**
despite this **trotzdem**
in effect **in Wirklichkeit**
however **aber**
incidentally **übrigens**
instead **an seiner Stelle**
instead of **statt** +gen
just as important **genauso wichtig**
likewise **gleichfalls**
no matter whether **egal, ob**
that may be so **ich glaube schon**
nevertheless **trotzdem**
otherwise **sonst**
in reality **in Wirklichkeit**
in many respects **in vielen Hinsichten**
in return **dafür**
as a rule **meistens**
so to speak **gewissermaßen**
in spite of **trotz** +gen
still, … **dennoch**

to tell the truth **um ehrlich zu sein**
whereas **indem, während**
on the whole **im großen und ganzen, alles in allem**

Cause & effect

all the more (because) **um so mehr, (da)**
as **da**
because **weil**
cause **die Ursache(n)**
consequence **die Folge(n)**
consequently **infolgedessen**
effect **die Wirkung(en), die Auswirkung(en)**
it follows that **hieraus folgt, daß**
how? **wie?**
if **wenn**
reason **der Grund(-e)**
for this reason **deshalb**
result **das Ergebnis(se)**
as a result **infolgedessen**
provided that **vorausgesetzt**
since **da**
so long as *(conj)* **solange**
that is why *(adv)* **deshalb adv**
therefore/so **so**
thus **so**
when(ever) **wenn**

In many respects things are not too bad.
As a rule people try to obey the law.
However, crime is still common, in spite of the efforts of the police.

In vielen Hinsichten ist die Lage nicht zu schlimm.
Meistens versuchen die Leute dem Gesetz zu gehorchen.
Aber die Verbrechen sind immer noch weit verbreitet, trotz der Bemühungen der Polizei.

– He is not very ill.
– Yes he is. His brother is not well either. And therefore we must wait.

– Er ist nicht sehr krank.
– Doch. Sein Bruder ist auch nicht gesund. Und deshalb müssen wir warten.

– I hope he will be better soon.

– Hoffentlich wird er bald wieder gesund.

when *(past event)* **als**
whether **ob**
why? **warum?, wozu?**

Emphasizing

above all **vor allem**
in addition **dazu**
all the more **um so mehr**
also **auch**
certainly **sicher**
clearly **offensichtlich**
under no circumstances **unter keinen Umständen**
completely **völlig, ganz**
especially **besonders**
even (more) **noch (mehr)**
without exception **ohne Ausnahme**
I emphasize **ich betone**
extremely **höchst, äußerst**
far and away **bei weitem**
fortunately **zum Glück**
honestly **ehrlich**
just when **gerade wo**
mainly **hauptsächlich**
moreover **übrigens**
naturally **natürlich, selbstverständlich**
not at all **keineswegs**
not in the least **keineswegs**

both ... and **sowohl ... wie/als**
obviously **offensichtlich, ja**
in particular **ins besondere**
particularly **besonders**
in every respect **in jeder Hinsicht**
I stress **ich betone**
thanks to **dank** +dat
undeniably **unleugbar**
very **sehr**
and what is more **und dazu**

Expressing reservations

even if **auch wenn**
even so **selbst dann**
to some extent **gewissermaßen**
at first sight **beim ersten Blick**
hardly **kaum**
in general **im allgemeinen**
in the main **zum größten Teil**
in part **zum Teil**
partly **teils, teilweise**
perhaps **vielleicht**
presumably **wohl, vermutlich**
probably **wahrscheinlich**
relatively **verhältnismäßig**
unfortunately **leider**
unusual(ly) **ungewöhnlich**
virtually **fast**
in a way **gewissermaßen**

– He is said to have gone abroad, in fact to the States.
– That really is the limit.
– What are the reasons for his behaviour/behavior?
– Maybe he is cross with me and that is why he went away.
As a result, I have problems at work, all the more so because he usually does so much.

So long as he writes soon I shall not worry.

– **Er soll ins Ausland gefahren sein, und zwar in die USA.**
– **Das ist ja die Höhe!**
– **Warum benimmt er sich auf diese Weise?**
– **Vielleicht ist er mir böse und ist deshalb weggegangen. Ich habe infolgedessen Probleme auf meiner Arbeitstelle, um so mehr, da er gewöhnlich so viel tut.**
Wenn er nur bald schreibt, werde ich mir keine Sorgen machen.

Human life & relationships

7a Family & friends

Friendship

acquaintance **der/die Bekannte** *(adj/n)*
boyfriend **der Freund(e)**
chum **der Kumpel(-)**
classmate **der Klassenkamerad** *(wk)*
companion **der Gefährte** *(wk)*, **die Gefährtin(nen)**
friend **der Freund(e) [-in]**
close friend **der enge Freund(e) [-in]**
friendship **die Freundschaft(en)**
gang **die Gang(s)**
I get along/on with **ich komme mit jdm. gut zurecht*/aus***
we get together **wir treffen uns**
girl friend **die Freundin(nen)**
I get to know **ich lerne kennen***
human relationships **die menschlichen Beziehungen** *(pl)*
I introduce **ich stelle vor***
mate/buddy **der Kamerad** *(wk)*
penfriend/pal **der Brieffreund(e)**
[-in]
relationship **die Verwandtschaft(en)**
schoolfriend/pal **der Schulfreund(e) [-in]**

The family and close relatives

adopted **adoptiert, Adoptiv-**
ancestor **der Vorfahr** *(wk)* **[-in]**
ancestry **die Abstammung(en)**
aunt **die Tante(n)**
maiden aunt **die unverheiratete Tante(n)**
baby **das Baby(s)**
brother **der Bruder(̈)**
brothers and sisters **die Geschwister** *(pl)*
brother-in-law **der Schwager(̈)**
child **das Kind(er)**
close relative **der/die enge Verwandte** *(adj/n)*
closely related **nah verwandt mit** +dat
common-law **eheähnlich**

We are good friends. We get on well together. We do a lot together.	**Wir sind gute Freunde. Wir kommen gut miteinander aus. Wir unternehmen viel gemeinsam.**
We are not talking. She's very difficult to get on with. We don't agree.	**Wir reden nicht mehr miteinander. Es ist sehr schwierig, mit ihr auszukommen. Wir sind nicht einverstanden.**
I live with my grandparents.	**Ich wohne bei meinen Großeltern.**
It runs in the family.	**Es liegt in der Familie.**

common-law partner **der Partner(-) [-in]**
cousin **der Cousin(s), die Cousine(n)**
dad/daddy **der Vati(s)**
daughter **die Tochter(⁻)**
daughter-in-law **die Schwiegertochter(⁻)**
elder **älter**
eldest **der/die/das älteste**
family **die Familie(n)**
family-tree **der Familienstammbaum(⁻e)**
father **der Vater(⁻)**
father-in-law **der Schwiegervater(⁻)**
fiance(e) **der/die Verlobte** (adj/n)
foster **Pflege-**
genealogy **die Genealogie(n)**
godmother **die Patin(nen)**
grandad **der Opa(s)**
grandchild **das Enkelkind(er)**
granddaughter **die Enkeltochter(⁻)**
grandfather **der Großvater(⁻)**
grandma **die Großmama(s)**
grandmother **die Großmutter(⁻)**
grandpa **der Großpapa(s)**
grandparents **die Großeltern** (pl)
grandson **der Enkelsohn(⁻e)**
granny **die Oma(s)**
guardian **der Vormund(⁻er)**
half-brother **der Halbbruder(⁻)**
half-sister **die Halbschwester(n)**

husband **der Ehemann(⁻er)**
member of the family **der/die Familienangehörige** (adj/n)
mother **die Mutter(⁻)**
mother-in-law **die Stiefmutter(⁻)**
mum/mom **die Mutti(s)**
nephew **der Neffe(n)** (wk)
niece **die Nichte(n)**
only child **das Einzelkind(er)**
parents **die Eltern** (pl)
partner **der Partner(-) [-in]**
related **verwandt**
relation **der/die Verwandte** (adj/n)
sister **die Schwester(n)**
son **der Sohn(⁻e)**
son-in-law **der Schwiegersohn(⁻e)**
spouse **der Gatte** (wk), **die Gattin(nen)**
step- **Stief-**
stepfather **der Stiefvater(⁻)**
twin **der Zwilling(e)**
twin brother **der Zwillingsbrüder(⁻)**
twin sister **die Zwillingsschwestern**
uncle **der Onkel(-)**
wife **die Ehefrau(en)**
younger **jünger**
youngest (adj) **der/die/das jüngste**

– Have you any family?
– I come from a large family. I have four brothers and sisters

I have no close family. I am an only child.

Have you any children?
He has family problems.
I'd like you to meet my parents.

– **Hast du eine Familie?**
– **Ich komme aus einer großen Familie. Ich habe vier Geschwister.**

Ich habe keine engen Verwandten. Ich bin (ein) Einzelkind.

Hast du Kinder?
Er hat Probleme in der Familie.
Ich möchte Sie meinen Eltern vorstellen.

➤ LOVE & CHILDREN 7b; LIFE & DEATH 7c

7b Love & children

Love & marriage

adultery **der Ehebruch(ˉe)**
affair **das Verhältnis(se)**
I have an affair with **ich habe ein Verhältnis mit** +dat
alimony **die Unterhaltszahlung(en)**
bachelor **der Junggeselle(n)** *(wk)*
betrothal **die Verlobung(en)**
betrothed **der/die Verlobte** *(adj/n)*
breakdown **der Zusammenbruch(ˉe)**
bride **die Braut(ˉe)**
bridegroom **der Bräutigam(e)**
bridesmaid **die Brautjungfer(n)**
I cheat on **ich betrüge**
couple **das Paar(e)**
married couple **das Ehepaar(e)**
I court **ich mache jdm. den Hof**
divorce **die Scheidung(en)**
divorced **geschieden**
I get divorced **ich lasse mich scheiden**
divorcee **der/die Geschiedene** *(adj/n)*
engaged **verlobt**
engagement **die Verlobung(en)**
I fall for **ich bin in jdn. vernarrt**
I fall in love (with) **ich verliebe mich (in** +acc)
I get divorced (from) **ich lasse mich (von jdm.) scheiden**
I get engaged to **ich verlobe mich mit** +dat
I get married (to) **ich verheirate mich (mit** +dat)
I go out with **ich gehe mit** +dat
we are incompatible **wir passen nicht zueinander**
love **die Liebe(n)**
I love **ich liebe**
lover **der/die Geliebte** *(adj/n)*
marriage **die Ehe(n), die Heirat(en)**
marriage guidance **die Eheberatung**
married **verheiratet**
I marry **ich heirate**
matrimony **der Ehestand** *(no pl)*
mistress **die Geliebte** *(adj/n)*
newly-married couple **die Neuvermählten** *(pl)*
orgasm **der Orgasmus (-en)**
promiscuity **die Promiskuität**
he is promiscuous **er wechselt häufig seine Partnerin**
relationship **das Verhältnis(se)**
we separate **wir trennen uns**
separation **die Trennung(en)**
sexual intercourse **der Geschlechtsverkehr** *(no pl)*
we have sex **wir lieben uns**

– Are you married?
– We are getting engaged.

– She doesn't understand me. She is always nagging. She gets me worked up.
– He shouts at me. He makes me mad.

– **Bist du verheiratet?**
– **Wir verloben uns.**

– **Sie versteht mich nicht. Sie meckert ständig. Sie regt mich auf.**
– **Er schreit mich an. Er macht mich verrückt.**

single **ledig**
single mother **die alleinstehende Mutter(-̈)**
unmarried **unverheiratet**
wedding **die Hochzeit(en)**
widow **die Witwe(n)**
widower **der Witwer(-)**

Birth & children

abortion **die Abtreibung(en)**
I have an abortion **ich lasse das Kind abtreiben**
I adopt **ich adoptiere**
adoption **die Adoption(en)**
baby **das Baby(s)**
babysitter **der Babysitter(-)**
baptism **die Taufe(n)**
I am baptized **ich werde/bin getauft**
birth **die Geburt(en)**
birth control **die Geburtenkontrolle**
birth-rate **die Geburtsrate(n)**
birthday **der Geburtstag(e)**
I was born **ich wurde geboren**
boy **der Junge(n)** *(wk)*
I bring up **ich erziehe**
I breast feed **ich stille**
caesarian section **der Kaiserschnitt(e)**
child **das Kind(er)**
child maintenance **das Kindergeld**
child-minder **der Kinderbetreuer(er) [-in]**
childhood **die Kindheit(en)**
christening **die Taufe(n)**
I conceive **ich empfange**
condom **das/der Kondom(e), das Präservativ(e)**
contraception **die Empfängnisverhütung**
contractions **die Wehen** *(pl)*
I deliver a baby **ich bringe zur Welt**
I am expecting a baby **ich erwarte ein Baby**

family planning **die Familienplanung**
fertile (in-) **(un)fruchtbar**
fertility **die Fruchtbarkeit**
fertility drug **die Fruchtbarkeitspille(n)**
I give birth **Ich gebäre/bringe zur Welt**
foetus/fetus **der Fötus (Foten/Fötusse)**
girl **das Mädchen(-)**
infancy **die Kindheit(en)**
infant **das Kleinkind(er)**
infantile **kindlich**
insemination **die Befruchtung(en)**
artificial insemination **die künstliche Befruchtung**
lad **der Bursche(n), der Junge(n)** *(wk)*
lass **das Mädchen(-)**
he looks like his mother **er sieht wie seine Mutter aus***
I have a miscarriage **ich habe eine Fehlgeburt**
midwife **die Hebamme(n)**
nappy/diaper **die Windel(n)**
nanny **das Kindermädchen(-)**
new-born child **das neugeborene Kind(er)**
orphan **die Waise(n), das Waisenkind(er)**
ovary **der Eierstock(-̈e)**
pregnancy **die Schwangerschaft(en)**
I get pregnant **Ich werde schwanger**
period *(monthly)* **die Periode(n)**
I remind of **ich erinnere an** +acc
I spoil my child **ich verwöhne mein Kind**
stillbirth **die Totgeburt(en)**
teenage **Jugend-**
teenager **der Teenager(-)**
toddler **das Kleinkind(er)**
triplets **der Drilling(e)**

➤ FAMILY 7a

7c Life & death

Growing up

adolescent **der/die Jugendliche** *(adj/n)*

adolescence **die Jugend**

adult **der/die Erwachsene** *(adj/n)*

age **das Alter(-)**

aged **bejahrt**

centenarian **der/die Hundertjährige** *(adj/n)*

child **das Kind(er)**

I come from **ich stamme aus** +dat

early retirement **der Vorruhestand**

elder(ly) **älter**

elderly *(adj)* **der/die/das ältere**

eldest *(adj)* **der/die/das älteste**

female **die Frau(en)**

female *(adj)* **weiblich**

foreigner **der Ausländer(-) [-in]**

generation **die Generation(en)**

generation gap **das Generationsproblem(e)**

I grow old/older **ich werde größer**

grown-up **der/die Erwachsene** *(adj/n)*

I grow up **ich wachse auf***

life **das Leben(-)**

life assurance **die Lebensversicherung(en)**

male/man **der Mann(-̈er)**

male *(adj)* **männlich**

maturity **die Reife** *(no pl)*

menopause **die Wechseljahre** *(pl)*

middle age **das mittlere Lebensalter**

new **neu**

nickname **der Spitzname(n)** *(wk)*

old **alt**

old age **das hohe Alter**

old man/woman **der/die Alte** *(adj/n)*

old people's home **das Altersheim(e)**

pension **die Rente(n)**

pensioner **der Rentner(-) [-in]**

people **die Leute** *(pl)*

person **die Person(en), der Mensch(en)** *(wk)*

in the prime of his/her life **in der Blüte seiner/ihrer Jahre**

puberty **die Pubertät** *(no pl)*

responsible for **verantwortlich für** +acc

I retire **ich lasse mich pensionieren**

retired **pensioniert**

retirement **der Ruhestand**

senility **die Senilität** *(no pl)*

single **ledig**

spinster **die ledige Frau(en)**

stranger **der/die Fremde** *(adj/n)*

surname **der Familienname(n)** *(wk)*

I take after **ich bin jdm. ähnlich**

– When I grow up, I want to be an astronaut.

– How old are you?

– I'm ten.

He respects his elders.

Young people often come into conflict with their parents.

– **Wenn ich groß bin, möchte ich Astronaut werden.**

– **Wie alt bist du?**

– **Ich bin zehn Jahre alt.**

Er respektiert ältere Menschen.

Junge Leute geraten oft in Konflikt mit ihren Eltern.

well-brought up **wohlerzogen**
woman **die Frau(en)**
young **jung**
young person **der junge
Mensch(en)** *(wk)*
younger **jünger**
youngest *(adj)* **der/die/das jüngste**
youth **die Jugend**
youth *(persons)* **der/die
Jugendliche** *(adj/n)*

Death

afterlife **das Leben nach dem Tod**
angel **der Engel(-)**
ashes **die Asche** *(no pl)*
autopsy **die Autopsie(n)**
I bequeathe **ich verebe**
body/corpse **die Leiche(n)**
burial **das Begräbnis(se)**
I bury **ich begrabe**
he is cremated **er wird
eingeäschert**
cremation **die Einäscherung(en)**
crematorium/crematory **die
Krematorium (-ien)**
dead **tot**
death **der Tod(e), das
Todesfall(¨e)**
death certificate **die
Sterbeurkunde(n)**
death rate **die Sterberate(n)**
I die **ich sterbe**
epitaph **die Grabinschrift(en)**
eulogy **die Lobesrede(n)**

fatal **tödlich**
funeral **die Beerdigung(en)**
grave **das Grab(¨er)**
gravestone/tombstone **der
Grabstein(e)**
graveyard/cemetery **der
Friedhof(¨e)**
heaven **der Himmel(-)**
he goes to heaven **er kommt
in den Himmel**
hell **die Hölle**
I inherit **ich erbe**
inheritance **die Erbschaft(en)**
I kill **ich töte**
I am killed **ich komme um***
late *(dead)* **selig**
last rites **die Letzte Ölung**
I lose my life **ich komme ums
Leben**
mortuary **die Leichenhalle(n)**
I mourn (for) **ich trauere um** +acc,
ich beklage
mourning **die Trauer** *(no pl)*
obituary **der Nachruf(e)**
he passes away **er scheidet hin***
remains **die Überreste** *(pl)*
tomb **das Grab(¨er), das
Grabmal(¨e)**
undertaker/mortician **der
Leichenbestatter(-) [-in]**
will **der Wille** *(no pl) (gen des
Willens) (wk)*
the last will and testament of …
der Letzte Wille des/der …

Many refugees are dying of
hunger, others of cholera. | **Viele Flüchtlinge sterben vor
Hunger, andere an Cholera.**

It's a matter of life and death. | **Es geht um Leben und Tod.**

There are many causes of death. | **Es gibt viele Todesursachen.**

➤ SICKNESS 11; WAR 27a

Daily life

8a The house

amenities **die Einrichtung(en)**
apartment **die Wohnung(en)**
block of flats/apartment house **der Wohnblock(-̈e)**
I build **ich baue**
building **das Gebäude(-)**
building plot **das Grundstück(e)**
building site **die Baustelle(n), das Baugelände(-)**
building society/savings & loan association **die Bausparkasse(n)**
bungalow **der Bungalow(s)**
caretaker **der Hausmeister(-)**
chalet **das Chalet(s)**
council flat **die Sozialwohnung(en)**
council/public housing **der soziale Wohnungsbau** *(no pl)*
detached house **das Einzelhaus(-̈er)**
I build an extension **ich baue ein Zimmer an***

flat/apartment **die Wohnung(en)**
furnished (un-) **(un)möbliert**
home **die Wohnung(en), das Haus(-̈er)**
   at home **zu Hause**
house **das Haus(-̈er)**
housing **die Wohnverhältnisse** *(pl)*
landlord **der Grundbesitzer(-), der (Haus)wirt(e)**
lease **der Mietvertrag(-̈e)**
leasehold property **der Pachtbesitz**
I let/rent out **ich vermiete**
I modernize **ich modernisiere**
mortgage **die Hypothek(en)**
mortgage rate **der Zinssatz(-̈e)**
I move (house) **ich ziehe um***
I occupy **ich bewohne**
I own **ich besitze**
owner-occupied flat/apartment **die Eigentumswohnung(en)**
owner-occupied house **das**

We are buying a new detached house. | **Wir kaufen ein neues Einfamilienhaus.**
We are having a house built. | **Wir lassen ein Haus bauen.**
I live in a rented, furnished apartment. | **Ich wohne in einer möblierten Mietwohnung.**

My tenancy has two weeks to run. | **Mein Mietvertrag hat noch zwei Wochen zu laufen.**

We moved house two years ago. The house has a pleasant view: it grows on you after a while! | **Wir zogen vor zwei Jahren um. Das Haus hat einen schönen Ausblick: mit der Zeit findet man Gefallen daran!**

➤ THE HOME 8b; FURNISHINGS 8c; DAILY ROUTINE 8d

Eigentumshaus(̈-er)
penthouse **die Dachterrassenwohnung(en)**
prefabricated house **das Fertighaus(̈-er)**
I rent **ich miete**
rent **die Miete(n)**
semi-detached house **das Zweifamilienhaus(̈-er)**
street lighting **die Straßenbeleuchtung** *(no pl)*
I take out a mortgage **ich nehme eine Hypothek auf***
tenancy **das Miet/Pachtverhältnis(se)**
tenant **der Mieter(-), der Pächter(-)**

Rooms

attic **die Dachstube(n), die Mansarde(n)**
balcony **der Balkon(s)**
basement **das Kellergeschoß (-sse)**
bathroom **das Badezimmer(-)**
bedroom **das Schlafzimmer(-)**
breakfast room **der Frühstücksraum(̈-e)**
cellar **der Keller(-)**
corridor **der Gang(̈-e)**
dining-room **das Eßzimmer(-)**

en-suite **mit Bad**
garage **die Garage(n)**
ground floor **das Erdgeschoß (-sse)**
hall(way) **der Hausflur(e)**
kitchen **die Küche(n)**
landing **der Treppenabsatz(̈-e), der Flur(e)**
lavatory/bathroom **die Toilette(n)**
living room **das Wohnzimmer(-)**
loft **der Dachboden(̈-)**
lounge **das Wohnzimmer(-)**
mezzanine floor **das Zwischengeschoß (-sse)**
passage **der Korridor(e)**
room **das Zimmer(-)**
shower room **der Duschraum(̈-e)**
sitting-room/living room **das Wohnzimmer(-)**
staircase **das Treppenhaus(̈-er)**
stairs **die Treppe(n)**
study **das Arbeitszimmer(-)**
sunroom **die Veranda (-en)**
terrace **die Terrasse(n)**
toilet **die Toilette(n)**
upper floor **das obere Stockwerk(e)**
utility room **die Waschküche(n)**
W.C. **das WC(s)**
verandah **die Veranda(s)**

Her penthouse is for rent.

Ihre Dachterrassenwohnung ist zu vermieten.

Let's go home.

Gehen wir nach Hause.

We are renting a flat/an apartment at the moment. The rent is very high and I do not like the estate/housing development.

Wir mieten zur Zeit eine Wohnung. Die Miete ist sehr hoch, und ich mag die Wohnsiedlung nicht.

It's a large three-room flat on the third floor.

Es ist eine geräumige Drei-Zimmer-Wohnung im dritten Stock.

➤ HOUSING & HOMELESSNESS 12c

8b The home

aerial **die Antenne(n)**
back-door **die Hintertür(en)**
big **groß**
blind **das Rouleau(s)**
button **der Knopf(-̈e)**
carpet **der Teppich(e)**
ceiling **die Decke(n)**
central **Zentral-**
central heating **die Zentralheizung(en)**
chimney/smokestack **der Schornstein(e)**
clean **sauber**
clothes hanger **der Kleiderbügel(-)**
comfortable (un-) **bequem**
cosy **gemütlich**
curtain **der Vorhang(-̈e), die Gardine(n)**
desk **der Schreibtisch(e)**
dirty **schmutzig**
door **die Tür(en)**
door-handle **der Türgriff(e)**
door-knob **der Türknauf(-̈e)**
door-mat **die Fußmatte(n)**
downstairs **(nach) unten**
dusty **staubig**
dustbin/trash can **die Mülltonne(n)**
electric **elektrisch**
electric plug **der (elektrische) Stecker(-)**
electric socket **die Steckdose(n)**
electricity **der Strom, die Elektrizität**
filthy **dreckig**
fire alarm **der Feueralarm(e)**
fire extinguisher **der Feuerlöscher(-)**
fireplace **der offene Kamin(e)**
flex/extension cord **das Verlängerungskabel(-)**
floor **der (Fuß)boden(-̈)**
floor (storey/story) **der Stock, das Stockwerk(e)**
    on the first floor **im ersten Stock**

front door **die Haustür(en)**
furnished **möbliert**
furniture **die Möbel** (pl)
    item of furniture **das Möbelstück(e)**
gas **das Gas**
glass (material) **das Glas(-̈er)**
handle **der Griff(e)**
    handle (of broom, pan) **der Stiel(e)**
    handle (on jug) **der Henkel(-)**
hearth **der Kamin(e)**
hearth and home **Haus und Herd**
household **der Haushalt(e)**
included **inbegriffen**
key **der Schlüssel(-)**
keyhole **das Schlüsselloch(-̈er)**
lamp **die Lampe(n)**
lampshade **der Lampenschirm(e)**
letterbox **der Briefkasten(-̈)**
lever **der Hebel(-)**
lift **der Lift(s), der Fahrstuhl(-̈e)**
light bulb **die Birne(n)**
light **das Licht(er)**
light-switch **der Lichtschalter(-)**
lock **das Schloß (-̈sser)**
mantelpiece **der Kaminsims(e)**
mat **die Matte(n)**
modern **modern**
new **neu**
nice **schön, nett**
off (switch) **aus**
    off (tap/faucet) **zu**
old **alt**
on (switch, tap/faucet) **an**
own **eigen**
pipe **das Rohr(e)**
plaster **der Verputz** (no pl)
plumbing **die Leitungen** (pl)
price **der Preis(e)**
radiator **der Heizkörper(-), die Heizung** (no pl)
roof **das Dach(-̈er)**
rubbish/garbage **der Abfall(-̈e)**
shelf **das Regal(e)**

shutters **der Fensterladen(-)**
situation **die Lage(n)**
skylight **das (Dach)Fenster(-)**
small **klein**
step **die Stufe(n)**
switch **der Schalter(-)**
tile *(roof)* **der Dachziegel(-)**
   tile *(ceramic)* **die Fliese(n)**
upstairs **(nach) oben**
vase **die Vase(n)**
view **die Aussicht(en)**
wall **die Mauer(n)**
   (inside) **die Wand(-e)**
   (partition) **die Trennwand(-e)**
waste paper basket **der Papierkorb(-e)**
water **das Wasser**
window **das Fenster(-)**
window-sill **die Fensterbank(-e)**
wire/flex **das Kabel(-)**
wiring **die elektrischen Leitungen** *(pl)*
wood **das Holz**

Electrical items

blender **der Mixer(-)**
cassette deck **das Kassettendeck(s)**
cassette recorder **der Kassettenrecorder(-)**
coffee machine **die Kaffeemaschine(n)**
compact-disc player **der CD-Spieler(-)**
deepfreeze **die Tiefkühltruhe(n)**

dishwasher **der Geschirrspüler(-)**
electric appliance **das Elektrogerät(e)**
electric razor/shaver **der Rasierapparat(e)**
electric cooker/stove **der Elektroherd(e)**
food mixer/processor **die Küchenmaschine(n)**
fridge/refrigerator **der Kühlschrank(-e)**
freezer **der Tiefkühlschrank(-e)**
hairdryer **der Fön(e)®**
hi-fi **die Hi-Fi-Anlage(n)**
iron **das Bügeleisen(-)**
micro-wave oven **der Mikrowellenherd(e)**
radio **das Radio(s)**
record player **der Schallplattenspieler(-)**
refrigerator **der Kühlschrank(-e)**
stereo system **die Stereoanlage(n)**
tape player **der Kassettenspieler(-)**
tape recorder **der Kassettenrecorder(-)**
television (TV) **das Fernsehen** *(no pl)*
tumble-drier **der Trockenautomat(en)**
TV set **der Fernseher(-)**
vacuum cleaner **der Staubsauger(-)**
video recorder **der Videorecorder(-)**
walkman® **der Walkman(s)®**
washing machine **die Waschmaschine(n)**

Shall we go up in the lift?	**Wollen wir mit dem Lift nach oben fahren?**
Careful, there's a step.	**Vorsicht, hier ist eine Stufe.**
Plug in the TV and switch on!	**Schließen Sie den Fernseher an, und schalten Sie ihn an!**
You can turn the heating up or down.	**Man kann die Heizung kleiner stellen oder höher drehen.**
The electricity has been cut off.	**Der Strom ist gesperrt.**

➤ DAILY ROUTINE 8d

8c Furnishings

Lounge

armchair **der Lehnstuhl(¨e)**
ashtray **der Aschenbecher(-)**
book-shelf/bookshelf **das Bücherregal(e)**
bookcase **das Bücherregal(e), der Bücherschrank(¨e)**
bureau **der Sekretär(e)**
coffee table **der Kaffeetisch(e)**
cupboard/closet **der Schrank(¨e)**
cushion **das Kissen(-)**
easy chair **der Sessel(-)**
ornament **der Schmuck, der Ziergegenstand(¨e)**
picture **das Bildnis(se), das Gemälde(-)**
   picture *(portrait)* **das Porträt(s)**
photo **das Foto(s)**
poster **das Poster(-)**
pouffe **der Puff(e)**
rocking-chair **der Schaukelstuhl(¨e)**
rug **der Läufer(-)**
settee **die Couch(en), das Sofa(s)**
sofa **das Sofa(s)**

Kitchen

bottle-opener **der Flaschenöffner(-)**
bowl **die Schüssel(n)**
broom **der Besen(-)**
cloth **der Lappen(-)**
   drying-up cloth **das Tuch(¨er)**
clothes line **die Wäscheleine(n)**
clothes peg **die Wäscheklammer(n)**
coffee pot **die Kaffeekanne(n)**
cooker/stove **der Herd(e), der Ofen(¨)**
crockery/dishes **das Geschirr** *(no pl)*
cup **die Tasse(n)**
cupboard **der Schrank(¨e)**
   wall-cupboard **der Wandschrank(¨e)**

cutlery **das Besteck(e)**
dish **die Schüssel(n)**
dishcloth **der Spüllappen(-)**
draining-board **das Ablaufbrett(er)**
duster **das Staubtuch(¨er)**
fork **die Gabel(n)**
gas cooker **der Gasherd(e)**
gas stove **der Gasofen(¨)**
glass **das Glas(¨er)**
   wine-glass **das Weinglas(¨er)**
jug **der Krug(¨e), die Kanne(n)**
knife **das Messer(-)**
   carving knife **das Tranchiermesser(-)**
leftovers **die Überreste** *(pl)*
mug **der Becher(-)**
oven **der Herd(e)**
peppermill **die Pfeffermühle(n)**
plate **der Teller(-)**
rubbish bin/garbage can **der Mülleimer(-)**
saltcellar/shaker **der Salzstreuer(-)**
saucer **die Untertasse(n)**
scouring pad **der Topfkratzer(-)**
sink **das Spülbecken(-)**
sink unit **die Spüle(n)**
spoon **der Löffel(-)**
tap/faucet **der Wasserhahn(¨e)**
teapot **die Teekanne(n)**
tea-towel **das Geschirrtuch(¨er)**
tray **das Tablett(s)**
washing powder **das Waschmittel(-)**
washing-up/washing liquid **das Spülmittel(-)**

Dining-room

chair **der Stuhl(¨e)**
candle **die Wachskerze(n)**
candlestick **der Kerzenhalter(-)**
dresser **die Anrichte(n), der Geschirrschrank(¨e)**
hot warmer **die Warmhalteplatte(n)**

place setting **das Gedeck(e)**
serviette **die Serviette(n)**
sideboard **das Büffett(s)**
table **der Tisch(e)**
table cloth **die Tischdecke(n)**
table napkin/serviette **die Serviette(n)**

Bedroom

alarm clock **der Wecker(-)**
bed **das Bett(en)**
    bunk bed **das Etagenbett(en)**
    double bed **das Doppelbett(en)**
bedclothes **das Bettzeug** *(no pl)*
bedside table **der Nachttisch(e)**
bedspread **der Bettüberwurf(¨e)**
blanket **die Decke(n)**
chest of drawers **die Kommode(n)**
dressing table **die Frisierkommode(n)**
duvet **das Federbett(en)**
pillow **das Kopfkissen(-)**
quilt **die Steppdecke(n)**
sheet **das Bettuch(¨er)**
wardrobe **der Kleiderschrank(¨e)**

Bathroom

basin **das (Wasch)becken(-)**
bath **das Bad(¨er)**
bathplug **der Stöpsel(-)**
bath-mat **die Badematte(n)**
clothes brush **die Kleiderbürste(n)**
flannel **der Waschlappen(-)**
handbasin **das Waschbecken(-)**
laundry basket **der Waschkorb(¨e)**
loo **das Klo(s)**
mirror **der Spiegel(-)**
nail-brush **die Nagelbürste(n)**
plug **der Stecker(-)**
shampoo **das Shampoo(s)**
shower **die Dusche(n)**
sink **das Waschbecken(-)**
soap **die Seife(n)**
tap **der Wasserhahn(¨e)**
toilet **die Toilette(n)**
toilet paper **das Toilettenpapier**
toothbrush **die Zahnbürste(n)**
toothpaste **die Zahnpasta(s)**
towel **das Handtuch(¨er)**
towel rail **der Handtuchhalter(-)**
washbasin **das Waschbecken(-)**

The washing machine doesn't work! Can you repair it?	**Die Waschmaschine funktioniert nicht. Können Sie sie reparieren?**
Come into the sitting-room.	**Kommen Sie ins Wohnzimmer.**
The bed has not been changed.	**Das Bettwäsche ist nicht sauber.**
Can I take a bath? Could we have some clean towels?	**Kann ich ein Bad nehmen? Könnten wir einige saubere Handtücher bekommen?**
There is no toilet paper. The toilet will not flush! The hot tap/faucet doesn't work!	**Es gibt kein Toilettenpapier. Die Toilette spült nicht! Der Heißwasserhahn funktioniert nicht!**
My toothpaste has run out.	**Meine Zahnpasta ist alle.**

➤ GARDENING 24c; TOOLS App.8b; TOILETRIES 9b

8d Daily routine

bath **das Bad(¨-er)**
bed **das Bett(en)**
breakfast **das Frühstück(e)**
clean **sauber**
cleaner **die Putzfrau(en)**
daily routine **der Alltag** *(no pl)*
dinner *(evening)* **das Abendessen(-)**
evening meal **das Abendbrot(e)**
home **das Heim(e), das Haus(¨-er)**
home *(at home)* **zu Hause**
home *(to one's home)* **nach Hause**
housekeeper/maid **die Haushälterin(nen)**
housework **die Hausarbeit(en)**
lunch **das Mittagessen(-)**
school **die Schule(n)**
shop **der Laden(¨)**
sleep **der Schlaf** *(no pl)*
spare *(left over)* **der Rest(e)**
spare *(available)* **übrig, frei**
spare time **die Freizeit**
spring cleaning **der Frühjahrsputz**
supper **das Abendessen(-)**
time **die Zeit(en)**
washing **die Wäsche** *(no pl)*
washing (dirty) **schmutzig**
washing up **das schmutzige Geschirr** *(no pl)*
work **die Arbeit(en)**

Actions

I break **ich breche**
I bring **ich bringe**
I buy **ich kaufe**
I carry **ich trage**
I change *(clothes)* **ich ziehe mich um***
I chat **ich plaudere**
I clean **ich putze, ich mache sauber***
I clear away **ich räume weg***
I clear the table **ich räume/decke den Tisch ab***

I cook **ich koche**
I close *(door)* **ich mache zu***
I darn **ich stopfe**
I dirty **ich mache schmutzig**
I do **ich tue, ich mache**
I drink **ich trinke**
I drop **ich lasse fallen***
I dry up **ich trockne ab***
I dust **ich wische Staub**
I eat **ich esse**
I empty **ich leere**
I enter **ich betrete**
I extend **ich baue aus*/an***
I fall **ich falle**
I fasten **ich verschließe**
I fasten *(attach)* **ich mache fest***
I fill **ich fülle**
I get dressed **ich ziehe mich an***
I get undressed **ich ziehe mich aus***
I get up **ich stehe auf***
I go to bed **ich gehe ins Bett**
I go to sleep **ich gehe schlafen***
I go to the toilet **ich gehe zur Toilette**
I have breakfast **ich frühstücke**
I have lunch **ich esse zu Mittag**
I have tea/coffee **ich trinke Tee/den Nachmittagskaffee**
I heat **ich heize**
I iron **ich bügele**
I knit **ich stricke**
I knock **ich klopfe, schlage**
I lay the table **ich decke den Tisch**
I leave **ich verlasse** +acc
I let *(allow)* **ich erlaube**
I let/rent **ich vermiete**
I live **ich wohne**
I lock **ich schließe ab***
I make **ich mache**
I make wet/dampen **ich befeuchte**
I mend **ich repariere, flicke**
I move (house) **ich ziehe um***

I move in **ich ziehe ein***
I move out **ich ziehe aus***
I move **ich bewege mich**
it is on **es ist an**
it is off **es ist aus**
I paint **ich streiche an***
I pick up **ich hebe auf***
I polish **ich poliere**
I prepare **ich bereite vor***
I press *(button)* **ich drücke (den Knopf)**
    I press *(iron)* **ich bügele**
I put on *(clothes)* **ich ziehe an***
    I put on *(radio, TV)* **ich mache an***
I put away **ich räume weg***
I put right **ich stelle zurecht***
I repair/fix **ich repariere**
I rest **ich ruhe mich aus***
I ring *(telephone)* **ich telefoniere**
    I ring *(doorbell)* **ich klingele**
I rinse **ich spüle**
I sew **ich nähe**
I share **ich teile**
I shine **ich poliere**
I shop **ich kaufe ein***
I shower **ich dusche**
I shut/close **ich schließe**

I sit down **ich setze mich (hin*)**
I sit **ich sitze**
I sleep **ich schlafe**
I speak **ich spreche**
I stand **ich stehe**
I stand up **ich stehe auf***
I start **ich beginne**
I stop **ich beende**
I sweep **ich kehre**
I switch/turn off **ich schalte aus***
I switch/turn on **ich schalte ein***
I take off **ich ziehe aus***
I tear **ich zerreiße**
I throw away **ich werfe weg***
I tidy/straighten up **ich räume auf***
I tie **ich binde**
I unblock **ich schließe auf***
I undo **ich mache auf***
I use **ich benutze**
I wake up **ich wache auf***
I wake up someone **ich wecke jdn.**
I wallpaper **ich tapeziere**
I wash **ich wasche**
I wash up/wash dishes **ich wasche ab***
I watch TV **ich sehe fern***
I wear **ich trage**

I get up, get dressed and go to work.

Ich stehe auf, ziehe mich an und gehe zur Arbeit.

We get up at 7 o'clock. We have breakfast at eight. Dinner will be at nine p.m.

Wir stehen um 7.00 Uhr auf. Wir frühstücken um acht. Das Abendessen wird um neun sein.

The table has not been cleared! Who is going to wash up/wash the dishes? I'll do the drying up.

Der Tisch wurde nicht abgeräumt! Wer wäscht ab? Ich werde abtrocknen.

She does the cleaning and dusting for us on Fridays.

Freitags macht sie bei uns sauber und staubt ab/wischt staub.

➤ GARDENING 24c

Shopping

9a General terms

article **der Artikel(-)**
assistant **der Verkäufer(-) [-in]**
automatic door **die automatische Tür(en)**
bank-note **der Geldschein(e)**
bargain **das Sonderangebot(e)**
basement **das Untergeschoß (-sse)**
business **das Geschäft(e)**
cash desk/register **die Kasse(n)**
change *(coinage)* **das Wechselgeld(er)**
cheap **billig, preiswert**
check-out **die Kasse(n)**
choice **die Auswahl** *(no pl)*
closed **geschlossen, zu**
coin **die Münze(n)**
colour/color **die Farbe(n)**
costly **kostspielig**
credit **der Kredit(e)**
credit card **die Kreditkarte(n)**
customer information **die Kundeninformation(en)**
customer service **der Kundendienst(e)**
day off/closed **am ... geschlossen**
dear **teuer**

department **die Abteilung(en)**
deposit **die Anzahlung(en)**
discount **der Rabatt(e)**
entrance **der Eingang(¨e)**
escalator **die Rolltreppe(n)**
exit **der Ausgang(¨e)**
expensive **teuer**
fashion **die Mode(n)**
fire door **die Feuertür(en)**
fire exit **der Notausgang(¨e)**
fitting room **der Anproberaum(¨e)**
free **frei, kostenlos**
free gift **(die Ware) umsonst**
it is good value **es ist preisgünstig**
handbag **die Handtasche(n)**
instructions for use **die Gebrauchsanweisung(en)**
item **die Ware(n), der Gegenstand(¨e)**
lift/elevator **der Fahrstuhl(¨e)**
manager **der Manager(-), der Geschäftsführer(-) [-in]**
open **geöffnet, auf**
opening hours **die Öffnungszeiten** *(pl)*
packet **das Päckchen(-)**

Anything else?/Is that all?	**Sonst noch etwas?/Ist das alles?**
Are you being served?	**Werden Sie bedient?**
Can I help you?	**Kann ich Ihnen helfen?**
Do you want anything in particular?	**Möchten Sie etwas Bestimmtes?**
Sliced or whole?	**Geschnitten oder im Stück?**
What would you like?	**Was möchten Sie?**
Whose turn is it?	**Wer ist dran?**

I pay **ich bezahle**
pocket **die Tasche(n)**
I pull **ich ziehe**
purse **der Geldbeutel(-)**
I push **ich drücke**
quality **die Qualität(en)**
real/genuine **echt**
receipt **die Quittung(en)**
reduced **ermäßigt**
reduction **die Ermäßigung(en)**
refund **das Geld zurück**
sale **der Ausverkauf(-e)**
security guard/store detective **der/
die Sicherheitsbeamte** *(adj/n)*
[-in]
self-service **die
Selbstbedienung(en)**
shop/store **der Laden(-)**
shop-assistant/sales person **der
Verkäufer(-) [-in]**
shop-keeper **der
Geschäftsinhaber(-) [-in]**
shop-lifter **der Ladendieb(e)**
shopping list **der Einkaufszettel(-)**
shopping basket **der
Einkaufskorb(-)**
shopping trolley **der
Einkaufswagen(-)**
shut **zu**
it shuts **es schließt**
special offer **das
Sonderangebot(e)**
I spend **ich gebe aus***
summer sale **der**

Sommerschlußverkauf *(no pl)*
till **die Kasse(n)**
till receipt **der Kassenbon(s)**
trader **der Händler(-)**
traveller's cheque/traveler's check
der Reisescheck(s)
wallet **die Brieftasche(n)**
way in **der Eingang(-e)**
way out **der Ausgang(-e)**

Actions

I change **ich wechsle**
I choose **ich wähle**
I decide **ich entscheide**
I dress **ich ziehe mich an***
I exchange **ich tausche**
I have on/wear **ich trage**
I push in **ich drücke ein***
I put on **ich ziehe an***
I queue/line up **ich stehe an***
I select **ich sortiere aus***
I sell **ich verkaufe**
I serve **ich bediene**
I shop **ich kaufe ein***
I shop-lift **ich stehle, ich klaue**
I show **ich zeige**
I spend (money) **ich gebe aus***
I steal **ich stehle**
I take off **ich ziehe aus***
I try on **ich probiere (an*)**
I wait **ich warte**
I wear **ich trage**
I weigh **ich wiege**
I wrap up **ich packe/wickle ein***

How much is it? Have you
anything cheaper?
Can I pay by cheque/check?
Do you take credit cards?
I've no change.
Can you change this note?

… back on the bottle
The bottle is non-returnable.

**Wieviel kostet das? Haben Sie
(irgendet)was Billigeres?
Kann ich mit Scheck bezahlen?
Nehmen Sie Kreditkarten?
Ich habe kein Kleingeld.
Können Sie mir diesen
(Geld)schein wechseln?
mit Pfand
Es ist eine Einwegflasche.**

➤ HOUSEHOLD GOODS & TOILETRIES 9b; CLOTHING 9c

9b Household goods & toiletries

Toiletries

acne cream   **die Aknesalbe(n)**
after-shave (lotion)   **das After-shave/Rasierwasser**
anti-perspirant   **das Anti-transpirant**
bubble bath   **das Schaumbad**
brush   **die Bürste(n)**
cologne   **das Kölnischwasser**
comb   **der Kamm(¨e)**
condom   **das Kondom(e)**
cotton wool   **die Watte**
cosmetics   **das Kosmetikum (-a)**
deodorant   **der (Deo-)spray(s)**
eye liner   **der Eyeliner**
face cream   **die (Haut)creme(s)**
foot powder   **der/das Fußpuder(-)**
glasses   **die Brille(n)**
hairbrush   **die Haarbürste(n)**
dental floss   **die Zahnseide(n)**
lipsalve   **die Lippenpomade(n)**
lipstick   **der Lippenstift(e)**
make-up   **das Make-up**
make-up remover pad   **die Abschminkwatte**
mascara   **die Wimperntusche(-)**
mouthwash   **das Mundwasser**
nail-file   **die Nagelfeile(n)**
paper handkercief   **das Papiertaschentuch(¨er)**
perfume   **das Parfüm(e/s)**
razor   **der Rasierapparat(e)**

razor blades   **die Rasierklinge(n)**
sanitary towels   **die Binde(n)**
shampoo   **das Shampoo(s), das Haarwaschmittel(-)**
soap   **die Seife(n)**
spray   **der/das Spray(s)**
sunglasses   **die Sonnenbrille(n)**
suntan lotion   **das Sonnenöl(e)**
talcum powder   **der/das Talkumpuder**
tampon   **der Tampon(s)**
tissues   **das Papiertaschentuch(¨er)**
toilet water   **das Toilettenwasser**
toilet-paper   **das Toilettenpapier**
toiletries   **die Toilettenartikel** *(pl)*
toothpaste   **die Zahnpasta(s)**
toothbrush   **die Zahnbürste(n)**

Household items

airfreshener   **der Luftreiniger(-)**
bleach   **das Reinigungsmittel(-)**
cling-film/cellophane wrapping   **die Frischhaltefolie**
clothes-pegs   **die Wäscheklammer(n)**
fire lighter   **der Feueranzünder(-)**
foil/aluminum foil   **die (Aluminium)folie(n)**
insect spray   **das Insektenbekämpfungsmittel(-)**
kitchen roll   **das**

Expressions of quantity

a bar of ...	**ein Stück/ein Riegel/eine Tafel...**
a bottle of ...	**eine Flasche ...**
a hundred gram(me)s of ...	**hundert Gramm ...**
a kilo of ...	**ein Kilo ...**
a litre/liter of ...	**ein Liter ...**
a packet of ...	**ein Päckchen ...**
a slice of ...	**eine Scheibe ...**
a tin/can of ...	**eine Büchse/Dose ...**
half a pound of ...	**ein halbes Pfund ...**

Papierhandtuch(¨er)
match das Streichholz(¨er)
mouse trap die Mausefalle(n)
paper napkin/serviette die Papierserviette(n)
paper towel das Papiertuch(¨er)
scouring pad der Topfkratzer(-)
string die Schnur(¨e)
washing/wash powder das Waschpulver(-)
washing-up/dishwashing liquid das Spülmittel(-)

Basic foodstuffs

bacon der Schinkenspeck
beef das Rindfleisch
beer das Bier(e)
biscuit/cookie der Keks(e)
bread das Brot(e)
  black bread der Pumpernickel, das Schwarzbrot(e)
  bread and butter das Butterbrot(e)
  rye bread das Roggenbrot(e)
  slice die Scheibe(n)
  sliced bread das Brot in Scheiben
  toast der Toast(e)
  white bread das Weizenbrot(e)
  wholemeal bread das .Vollkornbrot(e)
butter die Butter
cakes der Kuchen(-)
cereal das Getreide, die Getreideflocken
cheese der Käse
chips/french fries die Pommes Frites
chocolate spread der Schokoladenaufstrich(e)
cola die Cola(s)
coffee der Kaffee(s)
  instant coffee der Pulverkaffee(s)
crisps/chips *(US)* die Chips
custard die Vanillesoße(n)
egg das Ei(er)

fish der Fisch(e)
fruit die Frucht(¨e), das Obst
ham der Schinken
jam die Marmelade(n)
juice der Saft(¨e)
lemonade die Limonade(n)
loaf das Brot(e), der Laib(e)
macaroni die Makkaroni(s)
margarine die Margarine
marmalade die Orangenmarmelade(n)
mayonnaise die Mayonnaise
meat das Fleisch
milk die Milch
mustard der Senf
oil das Öl(e)
olive-oil das Olivenöl(e)
pasta die Nudel(n)
paté die Pastete(n)
peanut-butter die Erdnußbutter
pepper der Pfeffer
pizza die Pizza(s)
pork das Schweinefleisch
pudding der Pudding(s)
roll *(bread)* die Semmel(n), das Brötchen
salt das Salz(e)
sandwich das Sandwich(es)
  open sandwich das belegte Brot(e)
sardine die Sardine(n)
sauce die Soße(n)
sausage die Wurst(¨e)
soup die Suppe(n)
spaghetti die Spaghetti *(pl)*
spice das Gewürz(e)
sugar der Zucker
  cube/lump sugar der Würfelzucker
sunflower oil das Sonnenblumenöl(e)
tea der Tee(s)
teabags der Teebeutel(-)
vegetables das Gemüse(-)
vinegar der Essig
wine der Wein(e)

➤ FOOD & DRINK 10; MEAT 10b; VEGETABLES 10c

9c Clothing

anorak/parka **der Anorak(s)**
beautiful **schön**
big **groß**
bikini **der Bikini(s)**
blouse **die Bluse(n)**
boot **der Stiefel(-)**
bra **der BH, der Büstenhalter(-)**
brand new **funkelnagelneu**
briefs **der Slip(s)**
cagoule **das Windhemd(en)**
cap **die Mütze(n)**
cardigan **die Strickjacke(n)**
check **kariert**
clothes **die Kleider** *(pl)*
clothing **die Kleidung**
coat **der Mantel(-̈)**
colour/color-fast **waschecht**
colourful/colorful **bunt**
cravate **die Krawatte(n)**
dress **das Kleid(er)**
elegant **elegant**
embroidered **bestickt**
fashion **die Mode(n)**
fashionable **modisch**
glove **der Handschuh(e)**
handkerchief **das Taschentuch(-̈er)**
hat **der Hut(-̈e)**
headscarf **das Kopftuch(-̈er)**
heel **der Absatz(-̈e)**
jacket **die Jacke(n)**
jeans **die Jeans** *(pl)*
jersey **der Pullover(-)**
jumper **der Pulli(s)**
knitted **gestrickt**
knitwear **die Strickware(n)**
ladies' wear **die Frauenbekleidung**
the latest fashion **die neueste Mode**
linen **die Wäsche**
lingerie **die Damenunterwäsche**
long **lang**
long-sleeved **langärm(e)lig**
loose **locker, lose**

loud/brash **laut**
low-heeled **mit flachem Absatz**
man-made fibre/fiber **die Kunstfaser(n)**
matching **passend zu** +dat
men's wear **die Männerbekleidung**
non-iron **bügelfrei**
pair **das Paar(e)**
panties **der (Damen)slip(s)**
pants/underpants **die Unterhose(n)**
plain **einfach, schlicht**
printed **gedruckt, bedruckt**
pyjamas **der Schlafanzug(-̈e)**
raincoat **der Regenmantel(-̈)**
sandal **die Sandale(n)**
scarf **der Schal(s)**
shirt **das (Ober)hemd(e)**
shoe **der Schuh(en)**
shoe-lace **der Schnürsenkel(-)**
short-sleeves **kurzärm(e)lig**
silky **seidig**
size **die Größe(n)**
skirt **der Rock(-̈e)**
slip **der Unterrock(-̈e)**
small **klein**
smart **elegant, schick**
sneakers **der Freizeitschuh(e)**
sock **die Socke(n)**
soft **weich**
stocking **der Strumpf(-̈e)**
striped **gestreift**
suit **der Anzug(-̈e)**
sweater **der Pullover(-)**
sweatshirt **das Sweatshirt(s)**
swimming trunks **die Badehose(n)**
swimsuit **der Badeanzug(-̈e)**
T-shirt **das T-Shirt(s)**
tie **der Schlips(e)**
tight **eng**
tights **die Strumpfhose(n)**
trainers **der Sportschuh(e)**
trousers/pants *(US)* **die Hose(n)**
ugly **häßlich**
umbrella **der Regenschirm(e)**

underpants **die Unterhose(n)**
underwear **die Unterwäsche**
unfashionable **unmodern**
vest **die Weste(n), das Unterhemd(en)**

Alterations & repairs

alteration **die Änderung(en)**
I alter **ich ändere**
belt **der Gürtel(-)**
buckle **die Schnalle(n)**
button **der Knopf(¨e)**
collar **der Kragen(-)**
dressmaker **der Damenschneider(-) [-in]**
dressmaking **das Schneidern**
dry cleaning **die chemische Reinigung**
hat pin **die Hutnadel(n)**
hem **der Saum(¨e)**
I hem **ich säume**
I iron/press **ich bügele**
jewellery/jewelry **der Schmuck**

knitting machine **die Strickmaschine(n)**
knitting needle **die Stricknadel(n)**
material **der Stoff(e)**
needle **die Nadel(n)**
patch **der Flicken(-)**
pin **die Stecknadel(n)**
pocket **die Tasche(n)**
press stud/snap fastener **der Druckknopf(¨e)**
I repair **ich bessere aus***
safety pin **die Sicherheitsnadel(n)**
I sew **ich nähe**
sewing machine **die Nähmaschine(n)**
sleeve **der Ärmel(-)**
I stitch **ich nähe**
I take in/let out **ich mache enger/weiter**
tailor **der Schneider(-) [-in]**
tailored **geschneidert**
thread **der Faden(¨)**
turn-up/cuff **der Aufschlag(¨e)**
zip(per) **der Reißverschluß (¨sse)**

Expressions in clothes shops/stores

I'm next. **Ich bin der /die Nächste.**
I would like a ... **Ich möchte ...**
What colour/color? **Welche Farbe?**
Do you have the same in red? **Haben Sie das gleiche in Rot?**
I would like it in brown. **Ich hätte es gern in braun.**
I prefer ... **Ich bevorzuge ...**
I would rather have ... **Ich würde lieber das ... nehmen/haben.**
I take/wear size ... **Ich trage Größe ...**
I'd like it two sizes bigger. **Ich hätte es gern zwei Größen größer.**
Can I try it on? **Kann ich es anprobieren?**
That's not quite right. **Das ist nicht ganz richtig/das Richtige.**
They don't go together. **Das paßt nicht zusammen.**
It suits me. **Es paßt/steht mir.**
I like it. **Mir gefällt es.**
I'll take it. **Ich nehme es.**
I'll take the big one. **Ich nehme das große.**
I bought it at the sales. **Ich habe es im Schlußverkauf gekauft.**
I would like to change it. **Ich möchte es gern (um)tauschen.**

➤ PRECIOUS STONES & METALS App. 9c

Food & drink

10a Drinks & meals

Drinks

alcoholic **der Alkoholiker(-) [-in]**
alcoholic **alkoholisch**
aperitif **der Aperitif(s)**
beer **das Bier(e)**
black coffee **der schwarze Kaffee(s)**
brandy **der Weinbrand(¨e), der Kognak(s)**
champagne **der Champagner(-), der Sekt(e)**
chocolate (drinking) **die (heiße) Schokolade(n)**
cider **der Apfelwein(e)**
cocktail **der Cocktail(s)**
coffee **der Kaffee(s)**
cola **die Cola(s)**
draught beer **das Bier(e) vom Faß**
drink **das Getränk(e)**
dry **herb**
fruit-juice **der Fruchtsaft(¨e)**
heavy **schwer**
juice **der Saft(¨e)**
lemonade **die Limonade(n)**
light **leicht**
low-alcohol **alkoholarm**
orange juice/squash **der Orangensaft(¨e)**
milk **die Milch**
milk-shake **das Milchmixgetränk(e)**
mineral **Mineral-**
mineral water **das Mineralwasser(-)**
  fizzy **mit Kohlensäure**
  still **ohne Kohlensäure**
non-alcoholic **alkoholfrei**
punch **die Bowle(n)**
red wine **der Rotwein(e)**

sherry **der Sherry(s)**
sour **sauer**
sparkling wine **der Schaumwein(e)**
spirits **die Spirituosen** *(pl)*
sweet **süß**
tea **der Tee(s)**
water **das Wasser(-)**
whisky **der Whisky(s)**
white coffee **der Kaffee (mit Sahne)**
white wine **der Weißwein(e)**
wine **der Wein(e)**

Drinking out

bar **die Bar(s)**
barman/barmaid **der Kellner(-) [-in]**
beer hall **die Bierhalle(n)**
bottle **die Flasche(n)**
cafe **das Café(s)**
coffee bar **die Kaffeebar(s)**
cellar **der Keller(-)**
coffee-shop **der Kaffeeladen(¨)**
counter/bar **der Ladentisch(e), die Theke(n)**
I drink **ich trinke**
I get drunk **ich betrinke mich**
pub **die Kneipe(n)**
public-house **das Lokal(e)**
refreshments **die Erfrischungen** *(pl)*
saucer **die Untertasse(n)**
sip **das Schlückchen(s)**
straw **der Trinkhalm(e)**
teaspoon **der Teelöffel(-)**
wine cellar **der Weinkeller(-)**
wine glass **das Weinglas(¨er)**
wine-tasting **die Weinprobe(n)**

Meals

appetizer/starter **die Vorspeise(n)**
breakfast **das Frühstück(e)**
course **der Gang(¨e)**
dessert **der Nachtisch** *(no pl)*
I dine **ich speise**
dinner **das Mittag-/Abendessen**
dish **das Gericht(e)**
I eat **ich esse**
I have/take **ich nehme**
I have a snack **ich esse eine Kleinigkeit**
I have breakfast **ich frühstücke**
I have dinner **ich esse zu Abend**
I have lunch **ich esse zu Mittag**
lunch **das Mittagessen(-)**
main **Haupt-**
meal **das Essen(-), die Mahlzeit(en)**
snack **der Imbiß(e)**
supper **das Abendessen(-)**

Eating out

I add up the bill **ich mache die Rechnung**
bill/check **die Rechnung(en)**
bowl **die Schüssel(n)**
charge **der Preis(e)**
I charge **ich verlange**
cheap **billig, preiswert**
I choose **ich wähle**
it costs **es kostet**
cup **die Tasse(n)**
I decide **ich entscheide mich**
expensive **teuer**

first course **der erste Gang(¨e)**
fixed price **der Festpreis(e)**
fork **die Gabel(n)**
glass **das Glas(¨er)**
inclusive **inklusiv, einschließlich**
knife **das Messer(-)**
main course **das Hauptgericht(e)**
menu **die Speisekarte(n)**
menu of day **das Tagesangebot(e), das Tagesmenü(s)**
napkin **die Serviette(n)**
I order **ich bestelle**
order **die Bestellung(en)**
place-setting **das Gedeck(e)**
plate **der Teller(-)**
portion **die Portion(en)**
reservation **die Reservierung(en)**
I serve **ich bediene**
service **die Bedienung**
set menu **die Tageskarte(n)**
side-dish **die Beilage(n)**
spoon **der Löffel(-)**
sweet **der Nachtisch** *(no pl)*
table **der Tisch(e)**
tablecloth **die Tischdecke(n)**
I take away **ich nehme mit***
tip/gratuity **das Trinkgeld(er)**
I tip **ich gebe ein Trinkgeld**
toothpick **der Zahnstocher(-)**
tourist menu **die Touristenspeisekarte(n)**
tray **das Tablett(s)**
waiter/waitress **der Kellner(-) [-in]**
wine list **die Weinkarte(n)**

cafeteria **das Selbstbedienungsrestaurant(s)**
canteen **die Kantine(n)**
hot-dog stall **die Wurstbude(n)**
ice-cream parlour/parlor **die Eisdiele(n)**
pizza parlour/parlor **die Pizzeria(s)**
pub/inn **das Wirtshaus(¨er)**
restaurant **das Restaurant(s)**
self-service **die Selbstbedienung(en)**
snack-bar **die Imbißstube(n)**
take-away **zum Mitnehmen**

➤ COOKING, EATING 10d; BASIC FOODSTUFFS 9b

10b Fish & meat

Fish & seafood

anchovy	**die Sardelle(n)**
carp	**der Karpfen(-)**
clam	**die Venusmuschel(n)**
cockle	**die Herzmuschel(n)**
cod	**der Kabeljau(e)**
crab	**der Krebs(e)**
crayfish/crawfish	**die Languste(n)**
eel	**der Aal(e)**
fish	**der Fisch(e)**
hake	**der Seehecht(e)**
herring	**der Hering(e)**
langouste	**die Languste(n)**
lobster	**der Hummer(-)**
mussels	**die Miesmuschel(n)**
octopus	**der Tintenfisch(e)**
oyster	**die Auster(n)**
perch	**der Flußbarsch(e)**
pike	**der Hecht(e)**
plaice	**die Scholle(n)**
prawn	**die Krabbe(n)**
salmon	**der Lachs(e)**
sardine	**die Sardine(n)**
scampi	**die Scampi** *(pl)*
seafood	**die Meeresfrüchte** *(pl)*
shell	**die Muschel(n)**
shellfish	**die Meeresfrüchte** *(pl)*
shrimp	**die Krabbe(n), die Garnele(n)**
snails	**die Schnecke(n)**
sole	**die Seezunge(n)**
squid	**der Tintenfisch(e)**
sturgeon	**der Stör(e)**
trout	**die Forelle(n)**
tuna/tunny	**der Thunfisch(e)**
turbot	**der Steinbutt(e)**
whitebait	**der Breitling(e)**

Where can we get a drink around here?	**Wo können wir hier in der Nähe etwas zu trinken bekommen?**
I would like a white wine with soda.	**Ich möchte einen Weißwein gespritzt.**
Two white coffees, please.	**Zweimal Kaffee mit Sahne bitte.**
I'd like a pot of coffee, please.	**Ich hätte gerne ein Kännchen Kaffee.**
Can I have a mineral water, please?	**Könnte ich bitte ein Mineralwasser bekommen?**
I'd rather have tuna than crab.	**Ich nehme lieber den Thunfisch als den Krebs.**
Would you prefer cod or sole?	**Möchtest Du lieber Kabeljau oder Seezunge?**
One trout with boiled potatoes.	**Einmal Forelle mit Salzkartoffeln.**
Shall we try the chicken?	**Wollen wir das Hühnchen probieren?**
I'll have a rare steak with chips and salad, please.	**Ich möchte bitte ein leicht durchgebratenes Steak mit Pommes frites und Salat.**

Meat & meat products

bacon **der Schweinespeck**
beef **das Rindfleisch**
beefburger **der Beefburger(-)**
bolognese **die Bolognese**
chop **das Kotelett(s)**
cold meats **der Aufschnitt** *(no pl)*
cold table **das kalte Büffet(s)**
cutlet **der/das Schnitzel(-)**
escalope **das Schnitzel(-)**
ham **der Schinken**
hamburger **der Hamburger(-)**
hare **der Hase(n)**
hot-dog **der Hot-Dog(s)** *(wk)*, **das heiße Würstchen(-)**
kidney **die Niere(n)**
lamb **das Lammfleisch**
liver **die Leber**
liver sausage **die Leberwurst(-̈e)**
meat **das Fleisch**
meat-balls **die Fleischklops(-̈e)**
mixed grill **gemischte Grillplatte(n)**
mutton **das Hammelfleisch**
pate **die Pastete(n)**
pork **das Schweinefleisch**
rissole **die Frikadelle(n)**

salami **die Salami(s)**
sausage **die Wurst(-̈e)**
sirloin **das Rindfleischfilet(s)**
steak **das Steak(s)**
stew **der Eintopf(-̈e)**
veal **das Kalbfleisch**
venison **das Reh(e), das Wild** *(no pl)*

Poultry

chicken **das Hühnchen(-)**
duck **die Ente(n)**
goose **die Gans(-̈e)**
partridge **das Rebhuhn(-̈er)**
pheasant **der Fasan(e)**
pigeon **die Taube(n)**
poultry **das Geflügel**
quail **die Wachtel(n)**
turkey **die Pute(n)**

Egg dishes

egg **das Ei(er)**
boiled egg **das gekochte Ei(er)**
fried egg **das Spiegelei(er)**
omelette **das Omelett(s)**
poached egg **das pochierte Ei(er)**
scrambled egg **das Rührei(er)**

Traditional German dishes

die Gulaschsuppe beef soup
die Leberknödelsuppe liver dumpling soup
eingelegte Heringe pickled herrings
Forelle in Mandelbutter trout in almond butter
der Heringsalat herring salad
Lachs vom Grill grilled salmon
der Matjes young herring
der Rollmops(-̈e) pickled herring
der Salzhering(e) salted herring

der Aufschnitt cold, sliced meat
die Blutwurst blood sausage

die Bockwurst boiled sausage
das Eisbein mit Sauerkraut pork knuckle with sauerkraut
das Geschnetzelte meat cut in strips and stewed
das Gulasch beef stew
der Hasenpfeffer jugged hare
der Sauerbraten braised beef (marinaded in vinegar)
das Schweinekotelett(s) pork chop
die Thüringer Rostbratwurst fried sausage
das Wiener Schnitzel veal schnitzel
das Zigeunerschnitzel(-) veal in spicy sauce

➤ BASIC FOODSTUFFS 9b

10c Vegetables, fruit & dessert

Vegetables

artichoke **die Artischocke(n)**
asparagus **der Spargel**
aubergine/eggplant **die Aubergine(n)**
avocado **die Avocado(s)**
baked-beans **gebackene Bohnen**
beans **die Bohne(n)**
beetroot **die rote Bete(n)**
broccoli **die Brokkoli** *(pl)*
Brussels sprout **der Rosenkohl** *(no pl)*
cabbage **der Kohl** *(no pl)*, **der Kohlkopf(-̈e)**
carrot **die Mohrrübe(n)**
cauliflower **der Blumenkohl**
celeriac **die Knollensellerie**
celery **die Sellerie**
chick-pea **die Kichererbse(n)**
chicory/endive **der Endivensalat**
corn **der Mais**
corn on the cob **der Maiskolben(-)**
courgette/zucchini **die Zucchini** *(pl)*
cucumber **die Gurke(n)**
French bean **die Brechbohne(n)**
garlic **der Knoblauch**
gherkin **die saure Gurke(n)**
haricot bean **die Gartenbohne(n)**
herb **das Kraut(-̈er)**
leek **der Lauch(e), der Porree(s)**
lentil **die Linse(n)**
lettuce **der Kopfsalat(e)**
marrow **der Kürbis(e)**
mushroom **der Pilz(e), der Champignon(s)**
onion **die Zwiebel(n)**
parsley **die Petersilie**
parsnip **die Pastinake(n)**
pea **die Erbse(n)**

pepper **die Paprikaschote(n)**
potato **die Kartoffel(n)**
  boiled **die Salzkartoffel(n)**
  jacket **die Pellkartoffel(n)**
  mashed **der Kartoffelbrei**
  roast **die Röstkartoffel(n)**
pumpkin **der Kürbis(e)**
radish **das Radieschen(-)**
rice **der Reis**
salad **der Salat(e)**
spinach **der Spinat**
sweetcorn **der Mais**
tomato **die Tomate(n)**
turnip **die Steckrübe(n)**
vegetable **das Gemüse(-)**
watercress **die Kresse(n)**

Fruit

apple **der Apfel(-̈)**
apricot **die Aprikose(n)**
banana **die Banane(n)**
berry **die Beere(n)**
bilberry **die Heidelbeere(n)**
blackberry **die Brombeere(n)**
blackcurrant **die schwarze Johannesbeere(n)**
cherry **die Kirsche(n)**
chestnut **die Kastanie(n)**
coconut **die Kokosnuß (-sse)**
currant **die Korinthe(n)**
date **die Dattel(n)**
fig **die Feige(n)**
fruit **die Frucht(-̈e), das Obst** *(no pl)*
gooseberry **die Stachelbeere(n)**
grape **die Weinbeere(n)**
  bunch of grapes **die Weintraube(n)**
grapefuit **die Pampelmuse**

I want a tomato salad. Does it have garlic in it?	**Ich möchte einen Tomatensalat. Ist da Knoblauch drin?**

hazelnut **die Hazelnuß (¨-sse)**
kiwi-fruit **die Kiwi(s)**
lemon **die Zitrone(n)**
lime **die Limone(n)**
melon **die Melone(n)**
nut **die Nuß (¨-sse)**
olive **die Olive(n)**
orange **die Orange(n)**
passion fruit **die Passionsfrucht(¨-e)**
peach **der Pfirsich(e)**
peanut **die Erdnuß (¨-sse)**
pear **die Birne(n)**
peel **die Schale(n)**
I peel **ich schäle**
piece of fruit **das Obststück(e)**
pineapple **die Ananas(se)**
pip **der Kern(e)**
plum **die Pflaume(n)**
pomegranate **der Granatapfel(¨-)**
prune **die Backpflaume(n)**
raisin **die Rosine(n)**
raspberry **die Himbeere(n)**
redcurrant **die rote Johannisbeere(n)**
rhubarb **der Rhabarber** *(no pl)*
stone **der Kern(e)**
strawberry **die Erdbeere(n)**
sultana **die Sultanine(n)**
tangerine **die Mandarine(n)**
walnut **die Walnuß(¨-e)**

Dessert

biscuit/cookie **der Keks(e)**
blancmange **der Pudding(s)**
caramel **die Karamelle(n)**
chocolate **die Schokolade(n)**
chocolates **die Praline(n)**
cake **der Kuchen(-)**
cream **die Sahne, die Creme**
creme caramel **die Karamelcreme**
custard **die Vanillesoße(n)**
dessert **der Nachtisch**
flan **die Obsttorte(n)**
flour **das Mehl**
fresh fruit **das Frischobst** *(no pl)*
fruit of the day/season **die Früchte der Saison**
fruit salad **der Fruchtsalat(e)**
gateau **die Torte(n)**
ice cream **das Eis**
mousse **das Mousse**
pancake **der Pfannkuchen(-)**
pastry **der Blätterteig(e)**
pie **die Pastete(n)**
pudding **der Pudding(s)**
stewed apple **das/der Apfelmus**
stewed fruit **das Kompott(e)**
sweet **der Nachtisch**
tart **das Obsttörtchen(-)**
vanilla **die Vanille**
whipped cream **die Schlagsahne**
yoghurt **der Joghurt(s)**

Traditional dishes

Bratkartoffeln fried potatoes
Butterreis fried rice
Himmel und Erde potato and apples with black pudding
Kartoffelklöße/knödel potato dumplings
Kartoffelpuffer(-) potato pancake
Sauerkraut pickled cabbage

Spätzle Swabian noodles
der Kaiserschmarren pancake with raisins
die rote Grütze stewed soft fruit
Salzburger Nockerln sweet soufle
Schwarzwälder Kirschtorte Black Forest Gateau
Zwetschenknödel plum dumplings

➤ BASIC FOODSTUFFS 9b

10d Cooking & eating

Food preparation

I bake **ich backe**
I beat **ich schlage**
I boil **ich koche**
bone **der Knochen(-)**
    bone *(of fish)* **die Gräte(n)**
I bone **ich entferne die Knochen/Gräten**
I braise **ich schmore**
in breadcrumbs **paniert**
breast **die Brust(-̈e)**
I carve **ich tranchiere**
I chop **ich hacke**
I clear the table **ich räume den Tisch ab***
I cook **ich koche**
cooking/cuisine **die Küche, die Kochkunst**
creamed **-püree**
I cut **ich schneide**
I dice **ich schneide in Würfel**
diced **gehackt**
I dry up **ich trockne ab***
flavouring/flavoring **der Geschmack** *(no pl)*

I fry **ich brate**
I garnish with **ich garniere mit** +dat
I grate **ich reibe**
gravy **die Bratensoße(n)**
I grill **ich grille**
grilled **vom Grill**
with ice **mit Eis**
ingredients **die Zutaten** *(pl)*
large **groß**
leg **die Keule(n)**
I lay the table **ich decke den Tisch**
I marinate **ich mariniere**
I mix **ich mixe**
I mix in **ich mische ein***
I peel **ich schäle**
I pour **ich gieße**
preparation **die Vorbereitung(en)**
I prepare **ich bereite vor***
rare **leicht durchgebraten**
recipe **das Rezept(e)**
roast **der Braten**
I roast **ich brate**
roasted **gebraten**

Potato cakes
Peel and grate 1 kg raw potatoes.

Mix a grated onion, 50g flour and salt into the potato. Mix into a dough.

Heat plenty of cooking oil in a frying pan.
Put spoonfuls of the mixture into the hot pan and make about 4 cakes.
Fry golden brown on both sides and serve with stewed apple.

Kartoffelpuffer
1 kg rohe Kartoffeln schälen und grob reiben.
Eine geriebene Zwiebel, 50g Mehl, Salz unter den rohen Kartoffelbrei mischen. Zu einem Teig verrühren.
In einer Pfanne reichlich Backöl erhitzen.
Mit einem Löffel den Teig in die heiße Pfanne geben und etwa 4 Plätzchen machen.
Die Reibekuchen an beiden Seiten goldgelb backen und mit Apfelmus servieren.

in sauce   **in Soße(n)**
I sift/sieve   **ich siebe durch***
sliced   **in Scheiben**
I spread   **ich streiche**
stewed   **gedämpft**
I stir   **ich verrühre**
stuffed   **gefüllt**
I toast   **ich toaste**
toasted   **getoastet, überbacken**
I wash up   **ich wasche ab***
I weigh   **ich wiege**
well-done   **gut durchkocht**
I whip/whisk   **ich schlage**

Eating

additive   **der Zusatz(ᵊe)**
appetite   **der Appetit**
appetizing   **appetitanregend**
bad   **schlecht**
I bite   **ich beiße**
bitter   **bitter**
calorie   **die Kalorie(n)**
   low-calorie   **kalorienarm**
I chew   **ich kaue**
cold   **kalt**
delicious   **lecker**
diet   **die Diät**
   I'm on a diet   **ich mache eine Schlankheitskur**
fatty/oily   **fett**
food   **die Lebensmittel** *(pl)*
fresh(ly)   **frisch**
healthy   **gesund**
I help myself   **ich bediene mich**
hot   **heiß**
hunger   **der Hunger**

hungry   **hungrig**
   I am hungry   **ich bin hungrig, ich habe Hunger**
I like   **ich mag**
mild   **mild**
I offer   **ich biete**
I pass (the salt)   **ich reiche jdm. (das Salz)**
piece   **das Stück(e)**
I provide   **ich versorge (jdn.) mit** +dat, **ich besorge (etw.)**
salty   **salzig**
I serve   **ich serviere, ich trage auf***
serving   **die Portion(en)**
sharp   **scharf**
I smell   **ich rieche**
soft   **weich**
sour   **sauer**
spicy   **pikant, würzig**
stale *(bread)*   **altbacken**
strong   **stark, fest**
I swallow   **ich (ver)schlucke**
sweet   **süß**
taste   **der Geschmack**
   it tastes of   **es schmeckt nach** +dat
tasty   **schmackhaft**
thirst   **der Durst**
thirsty   **durstig**
   I am thirsty   **ich habe Durst**
I try   **ich probiere, ich versuche**
vegan   **der radikale Vegetarier(-) [-in]**
vegetarian   **der Vegetarier(-) [-in]**
   vegetarian *(adj)*   **vegetarisch**

Enjoy your meal!	**Guten Appetit!**
Did you enjoy it?	**Hat's geschmeckt?**
Dinner is served.	**Darf ich zu Tisch bitten?**
It tastes of lemon.	**Es schmeckt nach Zitrone.**
Pour the wine.	**Schenk' den Wein ein!**
Pass the salt, please.	**Reich` (mir) bitte das Salz rüber.**

➤ HOUSEHOLD ITEMS, BASIC FOODSTUFFS 9b

Sickness & health

11a Accidents & emergencies

accident **der Unfall(⁻e)**
alive **am Leben**
ambulance **der Krankenwagen(-)**
black eye **das blaue Auge**
bomb **die Bombe(n)**
break **der Bruch(⁻e)**
I break **ich breche**
I break my arm **ich breche mir den Arm**
I have broken my leg **ich habe mir ein Bein gebrochen**
break **die Bruchstelle(n)**
breakage **der Bruch(⁻e)**
broken **gebrochen**
bruise **der blaue Fleck(e/en)**
I bruise **ich bekomme einen blauen Fleck**
burn **die Verbrennung(en)**
I burn **ich verbrenne (mich)**

casualty **der/die Verunglückte (adj/n)**
casualty department **die Unfallabteilung(en)**
it catches fire **es fängt Feuer**
I collide **ich stoße zusammen***
collision **der Zusammenstoß(⁻e)**
I have cut my finger **ich habe mich in den Finger geschnitten**
I crash (into) **ich knalle (gegen +acc)**
I crush **ich quetsche**
dead **tot**
death **der Tod, der Todesfall(⁻e)**
I die **ich sterbe**
emergency **der Notfall(⁻e)**
emergency department **die Notaufnahme(en)**
emergency exit **der**

– What's happened?

– There has been an accident!
We need an ambulance quickly!

Call the fire brigade!

It was his fault, not mine!

My friend is injured!
Are you a doctor?
Where's the nearest hospital?

Calm down!

– **Was ist los?**

– **Es ist ein Unfall passiert!**
Wir brauchen schnellstens einen Krankenwagen!

Rufen Sie die Feuerwehr!

Er war schuld daran, ich nicht!

Mein Freund ist verletzt!
Sind Sie Arzt?
Wo befindet sich das nächste Krankenhaus?

Beruhigen Sie sich!

Notausgang(-̈e)
emergency services **der Notdienst(e)**
it explodes **es explodiert**
explosion **die Explosion(en)**
I extinguish **ich lösche**
I fasten my seatbelt **ich schnalle mich an***
fatal **tödlich**
fire **der Brand(-̈e)**
fire brigade **die Feuerwehr**
fire engine **das Feuerwehrauto(s)**
fire extinguisher **der Feuerlöscher(-)**
fireman **der Feuerwehrmann(-̈er)**
first aid **die erste Hilfe**
graze **die Schramme(n)**
I graze **ich schramme mich**
I have an accident **ich habe einen Unfall**
hospital **das Krankenhaus(-̈er)**
impact **der Zusammenprall(-̈e)**
incident **der Vor-/Zwischenfall(-̈e)**
I injure **ich verletze**
injury **die Verletzung(en)**
injured **verletzt**

insurance **die Versicherung(en)**
I insure **ich versichere**
I kill **ich töte**
killed **getötet**
life-belt **der Rettungsgurt(e)**
life-jacket **die Schwimmweste(n)**
oxygen **der Sauerstoff**
para-medic **der Sanitäter(-) [-in]**
I recover consciousness **ich komme wieder zu mir**
I rescue **ich rette**
rescue **die Rettung(en)**
rescue services **der Rettungsdienst(e)**
I run over **ich überfahre**
I rush **ich renne, ich eile**
safe **sicher**
safe and sound **gesund und wohlbehalten**
safety-belt **der Sicherheitsgurt(e)**
I save **ich rette**
seat-belt **der Sitzgurt(e)**
terrorist attack **das Terroristenattentat(e)**
third-party **die dritte Person(en)**
witness **der Zeuge(n)** *(wk)* **[-in]**

Fasten safety belts.

Bitten anschnallen!

I think I have broken my arm. It hurts a lot.

Ich glaube, ich habe mir den Arm gebrochen. Es tut sehr weh.

She has cut her hand badly.

Sie hat sich tief in die Hand geschnitten.

Statistics show that the most likely place for accidents is in the home.

Laut der Statistik sollen die meisten Unfälle zu Hause passieren.

➤ MEDICAL TREATMENT 11c

11b Illness & disability

arthritis **die Arthritis**
I am asleep **ich schlafe**
asthma **das Asthma**
awake **wach**
bacillus **die Bazillus (-en)**
bacteria **die Bakterie(n)**
I bleed **ich blute**
blind **blind**
blood **das Blut**
breath **der Atem, der Atemzug(¨e)**
I breathe **ich atme**
breathless **atemlos**
catarrh **der Katarrh(e)**
I catch cold **ich erkälte mich**
circulatory problem **die Kreislaufstörung(en)**
constipated **verstopft**
constipation **die Verstopfung(en)**
convalescence **die Genesung**
I am convalescing **ich genese**
cough **der Husten**
I cough **ich huste**
I cry **ich schreie**
I cut **ich schneide**
dead **tot**
deaf **taub**

deafness **die Taubheit**
death **der Tod(¨e)**
depressed **deprimiert**
depression **die Depression(en)**
diarrhoea **der Durchfall**
I die **ich sterbe**
diet **die Diät**
disabled **behindert**
disease **die Krankheit(en)**
dizziness **das Schwindelgefühl(e)**
dizzy **schwindelig**
Down's syndrome **das Down-Syndrom**
drug **die Droge(n), die Arznei(en)**
drugged **betäubt**
drunk **betrunken**
dumb **stumm**
earache **die Ohrenschmerzen** (pl)
I fall **ich falle**
I feel **ich fühle mich, mir ist …**
fever **das Fieber**
I'm feverish **ich habe Fieber**
flu **die Grippe(n)**
I get drunk **ich betrinke mich**
I got better **mir geht es besser**
I have an operation **ich habe eine**

– I don't feel at all well!
– You look very well to me!

I have a sore throat.
I have a migraine coming on.

I have been sick several times.

I feel dizzy if I stand up.

But I am not ill/sick very often!

– Ich fühle mich nicht sehr wohl!
– Ich finde, du siehst sehr gesund aus.

Ich habe Halsschmerzen.
Es bahnt sich eine Migräne bei mir an.

Ich habe mich mehrmals übergeben.

Wenn ich aufstehe, wird mir schwindlig.

Aber ich bin nicht sehr oft krank!

Operation

I have a cold   ich habe eine Erkältung

I have a temperature   ich habe Fieber

headache   die Kopfschmerzen (pl)

health   die Gesundheit

healthy   gesund

heart attack   der Herzanfall(-e), der Herzinfarkt(e)

high blood pressure   der Bluthochdruck

hurt   der Schmerz(en)

hurt (adj)   verletzt

I hurt   es tut mir weh

it hurts   es schmerzt

I am ill/sick   ich bin krank

illness   die Krankheit(en)

I live   ich lebe

I look ill   Ich sehe krank aus*

mental illness   die Geisteskrankheit(en)

mentally sick   geisteskrank

microbe   die Mikrobe(n)

migraine   die Migräne(n)

nervous breakdown   der Nervenzusammenbruch(-e)

overdose   die Überdosis (-en)

pain   der Schmerz(en)

painful   schmerzhaft

pale   blaß, bleich

pregnancy   die Schwangerschaft(en)

I recover/get well   ich erhole mich

recovery   die Erholung(en)

rheumatism   der Rheumatismus

I sneeze   ich niese

sore throat   die Halsschmerzen (pl)

sting   der Stich(e)

it stings   es sticht

stomach   der Magen(-/-)

stomach ache   die Magen-/Bauchschmerzen (pl)

stomach upset   die Magenverstimmung(en)

I take drugs   ich nehme Medikamente

temperature   die Temperatur(en)

I vomit   ich übergebe mich

What's wrong?   Wo tut es weh?

I wound   ich verletze

wounded   verletzt

My children have diarrhoea; I seem to be constipated	**Meine Kinder haben Durchfall; ich scheine verstopft zu sein.**
I don't know what is wrong with her.	**Ich weiß nicht, was mit ihr los ist.**
He seems to be recovering.	**Er scheint sich zu erholen.**
I can't breath very well	**Ich kann nur schwer atmen.**
I suffer from high blood-pressure.	**Ich leide an Bluthochdruck.**

➤ PARTS OF THE BODY App.5a

11c Medical treatment

antibiotic **das Antibiotikum (-a)**
appointment **der Termin(e)**
bandage **der Verband(̈-e)**
blood **das Blut**
blood test **die Blutprobe(n)**
blood pressure **der Blutdruck**
capsule **die Kapsel(n)**
chemist/pharmacist **der Apotheker(-) [-in]**
chemotherapy **die Chemotherapie(n)**
cure **die Heilung(en)**
danger to life **die Lebensgefahr(en)**
dangerous **gefährlich**
death **der Tod(e)**
I diet **ich halte eine Diät.**
doctor (Dr) **der Arzt(̈-e), die Ärztin(nen)**
dressing **der Verband(̈-e)**
drop **der Tropfen(-)**
drug **die Arznei(en)**
E111-form **der Krankenschein(e)**
I examine **ich untersuche**
examination **die Untersuchung(en)**
I fill **ich fülle**
I have **ich habe**
heating **die Heizung(en)**
hospital **das Krankenhaus(̈-er)**
I improve **ich erhole mich**
I inject **ich spritze**

injection **die Spritze(n)**
insurance certificate **der Krankenschein(e)**
intensive care **die Intensivpflege(n)**
I look after **ich pflege**
medical **medizinisch**
medicine **die Medizin, das Medikament(e), das Mittel(-)**
alternative medicine **die alternative Medizin**
midwife **die Hebamme(n)**
nurse **die Krankenschwester(n), der Krankenpfleger(-)**
I nurse **ich pflege**
I operate **ich operiere**
operation **die Operation(en)**
I have an operation **ich lasse mich operieren**
operating theatre/theater **der Operationsaal (-säle)**
pastille **die Pastille(n)**
patient **der Patient(en)** *(wk)* **[-in]**
physiotherapy **die Physiotherapie(n)**
physiotherapist **der Physiotherapeut(en)** *(wk)* **[-in]**
pill **die Tablette(n), die Pille(n)**
plaster (of Paris) **der Gipsverband(̈-e)**
I prescribe **ich verschreibe**
prescription **das Rezept(e)**

Call a doctor! Is he a good doctor?	**Rufen Sie einen Arzt! Ist er ein guter Doktor?**
Will I have to have an operation? I have my insurance certificate with me.	**Muß ich operiert werden? Ich habe mein Krankenver-sicherungszeugnis mit.**
He had to have stitches.	**Er mußte genäht werden.**
He does not like injections.	**Er mag keine Spritzen.**
He has never had an X-ray.	**Er wurde noch nie geröntgt.**

radio therapy **die Röntgentherapie(n)**
service **der Dienst(e)**
I set *(in plaster)* **ich richte ein*, ich gipse**
smear test **der Abstrich(e)**
spa resort **der Kur- und Erholungsort(e)**
specialist **der Facharzt(⁒e)**
stitch **der Faden(⁒)**
sticking plaster/Bandaid® **das Heftpflaster(-)**
surgery **das Sprechzimmer(-)**
surgery hour **die Sprechstunde(n)**
syringe **die Spritze(n)**
tablet **die Tablette(n)**
therapeutic **therapeutisch**
therapy **die Therapie(n)**
therapist **der Therapeut(en)** *(wk)* **[-in]**
thermometer **das Thermometer(-)**
transfusion **die Transfusion(en)**
I treat **ich behandle**
treatment **die Behandlung(en)**
ward **die (Kranken)station(en)**
wound **die Wunde(n)**
X-ray **die Röntgenaufnahme(n)**
I X-ray **ich röntge**

Dentist & optician

abscess **der Abszeß (-sse)**
bi-focals **die Bifokalbrille(n)**
contact lens **die Kontaktlinse(n)**

hard/soft lenses **harte/weiche Linsen**
contact lens fluid **die Flüssigkeit für Kontaktlinsen**
crown **die Krone(n)**
dental treatment **die zahnärtliche Behandlung(en)**
dentist **der Zahnarzt(⁒e) [-in]**
dentures **das Gebiß (-sse)**
I drill **ich bohre**
I extract **ich ziehe heraus***
eye **das Auge(n)**
eyesight **die Sehkraft**
eye test **der Augentest(e)**
false teeth **das künstliche Gebiß**
I fill **ich plombiere**
filling **die Plombe(n)**
frame **das Gestell(e)**
glasses/spectacles **die Brille(n)**
gum **das Zahnfleisch** *(no pl)*
lens **die Linse(n)**
long-sighted **weitsichtig**
optician **der Optiker(-)**
pupil **die Pupille(n)**
short-sighted **kurzsichtig**
spectacle case **das Brillenetui(s)**
stye **das Gerstenkorn(⁒er)**
sunglasses **die Sonnenbrille(n)**
tinted **dunkel**
tooth **der Zahn(⁒e)**
toothache **die Zahnschmerzen** *(pl)*

Can I have a prescription? I have lost my tablets.	**Kann ich ein Rezept bekommen? Ich habe meine Tabletten verloren.**
Can I make an urgent appointment to see Dr. Schmidt?	**Kann ich einen dringenden Termin bei Herrn/Frau Dr. Schmidt haben?**
– I had a stomach operation. – Take this medicine four times a day.	**– Ich wurde am Magen operiert.** **– Nehmen Sie dieses Mittel viermal täglich.**

➤ DISEASES & ILLNESSES App.11b; PARTS OF THE BODY App.5b

11d Health & hygiene

Physical state

ache **der Schmerz(en)**
aching **schmerzen**
　aching *(adj)* **schmerzend**
all right/OK **in Ordnung**
I am asleep **ich schlafe**
awake **wach**
blister **die Blase(n)**
boil **das Furunkel(-)**
bruise **der blaue Fleck(en)**
I am cold **mir ist kalt**
comfort **der Trost**
I comfort **ich tröste**
comfortable (un-) **(un)bequem**
corn **das Hühnerauge(n)**
discomfort **die Beschwerden** *(pl)*
drowsiness **die Schläfrigkeit**
drowsy **schläfrig**
faint **ohnmächtig**
I faint **ich falle in Ohnmacht**
I feel **ich fühle mich, mir ist ...**
I am hot **mir ist warm**
I get fat **ich werde dick, ich
　nehme zu***
I get fit **ich trimme mich**
I get thin **ich werde mager/dünn**
hunger **der Hunger**
hungry **hungrig**
　I am hungry **ich habe Hunger**
it hurts **es tut weh**
ill/sick **krank**
I lie down **ich lege mich hin***
I look **ich sehe, ich gucke**
I lose weight **ich nehme ab***
I put on weight **ich nehme zu***
queasy **übel, schlecht**
I relax **ich ruhe mich aus***
I rest/have a rest **ich mache eine
　Pause**
I sleep **ich schlafe**
sleepy **schläfrig**
I slim **ich mache eine
　Schlankheitskur**
strange **komisch**
thirst **der Durst**

thirsty **durstig**
I am thirsty **ich bin durstig, ich
　habe Durst**
tired **müde**
I am tired **ich bin müde**
tiredness **die Müdigkeit**
under the weather **angeschlagen**
unwell **nicht wohl**
I wake up **ich wache auf***
well **wohl**
well-being **das Wohlbefinden**

Beauty & hygiene

acne **die Akne**
bath **das Bad(-̈er)**
beauty **die Schönheit**
beauty contest **der
　Schönheitswettbewerb**
beauty queen **die
　Schönheitskönigin(nen)**
beauty salon/parlor **der
　Schönheitssalon(s)**
beauty specialist **der
　Kosmetiker(-) [-in]**
beauty treatment **die kosmetische
　Behandlung**
body odour/odor **der (übe)
　Körpergeruch**
I burp/belch **ich rülpse**
I brush **ich bürste**
brush **die Bürste(n)**
I clean **ich putze**
clean **sauber**
I clean my teeth **ich putze mir die
　Zähne**
comb **der Kamm(-̈e)**
I comb my hair **ich kämme meine
　Haare**
complexion **der Teint**
condom **das Kondom(e)**
contraceptive **das
　Verhütungsmittel(-)**
contraception **die
　Empfängnisverhütung(en)**
cosmetics **die Kosmetika** *(pl)*

cosmetic/plastic surgery **die Schönheitsoperation(en)**
I cut **ich schneide**
dandruff **die Schuppen** *(pl)*
dirty **schmutzig**
electric razor **der elektrische Rasierapparat(e)**
I exercise **ich bewege mich**
exercise bike **der Heimtrainer(-)**
face-lift **das Facelift(s)**
face-pack **die Gesichtspackung(en)**
fit (un-) **(nicht) gesund**
fitness **die Fitness**
flannel **der Waschlappen(-)**
flea **der Floh(-̈e)**
hair **das Haar(e)**
unwanted hair **das unerwünschte Haar**
hairbrush **die Haarbürste(n)**
haircut **der Haarschnitt(e)**
I have my hair cut **ich lasse mir die Haare schneiden**
hairdo **die Frisur(en)**
hairdryer **der Fön(e)**
head-lice **die Kopfläuse** *(pl)*
healthy *(person)* **gesund**
hygiene **die Hygiene**
hygienic **hygienisch**
laundry *(establishment)* **die Wäscherei(en)**
laundry *(linen)* **die Wäsche**
I'm losing my hair **die Haare fallen mir aus***
I make up **ich schminke mich**
I menstruate **ich menstruiere**
menstruation **die Menstruation(en)**
mole **der Leberfleck(e)**
nailbrush **die Nagelbürste(n)**
nit **die Nisse(n)**
period **die Periode(n)**
period pains **die Periodenschmerzen** *(pl)*
permanent wave **die Dauerwelle(n)**
pill **die Pille(n)**
razor **der Rasierer(-)**
I remove unwanted hair **ich enthaare**
sanitary **hygienisch**
sanitary towel **die Monatsbinde(n)**
scissors **die Schere(n)**
shampoo **das Shampoo(s)**
I shave **ich rasiere mich**
shower **die Dusche(n)**
soap **die Seife(n)**
spot **der Pickel(-)**
spotty **fleckig**
smell *(odour/odor)* **der Geruck(-̈e)**
I smell (bad) **ich rieche (übel)**
sweat **der Schweiß**
I sweat **ich schwitze**
I take a bath **ich nehme ein Bad**
I take a shower **ich dusche (mich)**
tampon **der Tampon(s)**
toothbrush **die Zahnbürste(n)**
toothpaste **die Zahnpasta(s)**
toupee **das Toupet(s)**
towel **das Handtuch(-̈er)**
wart **die Warze(n)**
I wash **ich wasche mich**
wig **die Perücke(n)**

I'd like a haircut, please. Don't cut it too short. | **Haare schneiden, bitte. Nicht zu kurz schneiden.**
A little more off the back and sides, please. | **Bitte hinten und an den Seiten etwas kürzer.**
I'm having a wash and blow dry. | **Ich lasse mir die Haare schneiden und fönen.**

➤ TOILETRIES 9b

Social issues

12a Society

abnormal **anormal, abnormal**
alternative **alternativ**
amenity **die Unterhaltungsmöglichkeit(en)**
anonymous **anonym**
attitude **die Einstellung(en)**
available **verfügbar**
  it is available **es steht zur Verfügung**
basic **grundlegend**
basis **die Grundlage(n)**
burden **die Last(en)**
campaign **die Initiative(n)**
care **die Sorge, die Fürsorge**
cause **die Ursache(n)**
change **der Wandel(-)**
circumstance **der Umstand(ːe)**
community **die Gemeinde(n), die Gemeinschaft(en)**
compulsory **Pflicht-**
contribution **der Beitrag(ːe)**
cost **die Kosten** *(pl)***, die Unkosten** *(pl)*
I counsel **ich berate**
counselling **die (soziale) Beratung**
criterion **das Kriterium (-ien)**
dependence **die Abhängigkeit**
dependent **abhängig**
depressed **deprimiert**
depression **die Depression(en)**
deprived **benachteiligt, depriviert**
difficulty **die Schwierigkeit(en)**
effect **die Auswirkung(en)**
effective **wirksam**
fact **die Tatsache(n)**
finance **die Finanzen** *(pl)*
financial **finanziell**
frustrated **frustriert**
frustration **die Frustration(en)**

guidance **die Orientierung(en)**
increase **die Zunahme**
inner city **die Innenstadt(ːe)**
institution **die Anstalt(en)**
loneliness **die Einsamkeit**
lonely **einsam**
long-term **langfristig**
measure **die Maßnahme(n)**
negative **negativ**
normal **normal**
policy **die Politik**
  policies **die Politik**
positive **positiv**
power **die Macht(ːe)**
prestige **das Prestige** *(no pl)*
problem **das Problem(e)**
protest movement **die Protestbewegung(en)**
I provide (with) **ich versorge jdn. (mit** +dat)
provision **die Versorgung**
psychological **psychologisch**
quality of life **die Lebensqualität**
question/issue **die Frage(n)**
rate **die Rate(n), die Quote(n)**
responsibility **die Verantwortung(en)**
responsible (ir-) **(un)verantwortlich**
result **die Folge(n)**
right **das Recht(e)**
role **die Rolle(n)**
rural **ländlich**
scarcity **der Mangel(ː)**
scheme **die Maßnahme(n)**
I am on the scrap heap **ich gehöre zum alten Eisen**
secure (in-) **(un)sicher**
security (in-) **die (Un)sicherheit(en)**

self-esteem **die Selbstachtung**
short-term **kurzfristig**
situation **die Lage(n)**
social **sozial**
society **die Gesellschaft(en)**
stable (un-) **(un)stabil**
stability (in-) **die (Un)stabilität**
statistics **die Statistik(en)**
status **der Status**
stigma **das Brandmal(e)**
stress **der Streß (-sse)**
stressful **stressig**
structure **die Struktur(en), der Aufbau**
superfluous **überflüssig**
support **die Unterstützung(en)**
urban **Stadt-**
urge to conform **der Anpassungsdruck**
value **der Wert(e)**

Some useful verbs

I adapt/conform **ich passe mich +dat an***
it affects **es beeinflußt**
I afford **ich leiste mir (etw.)**
I alienate **ich entfremde**
I am ashamed **ich schäme mich**
I break down **ich breche zusammen***
I campaign **ich kämpfe**
I care for **ich sorge für** +acc
I cause **ich verursache**

it changes **es wandelt sich**
I contribute **ich trage zu +dat bei***
I cope **ich komme gut zurecht***
I depend on **ich hänge von +dat ab***
I deprive **ich benachteilige**
I discourage **ich entmutige**
I dominate **ich beherrsche, ich dominiere**
I encourage **ich ermutige**
I help **ich helfe** +dat
I increase **ich vergrößere**
I lack **es mangelt mir an** +dat
I look after **ich kümmere mich um** +acc
I need **ich brauche**
I neglect **ich vernachlässige**
I owe **ich bin jdm. etw. schuldig**
I protest **ich protestiere**
I provide for **ich versorge jdn. mit** +dat
I put up with **ich gebe mich mit** +dat
I rely on **ich bin auf jdn. angewiesen.**
I respect **ich verachte**
I share **ich teile**
I solve **ich löse**
I suffer from **ich leide an** +dat
I support **ich unterstütze**
I tackle **ich befasse mich mit** +dat
I value **ich schätze**

– There are immense social problems in the inner city.
– What are the causes, do you think?
– People are frustrated and lonely, often as a result of unemployment. We attempt to offer guidance and counselling.

– **Es gibt ungeheuere Sozialprobleme in der Innenstadt.**
– **Wo liegen Ihrer Meinung nach die Ursachen?**
– **Die Menschen sind frustriert und einsam, oft infolge der Arbeitslosigkeit. Wir versuchen die Leute zu beraten.**

▶ ADDICTION & VIOLENCE 12d; PREJUDICE 12e

12b Social services & poverty

Social services

aid **die Sozialhilfe**
agency **die Agentur(en)**
authority **die Gemeinde(n)**
benefit **die Unterstützung(en)**
I benefit **ich profitiere**
charity **die Wohlfahrtsorganisation(en)**
I give to charity **ich spende**
claim **der Anspruch(-̈e), der Antrag(-̈e)**
I claim **ich beantrage**
claimant **der Antragsteller(-)**
disability **die Arbeitsunfähigkeit**
disabled **arbeitsunfähig**
eligible (for) **berechtigt zu** +dat
I am eligible for **ich habe Anspruch auf** +acc
frail **schwach**
frailty **die Schwäche(n)**
grant **der Zuschuß (-̈sse)**
handicap **die Behinderung(en)**
handicapped **behindert**
ill-health **die schlechte Gesundheit**
income support **die Beihilfe(n)**
loan **die Anleihe(n)**
maintenance **die finanzielle Unterstützung(en)**
official **amtlich, offiziell**

reception centre/center **das Aufnahmelager(-)**
Red Cross **das Rote Kreuz**
refuge **der Zufluchtsort(e)**
refugee **der Flüchtling(e)**
I register **ich melde mich an***
registration **die Anmeldung(en)**
Salvation Army **die Heilsarmee**
service **der Dienst(e)**
social security **die soziale Sicherheit**
social service **der Sozialdienst(e)**
social worker **der Sozialarbeiter(-) [-in]**
support **die Hilfe**
I support **ich unterstütze**
welfare **die Wohlfahrt**

Wealth & poverty

I beg **ich bettele**
beggar **der Bettler(-) [-in]**
I am broke **ich bin abgebrannt**
debt **die Schuld(en)**
I am in debt **ich habe Schulden**
deprivation **die Armut**
deprived **benachteiligt**
destitute **mittellos**
living standards **der Lebensstandard(s)**

The physically handicapped can apply for help. They are particularly vulnerable to unemployment.

Die körperlich Behinderten können einen Antrag auf Hilfe stellen. Sie sind der Arbeitslosigkeit besonders ausgesetzt.

Not everyone gets the dole.

Nicht jeder bekommt die Arbeitslosenunterstützung.

They are retired now. The pension is barely adequate.

Sie leben jetzt im Ruhestand. Die Rente genügt kaum zum Leben.

millionaire **der Millionär(e)**
need **die Not(⁻e)**
   those in need **die**
   Notleidenden *(adj/n) (pl)*
nutrition **die Ernährung**
poor **arm**
poverty **die Armut**
rich **reich**
subsistence **die Lebenshaltung**
tramp/vagrant **der**
   Landstreicher(-) [-in]
wealth **der Reichtum(⁻er), der**
   Wohlstand
well off **wohlhabend**

Unemployment

I cut back *(on jobs)* **ich baue ab***
I dismiss **ich entlasse**
dole **das Arbeitslosengeld**
I employ **ich beschäftige**
employee **der Arbeitnehmer(-) [-in]**
employer **der Arbeitgeber(-) [-in]**
employment **die Arbeit**
full-time **Vollzeit-**
I give notice **ich kündige jdm.**
income support **die Sozialhilfe**
job **der Job(s), die Arbeit, der**
   Arbeitsplatz(⁻e)
job centre/employment office **das**
   Arbeitsamt(⁻er)
job/workplace **die Arbeitsstelle(n)**

job-sharing **das Jobsharing**
job creation scheme **die Arbeits-**
   beschaffungsmaßnahme(n)
long-term unemployed **der/die**
   Langzeitarbeitslose *(adj/n)*
occupation **der Beruf(e)**
occupational **beruflich**
part-time **Teilzeit-**
qualification **die Qualifikation(en)**
qualified **qualifiziert**
redundancy **die Entlassung(en)**
redundant **arbeitslos**
   I am made redundant **mir wird**
   gekündigt
retraining **die Umschulung(en)**
   I am retrained **ich lasse mich**
   umschulen
short-time working **die Kurzarbeit**
skill **die Fertigkeit(en)**
staffing **die Arbeitskräfte** *(pl)*
I take on **ich stelle an***
training scheme/program **die**
   Ausbildungsmaßnahme(n)
unemployed **arbeitslos**
unemployment figure **die**
   Arbeitslosenzahl(en)
unemployment rate **die**
   Arbeitslosenrate(n)
unskilled worker **der Hilfsarbeiter(-)**
vacancy **die leere Stelle(n)**
wage costs **die Lohnkosten** *(pl)*

– How high is the level of
unemployment? – In some areas it
is about 15%.
– Can people retrain or work
part-time?

– Yes, sometimes, and many retire
early. My brother was made
redundant some months ago. He
has to report every two weeks to
the job centre/employment office.

**– Wie hoch ist die
Arbeitslosenrate? – In einigen
Gegenden ist sie ungefähr 15%.
– Können die Leute umgeschult
werden oder eine Teilzeitarbeit
machen?**

**– Ja, manchmal, und viele treten
vorzeitig in den Ruhestand. Mein
Bruder hat vor einigen Monaten
seine Arbeitsstelle verloren. Er
muß sich alle zwei Wochen beim
Arbeitsamt melden.**

➤ JOB APPLICATION 14c

12c Housing & homelessness

accommodation **die Unterkunft**
I build **ich baue**
building **das Gebäude(-)**
comfortable/homely **gemütlich**
commune **die Wohngemeinschaft(en)**
I commute **ich pendle**
commuter **der Pendler(-)**
council flat/public apartment **die Sozialwohnung(en)**
delapidated **baufällig**
I demolish **ich reiße ab***
demolition **der Abbruch**
it deteriorates **es verfällt**
digs/unfurnished rooms **die Bude(n)**
drab **trist, traurig**
estate/real estate agent **der Immobilienmakler(-)**
it falls down **es stürzt ab***
flat/apartment **die Wohnung(en)**

house **das Haus(¨er)**
council house **die Sozialwohnung(en)**
housing **die Wohnungen** *(pl)*
housing association **die Wohnungsbaugesellschaft(en)**
housing policy **die Wohnungspolitik**
inner city **die Innenstadt(¨e)**
landlord **der Vermieter(-)**
I let/rent out **ich vermiete**
I maintain **ich halte instand**
I modernize **ich modernisiere**
I move (house) **ich ziehe um***
own **eigen**
redevelopment **die Sanierung**
I renovate **ich saniere**
I rent **ich miete**
rent **die Miete(n)**
I repair **ich repariere**
repair **die Reparatur(en)**

– Are they intending to renovate the city centre/downtown?
– Yes, many houses will be pulled down.
Others will be modernized.

– **Wollen Sie die Stadtmitte sanieren?**
– **Ja, man wird viele Häuser abreißen.**
Man wird andere modernisieren.

– Are you hoping to buy your own home soon?
– Yes, we are trying to get a mortgage.
We have found an older property which we are going to modernize.

– **Wollen Sie bald ein Eigenheim kaufen?**
– **Ja, wir versuchen eine Hypothek aufzunehmen.**
Wir haben ein älteres Haus gefunden, das wir modernisieren wollen.

We are renting a flat/an apartment at the moment.

Wir mieten zur Zeit eine Wohnung.

It is impossible to find a furnished flat to rent.

Es ist unmöglich, eine möblierte Mietwohnung zu finden.

shelter **die Unterkunft(-̈e)**
speculator **der Spekulant(en)** *(wk)*
squalid **elend**
squatter **der Hausbesetzer(-)** [-in]
suburb **der Vorort(e)**
tenant **der Mieter(-)** [-in]
town planning **die Stadtplanung**
urban **städtisch**
urban renewal **die Stadterneuerung**

Housing shortage

camp **das Lager(-)**
commune **die Wohngemeinschaft(en)**
container town **die Containerstadt(-̈e)**
delapidated **verfallen**
I evict **ich weise aus***
homeless **obdachslos**
homelessness **die Wohnungsnot(-̈e), die Obdachlosigkeit**

hostel **das Wohnheim(e)**
housing shortage **die Wohnungsnot**
living conditions **die Wohnverhältnisse** *(pl)*
overcrowded **überfüllt**
overcrowding **die Überfüllung**
I pull down **ich reiße ab***
shanty town **die Slumstadt(-̈e), die Bidonville(s)**
I sleep rough **ich übernachte im Freien**
slum **die Baracke(n)**
slum clearance **die Slumsanierung(en)**
squalid **dreckig**
I squat **ich besetze ein Haus**
squatter **der Hausbesetzer(-)** [-in]
it stands empty **es steht leer**
waste land **das Ödland**

– Why do so many houses stand empty?
The houses deteriorate fast and squatters move in.
Aren't the town planners intending to demolish the houses?
– Yes, but so many people are homeless. They sleep rough or squat.

– Is the council/municipality still building council/public housing?
– Yes, but not enough. Living conditions in the blocks of flats/apartments are extremely poor. They are overcrowded and the landlords no longer repair them.

– Warum stehen so viele Häuser leer?
Die Häuser verfallen schnell und werden besetzt.
Wollen die Stadtplaner die Häuser nicht abreißen?
– Doch, aber so viele Leute sind obdachlos, sie schlafen im Freien oder besetzen ein Haus.

– Baut die Stadtbehörde immer noch Sozialwohnungen?
– Ja, aber nicht genug. Die Wohnverhältnisse in den Blocks sind sehr schlecht. Sie sind überfüllt, und die Vermieter machen keine Reparaturen mehr.

➤ SOCIAL SERVICES 12b

12d Addiction & violence

abuse **der Mißbrauch(-̈e)**
I abuse **ich mißbrauche**
act of violence **die Gewalttat(en)**
addict **der/die Abhängige** *(adj/n)*
addiction **die (Drogen)Abhängigkeit**
addictive **zur Abhängigkeit führend**
aggression **die Agression(en), die Agressivität(en)**
aggressive **aggressiv**
alcohol **der Alkohol**
alcoholic **der Alkoholiker(-) [-in]**
alcoholism **der Alkoholismus**
anger **die Wut**
angry **wütend**
I attack **ich greife an***
attack **der Angriff(e), das Attentat(e)**
I beat up **ich verprügele, ich haue zusammen***
I bully **ich tyrannisiere**
bully **der Schlägertyp(en)**
consumption **der Konsum**
I cure, I dry out **ich entwöhne mich**
dangerous **gefährlich**
I drink **ich trinke**

I get drunk **ich betrinke mich**
drunk **betrunken**
drunken driving **die Trunkenheit am Steuer**
effect **die Wirkung(en)**
fatal **tödlich**
fear **die Angst(-̈e)**
I fear **ich habe Angst (vor +dat)**
force **die Gewalt**
gang **die Bande(n)**
I harass **ich schikaniere, ich haue an***
hooligan **der Rowdy (-ies)**
hostile **feindlich**
hostility **die Feindseligkeit(en)**
insult **die Beleidigung(en)**
I insult **ich beleidige**
intoxication **der Rausch**
legal (il-) **(il)legal**
I legalize **ich gebe frei***
I mug **ich überfalle**
mugger **der Straßenräuber(-)**
nervous **ängstlich**
nervousness **die Ängstlichkeit**
pimp **der Zuhälter(-)**
porno **der Porno(s)**
pornography **die Porno(graphie)**

Many alcoholics meet in the inner city and they are often aggressive. Violence and vandalism are common.

Older people and women are sometimes afraid to go out alone.

Some young people have a drug problem. They start by sniffing solvents, or by taking soft drugs.

Viele Alkoholiker treffen sich in der Innenstadt, und sie verhalten sich oft sehr aggressiv. Gewalt und Rowdytum sind häufig zu sehen.

Ältere Leute und Frauen haben manchmal Angst davor, allein auszugehen.

Einige Jugendliche haben ein Drogenproblem. Es fängt damit an, daß sie schnüffeln oder weiche Drogen nehmen.

prostitution **die Prostitution**
punk **der Punk(s)**
rehabilitation **die Rehabilitation**
I revert **ich falle zurück***
rocker **der Rocker(-)**
I seduce **ich verführe**
sexual harassment **die sexuelle Belästigung(en)**
skinhead **der Skinhead(s)**
I smoke **ich rauche**
stimulant **das Anregungsmittel(-)**
stimulation **der Rausch**
I terrorize **ich terrorisiere**
I threaten **ich bedrohe**
thug **der Schlägertyp(en)**
vandal **der Vandale(n)** *(wk)*
vandalism **der Vandalismus**
victim **das Opfer(-)**
violent **gewalttätig**
    act of violence **die Gewalttat(en)**

Drugs

addicted to drugs **süchtig**
AIDS **AIDS**
cannabis **das Marihuana**
cocaine **das Kokain**
crack **das Crack**
I deal **ich handle**

dealer **der Dealer(-)**
drug **das Rauschmittel(-), die Droge(n)**
drug scene **die Drogenszene**
drug traffic **der Drogenhandel**
I get infected **ich infiziere mich**
glue **der Klebstoff(e)**
hard drug **die harte Droge(n)**
hashish **der Haschisch, das Heu**
I have a fix **ich setze mir einen Druck**
heroin **das Heroin**
HIV-positive **HIV-infiziert**
I inject **ich spritze**
junkie **der Fixer(-)**
I kick *(the habit)* **ich gewöhne mich ab***
LSD **das LSD**
narcotic **das Rauschgift(e)**
pusher **der Dealer(-)**
I sniff **ich schnüffele**
soft drugs **weiche Drogen**
solvent **das Lösungsmittel(-)**
stimulant **das Anregungsmittel(-)**
syringe **die Spritze(n)**
I take drugs/a fix **ich nehme ein***
tranquillizer **das Betäubungsmittel(-)**
withdrawal **die Entwöhnung**

Cannabis is the most common. It gives a feeling of intoxication. People become psychologically dependent. Then they go onto hard drugs.

All drugs are dangerous, but injecting them brings risks of AIDS.

Junkies inject or smoke drugs.

Marihuana wird am häufigsten gebraucht. Es gibt einen Rausch. Die Leute werden psychologisch abhängig. Dann greifen sie zu den harten Drogen.

Alle Drogen sind gefährlich, aber das Spritzen hat das Risiko, daß man sich mit AIDS infiziert.

Die Fixer spritzen oder rauchen die Drogen.

12e Prejudice

asylum seeker **der Asylant(en) (wk)**
I call names **ich beschimpfe**
citizenship **die Staatsangehörigkeit(en)**
country of origin **das Geburtsland(-̈er)**
cultural **kulturell**
culture **die Kultur(en)**
I discriminate **ich diskriminiere**
discrimination **die Diskriminierung**
dual nationality **die doppelte Staatsangehörigkeit**
emigrant **der Auswanderer(-)**
emigration **die Auswanderung**
equal (un-) **gleich (un-)**
equal opportunities **die Chancengleichheit**
equal pay **der gleiche Lohn(-̈e)**
equal rights **die Gleichberechtigung**
equality (in-) **die (Un)gleichheit**
ethnic **ethnisch**
far right **rechtsradikal**
fascism **der Faschismus**
fascist **der Faschist(en) (wk) [-in], der/die Rechtsradikale (adj/n)**
foreign **fremd, ausländisch**

foreign worker **der Gastarbeiter(-)**
freedom **die Freiheit**
freedom of movement **die Bewegungsfreiheit**
freedom of speech **die Redefreiheit**
ghetto **das Ghetto(s)**
I immigrate **ich wandere ein***
immigrant (from Eastern block) **der Aussiedler(-) [-in]**
immigration **die Einwanderung**
I integrate **ich integriere mich**
integration **die Integration**
intolerance **die Intoleranz**
intolerant **intolerant**
majority **die Mehrheit(en)**
minority **die Minderheit(en)**
mother tongue **die Muttersprache(n)**
I persecute **ich verfolge**
persecution **die Verfolgung**
prejudice **das Vorurteil(e)**
prejudiced **voreingenommen gegenüber +dat**
rabid **rabiat**
race riot **der Rassenkrawall(e)**
racism **der Rassismus**
racist **der Rassist(en) [-in]**
racist (adj) **rassistisch**

– Is racism a serious problem?

– **Ist der Rassisimus ein großes Problem?**

– Yes, black and dark-skinned people suffer particularly from discrimination.

– **Ja, schwarze und dunkelhäutige Menschen leiden besonders an der Diskrimination.**

Immigration is now restricted. Black or Asian immigrants are more often refused a residence permit or work permit.

Die Immigration ist jetzt eingeschränkt. Schwarze oder asiatische Einwanderer erhalten oft keine Aufenthalts- oder Arbeitserlaubnis.

---

refugee **der Flüchtling(e)**
I repatriate **ich sende in das Heimatland zurück***
residence permit **die Aufenthaltserlaubnis(se)**
right **das Recht(e)**
  right to asylum **das Asylrecht**
  right to residence **das Wohnrecht**
second language **die zweite Sprache(n)**
stereotypical **stereotypisch**
tolerance **die Toleranz**
tolerant **tolerant**
I tolerate **ich toleriere**
work permit **die Arbeitserlaubnis(se)**

Race

anti-Semitic **antisemitisch**
anti-Semitism **der Antisemitismus**
Asian **asiatisch**
black **schwarz**
  black **der/die Schwarze** *(adj/n)*
Caribbean **der Karibe(n), die Karibin(nen)**
  Caribbean **karibisch**
coloured/colored **farbig**
dark-skinned **dunkelhäutig**
Jew **der Jude(n)** *(wk)*
Jewess **die Jüdin(nen)**

Jewish **jüdisch**
National Front **die Nationale Front**
Neo-Nazism **der Neonazismus**
white **weiß**
  white **der/die Weiße** *(adj/n)*

Sexuality

female **weiblich**
feminine **weiblich**
feminism **der Feminismus**
feminist **feministisch**
gay **schwul**
heterosexual **der Hetero(s)**
  heterosexual *(adj)* **heterosexuell**
homosexual **der/die Homosexuelle** *(adj/n)*
  homosexual *(adj)* **homosexuell**
homosexuality **die Homosexualität**
lesbian **die Lesbierin(nen), die Lesbe(n)**
lesbian **lesbisch**
male **männlich**
sexual **sexuell**
sexuality **die Sexualität**
women's lib **die Frauenbewegung(en)**
women's libber **die Frauenrechtlerin(nen)**
women's rights **die Frauenrechte**

– What about the ethnic minority population resident here? – Many have no right to citizenship.

The law still discriminates against male homosexuals, although society is getting more tolerant.

The feminist movement is still demanding equal rights for women

– **Wie ist es mit den ethnischen Minderheiten, die hier seßhaft sind? – Viele haben kein Recht auf Staatsangehörigkeit.**

Das Gesetz diskriminiert immer noch männliche Homosexuelle, obwohl die Gesellschaft toleranter wird.

Die Frauenbewegung verlangt immer noch die Gleichberechtigung der Frauen.

➤ HUMAN RELATIONSHIPS 7; LOVE 7b

Religion

13a Ideas & doctrines

agnostic **der Agnostiker(-) [-in]**
anglican **der Anglikaner(-) [-in]**
anti-semmitism **der Antisemitismus**
apostle **der Apostel(-)**
atheism **der Atheismus**
atheist **der Atheist(en)** *(wk)* **[-in]**
atheistic **atheistisch**
authority **die Autorität(en)**
belief **der Glaube** *(gen -ns) (wk)*
I believe (in) **ich glaube (an +acc)**
believer **der/die Gläubige** *(adj/n)*
Bible **die Bibel**
biblical **biblisch**
blessed **gesegnet**
Buddha **der Buddha(s)**
Buddhism **der Buddhismus**
Buddhist **der Buddhist(en)** *(wk)* **[-in]**
Calvinist **der Calvinist(en)** *(wk)* **[-in]**
cantor **der Kantor(en)** *(wk)* **[-in]**
Catholic **der Katholik(en)** *(wk)* **[-in]**
catholic *(adj)* **katholisch**
charismatic **charismatisch**
charity **die Nächstenliebe**
charity *(adj)* **karitativ**
charity organization **die Wohlfahrtsorganisation(en)**
Christ **Christus**
Christian *(adj)* **christlich**
all Christians **alle Christen**
Christianity **die Christenheit**
church **die Kirche(n)**
commentary **der Kommentar(e)**
consciousness **das Bewußtsein**
covenant **der Bund(ᵉe)**
disciple **der Jünger(-)**
divine **göttlich**
doctrine **die Lehre(n)**

duty **die Aufgabe(n), die Pflicht(en)**
ecumenicism **der Ökumenismus**
ethical **ethisch**
evil **das Böse** *(adj/n)*
evil *(adj)* **böse, übel**
I forgive **ich vergebe** +dat
forgiveness **die Vergebung(en)**
free will **der freie Wille** *(gen -ns) (wk)*
fundamentalism **der Fundamentalismus**
fundamentalist **der Fundamentalist(en)** *(wk)* **[-in]**
god **der Gott(ᵉer)**
goddess **die Göttin(nen)**
Gospel **das Evangelium (-ien)**
grace **die Gnade**
heaven **der Himmel(-)**
Hebrew **der Hebräer(-)**
hell **die Hölle(n)**
heretical **ketzerisch**
Hindu **der Hindu(s)**
Hinduism **der Hinduismus**
holiness **die Heiligkeit**
holy **heilig**
Holy Spirit **der Heilige Geist**
hope **die Hoffnung(en)**
human **menschlich**
human being **der Mensch(en)** *(wk)*
humanism **der Humanismus**
humanity **die Menschheit, die Menschlichkeit**
infallibility **die Unfehlbarkeit**
infallible **unfehlbar**
Islam **der Islam**
Islamic **islamisch**
Jesus **Jesus**
Jew **der Jude(n)** *(wk)*, **die**

Jüdin(nen)
Jewish **jüdisch**
Judaic **judäisch**
Judaism **der Judaismus**
Lord **der Herr(en)** *(wk)*
merciful **gnadenvoll**
mercy **die Gnade(n)**
Messiah **der Messias**
Mohammed **Mohammed**
moral **moralisch**
morality **die Moral, die Moralität**
Muslim **der Moslem(s)**
   Muslim *(adj)* **moslemisch**
myth **der Mythos (-en)**
New Testament **das neue Testament**
nirvana **das Nirwana**
Old Testament **das alte Testament**
orthodox **orthodox**
pagan **der Heide(n)** *(wk)* **[-in]**
parish **der Pfarrer(-) [-in]**
Pentateuch **der Pentateuch**
prophet **der Prophet(en)** *(wk)* **[-in]**
Q'uran/Koran **der Koran**
redemption **die Erlösung**
religion **die Religion(en)**
Roman Catholic **römisch-**

katholisch
sacred **heilig**
saint **der/die Heilige** *(adj/n)*
Saint Peter **Sankt Peter, der Heilige Petrus**
Salvation Army **die Heilsarmee**
he sanctifies **er heiligt**
Satan **der Satan**
he saves **er rettet**
scripture **die Heilige Schrift(en)**
service **der Gottesdienst(e)**
Sikh **der Sikh(s)**
Sikhism **der Sikhismus**
sin **die Sünde(n)**
sinful **sündig**
soul **die Seele(n)**
spirit **der Geist(er)**
spiritual **geistlich**
spirituality **die Geistlichkeit**
Talmud **der Talmud**
Taoism **der Taoismus**
theological **theologisch**
theology **die Theologie(n)**
traditional **traditionell**
Trinity **die Trinität, die Dreiheiligkeit**
true **wahr**
truth **die Wahrheit(en)**

Religious fundamentalism can lead to fanaticism and intolerance in any religion.

Der religöse Fundamentalismus kann in jeder Religion zu Fanatismus und Intoleranz führen.

Freedom of faith, of conscience and freedom of religious and ideological belief are inviolable. (Article 4 of the German constitution).

Die Freiheit des Glaubens, des Gewissens und die Freiheit des religiösen und weltauschaulichen Bekenntnisses sind unverletzlich. (Artikel 4 des Grundgesetzes)

There is considerable disagreement about the ordination of women to the priesthood.

Es bestehen beträchtliche Differenzen über die Ordination von Frauen ins Priesteramt.

archbishop der Erzbischof(⁓e)
baptism die Taufe(n)
I baptise ich taufe
bar-mitzvah das Bar-Mizvah
I bear witness to ich bekenne
bishop der Bischof(⁓e)
bishopric/see das Bistum(⁓er)
he canonises er spricht heilig
cathedral die Kathedrale(n)
I celebrate ich feiere
chapel die Kapelle(n)
christening die Taufe(n)
clergy der Klerus
clergyman der Geistliche(n)
  (adj/n), der Pfarrer(-)
communion (catholic) die
  Kommunion
  holy communion die heilige
  Kommunion
  communion (protestant) das
  Abendmahl
community die Gemeinde(n)
I confess (faith) ich bekenne mich

zu +dat
I confess (sins) ich beichte
confession die Beichte(n)
confirmation die Konfirmation
congregation die Gemeinde(n)
  (of cardinals) die
  Kongregation
conversion die Bekehrung(en)
convent das Kloster(⁓)
I convert (others) ich bekehre
I convert (self) ich konvertiere
Eucharist die Eucharistie
evangelical evangelisch
evangelist der Evangelist(en) (wk)
faith der Glaube (gen -ns) (wk)
faithful treu, gläubig
the faithful die Gläubigen (pl)
I give alms ich gebe Almosen, ich
  spende
I give thanks ich sage Dank
Imam der Imam
intercession die Fürsprache(n)
laity der Laienstand (no pl)

Those who are called to ministry must demonstrate their vocation before being accepted in theological colleges.	**Wer Pfarrer werden will, muß seine Berufung demonstrieren, bevor er in eine theologische Fakultät aufgenommen wird.**
The sacrament of Holy Communion will be celebrated on Sunday at 9 o'clock.	**Das Sakrament der heiligen Kommunion wird am Sonntag um 9 Uhr gefeiert werden.**
We work for charity.	**Wir arbeiten für eine Wohlfahrtsorganization.**
We contribute to the Red Cross.	**Wir spenden für das Rote Kreuz.**
The Baptist tradition is very strong in the American South.	**Die baptistische Tradition ist sehr stark im Süden der USA.**

lay **Laien-**
layperson **der Laie(n)** *(wk)*
the Lord's Supper **das Abendmahl**
Mass **die Messe**
I meditate **ich meditiere**
meditation **die Meditation**
minister **der Pfarrer(-)**
I minister to the parish **ich diene der Gemeinde**
ministry **das geistliche Amt(-̈er)**
mission **die Mission(en)**
missionary **der Missionar(e) [-in]**
monastery **das Kloster(-̈)**
monk **der Mönch(e)**
mosque **die Moschee(n)**
mullah **der Mullah(s)**
nun **die Nonne(n)**
parish **die Gemeinde(n)**
parishioner **das Gemeindemitglied(er)**
pastor **der Pastor(en)** *(wk)*
pastoral **seelsorgerisch**
Pope **der Papst(-̈e)**
I praise **ich lobe**
I pray (for) **ich bete (für** +acc)

prayer **das Gebet(e)**
morning prayer **die Morgenandacht**
prayerful **fromm**
priest **der Priester(-)**
rabbi **der Rabbi(s)**
I repent **ich empfinde Reue**
repentance **die Reue**
repentant **reuevoll**
I revere **ich verehre**
reverence **die Verehrung(en)**
reverent **ehrfürchtig**
rite **der Ritus (Riten)**
ritual **das Ritual(e)**
sacrament **das Sakrament(e)**
sermon **die Predigt(en)**
synagogue **die Synagoge(n)**
synod **die Synode(n)**
temple **der Tempel(-)**
vision **die Vision(en)**
vocation **die Berufung(en)**
witness **der Zeuge(n)** *(wk)* **[-in]**
I witness **ich bezeuge**
I worship **ich bete an*, ich verehre**

About 85% of the population belongs to one of the Christian faiths.

The Protestants predominate in the north, the Catholics in the south of Germany.

In England there is an Established Church. In Germany state and church are separate.

Bishops in the Church of England are not afraid to speak about social problems.

Etwa 85% der Bevölkerung bekennen sich zu einer der christlichen Konfessionen.

Die Evangelischen überwiegen im Norden, die Katholiken im Süden Deutschlands.

In England gibt es eine Staatskirche. In Deutschland sind Staat und Kirche getrennt.

Die Bischöfe der anglikanischen Kirche scheuen sich nicht, über soziale Probleme zu sprechen.

➤ RELIGIOUS FESTIVALS App.13b

14 Business & economics

14a Economic life

I administer **ich verwalte**
we agree (to) **wir beschließen (zu +inf)**
agreement **die Übereinkunft(-̈e)**
bureaucracy **die Bürokratie(n)**
business **das Geschäft(e), die Unternehmung(en)**
a business **ein Geschäft(e)**
capacity *(industrial)* **die Kapazität(en)**
commerce **der Kommerz, der Handel**
commercial **kommerziell**
company **die (Handels)gesellschaft(en)**
competition **die Konkurrenz**
competitive **konkurrenzfähig**
deal **das Geschäft(e)**
I deliver **ich liefere**
demand **die Nachfrage(n)**
in demand **gefragt**
development **die Entwicklung(en)**
I dismiss **ich kündige**
I earn (a living) **ich verdiene**
economy **die Wirtschaft(en), die Konjunktur** *(no pl)*
I employ **ich beschäftige**
employee **der Arbeitnehmer(-)**
employer **der Arbeitgeber(-)**
employment **die Arbeit**
executive **der Geschäftsführer(-) [-in]**
I export **ich exportiere**
export(s) **der Export(e)**
it falls **es sinkt, es fällt**
firm **die Firma (Firmen), der Betrieb(e)**
goods **die Ware(n)**
it grows **es wächst**
I import **ich importiere**

I increase **ich erhöhe, ich erweitere**
increase **der Anstieg, die Zunahme**
industrial **industriell**
industrial output **die Produktion(en)**
industry **die Industrie(n), der Industriebetrieb(e)**
I invest **ich investiere**
investment **die Investition(en)**
job **der Arbeitsplatz(-̈e)**
job creation scheme **die Arbeits-beschaffungsmaßnahme(n)**
lay-off **die Entlassung(en)**
living standards **der Lebensstandard(s)**
I manage **ich leite**
management **das Management(s), die Leitung(en)**
multinational **multinational**
I negotiate **ich verhandle**
priority **die Priorität(en)**
I produce **ich produziere, ich stelle her***
producer **der Hersteller(-)**
product **der Produkt(e)**
production line **das Fließband(-̈er)**
productivity **die Produktivität(en)**
public company **die Aktiengesellschaft(en)**
quality **die Qualität(en)**
I raise (prices) **ich erhöhe (die Preise)**
reliability **die Zuverlässigkeit**
rise **der Anstieg(e)**
wages rise **die Gehaltserhöhung(en)**
semi-skilled **angelernt**
service **der Service**

service industry **der Dienstleistungsbetrieb(e)**
I set (priorities) **ich setze (Prioritäten)**
I am on sick-leave **ich bin krankgeschrieben**
sick pay **das Krankengeld(er)**
I sign (contracts) **ich unterzeichne (Verträge)**
skilled labour/labor **der Facharbeiter(-) [-in]**
I strengthen **ich stärke**
supply **das Angebot(e)**
trade-unionism **das Gewerkschaftswesen**
turnover **der Umsatz(¨e)**
unemployment **die Arbeitslosigkeit(en)**
unemployment benefit **das Arbeitslosengeld(er)**
unskilled labour/labor **der ungelernte Arbeiter(-)**
work **die Arbeit(en)**
worker **der Arbeiter(-) [-in]**
work ethic **die Arbeitsmoral** *(no pl)*
workforce **die Arbeitskräfte** *(pl)*
working week **die Arbeitswoche(n)**
workplace **der Arbeitsplatz(¨e)**
working conditions **die Arbeitsbedingungen** *(pl)*

Industrial/Labor dispute

ballot **die Abstimmung(en)**
I boycott **ich boykottiere**
demonstration **die Demonstration(en)**
dispute **der Streit(e), die Auseinandersetzung(en)**
I go slow/slow down **ich mache einen Bummelstreik**
industrial/labor dispute **der Arbeitskonflikt(e)**
industrial relations **die Beziehungen zwischen Arbeitgeber und Gewerkschaften**
I lock-out **ich sperre aus***
lock-out **die Aussperrung(en)**
minimum wage **der Mindestlohn**
I picket **ich stelle Streikposten auf***
picket **der Streikposten(-)**
productivity bonus **die Prämie(n)**
I resume work **ich nehme die Arbeit wieder auf***
social unrest **die soziale Not/Unruhe(n)**
stoppage **der Stopp(s)**
strike **der Streik(s)**
  unofficial strike **der wilde Streik(s)**
I am on strike **ich streike**
I go on strike **ich trete in den Streik**
striker **der Streiker(-)**
strikebreaker **der Streikbrecher(-)**
trade union **die Gewerkschaft(en)**
unfair dismissal **die ungerechtfertigte Entlassung(en)**
unrest **die Unruhe(n)**
wage costs **die Lohnkosten** *(pl)*
wage demand **die Lohnforderung(en)**
wage settlement **das Lohnabkommen(-)**

The unions called for a reduction in working hours.	**Die Gewerkschaften forderten eine Verkürzung der Arbeitszeit.**
Unemployment is rising to 12%.	**Die Arbeitslosenquote steigt auf 12 Prozent an.**

➤ AT WORK 14b; UNEMPLOYMENT 12c; JOBS & PROFESSIONS App.14a

14b Work today

agenda **die Tagesordnung(en)**
  on the agenda **auf dem Programm**
on business **geschäftlich**
boring **langweilig**
business lunch **das Geschäftsessen(-)**
business meeting **das Treffen(-), die Konferenz(en)**
business trip **die Geschäftsreise(n)**
I buy **ich kaufe**
canteen **die Kantine(n)**
career **der Beruf(e)**
I chair a meeting **ich führe den Vorsitz**
I delegate **ich delegiere**
disciplinary proceeding **das Disziplinarverfahren(-)**
I do **ich mache**
I follow a training course **ich lasse mich ausbilden**
free **kostenlos**
grant **das Stipendium (-ien)**
holiday/vacation **die Ferien** *(pl)*, **der Urlaub(e)**
job **der Job(s)**
I have job satisfaction **ich bin mit**
meiner Arbeit zufrieden
I market **ich bringe … auf den Markt, ich vermarkte**
meal **die Mahlzeit(en)**
meeting **die Sitzung(en)**
misconduct **das Vergehen(-)**
occupation **die Beschäftigung(en), der Beruf(e)**
I'm off work **ich fehle**
I pay taxes **ich zahle Steuern**
post **die Stelle(n), die Stellung(en)**
profession **der Beruf(e)**
professional **der Fachmann(-̈er)**
  professional *(adj)* **beruflich, professionell**
publicity **die Öffentlichkeit**
I qualify **ich qualifiziere**
I report to **ich unterstehe jdm.**
research **ich forsche**
I am responsible for **ich bin für** +acc **verantwortlich**
I sell **ich verkaufe**
I teach **ich lehre**
I toil **ich schufte**
training **die Ausbildung(en)**
training course **das**

I am the wage earner.	**Ich verdiene das Geld.**
– What are you doing now?	**– Was haben Sie jetzt für einen Beruf?**
– I'm training to be an accountant.	**– Ich lasse mich als Buchhalter ausbilden.**
I go to college and I'm taking my finals next month.	**Ich besuche die Hochschule, und nächsten Monat mache ich die Abschlußprüfung.**

Ausbildungsprogramm(e)
I transfer **ich werde versetzt**
unskilled **ungelernt**
vocation **die Berufung(en)**
warning *(verbal)* **die Verwarnung(en)**
   written warning **die schriftliche Warnung(en)/Abmahnung(en)**
I work as … **ich arbeite als …**

In the office

computer **der Computer(-)**
conference room **der Konferenzsaal (-säle)**
desk **der Schreibtisch(e)**
I dictate **ich diktiere**
dictating machine **das Diktiergerät(e)**
electronic mail **die elektronische Post**
extension **der Apparat(e)**
fax **das Fax**
fax machine **das Faxgerät(e)**
I fax **ich faxe**
file **die Akte(n)**
I file **ich ordne/lege Akten an***
filing cabinet **der Aktenschrank(ˉe)**
intercom **die Sprechanlage(n)**
memorandum **die Mitteilung(en)**
open-plan **offen angelegt**
photocopier **der Fotokopierer(-)**
photocopy **die Kopie(n)**
I photocopy **ich kopiere**
pigeonhole **das Lesefach(ˉer)**
reception **die Rezeption(en)**
receptionist **der Herr/die Dame am Empfang**
short-hand **die Stenographie**
swivel chair **der Drehstuhl(ˉe)**
telephone **das Telefon(e)**
typing pool **die Schreibzentrale(n)**
wastebasket **der Papierkorb(ˉe)**
word processor **der Textverarbeiter(-)**
work station **die Arbeitssplatz(ˉe)**

On the factory & on site

automation **die Automatisierung**
blue-collar worker **der manuelle Arbeiter(-) [-in]**
bulldozer **die Planierraupe(n)**
car/automobile industry **die Autoindustrie(n)**
component **der Bestandteil(e)**
concrete **der Beton**
construction industry **die Bauindustrie(n)**
crane **der Kran(ˉe)**
fork-lift truck **der Gabelstapler(-)**
I forge **ich schmiede**
industry **die Industrie(n)**
   heavy industry **die Schwerindustrie(n)**
   light industry **die Leichtindustrie(n)**
I manufacture **ich stelle her***
manufacture **das Herstellen**
mass production **die Massenproduktion**
mining **der Bergbau**
power industry **die Energieindustrie(n)**
precision tool **das Präzisionswerkzeug(e)**
prefabricated **vorgefertigt**
process **der Prozeß (-sse)**
I process **ich verarbeite**
product **das Produkt(e)**
on the production line **am Fließband**
raw materials **der rohe Werkstoff(e)**
road building **der Straßenbau**
robot **der Roboter(-)**
scaffolding **das Gerüst(e)**
shipbuilding **der Schiffbau**
I smelt **ich schmelze**
steamroller **die Dampfwalze(n)**
steel smelting **das Stahlschmelzen**
textile industry **die Textilindustrie(n)**

➤ WORKING CONDITIONS 14c; COMPUTERS 15f; STATIONERY App.22b

14c Working conditions

I am employed **ich bin angestellt**
apprenticeship **die Lehre(n), die Lehrzeit(en)**
benefit **der Nutzen(-)**
bonus **die Prämie(n), der Zuschlag(¨e)**
I clock (in/out) **ich stemple (den Arbeitsbeginn/beim Herausgehen)**
commission **die Kommission(en)**
on commission **auf Provision**
company car **der Firmenwagen(-)**
conditions of employment **die Arbeitsbedingungen** *(pl)*
contract **der Vertrag(¨e)**
expenses **die Spesen** *(pl)*
expense account **das Spesenkonto (-en)**
flexi-time/flextime **die flexible Arbeitszeit(en)**
freelance **freiberuflich**
I work freelance **ich arbeite freiberuflich**
full-time **ganztägig, ganztags**
full-time job **die Ganztagsstelle(n)**

income **das Einkommen**
overtime **die Überstunde(n)**
overworked **überfordert**
part-time **Teilzeit-**
pay **der Lohn(¨e)**
payday **der Zahltag(e)**
payslip **die Lohnabrechnung(en)**
payrise/pay raise **die Gehaltserhöhung(en)**
pension **die Rente(n), die Pension(en)**
perk **die Vergünstigung(en)**
permanent **permanent**
professional association **die Berufsgenossenschaft(en)**
remuneration **die Vergütung(en)**
I retire **ich trete in den Ruhestand**
retirement **der Ruhestand**
salary **das Gehalt(¨er)**
self-employed **selbständig**
shift **die Schicht(en)**
day shift **die Tagesschicht(en)**
night shift **die Nachtschicht(en)**

The conditions in this office are not good enough. The place is cold, badly lit, and poorly ventilated

Die Arbeitsbedingungen im Büro sind unzulänglich. Der Raum ist kalt, schlecht beleuchtet und nicht ausreichend gelüftet.

The majority of people who are in part-time work choose not to work full-time because of family commitments.

Die Mehrheit der Leute, die in Teilzeitjobs beschäftigt sind, wählen diese, um ihren Familienverpflichtungen nachzukommen.

Our policy is to create more part-time jobs, and to protect the rights of part-time workers.

Unsere Geschäftspolitik besteht darin, mehr Teilzeitstellen zu schaffen und die Rechte von Teilzeitkräften zu stärken.

shiftworking **die Schichtarbeit**
temporary **für kurze Zeit, befristet**
trial period **die Probezeit(en)**
working-hours **die Arbeitsstunden**
wage **der Lohn(-̈e)**

Job application

I advertise the post **ich inseriere die Stelle**
advertisement **die Anzeige(n)**
I apply for a job **Ich bewerbe mich für eine Stelle.**
classified ad **die Kleinanzeige(n)**
curriculum vitae/resumé **der Lebenslauf(-̈e)**
discrimination **die Diskriminierung(en)**
　racial discrimination **die Rassendiskriminierung(en)**
　sexual discrimination **das sexuelle Diskriminierung(en)**
employment agency **die Arbeitsvermittlungsagentur(en)**
job centre/employment office **das Arbeitsamt(-̈er)**
I find a job **ich finde einen Job**
interesting **interessant**

interview **das Vorstellungsgespräch(e)**
I interview **ich interviewe**
job application **die Bewerbung(en)**
job offer **das Stellungangebot(e)**
I look for **ich suche**
opening **die freie Stelle(n)**
I promote (someone) **ich befördere (jdn.)**
I am promoted **ich werde befördert**
promotion **die Beförderung(en)**
qualification **die Qualifikation(en)**
qualified **qualifiziert, ausgebildet**
situations vacant **die Stellenangebote** *(pl)*
I start work (for) **Ich fange (bei** +dat) **zu arbeiten an***
I take on *(employee)* **ich stelle ein***
vacancy **die offene Stelle(n)**
work experience **das Praktikum (-a)**

– Hello. Could I speak to the Personnel Manager, please.
– Speaking. What can I do for you?
– I saw your advertisement in the local paper for a sales executive. Could you send me the job description and application forms? How many referees are you asking for?

– Two, including your present or last employer.

– Hallo, könnte ich bitte den Personalchef sprechen.
– Am Apparat. Was kann ich für Sie tun?
– Ich sah Ihre Anzeige in der Lokalzeitung für einen Verkaufsleiter. Können Sie mir eine Stellenbeschreibung und die Bewerbungsunterlagen zusenden? Wieviele Referenzen benötigen Sie?
– Zwei, einschließlich Ihres jetzigen oder letzten Arbeitgebers.

➤ UNEMPLOYMENT 12c

14d Finance & industry

account **die Rechnung(en), das Konto (-en)**
advance **der Vorschuß (-̈sse)**
I audit **ich prüfe**
bill **die Rechnung(en)**
bond **die Staatsanleihe(n)**
branch *(of company)* **die Zweigstelle(n)**
budget **das Budget(s), der Haushalt(e)**
capital **das Kapital**
capital expenditure **die Kapitalaufwendungen** *(pl)*
Chamber of commerce **die Handelskammer(n)**
collateral **die Sicherheit(en)**
company **die Gesellschaft(en)**
competition **die Konkurrenz**
I consume *(resources)* **ich verbrauche**
consumer goods **die Konsumgüter** *(pl)*
consumer protection **der Verbraucherschutz**
consumer spending **die Verbraucherausgaben** *(pl)*
cost of living **die Lebenshaltungskosten** *(pl)*
costing **die Kostenberechnung(en)**
costs **die Kosten** *(pl)*
credit **der Kredit(e)**
debit **die Abhebung(en)**
deflation **die Deflation**
economic **wirtschaftlich**
economy **die Wirtschaft(en)**
government spending **die öffentlichen Ausgaben** *(pl)*
income **das Einkommen**
income tax **die Einkommenssteuer(n)**
instalment/installment **die Rate(n)**
interest rate **die Zinsrate(n)**
I invest in **ich investiere in** +acc

investment **die Investierung(en)**
invoice **die Rechnung(en)**
labour/labor costs **die Arbeitskosten** *(pl)*
liability **die Verpflichtung(en)**
limited liability company **die Gesellschaft mit beschränkter Haftung (GmbH)**
loan **der Kredit(e)**
manufacturing industry **die herstellende Industrie(n)**
market **der Markt(-̈e)**
market economy **die Marktwirtschaft**
marketing **das Marketing**
merchandise **die Güter** *(pl)*
national debt **die Staatsschulden** *(pl)*
I nationalize **ich verstaatliche**
output **die Leistung(en), die Produktion(en)**
pay **der Lohne(-̈e)**
price **der Preis(e)**
private sector **der Privatsektor(en)**
I privatize **ich privatisiere**
product **das Produkt(e)**
production **die Produktion(en)**
public sector **der öffentliche Sektor(en)**
quota **die Quote(n)**
rate (going) **der Kurs(e)**
real estate/realty **die Immobilien** *(pl)*
retail sales **der Einzelhandelsverkauf** *(no pl)*
retail trade **der Einzelhandel** *(no pl)*
salaries **das/der Gehalt(-̈er)**
sales tax **die Verkausfssteuer(n)**
service sector **der Dienstleistungssektor(en)**
share **die Aktie(n)**
shares are going up/down **die Aktien fallen/steigen**

share index **der Aktienindex(e)**
statistics **die Statistik(en)**
Stock Exchange **die Börse(n)**
I subsidize **ich subventioniere**
subsidy **der Zuschuß (ꞋïÂsse)**
supply and demand **Angebot und Nachfrage**
supply costs **die Lieferkosten** *(pl)*
I tax **ich versteuere**
tax **die Steuer(n)**
    after tax **nach Abzug und Steuer**
tax cut **die Steuersenkung(en)**
tax relief **die Steuerbegünstigung(en)**
tax increase **die Steuererhöhung(en)**
taxation **die Steuern** *(pl)*
taxation level **das Steuerniveau(s)**
turnover **der Umsatz(ꞋïÂe)**
VAT/sales tax **die Mehrwertsteuer, MwSt**
viable **rentabel**
wage(s) **der Lohn(ꞋïÂe)**

Financial personnel

accountant **der Wirtschaftsprüfer(-) [-in]**
actuary **der Versicherungsmathematiker(-) [-in]**
auditor **der Prüfer(-) [-in]**
banker **der Bankier(s)**
    investment banker **der Investitionsbankier(s)**
    merchant banker **der Handelsbankier(s)**
bank manager **der Bankmanager(-) [-in]**
broker **der Makler(-) [-in]**
    insurance broker **der Versicherungsmakler(-) [-in**
consumer **der Verbraucher(-) [-in]**
investor **der Investor(en)**
speculator **der Spekulant(en)** *(wk)*
stockbroker **der Börsenmakler(-) [-in]**
trader *(Wall St.)* **der Händler(-) [-in], der Makler(-) [-in]**

Industry is recovering.	**Die Industrie nimmt einen Aufschwung.**
In spite of the increase in the value of the Deutschmark, there is an export surplus.	**Trotz der DM-Aufwertungen gibt es einen Ausfuhrüberschuß.**
Inflation is slowing down.	**Die Inflation nimmt ab.**
A stable economy, free trade and an organised monetary system are important for the EU/European Union.	**Eine stabile Wirtschaft, freier Handel und ein geordnetes Währungssystem sind wichtig für die EU.**
We have to pay for the import of raw materials.	**Wir müssen die Einfuhr von Rohstoffen bezahlen.**
The fall in value of the dollar is the cause of the recession.	**Der Rückgang des Dollarkurses ist Ursache der Rezession.**
I have overdrawn my account.	**Ich habe mein Konto überzogen.**

➤ ADVERTISING 18d

14e Banking & the economy

Banking & personal finance

account **das Konto (-en)**
automatic teller/cash point **der Geldautomat(en)** *(wk)*
bank **die Bank(en)**
I bank *(money)* **ich zahle Geld ein***
banking **das Bankwesen**
bank loan **das Bankdarlehen(-)**
bank charge **die Bankgebühr(en)**
bank statement **der Kontoauszug(¨e)**
building society/savings and loan association **die Bausparkasse(n)**
cash **das Bargeld(er)**
I cash a cheque/check **ich löse einen Scheck ein***
cashcard **die Scheckkarte(n)**
cashdesk **die Kasse(n)**
I change **ich wechsle**
cheque/check **der Scheck(s)**
credit card **die Kreditkarte(n)**
I'm in credit **Ich habe Geld auf dem Konto**
currency **die Währung(en)**
deficit **das Defizit(e)**
deposit *(in a bank)* **die Einzahlung(en)**
deposit *(returnable)* **die Kaution(en)**

I deposit **ich zahle ... ein***
direct debit **die Einzugs-ermächtigung(en)**
down payment/deposit **die Anzahlung(en)**
Eurocheque **der Euroscheck(s)**
exchange rate **der Wechselkurs(e)**
hire purchase/installment plan **der Teilzahlungskauf(¨e)**
I invest **ich lege an***
I lend **ich leihe**
loan **das Darlehen(-)**
mortgage **die Hypothek(en)**
I mortgage **ich nehme eine Hypothek auf***
I open an account **ich eröffne ein Konto**
overdraft **der Überziehungskredit(e)**
I overdraw **ich überziehe**
I pay cash **ich bezahle bar**
in the red **in den roten Zahlen**
repayment **die Zurückzahlung(en)**
I save **ich spare**
savings **die Ersparnisse** *(pl)*
savings bank **die Sparkasse(n)**
standing order **der Dauerauftrag(¨e)**
I transfer (to) **ich überweise auf** +acc

I have opened an account at the (savings) bank. You only need an identity card and an initial deposit. I have my salary automatically transferred into my account.

I pay my rent and insurance by standing order. Gas and electricity are withdrawn from my account by direct debit.

Ich habe bei der Sparkasse ein Konto eröffnet. Man braucht nur einen Personalausweis und ein erste Einzahlung. Ich lasse mein Gehalt automatisch auf das Konto überweisen.
Ich begleiche Miete und Versicherung mit Daueraufträgen. Gas und Strom werden durch Einzugsermächtigungen von meinem Konto abgebucht.

travellers' cheque/traveler's check
der Reisecheck(s)
I withdraw **ich hebe ab***

Growth

appreciation **die Wertsteigerung(en)**
asset **der Aktivposten(-)**
assurance **die Versicherung(en)**
auction **die Auktion(en)**
boom **die Hochkunjunktur, der Boom(s), der Aufschwung(¨e)**
I diversify **ich diversifiziere**
economic miracle **das Wirtschaftswunder(-)**
efficiency **die Wirtschaftlichkeit**
I grow/expand **ich wachse**
growth **das Wachstum**
it increases **es steigt**
joint venture **die Gemeinschaftsarbeit(en)**
they merge **sie fusionieren**
we merge **wir schließen uns zusammen***
merger **die Fusion(en)**
plan **der Plan(¨e)**
profit **der Gewinn(e)**
profitable **rentabel**
progress **der Fortschritt(e)**
prosperity **der Wohlstand** *(no pl)*
prosperous **wohlhabend**

recovery **der neue Aufschwung**
takeover **die Übernahme(n)**
takeover bid **das Übernahmeangebot(e)**

Decline

bankrupt **bankrott, pleite**
I go bankrupt **ich mache bankrott**
credit squeeze **die Kreditbeschränkung(en)**
debt **die Schuld(en)**
it is declining **es fällt, es geht zurück**
deficit **das Defizit(e)**
depreciation **der Kaufkraftverlust(e)**
I dump **ich verkaufe zu Dumpingpreisen**
inflation **die Inflation(en)**
inflation rate **die Inflationsrate(n)**
loss **der Verlust(e)**
no-growth economy **die stagnierende Wirtschaft**
recession **die Rezession(en)**
it slows down **es geht zurück**
slump **der Rückgang(¨e)**
it slumps **es stürzt**
spending cuts **die Kürzungen im Etat**
stagnant **stagnierend**
stagnation **die Stagnation(en)**

Nobody accepts a cheque/check today without a cheque/check card. The bank guarantees that every cheque/check is honoured/honored. My credit-worthiness has been checked.

Niemand nimmt heute einen Scheck ohne eine Scheckkarte. Die Bank garantiert dafür, daß jeder Scheck eingelöst wird. Man hat meine Kreditwürdigkeit überprüft.

We have a record surplus of DM90,000 million.

Wir haben einen Rekordüberschuß von 90Mrd. DM

The cost of oil imports is rising steeply.

Die Kosten der Öleinfuhren steigen kräftig.

Communicating with others

15a Meetings & greetings

Meetings

I accept *(invitation)* **ich nehme an***
appointment **die Verabredung(en), der Termin(e)**
at home **zu Hause**
ball **der Ball(¨e)**
banquet **das Bankett(e)**
I bump into **ich begegne jdm.**
I'm busy **ich habe keine Zeit**
I celebrate **ich begehe, ich feiere**
celebration **die Feier(n) , die Gedenkfeier(n)**
club **der Klub(s), der Club(s)**
dance **der Tanz(¨e)**
date *(appointment)* **die Verabredung(en), das Rendezvous(-)**
diary/datebook **der (Termin)kalender(-)**
I drop in **ich komme vorbei**
I'm expecting … for dinner **ich erwarte +acc zum Abendessen**
I greet **ich begrüsse**
guest **der Gast(¨e)**
I have guests **ich habe**

Besuch

handshake **der Händedruck(¨e)**
I invite **ich lade ein***
invitation **die Einladung(en)**
I join **ich trete +dat bei***
we meet **wir treffen uns**
meeting **die Begegnung(en), das Treffen(-)**
party **die Party(s), die Feier(n), das Fest(e)**
I throw a party **ich gebe eine Party**
reception **der Empfang(¨e)**
I shake hands with (someone) **ich gebe (jdm.) die Hand**
social life **das gesellschaftliche Leben**
I socialize **ich komme viel unter die Leute**
I spend *(an evening)* **ich verbringe**
I take part **ich mache mit***
I talk to someone **ich unterhalte mich mit jdm.**
I visit *(someone)* **ich besuche**
visit **der Besuch(e)**

– Please come in! Do sit down!

I'm delighted you were able to come. How are you?
– I am well thank you, and you?

– Not so well, unfortunately.
– What's your son doing now? I am sorry we couldn't meet him. I am so disappointed.

– **Kommen Sie bitte herein! Bitte nehmen Sie Platz!**
Ich freue mich, daß Sie kommen konnten. Wie geht es Ihnen?
– **Es geht mir gut danke, und Ihnen?**
– **Leider nicht so gut.**
– **Was macht Ihr Sohn jetzt? Ich bedaure sehr, daß wir ihn nicht kennenlernen konnten. Das war eine große Enttäuschung.**

➤ APPROVING, DISAPPROVING 15b; PERMISSION, CLARIFICATION 15c

Greetings

Good day **Guten Tag!**
Good morning! **Guten Morgen!**
Good evening! **Guten Abend!**
Hello! **Guten Tag! Grüß Gott!**
 Hello! *(fam)* **Hallo! Servus!**
Hey you! **Heh! Du!**
Doctor Braun, … **Herr Doktor Braun, …**
greetings to you all **ich begrüße Sie alle**
I say, did you know? **Du, weißt du schon?**
welcome to our home! **herzlich willkommen bei uns!**
what is it? **was ist's?**
what's up? **was gibt's?**
yes? **ja, bitte?**

Introductions

I am called … **ich heiße …**
can I introduce you? **darf ich (Sie) bekanntmachen?**
delighted to meet you **es freut mich, Sie kennenzulernen**
do you know Doctor Schmidt? **kennen Sie schon Herrn Doktor Schmidt?**
I am a friend of Peter's **ich bin ein Freund von Peter**
how do you do! **angenehm! freut mich!**
may I introduce my friend Peter? **darf ich meinen Freund Peter vorstellen?**
my name is … **mein Name ist …**
what are you called? **wie heißt du?**
what's your surname? **wie heißt du mit Nachnamen?**

Congratulations

all the best! **alles Gute!**
cheers! **zum Wohl! prost!**
congratulations! **herzlichen Glückwunsch!**
happy Christmas! **frohe Weihnachten**
happy Easter! **frohe Ostern!**
happy New Year! **ein gutes neues Jahr!, einen guten Rutsch ins neue Jahr!**
I congratulate you on **ich gratuliere (Ihnen) zu** +dat
I wish you … **ich wünsche Ihnen …**
my deepest sympathy! **mein herzliches Beileid!**
thank you so much! **ich bedanke mich (sehr)!**
your good health! **auf Ihr Wohl!**

Pleasantries

I address (someone) **ich rede (jdn.) an*, ich spreche zu** +dat
I address as "du" **ich duze**
I address as "Sie" **ich sieze**
may I come in? **darf ich reinkommen?**
come in! **herein!**
am I disturbing you? **störe ich?**
Am I in your way? **Störe ich?**
not at all! **nein, keineswegs!**

– We were so lucky with the weather.
– I am glad for you.
– What a pity the children were ill. I hope they are better soon.

– **Wir haben wirklich Glück mit dem Wetter gehabt.**
– **Das freut mich für Sie.**
– **Schade, daß die Kinder krank waren. Hoffentlich sind sie bald wieder gesund.**

➤ FAREWELLS 15d; POST/MAIL, TELEPHONE 15e; COMPUTERS 15f

15b Approving, thanking & disapproving

Approval

all right	**in Ordnung**
that's all right	**es ist ganz in Ordnung**
all right by me!	**meinetwegen!**
that's all right by me!	**von mir aus!**
fabulous	**fabelhaft**
fantastic	**phantastisch**
I'm in favour/favor	**ich bin (wäre) dafür**
delighted	**erfreut**
I'm delighted	**das freut mich**
I enjoy	**ich genieße**
exactly	**genau**
I feel	**ich fühle mich**
I feel like (doing)	**ich habe Lust, zu** +inf
fun	**der Spaß(-e)**
that's fun	**das macht Spaß**
fine!	**schön!, prima!, gut!**
I am fond of him	**ich habe ihn sehr gern**
glad	**froh**
I'm glad	**ich bin froh, ich freue mich**
great!	**toll!, prima!, phantastisch!, Klasse!**
that would be great	**das wäre gut/prima!**
interesting	**interessant**
it interests me	**das interessiert mich**
I am interested in	**ich interessiere mich für** +acc
just so!	**so ist das einfach/eben**
I like it a lot	**ich mag es sehr**
I like reading	**ich lese gern**
I like it	**es gefällt mir**
I really like you	**ich mag dich wirklich gern**
I like her	**ich kann sie gut leiden**
I would like	**ich würde gern, ich möchte**
I look forward to	**ich freue mich auf** +acc
I love	**ich liebe**
lovely	**schön**
marvellous	**herrlich**
I don't mind	**das ist (mir) egal/gleich**
nice	**nett, schön, sympathisch**
how nice!	**wie schön!**
pleased	**zufrieden**
with pleasure	**mit Vergnügen**
rather	**lieber**
I would rather	**ich möchte lieber**
right	**korrekt**
that's right	**das stimmt**
I want	**ich will/möchte**
wonderful	**großartig, wunderbar**
it works out	**es klappt**

I am looking forward a lot to the holidays/vacation. It is exactly what I want. I am interested in architecture.
I really like it in Bavaria. I feel great there.

It worked out well last year.
I don't mind whether we go to Munich or Würzburg.

Ich freue mich sehr auf die Ferien. Es ist genau das, was ich brauche. Ich interessiere mich für die Architektur.
Es gefällt mir sehr gut in Bayern. Ich fühle mich dort sehr wohl.
Letztes Jahr hat es gut geklappt.
Es ist mir gleich, ob wir nach München oder Würzburg fahren.

Thanking

please! **bitte!**
I thank **ich danke** +dat
thank you! **danke!**
many thanks! **vielen Dank!, danke sehr!**
thank you very much! **danke schön!**
thank you very much indeed! **herzlichen Dank!**
thanks a lot! **schönen Dank auch!**
don't mention it! **nichts zu danken!**
glad to help! **gern geschehen!**
no need to thank me! **keine Ursache!**
not at all! **bitte!, bitteschön!**
it was the least I could do! **das ist doch selbstverständlich!**

Disapproval

I annoy **ich störe**
you're annoying me! **du störst mich!**
bad **schlecht**
that's too bad! **das geht zu weit**
bad luck **das Pech**
we had bad luck **wir hatten Pech**
what bad luck! **so ein Mist!**
damn! **verdammt!**
dreadful **schrecklich, furchtbar**
fed up **sauer**

furious **wütend**
how dreadful! **wie schrecklich!**
I hate doing **ich hasse es, zu** +inf
it hurts! **das tut weh!**
impossible **unmöglich**
that's impossible **das geht (doch) nicht**
leave me in peace! **laß mich in Ruhe!**
are you mad? **bist du verrückt?**
I mind a lot **es macht mir viel aus***
miserable **miserabel**
nonsense! **Quatsch!, (das ist) Unsinn!**
it's nothing to do with me **das geht mich nichts an***
ouch! **au!**
there's no point! **das hat keinen Zweck/Sinn**
rubbish **Quatsch!**
shit! **Scheiße!**
I can't stand him **ich kann ihn nicht leiden**
stop that! **laß das!, hör doch auf!**
stupid **dumm**
that's stupid! **das ist zu dumm!**
that won't do **das geht nicht**
that's enough **das genügt**

The weather was dreadful.	**Das Wetter war schrecklich.**
Such bad luck!	**So ein Mist!**
Hans was quite impossible.	**Hans war ganz unmöglich.**
It really won't do, he was so annoying.	**Es geht einfach nicht, er störte so.**
There's no point in taking him.	**Es hat keinen Zweck, ihn mitzunehmen.**
I like his girl friend. She is really nice.	**Ich finde seine Freundin wirklich sympathisch. Sie ist wirklich sehr nett.**

➤ INTERJECTIONS, APOLOGIZING & FAREWELLS 15d

15c Permission, obligation & clarification

Permission

can I?	**kann ich?**
could I?	**könnte ich?**
OK?	**geht das?**
may I?	**darf ich?**
might I?	**dürfte ich?**

will you allow me to **erlauben Sie mir zu** +inf?
would it be possible? **wäre es möglich?**
yes of course! **ja natürlich!**
sure! **ja klar!**
OK! **okay!, in Ordnung!**
yes, that's OK! **ja, das geht!**
allowed **erlaubt/gestattet**
I allow you to.... **ich erlaube Ihnen zu** +inf
it doesn't bother me, if you ... **es stört mich nicht, wenn Sie ...**
carry on! **machen Sie ruhig weiter!**
of course you can ... **Sie dürfen selbstverständlich ...**
you can if you want **du kannst, wenn du willst**
as far as I'm concerned, you can ... **meinetwegen können Sie ...**
do you mind if ...? **stört es Sie wenn ...?**
yes, if you must **ja, wenn es sein muß**
do you object? **haben Sie was dagegen?**
permission **die Erlaubnis(se)**
as you wish **wie Sie wollen**
you are not allowed to **du darfst nicht**
no, you can't ... **nein, du kannst/darfst nicht ...**
certainly not! **durchaus nicht!**
certainly not **auf keinen Fall, keinesfalls**
it is just not done! **das tut man nicht!**
forbidden **untersagt, verboten**

smoking forbidden **kein Rauchen, Rauchverbot**
impossible! **ausgeschlossen!**
no, certainly not **nein, keineswegs**
not at all **gar/überhaupt nicht**
it's not on **es geht leider nicht**
of course not! **überhaupt nicht!**
out of the question! **es kommt nicht in Frage!**
please don't! **bitte nicht!**
I'd rather you didn't! **lieber nicht!**
I have no right to ... **ich habe kein Recht zu** +inf
I'm sorry! **tut mir leid!**
under no circumtances **auf keinen Fall**

Obligation

it's compulsory **es ist Vorschrift/obligatorisch**
I have got to **ich muß unbedingt/auf jeden Fall**
you've got to! **das muß sein!**
I have to **ich muß**
do I have to? **muß ich?**
you don't have to **du mußt nicht**
I have a lot to do **ich habe viel zu tun**
I intend to ... **ich habe vor zu** +inf
I intend to **ich habe die Absicht**
I must **ich muß**
you must pay a fee **es ist gebührenpflichtig**
it is not necessary **es ist nicht nötig**
not necessarily **nicht unbedingt**
you do not need to **du brauchst nicht zu** +inf
you needn't do it **du kannst es ruhig lassen**
I am obliged to **ich bin verpflichtet zu** +inf
I am not supposed to **ich soll nicht**

I want to **ich will**
what is to be done? **was ist zu tun?**

Clarifying

and so on, etc. **und so weiter, usw.**
I ask **ich frage**
may I ask a question? **dürfte ich eine Frage stellen?**
example **das Beispiel(e)**
for example **zum Beispiel, beispielsweise**
I explain **ich erkläre**
I hear **ich höre**
can you still hear me? **hören Sie mich noch?**
are you still there? **sind Sie noch da?**
I didn't hear **ich habe nicht gehört**
I forget **ich vergesse**
in other words **mit anderen Worten, anders gesagt**
I know **ich weiß**
I don't know how you say ... **ich weiß nicht, wie man sagt ...**
loud **laut**
louder **lauter**
not so loud! **nicht so laut!**
I mean **ich meine**
it means **es bedeutet**
what does it mean? **was heißt das?**
what do you mean **was meinen Sie?**
what do you mean by that? **was meinen Sie damit?**

I pronounce **ich spreche aus***
how do you pronounce it? **wie spricht man das?**
I have a question **ich habe eine Frage**
quick(ly) **schnell**
not so quick **nicht so schnell**
quiet please! **Ruhe bitte!**
quietly! **leise!**
I repeat **ich wiederhole**
could you repeat that? **können Sie das wiederholen?**
I say **ich sage**
how do you say that in German? **wie sagt man das auf deutsch?**
what would you say? **was würden Sie sagen?**
what did you say? **was haben Sie gesagt?**
slow **langsam**
slower **langsamer**
sorry **Entschuldigung!**
I translate into German **ich übersetze ins Deutsche**
I understand **ich verstehe**
can you understand me? **können Sie mich gut verstehen?**
what is it in English? **wie/was heißt das auf Englisch?**
what do you call it in German? **wie nennt man das auf deutsch?**
what was that? **wie war das? was war das gleich**

Excuse me, I do not understand.
Excuse my interrupting you.

Bitte, ich verstehe Sie nicht gut.
Entschuldigen Sie, wenn ich unterbreche.

I haven't finished what I was saying.
What do you want to say?
It's my turn (to speak).

Ich bin noch nicht fertig.

Was möchten Sie noch sagen?
Ich bin dran/an der Reihe.

15d Interjections, apologizing & farewells

Surprise

at last! **endlich!**
amazed **erstaunt**
Fancy that! **Na, so was!**
funny **komisch!**
funny he never told me! **komisch, daß er mir nicht Bescheid sagte!**
God! **O Gott!**
God be praised! **Gott sei Dank!**
Good God! **meine Güte!**
goodness **um Himmels willen**
I surprise **ich überrasche**
impossible **unmöglich**
that's incredible! **das ist ja unglaublich!**
possible **möglich**
that can't be possible! **das ist doch nicht möglich!**
really? **(also) wirklich?**
so what? **na, und?**
surely **doch**
surely you know **du weißt doch ...**
surprised **überrascht**
surprising **überraschend**
what a surprise! **das ist aber eine Überraschung!**
I think **ich denke**
I would never have thought that **das hätte ich nicht gedacht**
true **wahr**

that can't be true! **das darf doch nicht wahr sein!**
is that true? **ist das wahr? stimmt das?**
Well I never! **Na, so was!**
what! **was!**
luck **das Glück**
what luck (that)! **ein Glück (daß)!**
wow! **Mensch!**

Hesitating

aha **aha, ach so**
as it were **sozusagen**
but ... **aber ...**
by the way **nebenbei**
definitely? **bestimmt? sicher?**
is that so? **ist das so?**
I don't know **ich weiß nicht**
you know **wissen Sie**
maybe **es kann sein**
moreover **übrigens**
oh! **ach!**
one minute please **eine Minute, einen Moment bitte**
one moment! **(einen) Moment mal**
or? **oder? gell?**
or not? **oder nicht?**
pardon **bitte? Verzeihung?**
I beg your pardon **bitte?**
perhaps **vielleicht**

– I just don't know what to do.

– How about repairing it?

– Well OK, but it will break again, won't it?
– I suppose it happens every year.
– I never knew that.
Funny that no-one told me.

– Ich weiß einfach nicht, was ich machen soll.

– Wie wäre es, wenn wir es reparieren sollten?

– Ja schon, aber es wird wieder kaputt gehen, nicht wahr?
– Es passiert wohl jedes Jahr.
– Das habe ich nicht gewußt. Komisch, daß keiner mir das gesagt hat.

please go on   **mach weiter**
really?   **wirklich? tatsächlich?**
something like that   **so etwas**
I suppose   **ich vermute**
supposedly   **vermutlich, wohl**
that is, i.e.   **das heißt, d.h.**
that is to say   **das heißt**
what next?   **was nun?**
what shall I do now?   **was mache ich jetzt?**
well ...   **na, nun ...**
well OK!   **na gut!**
well then ...   **also**
what now?   **was jetzt/nun?**
why?   **warum**
why not?   **warum nicht?**
yes, but ...   **(ja) schon aber, schon gut aber ...**

Agreeing

I agree   **das finde ich auch**
agreed!   **einverstanden!, abgemacht!**
both ... and   **sowohl ... als auch**
certain   **sicher**
certainly!   **bestimmt!, allerdings!, eben!**
definitely   **bestimmt, gewiß**
exactly!   **genau!**
firstly   **erstens**
in short   **kurz (gesagt)**
I know   **ich weiß**
no!   **nein!**
not only ... but also   **nicht nur ... sondern auch**
obviously!   **selbstverständlich!**
that's obvious   **das ist klar**
of course!   **freilich!**
it occurs to me   **es fällt mir ein***
right!   **richtig!**
is that right?   **ist das richtig?**
isn't that so/right?   **nicht wahr?**
secondly   **zweitens**
something else   **was anderes**
I tell   **ich erzähle**
tell us   **erzählen Sie mal**
I think so too!   **das glaub ich auch!**

do you think so?   **finden/glauben/ meinen Sie?**
true   **wahr**
that's true!   **das stimmt!**
is that true?   **ist das wahr?**
I want   **ich will**
as you want   **wie Sie wollen/meinen**
if you want   **wenn Sie Lust haben**
well, that's that   **so, das wär's**
yes!   **ja!**

Apologizing

I apologize (for)   **ich entschuldige mich (für** +acc)
apology   **die Entschuldigung(en)**
excuse me   **entschuldigen Sie**
sorry!   **Entschuldigung!, Verzeihung!**
I'm sorry   **das tut mir leid!**
I am so sorry!   **Entschuldigen Sie bitte!**
it doesn't matter!   **das macht nichts!**
that's OK!   **schon gut!**

Farewells

Goodbye!   **Auf Wiedersehen!**
Goodbye! *(telephone)*   **Auf Wiederhören!**
Bye!   **Tschüß!**
See you soon!   **Bis bald!**
See you tomorrow!   **Bis morgen!**
greetings to the family!   **viele Grüße an die Familie!**
greet Manfred from me!   **grüß Manfred von mir!**
all the best!   **alles Gute!, mach's gut!**
best wishes to your wife!   **einen schönen Gruß an Ihre Frau!**
have fun!   **viel Spaß!**
have a good time!   **viel Vergnügen!**
have a good journey!   **gute Reise!**
have a safe journey!   **komm gut nach Hause!**
have a good holiday!   **schöne Ferien!**
same to you!   **danke gleichfalls!**

15e Post/Mail & telephone

Post/Mail

abroad **im/ins Ausland**
addressee **der Addressat(en)**
   (wk) **[-in]**
answer **die Antwort(en)**
any news? **irgendwelche**
   Nachricht(en)?
by air **per Luftpost**
airmail **die Luftpost**
collection/pickup **die Leerung(en)**
I correspond **ich korrespondiere**
correspondent **der**
   Korrespondent(en) *(wk)* **[-in]**
counter **der Schalter(-)**
customs declaration **die**
   Zollerklärung(en)
express delivery **das Eilgut**
first-class **erster Klasse**
franking-machine/postage meter
   die Frankiermaschine(n)
freepost **Gebühr bezahlt**
   Empfänger
I get/receive **ich bekomme**
I hand in **ich reiche ein***
letter **der Brief(e)**
letter/mail-box **der Briefkasten(¨e)**
letter-rate **die Briefgebühr(en)**
I finish *(letter)* **ich beende**
news **die Neuigkeit(en), die**
   Nachricht(en)
I note down **ich schreibe nieder***

package **das Päckchen(-)**
parcel **das Paket(e)**
parcel-rate **die Paketgebühr(en)**
pen-friend/pen pal **der**
   Brieffreund(e) [-in]
post/mail **die Post**
post office **das Postamt(¨er)**
poste restante **postlagernd**
postage **die Postgebühr(en)**
postal order **der Geldgutschein(e)**
postcode/zip code **die**
   Postleitzahl(en)
postman/mail carrier **der**
   Briefträger(-) [-in]
I receive **ich erhalte**
recorded delivery **per Einschreiben**
registered mail **die**
   eingeschriebene Post
reply **die Antwort(en)**
sealed **versiegelt**
I send **ich schicke**
I send (greetings) **ich bestelle**
   (Grüße)
sender **der Absender(-)**
stamp **die Briefmarke(n)**
I write **ich schreibe**

Telephoning

I call **ich rufe**
I connect **ich verbinde**
I dial **ich wähle**

I haven't heard from her for ages.	**Ich habe seit langem nichts von ihr gehört.**
When does the post/mail arrive?	**Wann trifft die Post ein?**
I am writing on behalf of my father, concerning …	**Ich schreibe im Namen meines Vaters, bezüglich …**
I look forward to hearing from you.	**Ich hoffe bald von Ihnen zu hören.**

I fax   **ich faxe**
I hang up   **ich lege auf***
I hold   **ich warte**
I pick up   **ich hebe ab***
I press   **ich drücke**
I put ... through (to)   **ich stelle zu**
   +dat **... durch***
I speak to ...   **ich spreche mit** +dat
I telephone/phone   **ich telefoniere**

Telephone &
   telecommunications

answering machine   **der**
   Anrufbeantworter
booth   **die Telefonzelle(n)**
button   **der Knopf(¨e)**
   push the button   **auf den Knopf**
   drücken!
call-box   **die Telefonzelle(n)**
communication   **die**
   Kommunikation(en)
conversation   **das Gespräch(e)**
I dial   **ich wähle**
E-mail   **Daten-Fernübertragung**
   (DFÜ), das Teletex
electronic mail   **die elektronische**
   Post
engaged *(phone)*   **besetzt**
I am ex-directory   **ich stehe nicht**
   im Telefonbuch
extension   **der Anschluß (¨sse)**
fax   **das Fax-Gerät(e), das Fax**
fax modem   **das Fax-Modem**
information highway   **das Integrierte**

   Breitband-Fernmeldenetz
line   **die Telefonverbindung(en)**
link   **der Anschluß (¨sse)**
local call   **das Ortsgespräch(e)**
long-distance call   **das**
   Ferngespräch(e)
nought   **Null**
number   **die Nummer(n)**
operator   **die Zentrale(n)**
optical fibre/fiber   **das**
   Glasfaserkabel(-)
order   **in Betrieb**
out of order   **außer Betrieb**
receiver   **der Hörer(-)**
reverse charge call   **das R-**
   Gespräch(e)
satellite   **der Satellit(en)** *(wk)*
slot   **der Schlitz(e)**
subscriber   **der Telefonteilnehmer(-)**
telecommunications   **die**
   Telekommunikation(en)
telegram(me)   **das Telegramm(e)**
telegraph   **der Telegraf(en)**
telephone   **das Telefon(e)**
   car phone   **das Autotelefon(e)**
   cellular/mobile phone   **das**
   Funktelefon(e)
telephone directory   **das**
   Telefonbuch(¨er)
telephone kiosk   **die Telefonzelle**
teletext   **der Videotext**
telex   **das Telex**
I transmit   **ich übertrage**
wrong number   **falsch verbunden**

Can I dial direct?
Who's speaking?
This is John Smith (speaking).
Could you put me through to Mr
Müller?
Please wait/hold! Are you still
there? I'm afraid he's not in.
I will call back later.
Good-bye!

Kann ich direkt durchwählen?
Wer ist am Apparat?
Hier spricht John Smith.
Können sie mich mit Herrn
Müller verbinden?
Bleiben Sie am Apparat. Sind sie
noch dran? Er ist leider nicht da.
Ich werde später zurückrufen.
Auf Wiederhören.

➤ COMPUTERS 15f

15f Computers

Computer applications

adventure game **das Abenteuerspiel(e)**
application **die Anwendung(en)**
artificial intelligence **die künstliche Intelligenz**
bar code **der Bar-Code(s)**
bar code reader **der Bar-Code-Leser(-)**
bar coded **mit Bar-Code**
calculator **der Rechner(-)**
computer control **die Computerkontrolle(n)**
computer controlled lathe **die computergesteuerte Drehmaschine(n)**
computer science/studies **die Informatik**
computerized **computerisiert**
desk-top publishing/DTP **das DTP-Programm(e)**
game **das Spiel(e)**
grammar checker **der Grammatiküberprüfer**
information **die Information(en)**
information technology **die Informatik**
office automation **die Büroautomation**
simulation **die Simulatation(en)**
simulator **der Simulator(en)** *(wk)*
spell-check **die Rechtschreibkontrolle(n)**
synthesizer **der Synthesizer(-)**
thesaurus **das Synonymwörterbuch(-̈er)**
word processor **der Textverarbeiter(-)**
word processing **die Textverarbeitung**

Word-processing & operating

I abort **ich breche ab***
I access **ich rufe auf***
I append **ich hänge an***
I back-up **ich sichere**
I block *(text)* **ich markiere**
I boot up **ich boote**
I browse **ich schmöckere**
I cancel *(command)* **ich deaktiviere**
I click on **ich klicke an***
I communicate **ich kommuniziere**
I copy **ich kopiere**
I count **ich zähle**
I create **ich erstelle**

It's all done by computer.

Das geht alles per Computer.

In a spreadsheet you can fill the cells with text, figures or formulae.

In einer Tabellenkalkulation kann man die Zellen mit Text, Zahlen oder Formeln füllen.

You must analyze the problem and decide what formulae to use.

Sie müssen die Aufgabe analysieren und entscheiden, welche Formeln Sie einsetzen müssen.

– This disk is corrupted. It has wiped my file!
– Have you checked for a virus?

– Diese Diskette ist defekt. Sie hat meine Datei gelöscht!
– Haben Sie ein Virusprogramm ablaufen lassen?

I cut and paste **ich schneide aus***
I debug **ich beseitige den Fehler**
I delete **ich lösche**
I download **ich lade**
I drag **ich ziehe**
I embolden **ich formatiere in Fettschrift**
I emulate **ich emuliere**
I enter (text) **ich gebe (Text) ein***
I erase **ich lösche**
I exit (the program) **ich beende (das Programm)**
I export **ich exportiere**
I file **ich lege an***
I format **ich formatiere**
I handle *(text)* **ich verarbeite**
I import **ich importiere**
I insert **ich füge ein***
I install **ich installiere**
keyboard operator **der Tastaturbearbeiter(-) [-in]**
keyboarding skills **die Eingabefähigkeit**
I key in **ich gebe ein***
I list **ich liste auf***
I log off **ich beende das Progamm**
I log on/off **ich logge ein/aus***
I merge **ich schließe zusammen***
I move *(a file)* **ich versetze**

I move **ich versetze, ich verschiebe**
I network **ich vernetze**
I open (a file) **ich öffne (eine Datei)**
I paste **ich füge ein***
I print **ich drucke**
I print out **ich drucke aus***
I (word) process **ich verarbeite**
I program(me) **ich programmiere**
I read **ich lese**
I receive **ich empfange**
I record **ich nehme auf***
I remove **ich streiche**
I replace **ich ersetze**
I retrieve **ich rufe ab*/auf***
I run **ich lade, ich lasse laufen***
I save **ich speichere**
I search **ich suche**
I send **ich (ver)sende**
I shift **ich speichere**
I simulate **ich simuliere**
I sort **ich sortiere**
I store **ich speichere, ich lege an***
I switch on/off **ich schalte ein/aus***
I tabulate **ich tabuliere**
I underline **ich unterstreiche**
I update **ich aktualisiere**

The data are in memory.	**Die Daten befinden sich im Arbeitsspeicher.**
Copy the files onto a floppy disc.	**Kopieren Sie die Dateien auf eine Diskette.**
Make a back-up copy.	**Machen Sie eine Sicherheitskopie.**
Which operating system do you use?	**Welches Betriebssystem verwenden Sie?**
How easy is this spreadsheet to use?	**Wie einfach ist es, diese Bildschirmtabelle zu bedienen?**
I don't like the software package with this PC.	**Ich mag die Software an diesem PC nicht.**

Leisure & sport

16a Leisure

activity   **die Aktivität(en)**
I am free   **ich bin frei**
archery   **das Bogenschießen**
bar   **die Bar(s)**
I begin   **ich beginne**
book   **das Buch(¨-er)**
boring   **langweilig**
camera   **der Fotoapparat(e), die Kamera(s)**
card   **die (Spiel)karte(n)**
card game   **das Kartenspiel(e)**
card table   **der Spieltisch(e)**
carpentry   **das Tischlern**
casino   **das Kasino(s)**
chess   **das Schach, das Schachspiel(e)**
cinema   **das Kino(s)**
closed   **geschlossen**
club   **der Klub(s)**
I collect   **ich sammle**
coin   **die Münze(n)**
crosswords   **das Kreuzworträtsel(-)**
collection   **die Sammlung(en)**
collectors fair   **die Sammlerausstellung(en)**
discotheque   **die Diskothek(en)**

I draw *(etch)*   **ich zeichne**
holiday/vacation   **die Ferien** *(pl)*
interest   **das Interesse(n)**
energy   **die Energie(n)**
enthusiasm   **die Begeisterung**
enthusiastic   **begeistert**
entrance   **der Eingang(¨-e)**
entry fee   **die Eintrittsgebühr(en)**
excitement   **die Aufregung(en), die Erregung(en)**
exciting   **aufregend, erregend**
excursion   **der Ausflug(¨-e)**
excursionist   **der Ausflügler(-) [-in]**
exit   **der Ausgang(¨-e)**
fair   **die Ausstellung(en), die Messe(n)**
fascinating   **faszinierend**
finished   **beendet, zu Ende**
I fish   **ich angle**
free time   **die freie Zeit, die Freizeit**
fun   **der Spaß(¨-e)**
I gamble   **ich spiele um Geld**
I go out   **ich gehe aus***
guide   **der Reiseführer(-) [-in]**
guided tour   **die Reisetour(en)**

Do you do a lot of sport?
I like going for long walks.

Treibst du viel Sport?
Ich wandere gern.

Sometimes I go fishing, which is recommended for stressed executives!

Manchmal gehe ich fischen, was sehr empfehlenswert für gestreßte Manager ist.

I can meet you at the swimming pool or, if you prefer, at the gym.

Wir können uns an der Schwimmhalle oder, wenn du willst, an der Turnhalle treffen.

hobby **das Hobby(s)**
energetic **energisch**
interesting **interessant**
it is over **es ist vorbei**
I join **ich trete in +acc ein*, ich schließe mich (jdm.) an***
leisure **die Freizeit**
I get in line **ich ordne mich ein***
I listen to **ich höre +dat zu***
I look **ich sehe, ich blicke**
market **der Markt(¨e)**
  antiques market **der Antiquitätenmarkt(¨e)**
  flea market **der Flohmarkt(¨e)**
I meet **ich treffe**
meeting place **der Treffpunkt(e)**
member **das Mitglied(er)**
membership **die Mitgliedschaft(en)**
nightclub **der Nachtklub(s)**
open **offen, auf**
organization **die Organisation(en)**
I organize **ich organisiere**
photograph **die Fotografie(n), die Aufnahmen(n)**
picnic **das Picknick(s)**
place **der Ort(e)**
I play **ich spiele**
pleasure **das Vergnügen(-), die Freude(n)**
politics **die Politik**
I prefer **ich bevorzuge, ich ziehe vor***

private **privat**
public **öffentlich**
queue/line **die Schlange(n)**
I queue **ich stehe an***
I read **ich lese**
season **die Jahreszeit(en)**
secluded **abgelegen, ruhig**
I sew **ich nähe**
slide/chute **die Rutsche(n)**
I slide **ich rutsche**
sold out **ausverkauft**
spectator **der Zuschauer(-) [-in]**
I start (doing) **ich beginne, zu +inf**
I stop (doing) **ich höre auf*, zu +inf**
I stroll **ich schlendere, ich spaziere**
subscription **das Abonnement(s)**
I take photos **ich fotografiere**
television **der Fernseher(-)**
ticket **die Karte(n)**
time **die Zeit(en)**
theatre **das Theater(-)**
tour **die Tour(en)**
vacation **die Ferien, der Urlaub**
I visit **ich besuche**
visit **der Besuch(e)**
I walk **ich gehe spazieren***
I watch **ich schaue +dat zu*, ich sehe +dat zu***
youth club **der Jugendklub(s)**
zoo **der Zoo(s)**

– What do you like doing on a rainy day?
– Perhaps playing cards, but not with my brother: he cheats!

– Was machst du gern, wenn es regnet?
– Vielleicht Karten spielen, aber nicht mit meinem Bruder: er mogelt!

– Are there any special rates for students?
– Yes, but only on Friday nights.

– Gibt es besondere Studentenermäßigungen?
– Ja, aber nur Freitag abends.

➤ LEISURE WEAR, LEISURE EQUIPMENT 16c; PHOTOGRAPHY App.16a

16b Sporting activity

aerobics **das Aerobic**
against **gegen** +acc
athlete **der Athlet(en)** *(wk)* **[-in]**,
   der Sportler(-) [-in]
athletic **sportlich**
I attack **ich greife an***
bathtowel **das Badetuch(-er)**
I defend **ich verteidige**
I bet **ich wette**
boat **das Boot(e)**
I box **ich boxe**
boxer **der Boxer(-)**
I bowl **ich bowle, ich gehe**
   bowlen
captain **der Kapitän(e)**
I catch **ich fange**
champion **der Meister(-) [-in]**
championship **die**
   Meisterschaft(en)
changing/locker room **der**
   Umkleideraum(-e)
I climb **ich klettere**
climber **der Bergsteiger(-) [-in]**
club **der Klub(s)**
coach **der Trainer(-) [-in]**
crew **die Mannschaft(en)**
cup *(tournament)* **der Pokal(e)**
cycle **das Fahrrad(-er)**
I cycle **ich fahre Rad**
defeat **die Niederlage(n)**
I dive **ich tauche**
I do (sport) **ich treibe (Sport)**
I draw **ich spiele unentschieden**
it was a draw **es war**
   unentschieden
effort **die Anstrengung(en)**
   I make an effort **ich strenge**
   mich an*
endurance **die Ausdauer**
equipment **die Ausstattung(en)**
I exercize **ich bewege mich**
exercize **die Bewegung(en)**
I fall **ich falle, ich stürze**
fall **der Sturz(-e)**
field **das Feld(er)**

finals **das Finale(s), das**
   Endspiel(e)
fit **fit**
fitness **die Fitness** *(no pl)*
game **das Spiel(e)**
I get fit **ich trimme mich**
goal **das Tor(e)**
ground **der Boden**
gym(nasium) **die Turnhalle(n)**
I hit **ich schlage, ich treffe**
hit **der Schlag(-e), der Treffer(-)**
horse-race **das Pferderennen(-)**
I ice skate **ich laufe Schlittschuh**
ice-rink **die Eisbahn(en)**
injury **die Verletzung(en)**
instructor **der Lehrer(-) [-in]**
I jog **ich jogge**
jogger **der Jogger(-) [-in]**
I jump **ich springe**
jump **der Sprung(-e)**
lawn **der Rasen(-)**
league **die Liga(s)**
league leader **der Ligaführer(-)**
locker room **der**
   Umkleideraum(-e)
I lose **ich verliere**
marathon **der Marathon(s)**
match **das Spiel(e)**
medal **die Medaille(n)**
   bronze/gold/silver **Bronze-/**
   Gold-/Silber-
muscle **der Muskel(n)**
Olympic Games (Winter) **die**
   Olympischen (Winter)spiele
I pass (ball) **ich spiele jdm. (den**
   Ball) zu*
pedal **das Pedal(e)**
I pedal **ich strample, ich trete**
physical **körperlich**
I pitch **ich werfe**
pitcher **der Werfer(-)**
pitch/field **das Spielfeld(er)**
I play **ich spiele**
player **der Spieler**
point **der Moment(e), der**

Zeitpunkt(e)
professional **professionell**
I race **ich renne (um die Wette)**
race **das Wettrennen(-)**
referee **der Schiedsrichter(-) [-in]**
rest **die Pause(n)**
result **das Ergebnis(se)**
I ride **ich reite, ich fahre**
riding **das Reiten**
riding-school **die Reitschule(n)**
I row **ich rudere**
I run **ich renne, ich laufe**
run **der Lauf(-̈e)**
runner **der Läufer(-) [-in]**
sailing school **die Segelschule(n)**
I sail **ich segle**
I save *(goal)* **ich halte, ich verhindere**
I score (a goal) **ich schieße (ein Tor)**
score **das Spielergebnis(se), die Punktzahl(en)**
score **der Spielstand**
I ski **ich laufe Ski**
I shoot *(ball, puck)* **ich schieße**
show **die Show(s)**
skier **der Skiläufer(-) [-in]**
ski-lift **der Skilift(e)**
sponsor **der Sponsor(en)**
sponsorship **die Förderung**
sport **der Sport (Sportarten)**

sports field/pitch **der Sportplatz(-̈e)**
sprint **der Sprint(s)**
stadium **das Stadion (-ien)**
stamina **das Durchhaltevermögen**
strength **die Kraft(-̈e)**
supporter **der Anhänger(-) [-in]**
I swim **ich schwimme**
team **die Mannschaft(en)**
team sport **das Mannschaftsspiel(e)**
I throw **ich werfe**
timing **das Timing**
tournament **das Turnier(e)**
track **die Rennbahn(en), die Piste(n)**
I train **ich trainiere**
trainer **der Trainer(-) [-in]**
training **das Training**
triumph **der Sieg(e)**
trophy **die Trophäe(n)**
I am unfit **ich bin nicht fit**
victory **der Sieg(e)**
I win **ich gewinne**
weight training **das Krafttraining**
work-out **das Training**
world championship **die Weltmeisterschaft(en)**
world cup *(soccer)* **die Fußballweltmeisterschaft(en)**

It is a remarkable achievement for the national team, which has played extremely well.

Es ist eine bemerkenswerte Leistung der Nationalmannschaft, die besonders gut gespielt hat.

The team has been training in very trying weather conditions. Each athlete was ready to give his best.

Die Mannschaft hat unter äußerst schwierigen Wetterverhältnissen trainiert. Jeder Spieler war bereit, das Beste zu geben.

Unfortunately, a member of the team was seriously injured during the last race.

Unglücklicherweise hat sich ein Mitglied der Mannschaft während des letzten Rennens ernsthaft verletzt.

➤ SPORTING EQUIPMENT 16c

16c Sports & equipment

Sports

athletics **die Leichtathletik**
badminton **das Badminton, der Federball**
baseball **der Baseball**
basketball **der Basketball**
billiards **das Billiard**
bowling **das Bowling**
boxing **das Boxen**
climbing **das Bergsteigen, das Klettern**
 free climbing **freies Klettern**
 rock climbing **das Felsenklettern**
cricket **das Cricket**
cycling **das Radfahren**
decathlon **der Zehnkampf(⁻e)**
diving **das Tauchen**
deep-sea diving **das Tiefseetauchen**
football **der Fußball**
handball **der Handball**
hockey **das Hockey**
horse-racing **das Pferderennen**
horse-riding **das Pferdereiten**
ice-hockey **das Eishockeyspiel(e)**
ice-skating **das Schlittschuhlaufen**

jogging **das Joggen**
motor-racing **das Autorennen, der Rennsport**
paragliding **das Fallschirmgleiten**
pentathlon **der Fünfkampf(⁻e)**
polo **das Polo**
pool **das Poolbilliard**
racing **das Rennen, der Wettlauf(⁻e)**
roller-skating **das Rollschuhlaufen**
rugby **das Rugbyspiel(e)**
sailing **das Segeln**
skiing **das Skilaufen**
 alpine skiing **das Abfahrtslaufen**
 cross-country skiing **das Langlaufen**
 down-hill skiing **das Schußfahren**
snooker **das Snooker**
soccer **der Fußball**
swimming **das Schwimmen**
table tennis **das Tischtennis**
tennis **das Tennis**
volleyball **der Volleyball**
water-polo **der Wasserball**
weightlifting **das Gewichtheben**

– Did you watch the match?
– No, I had to leave before the end. Who won?
– We lost 3-1. I still cannot understand how such a capable team could lose so disastrously after a brilliant season.

– Hast du das Spiel gesehen?
– Nein, ich mußte vor dem Ende gehen. Wer hat gewonnen?
– Wir verloren 3 zu 1. Ich kann immer noch nicht verstehen, wie eine so tüchtige Mannschaft nach einer sehr guten Saison so unglücklich verlieren konnte.

Leisure wear and sports clothes

anorak **der Anorak(s)**
bathing suit **der Badeanzug(¨e)**
boots **die Stiefel(-)**
cycling shorts **die Radlerhose(n)**
dancing shoes **der Tanzschuh(e)**
gardening gloves **der
Gartenhandschuh(e)**
leotard **der Gymnastikanzug(¨e)**
parka **der Parka(s)**
swimsuit **der Badeanzug(¨e)**
swimming trunks **die Badehose(n)**
rugby shirt **das Rugbyshirt(s)**
track suit **der Trainingsanzug(¨e)**
trainers **der Turnschuh(e)**
walking boot **der Wanderschuh(e)**
waterproof jacket **die
Wetterjacke(n)**
Wellington boot **der
Gummistiefel(-)**
wet suit **der Wetteranzug(¨e)**

Leisure and sports equipment

arrow **der Pfeil(e)**
ball **der Ball(¨e)**
bat **der Schläger(-)**
binoculars **das Fernglas(¨er)**
boxing gloves **der
Boxhandschuh(e)**
bow **der Bogen(-)**
camera **die Kamera(s)**
crash helmet **der Schutzhelm(e)**

exercise bike **der Heimtrainer(-)**
equipment **die Ausrüstung(en)**
fishing rod **die Angelrute(n)**
headphone **der Kopfhörer(-)**
hi-fi **das Hi-Fi**
knapsack **der Rucksack(¨e)**
knitting needles **die Stricknadel(n)**
javelin **der Speer(e)**
mountain bike **das
Mountainbike(s)**
net **das Netz(e)**
oar **das Ruder(-)**
puck **die Scheibe(n), der Puck(s)**
racket **der Schläger(-)**
rifle **das Gewehr(e)**
roller skates **der Rollschuh(e)**
rowing machine **das Motorboot(e)**
rowing boat **das Ruderboot(e)**
rucksack **der Rucksack(¨e)**
sailing-boat **das Segelboot(e)**
sewing kit **das Nähzeug**
skate **der Schlittschuh(e)**
skis **der Ski(er)**
ski boot **der Skistiefel(-)**
ski stick/pole **der Skistock(¨e)**
stick *(hockey)* **der
Hockeyschläger(-)**
spinning wheel **das Spinnrad(¨er)**
sports bag **die Sporttasche(n)**
surf board **das Surfbrett(er)**
weights **das Gewicht(e)**
yacht **die Yacht(en)**

All sports commentators agree that they were particularly unlucky when the referee insisted on the penalty kick.

– Do you develop your own photos?
– I would like to, but I do not have a dark room.

Alle Sportreporter waren sich einig, daß es besonderes Pech war, als der Schiedsrichter auf dem Strafstoß bestand.

– Entwickelst du deine Fotos selbst?
– Ich würde gern, aber ich habe keine Dunkelkammer.

➤ PHOTOGRAPHY App.16a; GARDENING 8c

17 The Arts

17a Appreciation and criticism

abstract **abstrakt**
abstruse **schwerverständlich**
action **die Handlung(en)**
aesthete **der Ästhet(en)** *(wk)*
aesthetics **die Ästhetik**
I analyze **ich analysiere**
I appreciate **ich schätze**
appreciation **das Verständnis(se)**
art **die Kunst(⁻e)**
artist **der Künstler(-) [-in]**
artistic **künstlerisch**
atmosphere **die Atmosphäre(n)**
atmospheric **atmosphärisch**
author **der Verfasser(-) [-in]**
award **der Preis(e)**
avant-garde **die Avantgarde**
believable **glaubhaft**
character **der Charakter(e)**
characterization **die Charakterisierung(en)**
characteristic **charakteristisch**
climax **der Höhepunkt(e)**
I close **ich schließe**
comic **der Komiker(-) [-in]**
  comic *(adj)* **lustig**
commentary **der Kommentar(e)**
conflict **der Konflikt(e)**
contemporary **zeitgenössisch, modern**
contrast **der Kontrast(e)**
it creates **es schafft**
creative **kreativ**
creativity **die Kreativität** *(no pl)*
credible **glaubwürdig**
critic **der Kritiker(-) [-in]**
criticism **die Kritik(en)**
cultivated **gebildet**
culture **die Kultur(en)**
it deals with **es handelt von** +dat
it describes **es beschreibt**

it develops **es entwickelt (sich)**
development **die Entwicklung(en)**
device **der Kunstgriff(e)**
dialogue/dialog **der Dialog(e)**
disturbing **störend**
empathy **das Einfühlungsvermögen**
ending **der Schluß (⁻sse)**
endless **endlos**
it ends **es endet**
entertaining **amüsant**
entertainment **die Unterhaltung**
epic **die Epik**
  epic *(adj)* **episch**
event **das Ereignis(se)**
eventful **ereignisreich**
example **das Beispiel(e)**
excited **aufgeregt**
exciting **aufregend, spannend**
I explain **ich erläutere**
explanation **die Erläuterung(en)**
it explores **es untersucht**
it expresses **es drückt aus***
extravagant **überschwenglich**
fake **die Fälschung(en)**
  fake *(adj)* **gefälscht**
fantastic **phantastisch**
fantasy **die Phantasie(n)**
farcical **possenhaft**
figure **die Figur(en)**
funny **komisch**
genre **das Genre(s)**
image **das Bild(er)**
imaginary **frei erfunden**
imagination **die Phantasie(n)**
inspiration **die Inspiration(en)**
inspired by **inspiriert durch** +acc
intense **intensiv**
intensity **die Intensität**
interpretation **die Deutung(en)**

interpreter **der Interpret(en)** *(wk)* **[-in]**

interpretation **die Interpretation(en)**

invention **die Erfindung(en)**

inventive **erfinderisch**

inventiveness **die schöpferische Kraft(-̈e)**

ironic **ironisch**

irony **die Ironie(n)**

issue **die Frage(n)**

long-winded **umständlich**

lyrical **lyrisch**

modern **modern**

mood **die Stimmung(en)**

moral **die Moral, die Ethik**

moral *(adj)* **moralisch**

morality **die Sittlichkeit(en)**

moving **ergreifend**

mystery **das Geheimnis(se)**

mysterious **geheimnisvoll**

mystical **mystisch**

mysticism **die Mystik(en)**

nature **die Natur**

obscure **unklar, undeutlich**

obscene **obszön**

obscenity **die Obszönität(en)**

opinion **die Meinung(en)**

optimism **der Optimismus**

optimistic **optimistisch**

parody **die Parodie(n)**

passion **die Leidenschaft(en)**

passionate **leidenschaftlich**

pessimism **der Pessimismus**

pessimistic **pessimistisch**

poetic **poetisch**

it portrays **es zeigt, es schildert**

portrayal **die Schilderung(en)**

precious **gekünstelt**

protagonist **der Protagonist(en), der Held(en)** *(wk)*

I read **ich lese**

reader **der Leser(-) [-in]**

readership **die Leserschaft**

realistic **realistisch**

reference **die Erwähnung(en), die Anspielung(en)**

I reflect **ich denke nach***

it reflects **es widerspiegelt**

reflection **die Reflektion(en)**

relationship **die Beziehung(en)**

it represents **es stellt dar***

representation **die Darstellung(en)**

review **die Kritik(en)**

romantic **romantisch**

sad **traurig**

satire **die Satire(n)**

it satirizes **es verspottet**

satirical **satirisch**

style **der Stil(e)**

in the style of **im Stil des/der**

stylish **stilvoll**

subject **das Thema (-en)**

Surrealism **der Surrealismus**

technique **die Technik(en)**

tension **die Spannung(en)**

theme **das Thema (-en)**

tone **der Ton(-̈e)**

tragedy **die Tragödie(n)**

tragic **tragisch**

true **wahr**

vivid **lebhaft**

vividly **anschaulich**

viewpoint **der Gesichtspunkt(e)**

witty **witzig, geistreich**

work of art **das Kunstwerk(e)**

The predominant theme of the painting of the period was the landscape.

They try to represent moral values symbolically.

Das entscheidende Motiv in der Malerei der Zeit war die Landschaft.

Sie versuchen Moralwerte symbolisch zu veranschaulichen.

➤ MUSIC, DANCE 17d; THEATER & CINEMA/THEATER & MOVIES 17e

17b Art & architecture

antique **die Antiquität(en)**
  antique *(adj)* **antik**
antiquity **das Altertum, die Antike**
architect **der Architekt(en)** *(wk)*
  [-in]
art **die Kunst(ˉe)**
artefact **das Artefakt(e)**
artist **der Künstler(-)**
art student **der Kunststudent(en)**
  (wk) **[-in]**
I auction **ich versteigere**
auction sale **die Auktion(en)**
auctioneer **der Auktionator(en)**
balance **das Gleichgewicht(e)**
beam **der Balken(-)**
bronze **die Bronze(n)**
brush **der Pinsel(-)**
I build **ich baue**
building **das Gebäude(-)**
bust **die Büste(n)**
caricature **die Karikatur(en)**
I carve **ich schnitze, ich haue**
I cast **ich gieße**
ceramics **die Keramik(en)**
charcoal **die Holzkohle(n)**
chisel **der Meißel(-)**
clay **der Ton**
collage **die Collage(n)**
decorated **dekoriert**
decoration **die Verzierung(en)**
I design **ich entwerfe**
design **der Entwurf(ˉe), das**
  Design(s)
dimension **die Dimension(en)**
I draw **ich zeichne**
drawing **die Zeichnung(en)**
drawing board **das Reißbrett(er)**
easel **die Staffelei(en)**
elevation **der Aufriß (-sse)**
enamel **die Emaille(n)**
I engrave **ich graviere ein***
engraving **der (Kupfer-/**
  Stahl)stich(e)
I etch **ich ätze**

etching **der Kupferstich(e)**
exhibition **die Ausstellung(en)**
figure **die Form(en), Figur(en)**
figurine **die Figurine(n)**
fine arts **die schönen Künste** *(pl)*
form **die Gestalt(en)**
free-hand **Freihand-**
fresco **die Freskomalerei(en)**
frieze **das Fries(-)**
gouache **die Gouache**
graphic arts **die Grafik(en)**
holography **die Holographie(n)**
interior **das Innere, die**
  Innengestaltung
intricate **kompliziert, fein**
iron **das Eisen**
landscape *(painting)* **das**
  Landschaftsbild(er)
landscape architect **der**
  Landschaftsarchitekt(en) *(wk)*
landscape painter **der**
  Landschaftsmaler(-)
large-scale **in großem Maßstab**
late works **die späten Arbeiten**
light **das Licht**
  light *(adj)* **leuchtend, hell**
lithograph(y) **die Lithographie(n)**
luminosity **die Helligkeit**
luminous **leuchtend**
masterpiece **das Meisterwerk(e)**
metal **das Metall(e)**
miniature **die Miniatur(en)**
model **das Modell(e)**
monostyle **der Monostil(e)**
mosaic **das Mosaik(en)**
museum **das Museum (-en)**
oil painting **das Ölgemälde(-)**
ornate **geschmückt**
I paint **ich male**
paint **die Farbe(n)**
painting **das Gemälde(-)**
pastel **das Pastell(e)**
pattern **das Muster(-)**
portrait **das Porträt(s)**

potter der Töpfer(-) [-in]
pottery die Töpferware(n)
reproduction die Reproduktion(en)
restoration die Restaurierung(en)
I restore ich restauriere
restored restauriert
restorer der Restaurierer(-) [-in]
roughcast der Rauhputz
school die Schule(n)
I sculpt ich bildhauere
sculptor der Bildhauer(-) [-in]
sculpture die Skulptur(en)
seascape die Seegemälde(-)
shadow der Schatten(-)
shape die Form(en)
I shape ich forme, ich gestalte
sketch die Skizze(n)
I sketch ich skizziere
stained-glass das farbige Glas(⁻er)
statuary die Plastik(en)
statue die Statue(n)
still-life das Stilleben(-)
studio das Studio(s)
symbolic symbolisch
tapestry der Wandbehang(⁻e)
town-planning die Stadtplanung(en)
translucent lichtdurchlässig
transparent durchsichtig
visual arts die bildenden Künste (pl)
water-colour/color das Aquarell(e)
weathering die Verwitterung(en)
wood das Holz
wood-carving die Holzschnitzerei(en)
woodcut der Holzschnitt(e)

Historical periods

Alemannic alemannisch
Charlemagne Karl der Große
Enlightenment die Aufklärung
First World War der Erste Weltkrieg
Frankish fränkisch
Hitler period die Hitlerzeit, das Dritte Reich
Holy Roman Empire das Heilige Römische Reich
Hundred Years War der Hundertjährige Krieg
Middle Ages das Mittelalter
migration of peoples die Völkerwanderung
Reformation die Reformation
Roman age die Römerzeit
Roman Empire das Römische Reich

Second World War der Zweite Weltkrieg
Thirty Years War der Dreißigjährige Krieg
Weimar Republic die Weimarer Republik

Bronze Age die Bronzezeit
Iron Age die Eisenzeit
Neolithic Age die Jungsteinzeit
Palaeolithic Age die Altsteinzeit
prehistoric vorgeschichtlich
prehistory die Vorgeschichte
Stone Age die Steinzeit

the 20th Century das zwanzigste (20.) Jahrhundert
in the 13th Century im dreizehnten Jahrhundert

➤ ARTISTIC STYLES & PERIODS App.17a

137

17c Literature

autograph **die Originalhandschrift(en)**
book **das Buch(-̈er)**
bookshop/store **der Buchladen(-̈e)**
bookseller **der Buchverkäufer(-) [-in]**
character **die Figur(en), die Gestalt(en)**
comic **lustig**
it concerns **es handelt (sich) um** +acc
dialogue/dialog **der Dialog(e)**
fictional **frei erfunden**
hardback **eine gebundene Ausgabe(n)**
I imagine **ich stelle mir vor***
imagination **die Einbildungskraft(-̈e)**
inspiration **die Inspiration(en)**
inspired by **inspiriert durch**
it introduces **es führt ein***
introduction **die Einleitung(en)**
I leaf through **ich blättere durch***
librarian **der Bibliothekar(e) [-in]**
library **die Bibliothek(en)**
   public library **die öffentliche Bibliothek(en)**
   reference library **die Präsenzbibliothek(en)**

library ticket **der Leserausweis(e)**
literal(ly) **wörtlich**
main character **die Hauptfigur(en)**
myth **der Mythos (-en)**
mythology **die Mythologie(n)**
it narrates **es erzählt**
narrative **die Erzählung(en)**
narrator **der Erzähler(-) [-in]**
note **die Anmerkung(en)**
page **die Seite(n)**
paperback **das Taschenbuch(-̈er)**
poem **das Gedicht(e)**
poetic **poetisch**
poetry **die Poesie, die Dichtkunst**
quotation **das Zitat(e)**
I quote **ich zitiere**
I read **ich lese**
I recount **ich erzähle**
review **die Rezension(en), die Kritik(en)**
rhyme **der Reim(e)**
secondary character **die Nebenfigur(en)**
it is set in **es spielt in** +dat
subtitle **der Untertitel(-)**
table **der Tabelle(n)**
text **der Text(e)**
title **der Titel(-)**
verse **der Strophe(n)**

Buddenbrooks is the great epic novel of the early 20th Century.

After the war the Gruppe 47 played an important role. Poetry blossomed again, above all in East Germany.

Günter Graß shows intense political involvement and an inexhaustible imagination.

"Buddenbrooks" ist der große Bildungsroman des frühen zwanzigsten Jahrhunderts.

Nach dem Krieg spielte die "Gruppe 47" eine wichtige Rolle. Die Lyrik blühte wieder auf, vor allem in der DDR.

Günter Graß zeigt großes politisches Engagement und eine unerschöpfliche Phantasie.

Types of books

adventure story **die Abenteuergeschichte(n)**

atlas **der Atlas(se/Atlanten)**

(auto)biography **die (Auto)biographie(n)**

children's literature **die Kinderliteratur**

comic novel **die humoristische Erzählung(en)**

cookbook/cookery book **das Kochbuch(-̈er)**

crime novel **der Kriminalroman(e), der Krimi(s)**

dictionary **das Wörterbuch(-̈er)**
  bilingual **zweisprachiges**
  monolingual **einsprachiges**

diary **das Tagebuch(-̈er)**

encyclopedia **die Enzyklopädie(n)**

epic poem **das Epos (-en), das epische Gedicht(e)**

epic poetry **die Epik**

essay **der Aufsatz(-̈e)**

fable **die Fabel(n)**

fairy tale **das Märchen(-)**

feminist literature **die Frauenliteratur**

fiction **die Belletristik**

Greek tragedy **die griechische Tragödie(n)**

horror story **die Horrorgeschichte(n)**

letters **die Literatur(en)**

light reading **die Unterhaltungslektüre(n)**

manual **das Handbuch(-̈er)**

memoirs **die Memoiren** *(pl)*

mystery play **das Mysterienspiel(e)**

novel **der Roman(e)**

novella **die Novelle(n)**

non-fiction **das Sachbuch(-̈er)**

parody **die Parodie(n)**

picaresque novel **der Schelmenroman(e)**

poetry **die Dichtkunst**

reference book **das Nachschlagewerk(e)**

satire **die Satire(n)**

science fiction story **die Science-Fiction-Erzählung(en)**

short story **die Kurzgeschichte(n)**

spy story **die Spionagegeschichte(n)**

teenage fiction **die Jugendliteratur**

travel book **der Reisebericht(e)**

war novel **der Kriegsroman(e)**

Heinrich Böll received the Nobel prize for literature. A central theme of his novels is Roman Catholicism. He describes the troubles and worrries of little people.

Baroque richness, precision of description and autobiographical details are typical of the period.

Heinrich Böll erhielt den Nobelpreis für Literatur. Ein zentrales Thema seiner Romane ist das katholische Christentum. Er schildert die Nöte und Sorgen der "kleinen Leute".

Barocke Fülle, Genauigkeit der Darstellung, und autobiographische Details kennzeichnen diese Periode.

17d Music & dance

accompaniment die Begleitung
accompanist der Begleiter(-) [-in]
I accompany ich begleite
acoustics die Akustik
agent der Agent(en) *(wk)*
album das Album (-en)
alto der Alt(e), die Altstimme(n)
amplifier der Verstärker(-)
audience das Publikum
audition das Probespiel(e)
I audition ich spiele/singe vor*
auditorium das Auditorium (-ien)
ballet das Ballett
baton der Taktstock(-̈e)
brass band die Blaskapelle(n)
canned music die
  Musikberieselung
cassette tape die Kassette(n)
cassette-deck das
  Kassettendeck(s)
chamber music die
  Kammermusik
chart die Hitliste(n)
choir der Chor(-̈e)
choral society der
  Gesangverein(e)
choreography die
  Choreographie(n)
chorus der Refrain(s)
classical music die klassische
  Musik
compact disc/disk die Compact-

disc(s)
competition der Wettbewerb(e)
I compose ich komponiere
composer der Komponist(en)
composition die Komposition(en)
concert das Konzert(e)
concert hall die Konzertsaal
  (-säle)
dance der Tanz(-̈e)
I dance ich tanze
dancer der Tänzer(-) [-in]
dance music die Tanzmusik
discotheque die Diskothek(en)
disc jockey der Discjockey(s)
ensemble das Ensemble(s)
folk music die Volksmusik
folksong das Volkslied(er), der
  Folksong(s)
gig das Konzert(e)
group die Gruppe(n)
harmony die Harmonie(n)
harmonic harmonisch
hit *(song)* der Hit(s)
hit parade die Hitparade(n)
I hum ich summe
instrument das Instrument(e)
instrument maker der
  Instrumentenbauer
I interpret ich interpretiere
interpretation die
  Interpretation(en)
jazz der Jazz

He sings out of tune. I have perfect pitch.	**Er singt falsch. Ich habe das absolute Gehör.**
You must tune your violin. It is flat/sharp.	**Du mußt die Violine stimmen. Sie ist zu tief/zu hoch.**
The poem was set to music by Wolf.	**Das Gedicht wurde von Wolf vertont.**
I love going to concerts. We went to the opera last week.	**Ich gehe gern ins Konzert. Wir waren letzte Woche in der Oper.**

juke-box **die Musikbox(en)**
key **die Tonart(en)**
lesson **der Musikunterricht** *(no pl)*
librettist **der Librettist(en)** *(wk)*
I listen to **ich höre** +dat **zu***
microphone **das Mikrofon(e)**
music **die Musik**
musically **musikalisch**
musician **der Musiker(-) [-in]**
musicologist **der Musikwissenschaftler(-) [-in]**
note **die Note(n)**
orchestra **das Orchester(-)**
orchestration **die Orchesterbearbeitung(en)**
part **die Stimme(n)**
I perform **ich führe**
performance **die Aufführung(en)**
performer **der Künstler(-) [-in]**
piano tuner **der Klavierstimmer(-) [-in]**
piece **das Stück(e)**
I play **ich spiele**
player **der Spieler(-) [-in]**
popular music/pop **die Popmusik**
I practise **ich übe**
promotional video **das Werbevideo(s)**
I put on a record **ich lege eine Schallplatte auf***
recital **das Konzert(e), der Liederabend(e)**
record **die Schallplatte(n)**

I record **ich nehme auf***
recording **die Aufnahme(n)**
recording studio **das Aufnahmestudio(s)**
I rehearse **ich probe**
rehearsal **die Probe**
rhythm **der Rhythmus (-en)**
rhythmic **rhythmisch**
rock music **der Rock**
I rock **ich rocke**
show **die Show**
I sing **ich singe**
singer **der Sänger(-) [-in]**
solo **das Solo(s)**
soloist **der Solist(en)** *(wk)* **[-in]**
song **das Lied(er)**
song-writer **der Liederschreiber(-) [-in]**
string **die Saite(n)**
string orchestra **das Streichorchester(-)**
tape **das Tonband(ִֵer)**
tour **die Tournee(n)**
 on tour **auf Tournee**
tune **der Klang**
 I sing in tune **ich singe richtig**
 out of tune **falsch, verstimmt**
I tune **ich stimme**
tuning fork **die Stimmgabel(n)**
voice **die Stimme(n)**
I whistle **ich pfeife**
wind band **die Blaskapelle(n)**
wind instrument **das Blasinstrument(e)**

– We make a lot of music at home.
– Do you play an instrument?
– Our son plays the violin.

– **Wir musizieren viel zu Hause.**
– **Spielst du ein Instrument?**
– **Unser Sohn spielt Geige.**

Our daughter is going to the open-air concert. Her favourite/favorite group is playing. She is a fan of the Rolling Stones. It really freaked her out.

Unsere Tochter geht ins Freiluftkonzert. Ihre Lieblingsgruppe spielt mit. Sie ist ein Fan der Stones. Dabei ist sie total ausgeflippt.

➤ MUSICAL FORMS, MUSICAL TERMS App.17d

17e Theatre and Film/Theater & the Movies

act   der Akt(e)
I act   ich spiele
acting school   die
   Schauspielschule(n)
actor   der Schauspieler(-) [-in]
I applaud   ich klatsche Beifall
applause   der Beifall
audience   die Zuschauer(-)
auditorium   der Zuschauerraum(-̈e)
I book   ich buche
box   die Loge(n)
box-office   die (Theater)kasse(n)
cabaret   das Kabarett(s)
camera   die Kamera(s)
camera crew   das Kamerateam(s)
cameraman   der
   Kameramann(-̈er)
cartoon   der Trickfilm(e)
choreographer   der
   Choreograph(en) (wk) [-in]
cinema/movies   das Kino(s)
cinema/movie buff   der Kinofan(s)
circle   der Rang(-̈e)
circus   der Zirkus(se)
I clap   ich klatsche Beifall
cloakroom   die Garderobe(n)
comedian   der Komiker(-) [-in]
contract   der Vertrag(-̈e)
critic   der Kritiker(-) [-in]
curtain   der Vorhang(-̈e)
I design   ich entwerfe
designer   der Bühnenbilder(-) [-in]

I direct   ich führe Regie
director   der Regisseur(e)
distribution system   das
   Vertriebssystem(e)
drama   das Drama (-en)
dress rehearsal   die
   Generalprobe(n)
dubbed   synchronisiert
dubbing   die Synchronisation
effects   die Spezialeffekte (pl)
I enter   ich trete auf*
exciting   spannend
I exit   ich gehe ab*
expectation   die Erwartung(en)
farce   der Schwank(-̈e), die
   Farce(n)
film/movie   der Film(e)
I film   ich filme, ich verfilme
film/movie maker   der
   Filmemacher(-)
filmstar/movie star   der Filmstar(s)
film/movie producer   der
   Filmproduzent(en) (wk)
first night   die Uraufführung(en)
floor-show   die Vorstellung(en)
flop   der Reinfall(-̈e)
intermission/interval   die Pause(n)
lights   die Beleuchtung(en)
limelights   das Rampenlicht(er)
lobby   das Foyer(s)
location work   die
   Außenaufnahmen (pl)

The play begins at 8:00 p.m.

**Das Theater beginnt um acht
Uhr abends.**

Have you seen the latest
production of Faust? The main
parts are excellently acted. It plays
to full houses.

**Hast du die neueste
Inszenierung vom Faust
gesehen? Die Hauptdarsteller
sind vortrefflich. Das Stück läuft
vor ausverkauften Häusern.**

I make a film/movie **ich drehe einen Film**
masterpiece **das Meisterwerk(e)**
matinée **die Matinee(s)**
melodrama **das Melodrama (-en)**
mime **die Pantomime(n)**
movie **der Film(e)**
music-hall **das Varieté(s)**
off-stage **hinter den Kulissen**
one-act play **der Ein-Akter(-)**
opening night **die Eröffnungsvorstellung(en)**
ovation **der Beifallssturm(-e)**
performance **die Aufführung(en)**
photography **die Aufnahmen** (pl)
play **das (Theater)stück(e)**
I play **ich spiele**
playwright **der Dramatiker(-) [-in]**
premiere **die Premiere(n)**
I produce **ich produziere, ich inszeniere**
producer **der Regisseur(e)**
production **die Inszenierung(en)**
projector **der Projektor(en)**
public **die Öffenlichkeit, die Zuschauer** (pl)
retrospective **der Rückblick**
retrospective (adj) **rückblickend**
review **die Rezension(en)**
role **die Rolle(n)**
row **die Reihe(n)**
scene **die Szene(n)**
scenery **das Bühnenbild(er)**
screen **die Leinwand(-e)**

screen test **die Probeaufnahmen** (pl)
screening **die Vorführung(en)**
I shoot (a film/movie) **ich drehe, ich filme**
script **das Drehbuch(-er)**
scriptwriter **der Drehbuchautor(en)**
script-girl **das Scriptgirl(s)**
seat **der Sitzplatz(-e)**
sequel **die Folge(n)**
sequence **die Reihenfolge(n)**
I show (film/movie) **ich führe auf*, ich bringe**
it is shown at **es wird im ... gezeigt/gegeben**
sold-out **ausverkauft**
sound-track **der Ton, die Filmmusik**
special effects **die Spezialeffekte** (pl)
stage **die Bühne(n)**
stage directions **die Bühnenanweisungen** (pl)
stage effects **die Bühneneffekte** (pl)
stage-fright **das Lampenfieber**
stalls **die Parterre**
stunt person **der Stuntman**
it takes place in **es spielt in**
trailers **die Vorschau**
understudy **die zweite Besetzung**
usherette **die Platzanweiserin(nen)**
walk-on part **die Statistenrolle(n)**
I zoom **ich zoome**

An exciting black and white film was shown on TV. It is set in Vienna.	**Ein spannender Schwarz-Weiß-Film kam im Fernsehen. Er spielt in Wien.**
The time and place of the action are Berlin in the 20s.	**Ort und Zeit der Handlung sind Berlin in den 20er Jahren.**
The book is being filmed.	**Das Buch wird verfilmt.**
We are filming in Africa.	**Wir filmen in Afrika.**

➤ APPRECIATION & CRITICISM 17a

The Media

18a General terms

admission **der Eintritt(e), der Einlaß**
I analyze **ich analysiere**
analysis **die Analyse(n)**
I appeal to **ich appelliere an** +acc
I argue **ich argumentiere**
argument **das Argument(e)**
attitude **die Einstellung(en), die Weltanschauung(en)**
biased **voreingenommen**
campaign **die Aktion(en)**
censorship **die Zensur**
  press censorship **die Pressezensur**
cogent **überzeugend**
comment **der Kommentar(e)**
conspiracy **die Verschwörung(en)**
criticism **die Kritik(en)**
cultural **kulturell**
culture **die Kultur(en)**
cultured **kultiviert**
current events **die aktuellen Ereignisse** *(pl)*
declaration **die Erklärung(en)**

I declare **ich erkläre**
detailed **detailliert**
it discriminates **es diskriminiert**
disaster **die Katastrophe(n)**
disinformation **die Fehlinformation(en)**
educational **Bildungs-**
I entertain **ich unterhalte**
ethical **ethisch**
event **das Ereignis(se)**
example **das Beispiel(e)**
expectation **die Erwartung(en)**
I exploit **ich beute aus***
fallacious **trügerisch**
fallacy **der Irrtum(¨er)**
freedom **die Freiheit(en)**
  freedom of the press **die Pressefreiheit**
full/detailed **voll**
gullible **leichtgläubig**
hidden **versteckt**
homophobic **homophobisch**
ignorance **die Unwissenheit**
I ignore **ich sehe über** +acc

During the recent elections it was difficult to find an example of unbiased reporting.

Während der letzten Wahlen war es schwierig, ein Beispiel an unbeeinflußter Berichterstattung zu finden.

In recent years many war correspondents have lost their lives while reporting from the front or have been taken hostage.

In den letzten Jahren wurden viele Kriegskorrespondenten bei der Berichterstattung getötet oder als Geiseln genommen.

I am a freelance journalist.

Ich bin ein freischaffender Journalist.

hinweg*
influential **einflußreich**
information **die Information(en)**
informative **informativ**
interview **das Interview(s)**
I intrude **ich störe**
intrusion **die Zudringlichkeit(en)**
intrusive **zudringlich**
issue *(problem)* **das Problem(e)**
journalese **der Pressejargon**
I keep up with (news) **ich bleibe
auf dem laufenden**
libel **die Verleumdung(en)**
libellous **verleumderisch**
local **Orts-, Regional-**
material **der Stoff(e)**
I meddle **ich mische mich ein***
medium **das Medium (-ien)**
media **die Medien** *(pl)*
news **die Nachrichten** *(pl)*
news agency **die
Nachrichtenagentur(en)**
news item **die Neuigkeit(en)**
partisan **parteiisch**
persuasion **die Überzeugung(en)**
persuasive **überzeugend**
prejudice **das Vorurteil(e)**
political **politisch**
politician **der Politiker(-) [-in]**
politics **die Politik** *(no pl)*
policy **die Politik** *(no pl)*

press **die Presse**
privacy **das Privatleben**
problem **das Problem(e)**
I report **ich berichte**
reportage **der Bericht(e)**
reporter **der Reporter(-) [-in]**
review **die Kritik(en)**
I review **ich bespreche**
it comes under review **es wird
geprüft**
scoop **der Knüller(-)**
sensational **sensationell**
sensationalism **die
Sensationsgier**
sexism **der Sexismus**
sexist **der Sexist(en)** *(wk)*
shrewd **klug, scharf**
summary **der Überblick(e)**
summary *(adj)* **kurzgefaßt**
it takes place **es findet statt***
trust **das Vertrauen**
I trust **ich glaube** +dat
trustworthy **glaubwürdig**
truth **die Wahrheit(en)**
truthful **ehrlich**
unbiased **unparteiisch**
untrustworthy **unzuverlässig**
up to date **aktuell**
weekly **wöchentlich**

Although British newspapers have
correspondents in all the European
capitals, they do not always
report/cover current events.

Media barons dominate the press
in many western countries.

**Obwohl die britische Presse in
allen europäischen
Hauptstädten Berichterstatter
hat, berichten diese nicht immer
über aktuelle Ereignisse.**

**Die Medienbarone beherrschen
die Presse in vielen westlichen
Ländern.**

18b The Press

article   der Artikel(-)
back page   die Rückseite(n)
barons   der Pressezar(en) *(wk)*
broadsheet   das Flugblatt(¨-er)
cartoon   der/das Cartoon(s), der
   Zeichentrick(s)
chief editor   der Chefredakteur(e)
circulation   die Auflagenziffer(n)
colour/color supplement   das
   Magazin(e), die Beilage(n)
column (of print)   die Spalte(n)
column *(article)*   die Kolumne(n)
comic   das Comic-Heft(e)
correspondent   der
   Korrespondent(en) *(wk)* [-in]
   foreign correspondent   der
   Auslandskorrespondent
   sports correspondent   der
   Sportkorrespondent
   war correspondent   der
   Kriegskorrespondent
daily newspaper   die
   Tageszeitung(en)
I edit   ich gebe heraus*
edition   die Ausgabe(n)
editor   der Redakteur(-) [-in]

glossy magazine   das
   Hochglanzmagazin(e)
gutter press   die Boulevardpresse
headline   die Schlagzeile(n)
heading   die Überschrift(en)
illustration   die Illustration(en)
I publish   ich veröffentliche
it is published   es ist erschienen
journalist   der Journalist(en) *(wk)*
   [-in]
layout   das Layout(s)
local paper   die Lokalzeitung(en)
magazine   die Illustrierte(n)
monthly   die Monatsschrift(en)
national newspaper   die nationale
   Zeitung(en)
newsagent   der Zeitungs-
   händler(-)
newspaper   die Zeitung(en)
news stand   der Zeitungskiosk(e)
page   die Seite(n)
pamphlet   das Flugblatt(¨-er)
periodical   die Zeitschrift(en)
power   die Macht(¨-e)
powerful   einflußreich
press agency   die

The constitution guarantees the right of freedom of expression and the freedom of the press.

Das Grundgesetz garantiert das Recht der freien Meinungsäußerung und die Pressefreiheit.

Die Frankfurter Allgemeine, die Süddeutsche Zeitung and *die Welt* are the best known newspapers in the country. They are national newspapers.

***Die Frankfurter Allgemeine, die Süddeutsche Zeitung* und *die Welt* sind die bekanntesten Zeitungen im Ausland. Sie sind überregionale Zeitungen.**

Die Bild-Zeitung is the most widely read newspaper in Germany.

***Die Bild-Zeitung* ist die meist-gelesene Zeitung in Deutschland.**

Presseagentur(en)
press conference **die Pressekonferenz(en)**
I print **ich drucke**
I publish **ich veröffentliche**
publisher **der Verleger(-) [-in]**
publishing company **der Verlag(e)**
quality press **die Qualitätspresse**

reader **der Leser(-) [-in]**
special issue **die Sonderausgabe(n)**
I subscribe to **ich abonniere**
subscription **das Abonnement(s)**
tabloid **die Boulevardzeitung(en)**
type(face) **die Schriftart(en)**
weekly **die Wochenzeitung(en)**

Newspaper sections & features

announcements **Anzeigen**
arts **bildenden Künste**
crossword puzzles **Kreuzwort-rätsel**
economy **Wirtschaft**
editorial **Kommentar**
entertainment **Kulturangebot**
finance **Finanzen, Börse**
food and drink **Speise und Getränk**
front page **die erste Seite**
editorials **Leitartikel**
gossip column **Klatschspalte**
home news **Landesspiegel,**

Meldungen aus dem Inland
horoscope **Horoskop**
international news **internationale Nachrichten**
leaders **Leitartikel**
obituaries **Todesanzeigen**
politcs **Politik**
problem page **Problemseite**
property **Immobilien**
small ads **Kleinanzeigen, Inserate**
sports page **Sport**
travel **Reisen**
women's page **Frauen**

Der Spiegel is an influential news magazine.

Der Spiegel ist ein einfluß-reiches Nachrichtenmagazin.

Many local newspapers are disappearing through mergers.

Viele Lokalzeitungen sind infolge Fusionen verschwunden.

Many people think that diversity and independence will be lost.

Viele Leute meinen, daß Vielfalt und Unabhängigeit verloren gehen.

The gutter press has a surprisingly high readership.

Die Klatschpresse hat eine überraschend hohe Leserzahl.

I subscribe to *Spiegel*.

Ich bin auf *Spiegel* abonniert.

➤ PUBLISHING 17c; ADVERTISING 18d

18c Television & radio

aerial **die Antenne(n)**
anchorman **der Koordinator(en)**
anchorwoman **die Koordinatorin(nen)**
announcer **der Ansager(-) [in]**
audience **die Zuhörer/-schauer** *(pl)*
I broadcast **ich sende**
broadcasting station **die Sendestation(en)**
cable TV **das Kabelfernsehen**
  by cable **über Kabel**
cameraman **der Kameramann(-̈er) [-frau]**
I change channel **ich schalte um***
channel **der Kanal(-̈e), das Programm(e)**
commercial **die Fernsehwerbung**
couch potato **der Dauerglotzer(-) [-in]**
dubbed **synchronisiert**
earphone **der Kopfhörer(-)**
episode **die Fortsetzung(en)**
goggle box **die Glotzkiste(n)**
high frequency **die Hochfrequenz(en)**
interactive **interaktiv**

light entertainment **die Unterhaltungssendung(en)**
listener **der Zuhörer(-) [-in]**
live broadcast **die Liveübertragung(en)**
live coverage/commentary **die Liveberichterstattung(en)**
loudspeaker **der Lautsprecher(-)**
low frequency **die niedrige Frequenz(en)**
microphone **das Mikrofon(e)**
news flash **die Kurzmeldung(en)**
newsreader/caster **der Nachrichtensprecher(-) [-in]**
production studio **das Aufnahmestudio(s)**
program(me) **die Sendung(en)**
radio **das Radio(s), der Hörfunk**
  on radio **im Radio**
I receive **ich empfange**
I record **ich nehme auf***
recording **die Aufnahme(n)**
remote control **die Fernbedienung(en)**
I repeat **ich wiederhole**
repeat **die Wiederholung(en)**
satelite **der Satellit(en)** *(wk)*

– What! Still glued to the set? You have been watching the box all evening! You have become a real couch potato!

– I'm just going to record this film then I'll join you. Have we got a blank videocassette.

Was the Pink Floyd concert broadcast live from Venice?

– Was! Klebst du immer noch am Fernseher? Du hast den ganzen Abend in die Glotze geschaut! Du bist ein richtiger Stubenhocker geworden!
– Ich möchte nur diesen Film aufnehmen, danach mache ich bei euch mit. Haben wir irgendeine leere Videokassette?

Wurde das Pink-Floyd-Konzert live aus Venedig übertragen?

satellite dish **die Satellitenschüssel(n)**
satellite TV **das Satellitenfernsehen**
screen **der Bildschirm(e)**
I show **ich zeige**
signal **das Signal(e)**
station **der Sender(-)**
subtitles **der Untertitel(-)**
I switch off **ich schalte ab***
I switch on **ich schalte an***
teletext **der Bildschirmtext(e)**
television/TV **das Fernsehen**
on TV **im Fernsehen**
television set **das Fernsehgerät(e), der Fernseher(-)**
television studio **das Fernsehstudio(s)**
I transmit **ich übertrage, ich sende**
video clip **der Videoclip(s)**
videogame **das Videospiel(e)**
video library **die Videothek(en)**
video nasty **die verbotene Aufnahme(n)**
video recorder **der Videorecorder(-)**
video recording **die Videoaufnahme(n)**
viewer **der Zuschauer(-) [-in]**
I watch **ich schaue zu***

TV and radio program(me)s

cartoon **der Zeichentrickfilm(e), der/das Cartoon(s)**
children program(me) **das Kinderprogramm(e)**
comedy **die Komödie(n)**
current affairs program(me) **die Tagesschau**
drama **das Drama (-en)**
documentary **der Dokumentarfilm(e)**
education program(me) **das Bildungs-/Lehrprogramm(e)**
feature film/movie **der Spielfilm(e)**
light entertainment **die leichte Unterhaltung** *(no pl)*
newscast **die Nachrichtensendung(en)**
quiz program(me) **das Quizprogramm(e), die Quizsendungen** *(pl)*
radio play **das Hörspiel(e)**
regional news **die Regionalnachrichten** *(pl)*
soap **die Fernsehserie(n)**
science program(me) **die Wissenschaftssendung(en)**
school broadcasting **die Schulsendung(en), der Schulfunk**
sports program(me) **die Sportsendung(en)**
TV film/movie **der Fernsehfilm(e)**
weather report **der Wetterbericht(e)**

Public broadcasting companies

ARD Arbeitsgemeinschaft der öffentlich-rechtlichen Rundfunkanstalten Deutschlands
ORF der Österreichische Rundfunk
SRG die Schweizerische Radio- und Fernsehgesellschaft
ZDF Zweites Deutsches Fernsehen
Deutsche Welle *(radio)*
Deutschlandfunk *(radio)*

➤ FILM/MOVIE GENRES App.17e

18d Advertising

I advertise **ich werbe für** +acc
advertisement **die Anzeige(n), die Reklame(n)**
advertising **die Werbung(en)**
advertising column **die Litfaßsäule(n)**
advertising industry **die Werbeindustrie**
appeal **der Reiz(e)**
it appeals to **es spricht jdn. an***
billboard **das Werbeplakat(e)**
brand **die Marke(n)**
brand awareness **das Markenbewußtsein**
brochure **die Broschüre(n)**
campaign **die Kampagne(n)**
it catches the eye **es zieht das Auge an***
commercial **der Werbespot(s)**
  commercial *(adj)* **kommerziell**
commercial break **die Werbepause(n)**
competition *(rival)* **die Konkurrenz** *(no pl)*
  competition *(game)* **das Preisausschreiben(-)**

consumer **der Verbraucher(-)**
consumer society **die Verbrauchergesellschaft(en)**
copywriter **der Werbetexter(-)**
I covet **ich begehre**
it creates a need **es schafft den Bedarf**
demand **die Nachfrage**
direct/junk mail **die Postwurfsendung(en)**
disposable income **das verfügbare Einkommen**
distributor **der Händler(-) [-in]**
ethical **ethisch**
good(s) **die Ware(n)**
hidden persuasion **die versteckte Beeinflussung**
image **das Image(s)**
launch **die Einführung**
life-style **der Lebensstil(e)**
I manipulate **ich manipuliere**
market **der Markt(ᵃe)**
model **das Modell(e)**
I motivate **ich motiviere**
need **das Bedürfnis(se), der Mangel(ᵃ)**

I advertised the job.	**Ich habe die Stelle ausgeschrieben.**
You must put a small ad in the paper.	**Sie müssen in der Zeitung inserieren.**
It pays to advertise!	**Inserieren bringt Gewinn!**
The buildings are covered in ugly advertising billboards.	**Die Gebäude sind mit häßlichen Werbeplakaten bedeckt.**
Until recently most TV spots portrayed women in exclusively traditional roles.	**Bis vor kurzem schilderten die meisten Fernsehspots Frauen in ausschließlich traditionellen Rollen.**

persuasion **die Überredung**
poster **das Poster(-)**
product **das Produkt(e)**
I promote **ich fördere, ich werbe**
   für +acc
promotion (of) **das Werbung (für)**
publicity **die Werbung(en)**
I publicize **ich mache Werbung**
   für +acc
purchasing power **die Kaufkraft**
radio advertisement **die**
   Radiowerbung(en)
slogan **der Slogan(s), der**
   Werbespruch(-̈e)
status symbol **das**
   Statussymbol(e)
stunt **der Gag(s)**
I target **ich ziele auf** +acc **ab***
target group **die Zielgruppe(n)**
I tempt **ich locke an***
trademark **der Handelsname(n)**
trend **der Trend(s)**
truthful **wahrhaft**
TV advertisement **die**
   Fernsehwerbung(en)
unethical **unethisch**

Small ads

accommodation **Häusermarkt**
appointments
   Stellenangebote
births **Geburten**
courses and conferences
   Kurse und Konferenzen
deaths **Todesanzeigen**
engagement(s)
   Verlobungsannonce(n)
exchange **Wechselkurs**
exhibitions **Ausstellungen**
for sale **zum Verkauf**
health **Gesundheit**
holidays **Ferien**
lonely hearts
   Kontaktanzeigen
marriages **Heiratsanzeigen**
personal services
   Persönliches
property **Immobilien** *(pl)*
travel **Reisen**
wanted **Kaufgesuche,**
   gesucht

This publicity may be offensive to some ethnic groups.

Für einige ethnische Gruppen kann diese Werbung beleidigend sein.

This has been his least successful campaign: next time we will use another agency or perhaps a freelance copywriter.

Das ist seine am wenigsten erfolgreiche Kampagne gewesen: das nächste Mal nehmen wir eine andere Agentur oder vieleicht einen freischaffenden Werbetexter.

Do you think that TV advertisements are more effective than advertisements in newspapers?

Denkst du, daß die Fernsehwerbung effektiver als Zeitungsanzeigen ist?

➤ THE PRESS 18b; TELEVISION & RADIO 18c

TRAVEL

19a General

accident **der Unfall(ˉe)**
adult **der/die Erwachsene** *(adj/n)*
announcement **die Ansage(n)**
  special announcement **die Sondermeldung(en)**
arrival **die Ankunft(ˉe)**
I arrive at **ich komme in ... an**
assistance **die Hilfe** *(no pl)*
automatic **automatisch**
available **zu haben**
bag **die Tasche(n), der Beutel(-)**
baggage **das Gepäck** *(no pl)*
bar **die Bar(s)**
I book **ich buche**
booking office **der Fahrkartenschalter(-)**
business trip **die Geschäftsreise(n)**
I buy a ticket **ich kaufe/löse eine Fahrkarte**
it calls at **er hält in** +dat
I cancel *(trip)* **ich sage ab***
  I cancel *(ticket)* **ich entwerte**
I carry **ich trage**
I catch **ich erwische, ich erreiche**
I check *(tickets)* **ich überprüfe, ich kontrolliere**
child **das Kind(er)**
class **die Klasse(n)**
coin **die Münze(n)**
I confirm **ich bestätige**
connection **die Verbindung(en)**
I cross **ich überquere**
delay **die Verspätung(en)**
delayed **verspätet, verzögert**
it is delayed **er hat Verspätung**
I depart **ich fahre ab***
departure **die Abfahrt(en)**
destination **das Reiseziel(e)**
direct **direkt**

direction **die Richtung(en)**
disabled **behindert**
distance **die Entfernung(en)**
document **das Dokument(e)**
early **früh**
emergency **der Notfall(ˉe)**
emergency call **der Notruf(e)**
I enquire about **ich erkundige mich nach** +dat
enquiry **die Erkundigung(en)**
en route **auf dem Weg**
entrance **der Eingang(ˉe)**
exit **der Ausgang(ˉe)**
extra charge **der Zuschlag(ˉe)**
fare **der Fahrpreis(e)**
fast **schnell**
I fill in a form **ich fülle ein Formular aus***
free *(not occupied)* **frei**
I go away **ich verreise**
information **die Information(en), die Auskunft**
information office **das Informationsbüro(s)**
insurance **die Versicherung(en)**
help **die Hilfe**
helpful **hilfsbereit**
holdall **die Reisetasche(n)**
late **(zu) spät**
I leave **ich fahre ab***
I leave *(person/object)* **ich verlasse**
left-luggage office **die Gepäckaufbewahrung(en)**
lost **verloren**
lost property/lost & found office **das Fundbüro(s)**
loudspeaker **der Lautsprecher(-)**
luggage **das Gepäck** (no pl)
message **die Nachricht(en)**
I miss *(train)* **ich verpasse**

money **das Geld(er)**
non-smoker **der Nichtraucher(-) [-in]**
notice **die Anzeige(n), die Mitteilung(en)**
nuisance **das Ärgernis(se)**
occupied **besetzt**
on board **an Bord**
on time **pünktlich**
I pack **ich packe**
passenger **der Passagier(e)**
porter *(hotel)* **der Portier(s)**
reduced fare **zu ermäßigtem Preis**
reduction **die Ermäßigung(en)**
reservation **die Reservierung(en)**
I reserve **ich reserviere**
I return **ich komme zurück***
return **die Rückkehr**
return/round-trip ticket **die Rückfahrkarte(n)**
round-trip **die Rundreise(n)**
safe **sicher**
safety **die Sicherheit(en)**
seat **der (Sitz)platz(⁻e)**
seatbelt **der Sicherheitsgurt(e)**
I set off **ich setze mich in Gang, ich mache mich auf den Weg**
slow **langsam**
I slow down **ich fahre langsamer**
small change **das Wechselgeld**
smoking **das Rauchen**
speed **die Geschwindigkeit(en)**
I speed up **ich fahre schneller**

staff **das Personal**
I start from **ich fahre von ... ab***
stop **der Halt, die Haltestelle(n)**
I stop **ich halte**
suitcase **der Koffer(-)**
I take *(bus, train)* **ich nehme**
ticket **die Fahrkarte(n)**
ticket desk **der/die Fahrkartenschalter(-)**
timetable **der Fahrplan(⁻e)**
to **nach, Richtung**
toilet/restroom **die Toilette(n)**
I travel **ich reise**
travel **die Reise(n)**
    document **das Reisedokument(e)**
    office **das Reisebüro(s)**
    pass **der Reisepaß (⁻sse)**
    sickness **die Reisenkrankheit**
traveller **der/die Reisende(n) *(adj/n)***
tunnel **der Tunnel(s/-)**
unexpected **unerwartet**
I unpack **ich packe aus***
valid **gültig**
visitor **der Besucher(-) [-in]**
warning **die Warnung(en)**
way in **der Eingang(⁻e)**
way out **der Ausgang(⁻e)**
on weekdays **an Wochentagen**
week-end **das Wochenende(n)**
welcome **der Empfang(⁻e)**
welcoming **freundlich**

---

by air **mit dem Flugzeug**
by car **mit dem Auto**
by ferry **mit der Fähre**
on foot **zu Fuß**

on horseback **mit dem Pferd**
by sea **auf dem Seeweg**
by train **mit dem Zug, mit der Bahn**

I usually fly, but today I am taking the train.

Ich fliege meistens, aber heute nehme ich den Zug.

– Are you walking or driving? – I am going by car.

– Fährst du oder gehst du zu Fuß? – Ich fahre mit dem Auto.

➤ HOLIDAYS/VACATION 20a; DIRECTIONS 2b; MOVEMENT 2c

19b Going abroad & travel by boat

Going abroad

Channel Tunnel **der Kanaltunnel(s/-)**
I cross the English Channel **ich überquere den Ärmelkanal**
currency **die Währung(en)**
currency exchange office **die Wechselstube(n)**
customs **der Einfuhrzoll(¨e)**
customs control **die Zollkontrolle(n)**
customs officer **der Zollbeamte(n)** *(wk)*
customs regulation **die Zollbestimmung(en)**
declaration **die Zollerklärung(en)**
I declare **ich verzolle**
duty **der Einfuhrzoll(¨e)**
duty-free goods **die zollfreie Ware(n)**
duty-free shop **das zollfreie Geschäft(e)**
exchange rate **der Wechselkurs(e)**
foreign currency **die Devisen** *(pl)*
frontier **die Grenze(n)**
I go through customs **ich gehe durch den Zoll**
I go through passport control **ich gehe durch die Paßkontrolle**

immigration office **die Einwanderungsbehörde(n)**
immigration rules **die Einwanderungsgesetze** *(pl)*
passport **der Paß(¨sse)**
I pay duty on **ich zahle Zoll auf** +acc
smuggler **der Schmuggler(-)**
smuggling **das Schmuggeln**
visa **das Visum (-en/-a)**

Travel by boat

bridge **die Brücke(n)**
cabin **die Kabine(n)**
calm **still**
captain **der Kapitän(e)**
car-ferry **die Autofähre(n)**
Channel **der (Ärmel)kanal**
choppy **bewegt**
coast **die Küste(n)**
crew **die Besatzung(en)**
crossing **die Überfahrt(en)**
cruise **die Kreuzfahrt(en)**
deck **das Deck(s)**
  below decks **unter Deck**
  lower deck **das Unterdeck**
  on deck **auf Deck**
  upper deck **das Oberdeck**
deck chair **der Liegestuhl(¨e)**
I disembark **ich gehe von Bord**

I've been through passport and customs.	**Die Paß- und Zollformalitäten sind erledigt.**
What is the best way to Zürich?	**Wie kommt man am schnellsten nach Zürich?**
My final destination is Milan.	**Mein Reiseziel ist Mailand.**

disembarkation **die Landung(en)**
dock **die Landungsbrücke(n)**
I embark (for) **ich schiffe mich (nach** +dat) **ein***
embarkation card **die Bordkarte(n)**
I go on board **ich gehe an Bord**
harbour **der Hafen(-)**
heavy *(sea)* **schwer**
lifejacket **die Schwimmweste(n)**
lifeboat **das Rettungsboot(e)**
lounge **der Salon(s)**
luggage **das Gepäck**
ocean **der Ozean(e), das Meer(e)**
officer **der Offizier(e)**
off-shore **vor der Küste**
on board **an Bord**
overboard **über Bord**
port **der Hafen(-)**
purser **der Zahlmeister(-)**
quay **der Kai(s)**
reclining seat **der Liegesitz(e)**
sea **die See**
sea-sickness **die Seekrankheit(en)**
seaman **der Seemann (-leute)**
shipping forecast **die Wettervorhersage(n)**
shipyard **die Werft(en)**
smooth **ruhig**
storm **der Sturm(-e)**
stormy **stürmisch**

tide **die Gezeiten** *(pl)*
high tide **die Flut**
low tide **die Ebbe**
waves **die Wellen**
wind **der Wind(e)**
windy **windig**

Ships & boats

aircraft carrier **der Flugzeugträger(-)**
canoe **das Kanu(s)**
cargo boat **das Transportschiff(e)**
dinghy *(rubber)* **das Schlauchboot(e)**
ferry **die Fähre(n)**
hovercraft **das Hovercraft(s)**
hydrofoil **das Tragflächenboot(e)**
life boat **das Rettungsboot(e)**
merchant ship **das Handelsschiff(e)**
motorboat **das Motorboot(e)**
ocean liner **der Überseedampfer(-)**
oil tanker **der Öltanker(-)**
rowing boat **das Ruderboot(e)**
sailing boat **das Segelboot(e)**
ship **das Schiff(e)**
speed boat **das Rennboot(e)**
submarine **das U-Boot(e)**
towboat **der Schlepper(-)**
warship **das Kriegsschiff(e)**
yacht **die Yacht(en)**

Shall we meet on deck?	**Treffen wir uns auf Deck?**
In stormy weather the boat pitches a lot.	**Bei stürmischem Wetter schaukelt das Schiff sehr.**
I felt so ill/sick on the crossing.	**Bei der Überfahrt war mir so übel.**
We docked at 10:00 p.m.	**Das Boot legte um 22.00 an.**

➤ COUNTRIES App.20a; CURRENCIES 9a

19c Travel by road

I accelerate **ich gebe Gas**
access **der Zugang(ˉe)**
alley **die Gasse(n), der Durchgang(ˉe)**
I allow **ich erlaube**
articulated lorry **der Sattelschlepper(-)**
avenue **die Allee(n)**
I back up/reverse **ich setze zurück***
bend/curve **die Kurve(n)**
bike/bicycle **das Fahrrad(ˉer)**
black ice **das Glatteis**
bottleneck **der Engpaß(ˉsse)**
breathalyzing test **die Alkoholkontrolle(n)**
I break down **ich habe eine Panne**
breakdown **die Panne(n)**
breakdown service **der Pannendienst(e)**
bridge **die Brücke(n)**
broken **kaputt**
built-up area **das Wohngebiet(e)**
bump **die Beule(n), der Stoß(ˉe)**
bus **der Bus(se)**
bus fare **der Busfahrpreis(e)**
bus stop **die Bushaltestelle(n)**
bypass **die Umgehungsstraße(n)**
car **das Auto(s)**
car hire/rental **der Autoverleih**
car park/parking lot **der Parkplatz(ˉe)**
multi-storey car park/high-rise parking lot **die Hochgarage(n)**
underground car park/parking lot **die Tiefgaragen(n)**
car part **das Ersatzteil(e)**
carwash **die Autowaschanlage(n)**
caravan/trailer **der Wohnwagen(-)**
careful **vorsichtig**
caution **die Vorsicht** *(no pl)*
caution *(legal)* **die Warnung(en)**
central reservation **der Mittelstreifen(-)**

I change gear **ich schalte um***
chauffeur **der Chauffeur(e)**
I check **ich (über)prüfe**
closed *(road)* **gesperrt**
I collide with **ich stoße mit** +dat **zusammen***
collision **der Zusammenstoß(ˉe)**
company car **der Firmenwagen(-)**
conductor/conductress *(bus)* **der Schaffner(-) [-in]**
corner **die Ecke(n), die Kurve(n)**
I cross **ich überquere**
crossing **die Übergang(ˉe)**
crossroad **die Kreuzung(en)**
cul-de-sac **die Sackgasse(n)**
dangerous **gefährlich**
detour **der Umweg(e)**
diesel **der Diesel, das Dieselöl**
I do 30 km.p.h. **ich fahre 30**
I drive **ich fahre**
drive **die Fahrt(en)**
driver **der Fahrer(-) [-in]**
driving **Fahr-**
instructor **der Fahrlehrer(-)**
lesson **die Fahrstunde(n)**
licence/diver's license **der Führerschein(e)**
school **die Fahrschule(n)**
test **die Fahrprüfung(en)**
drunken driving **betrunken am Steuer**
emergency stop **die Vollbremsung**
engine trouble **der Motorschaden** *(no pl)*
eye-witness **der Augenzeuge(n)** *(wk)*
I fasten my seatbelt **ich schnalle mich an***
fatality **das Todesopfer(-)**
I fill up **ich tanke**
filling station **die Tankstelle(n)**
I find my way **ich finde mich zurecht***
I fix **ich repariere**

forbidden **verboten**
for hire/rent **zu vermieten**
garage **die Garage(n)**
gear **der Gang(¨e)**
   in gear **der Gang ist eingelegt**
   in first gear **im ersten Gang**
   in neutral **im Leerlauf**
   in reverse **im Rückwärtsgang**
I get in the car **ich steige ein***
I get in lane **ich ordne mich ein***
I get out **ich steige aus***
I give way **ich lasse (jdm.) die Vorfahrt**
green card *(insurance)* **die grüne Karte**
I have it repaired **ich lasse es reparieren**
highway **die Landstraße(n)**
Highway Code **die Straßenverkehrsordnung**
Highway police **die Autobahnpolizei**
I hire **ich miete**
hired car **der Mietwagen(-)**
I hitchhike **ich trampe, ich fahre per Anhalter**
hitchhiker **der Tramper(-) [-]**
I honk **ich hupe**
inside lane **die Innenspur(en)**
insurance **die Versicherung(en)**
insurance policy **die Versicherungspolice(n)**
I am insured **ich bin versichert**
intersection **die Kreuzung(en)**
international driving licence **der Internationale Führerschein(e)**
jack **der Wagenheber(-)**
it is jammed **es klemmt**
junction **der Kreuzweg(e)**
key **der Schlüssel(-)**
key-ring **der Schlüsselring(e)**
kilometre/kilometer **der Kilometer(-)**
lane **die Fahrspur(en)**
lay-by **der Rastplatz(¨e)**
lead-free **bleifrei**
leaded **verbleit**

learner driver **der Fahrschüler(-)**
level crossing **der Bahnübergang(¨e)**
limit **die (Geschwindigkeits)-begrenzung(en)**
line of cars **die Autoschlange(n)**
litre/liter **der Liter(-)**
logbook **der Kraftfahrzeugbrief(e)**
lorry/truck **der Lastwagen(-)**
lorry/truck driver **der LKW-Fahrer(-) [-in]**
main **Haupt-**
main street **die Hauptstraße(n)**
I make a statement **ich mache eine Aussage**
make of car **die Automarke(n)**
MOT/vehicle validation **der TÜV**
maximum speed **die Höchstgeschwindigkeit(en)**
mechanic **der Mechaniker(-) [-in]**
mechanic *(adj)* **mechanisch**
motel **das Motel(s)**
motor caravan/trailer **der motorisierte Wohnwagen**
motor show **die Automobilausstellung(en)**
motorway/expressway **die Autobahn(en)**
   entry **die Auffahrt(en)**
   exit **die Ausfahrt(en)**
   hard shoulder **die Standspur(en)**
   junction **der Autobahnknotenpunkt(e)**
   police **die (Autobahn)polizei**
   services **die Raststätte(en)**
   toll **die Autobahngebühr(en)**
one-way **Einbahn-**
one-way street **die Einbahnstraße(n)**
outside lane **die Überholspur(en)**
I overtake/pass **ich überhole**
overtaking/passing **das Überholen**
I park **ich parke**
parking **das Parken**
parking ban **das Parkverbot(e)**
parking meter **die Parkuhr(en)**

parking ticket **der Strafzettel(-)**
I pass **ich fahre vorbei***
passenger **der Passagier(e)**
pedestrian **der Fußgänger(-) [-in]**
pedestrian crossing **der Fußgängerübergang(¨e)**
pedestrian zone **die Fußgängerzone(n)**
petrol/gasoline **das Benzin**
  four-star **das Superbenzin**
  two-star **das Normalbenzin**
picnic area **der Picknickplatz(¨e)**
police **die Polizei**
policeman **der Polizist(en)** *(wk)* **[-in]**
police station **das Polizeirevier(e)**
private car **der eigene Wagen(-)**
private property **das Privateigentum**
public transport **das öffentliche Verkehrsmittel(-)**
puncture/flat **der platte Reifen(-)**
I put on my seat belt **ich schnalle mich an***
ramp **die Rampe(n)**
registration papers **die Autopapiere** *(pl)*
rental charge **der Mietpreis(e)**
repair **die Reparatur(en)**
I repair **ich repariere**
I reverse **ich fahre zurück***
(in) reverse **im Rückwärtsgang**
right of way **die Vorfahrt**
ring road **die Umgehungsstraße(n)**
road **die Straße(n)**
  accident **der Unfall(¨e)**
  block **die (Straßen)sperrung(en)**
  hog **der Verkehrsrowdy(s)**
  map **die Straßenkarte(n)**
  sign **das Straßenschild(er)**
  signals **die Ampel(n)**
  side **die Straßenrand(¨er)**
  works **der Straßenbau**
roundabout **der Kreisverkehr**
route **die Route(n)**
I run over **ich überfahre**
rush hour **der Berufsverkehr**
second-hand car **der Gebrauchtwagen(-)**
service **die Inspektion(en)**
I set off **ich mache mich auf den**

You must fill up, test the oil and pump up the tyres/tires.	**Sie müssen Benzin tanken, den Ölstand prüfen und die Reifen aufpumpen.**
Fill her up!	**Bitte volltanken!**
When the engine starts, use the clutch, go into first gear and accelerate.	**Wenn der Motor anspringt, treten Sie die Kupplung, legen Sie den ersten Gang ein, und geben Sie Gas.**
When the traffic is heavy you must go slowly.	**Im dichten Straßenverkehr muß man langsam fahren.**
Keep to the right!	**Rechts halten!**
One must not drive when one is drunk.	**Man darf nicht betrunken am Steuer fahren.**

Weg
side street **die Nebenstraße(n)**
signpost **der Wegweiser(-), das Schild(er)**
I skid **ich rutsche aus***
slip road **die Auf-/Ausfahrt(en)**
slippery **glatt**
slow **langsam**
I slow down **ich fahre langsamer**
speed **die Geschwindigkeit(en)**
I speed up **ich fahre schneller**
speed limit **die Geschwindigkeits-begrenzung(en)**
spot fine **die Geldstrafe(n)**
I start *(engine)* **ich lasse an***
street **die Straße(n)**
I switch off **ich schalte ab***
taxi/cab **das Taxi(s)**
taxi driver **der Taxifahrer(-)**
taxi rank/stand **der Taxistand(-̈e)**
I test **ich prüfe**
tool **das Werkzeug(e)**
I tow away **ich schleppe ab***
town plan **der Stadtplan(-̈e)**
town traffic **der Stadtverkehr**
traffic **der Verkehr**
traffic jam **der Stau(s)**

traffic light **die Ampel(n)**
traffic offence **das Verkehrsdelikt(e)**
traffic news **die Verkehrsmeldung(en)**
traffic police **die Verkehrspolizei**
traffic warden **die Politesse(n)**
traffic-free zone **die verkehrsfreie Zone(n)**
I turn **ich biege**
I turn left **ich biege nach links**
I turn right **ich biege nach rechts**
I turn off at **ich biege ab***
I turn off *(engine)* **ich schalte ... ab***
underground garage **die Tiefgarage(n)**
underground passage **die Unterführung(en)**
unleaded **bleifrei**
U-turn **das Wenden** *(no pl)*
vehicle **das Fahrzeug(e)**
I wait **ich warte**
warning **die Warnung(en)**
warning triangle **das Warndreieck(e)**
workshop **die Werkstatt(-̈e)**

When it is wet the bend gets dangerously slippery.	**Bei Nässe wird die Kurve gefährlich glatt.**
We must make a detour because of the road works.	**Wir müssen wegen der Baustelle einen Umweg fahren.**
He went across the intersection at 120. The speed limit here is 100 kph.	**Er ist bei 120 über die Kreuzung gefahren. Die Höchstgeschwindigkeit hier ist 120 Kilometer pro Stunde.**
He did not dip his lights.	**Er hat nicht abgeblendet.**
He did not switch on the indicator.	**Er hat den Blinker nicht betätigt.**
– He jumped the lights. – Surely the lights were green?	**– Er ist bei Rot über die Ampel gefahren. – Die Ampel stand doch auf Grün?**

➤ PARTS OF THE CAR, ROAD SIGNS App.19c; DIRECTIONS 2b

19d Travel by air

aeroplane/airplane **das Flugzeug(e)**
air hostess/stewardess **die Stewardeß (-ssen)**
airline **die Fluglinie(n)**
airline desk **der Flugschalter(-)**
air travel **der Flugverkehr**
airport **der Flughafen(-)**
I am airsick **mir wird schlecht beim Fliegen**
baggage **das Gepäck**
baggage reclaim **die Gepäckausgabe**
body search **die Leibeskontrolle(n)**
I board a plane **ich gehe an Bord eines Flugzeugs**
boarding card **die Bordkarte(n)**
business class **die Businessklasse(n)**
by air **per Flugzeug**
cabin **die Kabine(n)**
cancelled **gestrichen**
carousel **das Gepäckband(-er)**
charter flight **der Charterflug(-e)**
I check in **ich checke ein***

check-in operations **das Einchecken**
control tower **der Kontrollturm(-e)**
co-pilot **der Co-Pilot(en)** *(wk)* **[-in]**
crew **die Besatzung(en)**
direct flight **der Direktflug(-e)**
domestic flights **der Inlandflug(-e)**
during landing **während der Landung**
during take-off **während des Starts**
during the flight **während des Fluges**
duty-free goods **die zollfreie Ware(n)**
economy class **die Touristenklasse(n)**
emergency exit **der Notausgang(-e)**
emergency landing **die Notlandung(en)**
excess baggage **das Übergewicht**
flight **der Flug(-e)**
flight attendant **der Flugbegleiter(-) [-in]**
I fly **ich fliege**

We are about to land in Zürich.	**Wir befinden uns im Anflug auf Zürich.**
Please fasten your safety belt and stop smoking.	**Wir bitten Sie, sich jetzt anzuschnallen und das Rauchen einzustellen.**
We are flying on the early flight to the Sudan.	**Wir fliegen mit der Frühmaschine in den Sudan.**
The ticket is waiting at the Lufthansa desk.	**Der Ticket liegt am Lufthansa-Schalter bereit.**
The plane landed punctually.	**Die Maschine setzte pünktlich auf.**
Can I change my reservation?	**Kann ich umbuchen?**

I fly at a height of **ich fliege in einer Höhe von**
flying **das Fliegen**
fuselage **der Flugzeugrumpf(ᵉe)**
gate **der Ausgang(ᵉe)**
instructions **die Gebrauchsanweisung(en)**
hand luggage **das Handgepäck**
headphone **der Kopfhörer**
highjacker **der Luftpirat(en)** *(wk)*
immigrant **der Immigrant(en)** *(wk)* **[-in]**
immigration **die Einwanderung**
immigration rules **die Einwanderungsgesetze**
information desk **die Information**
I land **ich lande**
landing **die Landung(en)**
landing lights **die Landebeleuchtung**
no-smoking sign **das Rauchen-verboten-Schild**
non-stop **Non-stop-**
on board **an Bord**
parachute **der Fallschirm(e)**
passenger **der Passagier(e)**
passengers lounge **die Wartehalle(n)**
passport control **die Paßkontrolle(n)**
pilot **der Pilot(en)** *(wk)*
plane **die Maschine(n)**
refreshments **die Erfrischungen** *(pl)*
runway **die Start- und Landebahn(en)**
safety jacket **die Sicherheitsjacke(n), die Rettungsweste(n)**
security measures **die Sicherheitsmaßnahmen** *(pl)*
security staff **das Sicherheitspersonal**
steward **der Steward(s)**
stewardess **die Stewardeß (-ssen)**
I take off **ich starte, ich fliege ab***
take-off **der Abflug(ᵉe)**
terminal **das Terminal(s)**
tray **das Tablett(s/e)**
turbulence **die Turbulenzen** *(pl)*
view **die Aussicht(en)**
window **das Fenster(-)**
window seat **der Fensterplatz(ᵉe)**

There was a problem in the baggage hall. The flight to London is delayed by half an hour.	**Es gab ein Problem bei der Gepäckausgabe. Der Flug nach London hat eine halbe Stunde Verspätung.**
There are some seats free on the plane.	**In der Maschine sind noch Plätze frei.**
Passengers continuing to Rome please go to gate 18.	**Passagiere im Weiterflug nach Rom bitte nach Ausgang 18 gehen.**
I need a wheelchair for a disabled passenger.	**Ich brauche einen Rollstuhl für einen behinderten Passagier.**
Frankfurt Airport is called the gateway to the world.	**Man nennt den Rhein-Main-Flughafen das Tor zur Welt.**

➤ HOLIDAYS/VACATION 20

19e Travel by rail

buffet **das Büffet(s)**
buffet-car **der Speisewagen(-)**
coach **der Waggon(s)**
compartment **das Abteil(e)**
connection **der Anschluß (̈-sse)**
dining-car **der Speisewagen(-)**
direct train **der durchgehende Zug(̈-e)**
express train **der Schnellzug(̈-e)**
fare **der Fahrpreis(e)**
first class **erster Klasse**
inspector **der Kontrolleur(e)**
Intercity train **der Intercity, der IC-Zug**
level crossing **der Bahnübergang(̈-e)**
luggage/baggage rack **die Gepäckablage(n)**
non-refundable **keine Rückzahlung**
occupied **besetzt**
on time **pünktlich**
platform **der Bahnsteig(e), das Gleis(e)**
porter **der Gepäckträger(-)**
I punch *(ticket)* **ich entwerte**
railway/railroad **die Eisenbahn(en)**
station **der Bahnhof(̈-e)**
track **das Gleis(e)**
reduction **die Ermäßigung(en)**
reservation **die Reservierung(en)**
reserved **reserviert**
return/round trip ticket **die Rückfahrkarte(n)**
second class **zweiter Klasse**
single/one-way ticket **die einfache Karte(n)**
sleeper **der Schlafwagen(-)**

Have you checked the timetable?

Hast du im Fahrplan nachgesehen?

– When is the first train? – At 4:00 p.m. from platform 3.

– Wann fährt der erste Zug? – Um sechzehn Uhr von Gleis 3.

The train arrived punctually.

Der Zug ist pünktlich eingelaufen.

Have you got your ticket?

Haben Sie Ihren Fahrschein?

Paul travelled without a ticket.

Paul ist schwarzgefahren.

Don't forget to pay the supplement for the Inter-City.

Vergessen Sie nicht, den Zuschlag für den Inter-City-Zug zu bezahlen.

Where do I change?

Wo muß ich umsteigen?

(non) smoking compartment **das (Nicht)raucherabteil(e)**

station master **der Bahnhofsvorsteher(-)**

stop **die Station(en)**

I stop **ich halte**

suitcase **der Koffer(-)**

supplement **der Zuschlag(¨e)**

taxi rank/stand **der Taxistand(¨e)**

ticket **die Fahrkarte(n)**

  collector **der Schaffner(-)**

  office **der Fahrkartenschalter(-)**

timetable **der Fahrplan(¨e)**

  change **die Fahrplanänderung(en)**

  summer timetable **der Sommerfahrplan(¨e)**

  winter timetable **der Winterfahrplan(¨e)**

toilets **die Toilette(n)**

track **das Gleis(e)**

traveller **der/die Reisende** *(wk)*

train **der Zug(¨e)**

  express train **der Schnellzug(¨e)**

  fast stopping train **der Eilzug(¨e)**

  Intercity train **der Intercity-Zug(¨e)**

  local train **die Ortsbahn, die Stadtbahn(en)**

  night train **der Nachtzug(¨e)**

  through train **der D-Zug(¨e)**

trolley **der Kofferkuli(s)**

waiting-room **der Wartesaal (-säle)**

wagon-lits **der Waggon(s)**

warning **die Warnung(en)**

window **das Fenster(-)**

window seat **der Fenstersitz(e)**

– Is there a connection to Basle? – It only runs on Sundays and holidays.

– Gibt es eine Verbindung nach Basel? – Er fährt nur an Sonn- und Feiertagen.

It's a no-smoking compartment.

Es ist ein Nichtraucher-Abteil.

The German Federal Railway is the largest transport business in Germany.

Die Deutsche Bundesbahn (DB) ist das größte Transport-unternehmen in Deutschland.

There is a lot of commuter traffic, above all in large built up areas.

Es gibt einen starken Pendelverkehr, vor allem in den großen Ballungsgebieten.

On Sundays and holidays ...

An Sonn- und Feiertagen ...

On weekdays ...

An Werktagen ...

Holidays/Vacation

20a General terms

abroad **im/ins Ausland**
accommodation **die Unterkunft(̈e)**
alone **allein**
amenities **die Möglichkeiten** *(pl)*
area **das Gebiet(e)**
arrival **die Ankunft(̈e)**
it is available **er steht zur Verfügung**
beach **der Strand(̈e)**
camera **die Kamera(s), der Fotoapparat(e)**
clean **sauber**
climate **das Klima(s)**
closed **geschlossen**
clothes **die Kleidung**
cold **kalt**
comfortable **bequem**
congested **überfüllt**
cost **die Kosten** *(pl)*
country **das Land(̈er)**
in the country **auf dem Land(e)**
countryside **die Landschaft(en)**
departure **die Abfahrt(en)**
dirty **schmutzig**
disorganized *(untidy)* **unordentlich**
I am disorganized **ich bin schlecht organisiert**
exchange *(money)* **die Wechselstube(n)**
folding chair **der Klappstuhl(̈e)**
folding table **der Klapptisch(e)**
food **das Essen**
free **frei, kostenlos**
full **voll**
full-up *(hotel)* **ausgebucht**
I get brown/tan **ich werde braun**
I go away **ich verreise**
group **die Gruppe(n)**
group travel **die Gruppenreise(n)**
guide **der Reiseführer(-) [-in]**

guided tour **die Reisetour(s)**
guided walk **die Führung(en)**
holidays/vacation **die Ferien** *(pl)*, **der Urlaub** *(no pl)*
I go on holiday/vacation **ich fahre in Urlaub**
holiday/vacation dates **die Ferientermine** *(pl)*
land **das Land(̈er)**
landscape **die Landschaft(en)**
journey **die Reise(n)**
map **die Landkarte(n)**
mild *(climate)* **mild**
money **das Geld(er)**
in the mountains **im Gebirge**
open **offen, geöffnet**
it is open **es ist auf**
organization **die Organisation(en)**
I organize **ich organisiere**
organized **organisiert**
I pack **ich packe ein***
I plan **ich plane**
portable **tragbar**
postcard **die Ansichtskarte(n)**
rucksack/knapsack **der Rucksack(̈e)**
sea **das Meer(e)**
seaside resort **der Badeort(e)**
shade **der Schatten(-)**
I shop **ich kaufen ein***
show **die Vorstellung(en)**
sight **die Sehenswürdigkeit(en)**
I spend (time) **ich verbringe (Zeit)**
stay **der Aufenthalt(e)**
I stay **ich wohne**
sun **die Sonne(n)**
I sunbathe **ich liege in der Sonne**
tour **die Tour(en), die Fahrt(en)**
tourism **der Tourismus**
tourist **der Tourist(en)** *(wk)*

tourist menu **die Touristenspeisekarte(n)**
tourist office **das Verkehrsamt(⁻er)**
town **die Stadt(⁻e)**
town plan **der Stadtplan(⁻e)**
travel **das Reisen**
I travel **ich reise**
travel adaptor **der Adapter(-)**
trip **der Ausflug(⁻e)**
uncomfortable **unbequem**
I understand **ich verstehe**
I unpack **ich packe aus***
visit **der Besuch(e)**
I visit **ich besuche**
visiting hours **die Besuchszeit(en)**
visitor **der Besucher(-)**
welcome **der Empfang(⁻e)**
I welcome **ich begrüße**
worth seeing **sehenswert**

Holidays/Vacation activities

beach holiday/vacation **der Urlaub am Meer**
boating holiday/vacation **die Bootsfahrt(en)**
camping **das Zelten**
canoeing **das Kanufahren**
coach holiday/vacation **die Busreise(n)**
cruise **die Kreuzfahrt(en)**
cycling **das Radfahren**
exchange (school) **der Austausch(e)**
fishing **das Angeln, das Fischen**
fruit picking **das Obstpflücken**
hunting **die Jagd** *(no pl)*
I go hunting **ich gehe auf die Jagd**
mountain climbing **das Bergsteigen**
package holiday/tour **die Pauschalreise(n)**
rock climbing **das Klettern**
safari **die Safari(s)**
sailing **das Segeln**
shopping **das Einkaufen**
sightseeing **die Besichtigungstour(en)**
skiing **das Skilaufen**
study holiday **die Informationstour(en)**
sunbathing **das Sonnenbaden**
trekking **das Trekking**
volunteer work **für die Wohlfahrt arbeiten**
walking **das Wandern**
wine tasting **die Weinprobe(n)**

– When are you on holiday/ vacation? Have you got your holiday/vacation dates yet?

– We are going on holiday/ vacation in July.

– I hope you had a restful holiday/ vacation.
– We spent it in the mountains. We had bed and breakfast on a farm. We had to pay in cash, as they would not take a cheque/ check.

– Wann hast du Urlaub? Hast du deine Ferientermine schon?

– Wir fahren im Juli in/auf Urlaub.

– Hoffentlich haben Sie einen erholsamen Urlaub verbracht.
– Wir haben ihn im Gebirge verbracht. Wir hatten Übernachtung mit Frühstück auf einem Bauernhof. Wir mußten bar bezahlen, da sie keinen Scheck annehmen wollten.

➤ COUNTRIES App.20a; HOBBIES 16a; ON THE BEACH App.20a

20b Accommodation & hotel

Accommodation

accommodation **die Unterkunft(⁻e)**
apartment **die Wohnung(en)**
bed and breakfast **die**
    Übernachtung mit Frühstück
    "Bed & Breakfast"
    "Fremdenzimmer"
campsite **der Campingplatz(⁻e)**
caravan/trailer **der Wohnwagen(-)**
guest **der Gast(⁻e)**
farm **der Bauernhof(⁻e)**
full board **die Vollpension**
half board **die Halbpension**
holiday flat/vacation apartment **die**
    Ferienwohnung(en)
home exchange **der Haustausch(e)**
hotel **das Hotel(s)**
mobile home **das Wohnmobil(e)**
inn **das Wirtshaus(⁻er)**
self-catering/service **mit**
    Selbstverpflegung
villa **die Villa(s)**
youth hostel **die**
    Jugendherberge(n)

Booking & payment

I afford **ich leiste mir**
all included **(alles mit)**
    inbegriffen, inklusiv
bill **die Rechnung(en)**
I book **ich buche**
cash *(money)* **das (Bar)geld**
I cash **ich löse ein***
cheap **billig, preiswert**
cheque/check **der Scheck(s)**
cost **der Preis(e)**
credit **der Kredit(e)**
credit card **die Kreditkarte(n)**
Eurocheque **der Euroscheck(s)**
exclusive **exklusiv**
expensive **teuer**
extra charge **zusätzliche Kosten**
    (pl)
I fill in **ich fülle aus***
form **das Formular(e)**

free **kostenlos, frei**
I pay **ich bezahle**
payment **die Bezahlung(en)**
    by cheque/check **mit Scheck**
    with cash **in bar**
price **der Preis(e)**
price-list **die Preisliste(n)**
receipt **die Quittung(en)**
reduction **der Ermäßigung(en)**
refund **die Rückvergütung(en)**
reservation **die Reservierung(en)**
I reserve **ich reserviere**
I sign **ich unterschreibe**
signature **die Unterschrift(en)**
traveller's cheque/check **der**
    Reisescheck(s)
VAT/sales tax **die**
    Mehrwertsteuer, MWS

In the hotel

amenities **die Einrichtungen** *(pl)*
balcony **der Balkon(s)**
ball **der Ball(⁻e)**
bank card **die Bankkarte(n)**
basement **das Kellergeschoß(⁻e)**
bath **das Bad(⁻er)**
bed **das Bett(en)**
    double bed **das Doppelbett(en)**
    single bed **das Einzelbett(en)**
    twin beds **mit zwei Betten**
bedding **das Bettzeug** *(no pl)*
bedspread **die Überwurf(⁻e)**
billiard room **der Billardraum(⁻e)**
breakfast **das Frühstück(e)**
    English breakfast **das**
    englische Frühstück
broken **kaputt**
it is broken **es ist zerbrochen**
business conference **die**
    Geschäftskonferenz(en)
button **der Knopf(⁻e)**
call **der Anruf(e)**
I call **ich rufe an***
I check in **ich melde mich an***
I check out **ich fahre ab***

coathanger **der Kleiderbügel(-)**
comfortable **bequem**
I complain (about) **ich beschwere mich (über** +acc)
complaint **die Beschwerde(n)**
conference **die Konferenz(en)**
conference facilities **die Konferenzeinrichtungen** (pl)
damage **der Schaden(-̈)**
dining-room **der Speiseraum(-̈e)**
dry cleaning **die Reinigung**
early morning call **der Weckruf(e)**
en-suite bathroom **mit Bad**
evening meal **das Abendessen(-)**
extravagant **luxuriös**
facilities **die Einrichtungen** (pl)
fax **das (Tele)fax(e)**
it is on fire **es brennt!**
fire alarm **der Feueralarm**
fire exit **der Notausgang(-̈e)**
fire extinguisher **der Feuerlöscher(-)**
first floor **die erste Etage**
ground floor **das Erdgeschoß (-sse)**
guest **der Gast(-̈e)**
hairdresser **der Friseur(e)**
hairdryer **der Fön(s)**
heating **die Heizung(en)**
key **der Schlüssel(-)**
laundry **die Wäsche** (no pl)
laundry-bag **der Wäschebeutel(-)**

laundry service **der Wäscheservice**
lift/elevator **der Fahrstuhl(-̈e), der Aufzug(-̈e)**
night porter **der Nachtportier(s)**
noisy **laut**
nuisance **das Ärgernis(se)**
overnight bag **die Übernachtungstasche(n)**
parking space **der Parkplatz(-̈e)**
pleasant **angenehm, freundlich**
plug **der Stecker(-)**
porter **der Portier(s)**
private **privat**
privacy **die Ruhe**
proof of identity **der Ausweis(e)**
quality **die Qualität(en)**
quiet **still, ruhig**
reception **die Rezeption(en)**
receptionist **der Empfangschef/dame**
room **das Zimmer(-)**
  double room **das Doppelzimmer**
  family room **der Familienraum(-̈e)**
room service **der Zimmerservice**
service **die Bedienung**
stay **der Aufenthalt(e)**
I stay **ich wohne**
suitcase **der Koffer(-)**
terrace **die Terrasse(n)**
view **die Aussicht(en)**

Our hotel room was large and sunny, with a view, a balcony and running water. Our stay was very pleasant.

Unser Hotelzimmer war groß und sonnig, mit Aussicht, Balkon und fließendem Wasser. Unser Aufenthalt war sehr schön.

The children spent a lot of time in the swimming pool.

Die Kinder verbrachten viel Zeit im Swimmingpool.

I prefer an en suite bathroom.

Ich ziehe es vor, ein Zimmer mit Bad zu haben.

We parked outside the hotel.

Wir parkten vor dem Hotel.

➤ ROOMS 8a; FURNISHINGS 8c; EATING OUT 10a

20c Camping & self-catering/service

At the campsite

air bed   **die Luftmatratze(n)**
antihistamine cream   **die Antihistamincreme(n)**
ant   **die Ameise(n)**
barbeque   **der Grill(s), das Grillfest(e)**
battery   **die Batterie(n)**
I camp   **ich zelte**
camp bed   **das Campingbett(en)**
camper   **der Camper(-)**
camping   **das Zelten**
camping equipment/gear   **die Campingausrüstung(en)**
camping gas   **das Campinggas**
campsite   **der Zeltplatz(-̈e)**
caravan/trailer   **der Wohnwagen(-)**
connected   **mit elektrischem Anschluß**
cooking facilities   **die Kochmöglichkeiten** *(pl)*
dark   **dunkel**
disconnected   **ohne elektrischen Anschluß**
drinking water   **das Trinkwasser**
dry   **trocken**
dustbin   **der Mülleimer(-)**

extension lead   **das Verlängerungskabel(-)**
forbidden   **verboten**
fun   **der Spaß** *(no pl)*
gas cooker   **der Gaskocher(-)**
gas cylinder   **die Gasflasche(n)**
ground-sheet   **der Zeltboden(-̈)**
we make friends   **wir freunden uns an***
medicine box   **der Arzneikasten(-̈)**
mosquito   **der Moskito(s)**
mosquito bite   **der Moskitostich(e)**
mosquito net   **das Moskitonetz(e)**
pan   **der Kochtopf(-̈e)**
peg   **der Pflock(-̈e)**
pillow   **das Kissen(-)**
I pitch/put up *(tent)*   **ich stelle auf***
potty   **das Töpfchen(-)**
private   **privat**
proprietor   **der Eigentümer(-) [-in]**
registration   **die Anmeldung(en)**
reservation   **die Reservierung(en)**
services   **der Strom- und Wasseranschluß (-̈sse)**
shadow   **der Schatten(-)**
sheet   **das Bettlaken(-)**
site   **der Platz(-̈e)**

We went camping.	**Wir haben gezeltet.**
We were right by the beach.	**Wir waren dicht am Strand.**
We pitched the tent in the shade.	**Wir haben das Zelt im Schatten aufgeschlagen.**
The ground was boggy and there were too many midges.	**Der Boden war sumpfig und es gab zu viele Mücken.**
It was very noisy at night.	**Nachts war es sehr laut.**

sleeping bag **der Schlafsack(¨e)**
space **der Platz(¨e)**
I take down (tent) **ich baue (das Zelt) ab***
tent **das Zelt(e)**
tin opener **der Dosenöffner(-)**
toilet **die Toilette(n)**
torch/flashlight **die Taschenlampe(n)**
uncomfortable **unbequem, ungemütlich**
vehicle **das Fahrzeug(e)**
washing facilities **die Waschgelegenheiten** *(pl)*
water filter **der Wasserfilter(-)**

Self-catering/service

agency **die Agentur(en)**
agreement **der Vertrag(¨e)**
amenity **die Annehmlichkeit(en)**
apartment **die Wohnung(en)**
clean **sauber**
I clean **ich mache sauber***
I cook **ich koche**
damaged **defekt**
damages **der Schadensersatz** *(no pl)*
electricity **die Elektrizität**
equipment **die Austattung(en)**

facilities **die Einrichtungen** *(pl)*
farm **der Bauernhof(¨e)**
furniture **die Möbel** *(pl)*
ironing board **das Bügelbrett(er)**
landlord **der Wirt(e) [-in]**
maid **das Dienstmädchen(-)**
meter **der Zähler(-)**
owner **der Besitzer(-) [-in]**
rent **die Miete(n)**
I rent **ich miete**
I rent out **ich vermiete**
repair **die Reparatur(en)**
I repair **ich repariere**
I return *(give back)* **ich gebe wieder***
ruined **zerstört**
self-service **die Selbstbedienung**
set of keys **der Schlüsselbund(¨e)**
I share **ich teile**
shutters **die Fensterläden** *(pl)*, **die Rolladen** *(pl)*
smelly **übelriechend**
spare key **der Ersatzschlüssel(-)**
well **der Brunnen(-)**
well kept **gutgepflegt**

We rented a cottage.	**Wir mieteten ein Ferienhaus.**
It was really worthwhile.	**Es hat sich wirklich gelohnt.**
We had to pay by the day.	**Wir mußten pro Tag bezahlen.**
It had two double bedrooms, one with bunk beds, a modern kitchen and a bathroom with shower and loo.	**Es hatte zwei Doppelzimmer, ein Zimmer mit Etagenbetten, eine modern eingerichtete Küche und Bad mit Dusche und WC.**
It was in a quiet situation. The advertisement said there was a view, but that was not really true.	**Die Lage war ruhig. In der Anzeige hieß es, daß sie eine gute Aussicht hatte, aber das stimmte eigentlich nicht.**

➤ FURNISHINGS 8c; COOKING UTENSILS App. 10d

Language

21a General terms

accuracy **die Genauigkeit**	grammatical **grammatisch**
accurate **genau sein**	I improve **ich verbessere (mich)**
I adapt **ich passe mich an***	influence **der Einfluß (-̈sse)**
I adopt **ich übernehme**	isolation **die Isoliertheit**
advanced **fortgeschritten**	known **bekannt**
aptitude **die Begabung**	language **die Sprache(n)**
artificial language **die künstliche**	language course **der**
Sprache(n)	**Sprachkurs(e)**
it is based on **es basiert auf** +dat	language family **die**
bilingual **zweisprachig**	**Sprachfamilie(n)**
bilingualism **die Zweisprachigkeit**	language school **die**
borrowing **das Lehnwort(-̈er)**	**Sprachschule(n)**
branch **der Zweig(e)**	language skill **die**
classical language **die klassische**	**(Sprach)fertigkeit(en)**
Sprache(n)	I learn **ich lerne**
it derives from **es stammt aus**	learning **das Lernen**
+dat	level **das Sprachniveau(s)**
development **die Entwicklung(en)**	linguistics **die**
difficult **schwer**	**Sprachwissenschaft(en)**
easy **leicht**	link **die Verbindung(en)**
error **der Fehler(-)**	living **lebendig**
foreign language **die**	major language **die**
Fremdsprache(n)	**Weltsprache(n)**
I forget **ich vergesse**	it means **das bedeutet**
grammar **die Grammatik(en)**	I mime **ich mime**

– You speak good German. Are you bilingual?

– German is my mother tongue. We spoke German at school.

I am not very good at languages, but my sister is a good linguist.

– **Sie sprechen ein gutes Deutsch. Sind Sie zweisprachig?**
– **Deutsch ist meine Muttersprache. Wir haben deutsch in der Schule gesprochen.**

Ich bin nicht sehr gut in Sprachen, aber meine Schwester ist sehr sprachbegabt.

minor language **die weniger bedeutende Sprache(n)**
mistake **der Fehler(-)**
modern language **die Fremdsprache(n)**
monolingual **einsprachig**
mother tongue **die Muttersprache(n)**
mutation **der Wandel** *(no pl)*
name **der Name(n) (gen des Namens)** *(wk)*
nation **das Volk(-̈er)**
national **national**
native **Mutter-, Heimat-**
natural **natürlich**
official **offiziell**
offshoot **der Zweig(e)**
origin **die Herkunft(-̈e)**
phenomenon **die Erscheinung(en)**
I practise/practice **ich übe**
preserved **erhalten**
question **die Frage(n)**
register **das Verzeichnis (-sse), das Register(-)**
separate **einzeln**
sign language **die Zeichensprache(n)**
survival **das Überleben**
it survives **es überlebt**
I translate **ich übersetze, ich übertrage**
translation **die Übersetzung(en)**
I understand **ich verstehe**
unknown **unbekannt**
widely used **weit verbreitet**
witticism **die witzige Bemerkung(en)**

Words & vocabulary

antonym **das Antonym(e)**
colloquial **umgangssprachlich**
consonant **der Konsonant(en)**
dictionary **das Wörterbuch(-̈er)**
expression **der Ausdruck(-̈e)**
idiom **die Redewendung(en)**
idiomatic **idiomatisch**
jargon **der Jargon(s)**
lexicographer **der Lexikograph(en)** *(wk)* **[-in]**
lexicon **das Lexikon(s/-a)**
phrase **die Phrase(n)**
phrase book **der Sprachführer(-)**
sentence **der Satz(-̈e)**
slang **der Slang** *(no pl)*
syllable **die Silbe(n)**
synonym **das Synonym(e)**
vocabulary **der Wortschatz(-̈e)**
vowel **der Vokal(e)**
word *(individual)* **das Wort(-̈er)**
word *(in text)* **das Wort(e)**
word game **das Wortspiel(e)**

We always talk French. | **Wir unterhalten uns immer auf französisch.**

I practise/practice my Spanish with a native speaker. | **Ich übe mein Spanisch mit einem Muttersprachler.**

Writing Urdu is a problem for me as the alphabet is quite different.. They use the Arabic script. | **Es ist für mich ein Problem, Urdu zu schreiben, da das Alphabet ganz anders ist. Sie verwenden die arabische Schrift.**

21b Using language

Speaking & listening

accent **der Akzent(e)**
   regional accent **die regionale Aussprache(n)**
I am articulate **ich spreche (mich) klar aus***
I articulate **ich artikuliere**
clear **klar, deutlich**
colloquial language **die Umgangssprache**
I communicate **ich kommuniziere, ich teile jdm. mit*** +dat
conversation **das Gespräch(e)**
I converse (with) **ich unterhalte mich (mit** +dat)
dialect **der Dialekt(e)**
diction **die Ausdrucksweise(n)**
I express (myself) **ich drücke (mich) aus***
fluent(ly) **fließend**
I interpret **ich dolmetsche**
interpreter **der Dolmetscher(-) [-in]**
intonation **die Betonung(en)**
lisp **das Lispeln**
I lisp **ich lisp(e)le**
I listen to **ich höre jdm. zu*** +dat
listening **das Hören**
listening skills **das Hörverständnis(se)**

I mispronounce **ich spreche falsch aus***
mispronunciation **die falsche Aussprache**
oral **mündlich**
I pronounce **ich spreche aus***
pronunciation **die Aussprache(n)**
rhythm **der Rhythmus (-en)**
I say **ich sage**
sound **der Laut(e)**
I sound **ich klinge**
I speak **ich spreche, ich rede**
speaking **das Sprechen**
speaking skills **die Sprechfähigkeit(en)**
speech **die Sprache(n)**
I give a speech **ich halte eine Rede**
speed **die Schnelligkeit(en)**
spoken **gesprochen**
spoken language **die gesprochene Sprache**
stress **die Betonung(en)**
stressed (un-) **(un)betont**
I stutter/stammer **ich stottere**
I talk **ich spreche**
I tell **ich sage, ich erzähle**
unpronounceable **unaussprechbar**
verbal(ly) **verbal**

What does that mean?	**Wie übersetzt man das?**
What does that mean in English?	**Was heißt/bedeutet das auf englisch?**
How do you pronounce that?	**Wie spricht man das aus?**
How do you spell that?	**Wie schreibt/buchstabiert man das?**
Could you translate that into English?	**Könnten Sie das bitte ins Englische übersetzen?**

Writing & reading

accent **das Akzentzeichen(-)**
   umlaut **der Umlaut(e)**
alphabet **das Alphabet(e)**
alphabetically **alphabetisch**
in bold **fett**
Braille **die Blindenschrift**
character **der Charakter(e)**
code **der Kode**
I correct **ich korrigiere**
I correspond with **ich**
   korrespondiere mit +dat
correspondence **die**
   Korrespondenz
I decypher **ich entziffere**
I draft **ich entwerfe**
graphic **graphisch**
handwriting **die Handschrift**
illiterate **der Analphabet(en)** *(wk)*
   [-in]
italic **der Kursivdruck**
in italics **kursivgedruckt**
letter *(alphabet)* **der Buchstabe(n)**
   (wk)
he is literate **er kann lesen und**
   schreiben
literature **die Literatur(en)**
note **die Anmerkung(en)**
paragraph **der Absatz(ë)**
philology **die**
   Sprachwissenschaft(en)
philologist **der**

Sprachwissenschaftler(-) [-in]
pictogram(me) **das**
   Piktogramm(e)
I print **ich drucke**
I read **ich lese**
reading **das Lesen, die Lektüre**
reading matter **die Lektüre(n), der**
   Lesestoff
reading skills **das**
   Leseverständnis(se)
I re-write **ich schreibe neu, ich**
   schreibe um*
scribble **das Gekritzel**
I scribble **ich kritz(e)le**
sign **das Zeichen(-)**
I sign **ich unterschreibe**
signature **die Unterschrift(en)**
I spell **ich buchstabiere**
spelling **die Rechtschreibung**
text **der Text(e)**
I transcribe **ich schreibe**
   ab*/nieder*
transcription **die Abschrift(en),**
   die Umschrift(en)
I underline **ich unterstreiche**
I write **ich schreibe**
writing **das Schreiben**
writing skills **die**
   Schreibfähigkeit(en)
written language **die**
   Schriftsprache(n)

What is the right spelling?	**Was ist die richtige Schreibweise?**
Don't worry about spelling mistakes.	**Mach dir keine Sorgen über Schreibfehler.**
The stem is modified by an umlaut.	**Der Stamm wird umgelautet.**
The verb goes to the end.	**Das Verb steht am Ende.**
That is colloquial German.	**Das ist Umgangssprache.**

➤ WORDS & VOCABULARY 21a; GRAMMAR, PUNCTUATION App.21b

Education

22a General terms

absent **abwesend**
achievement **die Leistung(en)**
admission **die Einschulung**
    I am admitted to school **ich werde eingeschult**
age group **die Altersstufe(n)**
aptitude **die Fertigkeit(en), das Talent(e)**
I analyze **ich analysiere**
answer **die Antwort(en)**
I answer **ich antworte**
    I answer (someone) **ich beantworte (jdn.)**
    I answer (a question) **ich antworte auf (eine Frage)**
I ask (a question) **ich stelle (eine Frage)**
    I ask (someone) **ich frage (jdn.)**
I attend (a school) **ich besuche (eine Schule)**
career **der Beruf(e)**
careers advice **die Berufsberatung(en)**
careers education **die Berufsorientierung(en)**
careers teacher **der Berufsberater(-)**
caretaker **der Hausmeister(-)**
I catch up **ich hole nach***
chapter **das Kapitel(-)**
I cheat **ich mogele**
class **die Klasse(n)**
class council **der Klassenrat(-̈e)**
class representative **der Klassensprecher(-)**
class teacher **der Klassenlehrer(-)**
class trip **die Klassenfahrt(en)**
club **der Klub(s), der Verein(e)**
I complete **ich vollende**
comprehension **das**
Verständnis(se)
compulsory schooling **die Schulpflicht**
computer **der Computer(-)**
concept **das Konzept(e)**
I copy (out) **ich kopiere ... aus***
copy **die Kopie(n)**
course **der Kurs(e), das Seminar(e)**
deputy head **der/die stellvertretende Schulleiter(-)**
detention **das Nachsitzen**
    I am in detention **ich sitze nach***
difficult **schwierig**
discuss **besprechen**
easy **leicht**
education **die Bildung, die Erziehung**
educational system **das Bildungssystem(e)**
I encourage **ich fördere**
essay **der Aufsatz(-̈e)**
example **das Beispiel(e)**
excellent **ausgezeichnet, vortrefflich**
favourite/favorite **der Liebling(e), Lieblings-**
favourite/favorite subject **das Lieblingsfach(-̈er)**
I forget **ich vergesse**
governing body **der Schulausschuß(-̈e)**
grade **die Klasse(n)**
holidays **die Ferien** (pl)
headteacher/principal **der Schulleiter(-)[-in]**
homework **die Hausaufgabe(n)**
instruction **der Unterricht**
interesting **interessant**
I learn **ich lerne**

I leave **ich verlasse**
lesson **die Stunde(n)**
   lesson *(chapter)* **die Lektion(en)**
   lessons **der Unterricht**
I listen **ich höre** +dat **zu***
local education authority **die Schulbehörde(n)**
I look at **ich sehe ... an***
I misunderstand **ich mißverstehe**
mixed ability group **die undifferenzierte Gruppe(n)**
modular **aus Elementen zusammengesetzt**
module **die Einheit(en), das Element(e)**
oral **mündlich**
outdoor **im Freien**
out of school activity **die Arbeitsgemeinschaft(en)**
parents' evening **der Elternabend(e)**
pastoral care **das Tutorensystem(e)**
I play truant **ich schwänze die Schule**
principal **der Direktor(en) [-in]**
project **das Projekt(e), die Projektarbeit(en)**
punctual **pünktlich**
I punctuate **ich setze die Satzzeichen**
punctuation mark **das Satzzeichen(-)**
I punish **ich bestrafe**
punishment **die Strafe(n)**
pupil **der Schüler(-)[-in]**
qualification **die Qualifikation(en)**
I qualify **ich qualifiziere**
question **die Frage(n)**
I question **ich befrage (jdn.)**
I read **ich lese**
reading **das Lesen**
I repeat a year **ich wiederhole das Jahr**
report **das Zeugnis(se)**
research **die Forschung(en)**
I research **ich forsche**

resources centre/center **die Mediathek(en)**
scheme of work **der Lehrplan(-̈e)**
school book **das Schulbuch(-̈er)**
school council **der Schulausschuß (-̈sse)**
school-friend **der Klassenkamerad(en)**
set **die Leistungsgruppe(n)**
   the school sets **die Schule differenziert**
   setted *(by ability)* **differenziert nach Leistung**
skill **die Fertigkeit(en)**
specialist teacher **der Fachlehrer(-)**
spelling **die Rechtschreibung, die Orthographie**
staff **das Lehrerkollegium (-ien)**
I stay in **ich sitze nach***
I stay down **ich bleibe sitzen***
stream **die Leistungsgruppe(n)**
strict **streng**
I study **ich studiere, ich lerne**
sum **die Rechenaufgabe(n)**
I summarize **ich fasse zusammen***
I swot **ich büffele, ich pauke**
task **die Aufgabe(n)**
I teach **ich lehre, unterrichte**
teacher **der Lehrer(-) [-in]**
teaching **der Unterricht**
term/semester **das Semester(-)**
I train **ich lasse mich ausbilden**
training **die Ausbildung(en)**
I translate **ich übersetze**
translation **die Ubersetzung(en)**
tutor **der Klassenlehrer(-) [-in]**
I understand **ich verstehe**
understanding **das Verständnis(se), der Verstand**
unit (of work) **die Einheit(en)**
I work **ich arbeite**
   I work at ... **ich arbeite an** +dat
work experience **das Betriebspraktikum (-a)**
I write **ich schreibe**
written work **die schriftliche Arbeit(en)**

➤ FURTHER & HIGHER EDUCATION 22d

22b School

blackboard **die Tafel(n)**
black-out **das Blackout**
book **das Buch(¨er)**
break **die Pause(n)**
briefcase **die Mappe(n)**
canteen **die Kantine(n)**
cassette *(audio/video)* **die Kassette(n)**
cassette recorder **der Kassettenrecorder(-)**
classroom **das Klassenzimmer(-)**
computer **der Computer(-)**
desk **das Pult(e)**
dormitory **das Schlafsaal (-säle)**
gym(nasium) **die Turnhalle(n)**
headphone **der Kopfhörer(-)**
interactive TV **das interaktive Fernsehen**
laboratory **das Laboratorium (-ien)**
language laboratory **das Sprachlabor(s)**
library **die Bibliothek(en)**
lunch-hour **die Mittagspause(n)**
note **die Anmerkung(en)**
office **das Büro(s)**
playground **der Schulhof(¨e)**
radio **das Radio(s)**
rubber/eraser **das Radiergummi(s)**
ruler **das Lineal(e)**
slide **das Dia(s)**
satellite TV **das Satellitenfernsehen**

school hall **der Saal(Säle), die Halle(n)**
schoolbag/satchel/bookbag **die Schulmappe(n)**
sports field **der Sportplatz(¨e)**
sports hall **die Sporthalle(n)**
staffroom **das Lehrerzimmer(-)**
studio **das Studio(s)**
timetable **der Stundenplan(¨e)**
video **das Video(s)**
video-player **das Videogerät(e)**
video camera **die Videokamera(s)**
video cassette **die Videokassette(n)**
video recorder **der Videorecorder(-)**
workshop **das Werkstatt(¨en)**

Type of school

boarding school **das Internat(e)**
comprehensive school **die Gesamtschule(n)**
day school **das Externat(e)**
further education **die Weiterbildung**
grammar school **das Gymnasium (-ien)**
infant school **die Vorschule(n)**
nursery school **der Kindergarten(¨)**
playgroup **die Spielgruppe(n)**
primary school **die Grundschule(n)**
school **die Schule(n)**

– At what age do children start school?
– They have to go to school when they are six. Our son already goes to the kindergarten and is looking forward to school.

I would like to go to college to study environmental science.

– In welchem Alter kommen die Kinder in die Schule?
– Mit sechs werden sie schulpflichtig. Unser Sohn geht schon zum Kindergarten und freut sich auf die Schule.

Ich möchte gern auf die Hochschule gehen, um die Umweltswissenschaften zu studieren.

➤ SCHOOL SUBJECTS, EXAMINATIONS 22c; STATIONERY App.22b

school type **die Schulform(en)**
of school age **schulpflichtig**
secondary **Sekundar-**
secondary school/junior high school
die Sekundarschule(n)
secondary modern school/senior
high school **die Hauptschule(n)**
sixth form/senior year **die
Oberstufe(n)**
sixth-form college **das
Oberstufenzentrum (-en)**
special school **die Sonderschule(n)**
technical school **die Realschule(n)**

Classroom commands

Answer the question! **Beantworte
die Frage!**
Be careful! **Vorsicht!, Passen Sie
auf!**
Be quiet! **Ruhe!**
Be quick! **Macht schnell!**
Bring me your work! **Bring' mir
deine Aufgabe!**
Clean the blackboard! **Mach' die
Tafel sauber!**
Close the door! **Machen Sie die Tür
bitte zu!**
Come here! **Komm' mal her!**
Come in! **Kommen Sie bitte herein!**
Copy these sentences! **Kopieren
Sie diese Sätze!**
Do your homework! **Macht eure
Hausaufgaben!**

Don't talk/chatter! **Bitte nicht reden!**
Go out! **Geht hinaus!**
Learn by heart! **Lernt auswendig!**
Learn the vocabulary! **Lern' die
Vokabeln!**
Listen carefully! **Hören Sie gut zu!**
Make less noise! **Machen Sie nicht
so viel Krach!**
Make notes! **Macht Notizen!**
Open the window! **Mach' das
Fenster auf!**
Pay attention! **Paßt gut auf!**
Put on the headphones! **Legt die
Kopfhörer auf!**
Read the text! **Lies' den Text (vor)!**
Show me your book! **Zeig' mir dein
Heft!**
Sit down! **Setzt euch!**
Stand up! **Aufstehen!**
Tick the boxes! **Abhaken!**
Work in pairs! **Jetzt Partnerarbeit!**
Work in groups! **Jetzt
Gruppenarbeit!**
Write an essay! **Jetzt schreiben wir
einen Aufsatz!**
Write it down! **Schreiben Sie es auf!**
Write out in rough! **Macht einen
Entwurf!**
Write out in neat/neatly! **Bitte
schön ausschreiben!**

Our daughter goes to the primary/
elementary school. She reads to
her teacher every day and can
read well now.

– Do you move up a class every
year?
– No, last year I had to stay down
a year.

**Unsere Tochter geht zur
Grundschule. Jeden Tag liest
sie ihrer Lehrerin vor und kann
jetzt gut lesen.**

– Bist du jedes Jahr versetzt?

**– Nein, letztes Jahr mußte ich
sitzenbleiben.**

➤ THE CLASS IN GERMANY App.22b; GENERAL EDUCATIONAL TERMS 22a

22c School subjects & examinations

School subjects

arithmetic **das Rechnen**
art **die Kunst, das Zeichnen**
biology **die Biologie**
business studies **die Wirtschaftkunde**
careers education **die Arbeitslehre**
chemistry **die Chemie**
CDT/crafts, design and technology **das Werken**
commerce **die Betriebswirtschaft**
compulsory subject **das Pflichtfach(-er)**
computer studies **die Informatik**
design technology **die Technologie**
economics **die Wirtschaftskunde**
English **das Englisch**

foreign language **die Fremdsprache(n)**
French **das Französisch**
geography **die Erdkunde, die Geographie**
German **das Deutsch**
Greek **das Griechisch**
gymnastics **das Turnen**
history **die Geschichte**
home economics **die Hauswirtschaft**
Italian **das Italienisch**
information technology **die Informatik**
Latin **das Latein**
law **die Rechtskunde**
main subject **der Leistungskurs(e)**

Examinations in Germany

das Abitur A level exam
der Abiturient(en) [-] A level candidate
das Staatsexamen(-) final examination
die mittlere Reife 16+ examination
die Abschlußprüfung(en) school leaving exam
der Hauptschulabschluß(üsse)

school leaving certificate
der Realschulabschluß(üsse) school leaving certificate

Marks

1 sehr gut very good
2 gut good
3 befriedigend satisfactory
4 ausreichend pass
5 mangelhaft poor
6 ungenügend unsatisfactory

– Which school do you go to?
– I go to the comprehensive. I enjoy it a lot. There are lots of clubs and activities.
– Which is your favourite subject?
– I like maths/math, but prefer physics. I don't like history, it is so boring.

– **Welche Schule besuchst du?**
– **Ich besuche die Gesamtschule. Es gefält mir sehr. Es gibt viele Klubs und Arbeitsgemeinschaften.**
– **Was ist dein Lieblingsfach?**
– **Ich mag gern Mathe, aber mache lieber Physik. Geschichte mag ich überhaupt nicht, es ist so langweilig.**

mathematics **die Mathematik**
metalwork **die Metallarbeit**
music **die Musik**
option(al subject) **das
    Wahlfach(⸚er)**
philosophy **die Philosophie**
physical education **der Sport**
physics **die Physik**
religious education **die Religion**
science **die Naturwissenschaft(en)**
sex education **die Sexualerziehung**
social studies **die
    Gemeinschaftskunde**
sociology **die Sozialkunde**
Spanish **das Spanisch**
sport **der Sport**
    type of sport **die Sportart(en)**
subject **das Fach(⸚er)**
subsidiary subject **der
    Grundkurs(e), das
    Nebenfach(⸚er)**
technical drawing **das technische
    Zeichnen**
technology **die Technologie**
textiles **die Textilarbeit(en)**
woodwork **die Holzarbeit(en)**

Examinations

I assess **ich bewerte, ich benote**
assessment **die Bewertung(en)**
certificate **das Zertifikat(e)**
degree **das Diplom(e)**
diploma **das Diplom(e)**

dissertation **die Dissertation(en)**
distinction **die Auszeichnung(en)**
doctorate **das Doktorat(e)**
examination **die Prüfung(en), das
    Examen(-)**
    external **extern**
    final **Schluß-**
grade **die Zensur(en), die Note(n)**
I grade **ich benote, ich zensiere**
graduate engineer **der
    Diplomingenieur(-)**
listening comprehension **das
    Hörverständnis(se)**
mark **die Note(n)**
mark system **das Notensystem(e)**
masters **die Magisterarbeit(en)**
merit **die Auszeichnung(en)**
oral **mündlich**
point **der Punkt(e)**
post-graduate course **der
    Anschlußkurs(e)**
reading comprehension **das
    Leseverständnis(se)**
I pass (an exam) **ich lege (ein
    Examen) ab***
I test **ich teste, ich prüfe**
test **der Test(s)**
thesis **die Doktorarbeit(en)**
trainee **der Azubi(s)/
    Auszubildende(n)** *(adj/n)*
written test **die schriftliche
    Prüfung(en)**

My favourite/favorite subject is PE.

Mein Lieblingsfach ist Sport.

I'm good at English, since I did an exchange. I work very hard at it.

Ich kann gut Englisch, da ich einen Austausch gemacht habe. Ich arbeite sehr fleißig daran.

After school I do sports and I am in the football/soccer team.

Nach der Schule mache ich Sport, und ich bin Mitglied der Fußballmannschaft.

➤ SCHOOL 22b; USING LANGUAGE 21b

22d Further and higher education

adult **der/die Erwachsene(n)** *(adj/n)*
  adult *(adj)* **erwachsen**
adult education **die**
  Erwachsenenbildung
alumnus **der ehemalige Schüler(-)**
apprentice **der Lehrling(e)**
apprenticeship **die Lehre(n)**
chair **der Lehrstuhl (¨e)**
college **die Hochschule(n)**
  college of FE **die**
  berufsbildende Schule(n)
  college of HE **die**
  Hochschule(n)
course of study **das Studium (-ien)**
diploma **das Diplom(e)**
dual system **das duale System**
faculty **das Seminar(e), die**
  Fakultät(en)
hall of residence/residence hall
  das Wohnheim(e)
in-service training **die Weiterbildung**
lecture **das Referat(e), die**
  Vorlesung(en)
lecture hall **der Hörsaal (-säle)**
lecturer **der Referent(en)** *(wk)* **[-in]**

masters degree **der**
  Magisterabschluß(¨e)
part-time FE **die Berufschule(n)**
part-time education **die**
  Teilzeitschule(n)
polytechnic **die technische**
  Hochschule(n)
practical **das Praktikum (-a)**
principal **der Direktor(en) [-in]**
professor/college professor **der**
  Professor(en) [-in]
quota (for university entry) **der**
  Numerus clausus
research **die Forschung(en)**
retraining **die Umschulung**
I retrain **ich lasse mich umschulen**
scholarship **die Stipendium (-ien)**
seminar **das Seminar(e)**
sorority/fraternity **die**
  Studentenverbindung(en)
student **der Student(en)[-in]**wk
student council **der**
  Studentenrat(¨e)
student grant **das Bafög**
  (Bundesausbildungsausförde-

We have increased the number of
universities and are aiming for a
broader provision.

Wir haben die Anzahl der
Hochschulen erhöht und
erzielen ein breiteres Angebot.

The technical colleges now belong
to the university sector.

Die Fachhochschulen gehören
jetzt zum Hochschulbereich.

Admission to the technical colleges
is possible without the *Abitur*.
The length of course is four years
(eight terms/semesters).

Der Zugang zu den
Fachhochschulen ist auch ohne
Abitur möglich. Die
Studiendauer beträgt vier Jahre
(acht Semester).

Financial support is of the greatest
importance.

Die finanzielle Förderung ist von
großer Bedeutung.

rungsgesetz)
student association **die Studentenverbindung(en)**
teacher training college **die pädagogische Hochschule(n)**
technical college **die technische Hochschule(n)**
university/college **die Universität(en)**
university entrance qualification **die Hochschulreife**
vocational route **der zweite Bildungsweg**

Subjects

accountancy/accounting **die Buchführung**
architecture **die Architektur**
business management **die Betriebswirtschaftslehre**
catering **das Gaststättengewerbe**
classics **die Altphilologie**
civil engineering **der Hoch- und Tiefbau**
commerce **das Betriebswesen**
construction **das Bauwesen**
education **die Pädagogik**

electronics **die Elektronik**
electrical engineering **die Elektroinstallation**
economics **die Ökonomie**
engineering **das Ingenieurwesen**
environmental sciences **die Umweltkunde**
history of art **die Kunstgeschichte**
hotel management **das Hotelwesen**
languages **die Fremdsprachen** *(pl)*
law **die Rechswissenschaft, die Jura**
leisure and tourism **(die) Freizeit und (der)Tourismus**
literature **die Literatur**
mechanical engineering **der Maschinenbau**
medicine **die Medizin**
pharmacy **die Pharmarzie**
nuclear science **die Kernwissenschaft**
office skills **das Bürowesen**
philosophy **die Philosophie**
psychology **die Psychologie**
sociology **die Soziologie**
theology **die Theologie**

Many students get a state grant.	**Viele Studenten erhalten BAFöG-Förderung.**
Many students apply for places but they cannot all be admitted.	**Viele Studenten machen den Antrag auf einen Platz, aber sie können nicht alle zugelassen werden.**
There is now an entrance restriction. The right to a place depends on marks in the *Abitur*. They require particularly high marks for medicine.	**Es gibt jetzt den numerus clausus. Das Recht auf einen Platz hängt von den Noten im Abitur ab. Für Medizin braucht man besonders gute Zensuren.**
Our results are always outstanding.	**Unsere Prüfungsergebnisse sind immer hervorragend.**

➤ LANGUAGES App.21a; SCIENTIFIC DISCIPLINES App.23a

Science: the changing world

23a Science & biology

Scientific method

academic paper **die theoretische/ akademische Arbeit(en)**
I analyze **ich analysiere**
authentic **authentisch**
I challenge **ich stelle in Frage**
I check **ich prüfe**
classification **die Klassifizierung(en), die Einteilung(en)**
I classify **ich klassifiziere, ich ordne**
I conduct *(an experiment)* **ich führe durch*, ich leite**
control **die Kontrolle(n)**
I control **ich kontrolliere**
dial **die Skala (-en)**
experiment **das Experiment(e), der Versuch(e)**
I experiment **ich experimentiere**
flask **der Kolben(-)**
gauge **das Meßgerät(e)**
hypothesis **die Hypothese(n)**
I identify **ich identifiziere**
invention **die Erfindung(en)**

I investigate **ich untersuche**
laboratory **das Laboratorium (-ien)**
material **das Material(ien)**
I measure **ich messe**
measurement **die Messung(en), das Maß(e)**
(electron) microscope **das (Elektronen)mikroskop(e)**
I observe **ich beobachte**
observation **die Beobachtung(en)**
origin **der Ursprung(¨e)**
pipette **die Pipette(n)**
research **die Forschung(en)**
I research **ich (er)forsche**
result **das Resultat(e)**
scientific **wissenschaftlich**
I solve (a problem) **ich löse (ein Problem)**
I sort **ich sortiere**
test **die Probe(n)**
I test **ich teste, ich prüfe**
test-tube **das Reagenzglas(¨er)**
theory **die Theorie(n)**
I transfer **ich versetze**

Research on human embryo tissue is likely to remain highly controversial.

Die Forschung am menschlichen Embryogewebe wird wohl sehr umstritten bleiben.

The researcher took a sample, mounted it on a slide and put it under the microscope for examination. All the results from the experiments support her hypothesis.

Die Forscherin nahm eine Probe, gab sie auf einen Objektträger und legte sie zum Untersuchen unter das Mikroskop. Alle Untersuchungsergebnisse unterstützen ihre Hypothese.

Life sciences

bacteria **die Bakterie(n)**
botanical **botanisch**
I breathe **ich atme**
cell **die Zelle(n)**
chlorophyll **das Chlorophyl**
it circulates **es zirkuliert, es fließt**
decay **der Verfall**
it decays **es verfault**
decline **der Nieder-/Rückgang(-̈e)**
it declines **es geht zurück***
it excretes **es scheidet aus***
excretion **die Ausscheidung(en)**
it feeds (on) **es frißt, es ernährt
  sich (von** +dat)
food chain **die Nahrungskette(n)**
gene **das Gen(e)**
gene bank **die Gen-Bank(en)**
genetic **genetisch**
genetics **die Genetik**
genetic disorder **die genetische
  Krankheit(en)**
it grows **es wächst**
growth **das Wachstum**
habitat **der Lebensraum(-̈e)**
I inherit **ich erbe**
mammal **das Säugetier(e)**
membrane **die Membran(en)**
it mutates **es verändert sich, es
  mutiert**
nucleus **der Nukleus (Nuklei)**
organic **organisch**
organism **der Organismus (-en)**
photosynthesis **die
  Photosynthese(n)**
population **die Menge(n), die
  Bevölkerung**
process **der Prozeß (-sse)**
it reproduces **es reproduziert sich**
respiration **die Atmung(en)**
sample **die Probe(n)**
sensitivity **die Empfindlichkeit(en)**
slide **der Objektträger(-)**
survival **das Überleben**
it survives **es überlebt**
virus **der Virus (-en)**

Medical science & research

ante-natal tests (on foetus) **die
  Schwangerschaftsunter-
  suchung(en)**
cosmetic surgery **die
  Schönheitsoperation(en)**
DNA **die DNS**
donor **der Blutspender(-) [-in]**
embryo **der Embryo(s)**
embryo research **die
  embryonische
  Untersuchung(en)**
ethical consideration **ethische
  Ansichten** (pl)
ethics of human reproduction **die
  Ethik** (pl) **der menschlichen
  Fortpflanzung**
experiment on animals **der
  Tierversuch(e)**
hereditary illness **die
  Erbkrankheit(en)**
IVF (in vitro fertilization) **die in
  vitro Befruchtung**
I justify **ich rechtfertige**
microorganism **der
  Mikroorganismus (-en)**
organ transplant **die
  Organtransplantation(en), das
  Transplantat(e)**
pacemaker **der
  (Herz)schrittmacher(-)**
I permit **ich erlaube jdm.**
plastic surgery **die plastische
  Chirurgie**
psychology **die Psychologie**
recipient **der Empfänger(-) [-in]**
I reject (an organ) **ich stoße (ein
  Organ) ab***
risk **das Risiko (-en)**
I risk **ich riskiere**
survival rate **die Überlebensrate**
test-tube baby **das Retortenbaby
  (-ies)**
transplant **das Transplantat(e)**
X-ray **die Röntgenstrahlung(en)**
I X-ray **ich röntge**

➤ MEDICAL TREATMENT 11c; THE ANIMAL WORLD 24b

23b Physical sciences

Chemistry

acid **die Säure(n)**
air **die Luft(-e)**
alkali **das Alkali**
alkaline **basisch**
alkaline solution **die Lauge(n)**
boiling-point **der Siedepunkt(e)**
Bunsen burner **der
    Bunsenbrenner(-)**
I calculate **ich berechne, ich
    kalkuliere**
chemical **chemisch**
compound **die Verbindung(en)**
composition **die
    Zusammensetzung(en)**
it dissolves **es löst sich (auf)***
it dissolves in water **es ist
    wasserlöslich**
element **das Element(e)**
emulsion **die Emulsion(en)**
equation **die Gleichung(en)**
gas **das Gas(e)**
inorganic **anorganisch**
insoluble **unlöslich**
liquid **die Flüssigkeit(en)**
    liquid *(adj)* **flüssig**
Litmus paper **das Lackmuspapier**
matter **die Materie, der Stoff(e)**
metal **das Metall(e)**
natural gas **das Erdgas(e)**
opaque **undurchsichtig**
periodic table **das
    Periodensystem**
physical **physikalisch**
pure **rein**
it reacts **es reagiert**
reaction **die Reaktion(en)**
salt **das Salz(e)**
solid **der Festkörper(-)**
    solid *(adj)* **fest**
soluble **löslich**
solution **die Lösung(en)**
stable **fest, stabil**
substance **die Substanz(en)**
transparent **durchsichtig**

Physics & mechanics

it accelerates **es beschleunigt**
acceleration **die
    Beschleunigung(en)**
acoustic(s) **die Akustik**
analysis **die Analyse(n)**
artificial **künstlich**
automatic **automatisch**
ball-bearing **das Kugellager(-)**
conservation **die Erhaltung**
density **die Dichte(n)**
distance **die Distanz(en)**
energy **die Energie**
engine **der Motor(en)**
it expands **es dehnt sich aus***
fibre/fiber **die Faser(n)**
force **die Kraft(-e), die Stärke(n)**
it freezes **es gefriert**
formula **die Formel(n)**
freezing-point **der Gefrierpunkt(e)**
friction **die Reibung(en), die
    Friktion**
gear **das Getriebe**
gravity **die Schwerkraft(-e)**
    centre/center of gravity **der
    Schwerpunkt(-)**
    law of gravity **das
    Gravitationsgesetz**
I heat **ich erhitze**
heat **die Hitze, die Wärme**
heat loss **der Wärmeverlust(e)**
laser **der Laser(-)**
laser beam **der Laserstrahl(en)**
light **das Licht(er)**
light beam **der Lichtstrahl(en)**
lubricant **das Schmiermittel(-)**
machinery **der Mechanismus
    (-en)**
magnetism **der Magnetismus**
magneto **der Magnetzünder(-)**
mass **die Masse(n)**
mechanics **der Maschinenbau**
mechanical **mechanisch**
mechanism **der Mechanismus (-en)**
mechanics **die Mechanik**

metallurgy **die Metallurgie**
microscope **das Mikroskop(e)**
microwave **die Mikrowelle(n)**
mineral **das Mineral(e)**
missile **das Geschoß (-sse), die Rakete(n)**
model **das Modell(e)**
motion **die Bewegung(en)**
I operate *(machinery)* **ich bediene**
optics **die Optik**
pressure **der Druck(-e)**
property **die Eigenschaft(en)**
proportional **proportional**
ray **der (Licht)strahl(en)**
reflection **die Reflexion(en)**
refraction **die Brechung(en)**
relativity **die Relativität**
  relativity theory **die Relativitätstheorie**
resistance **der Widerstand(-e)**
resistant **widerstandsfähig**
robot **der Roboter(-)**
sound **der Schall(-e)**
speed **die Geschwindigkeit(en)**
structure **die Struktur(en)**
synthetic **synthetisch, künstlich**
temperature **die Temperatur(en)**
theory **die Theorie(n)**
transmission **die Übertragung(en)**
I transmit **ich übertrage**
vapour/vapor **der Dampf(-e)**
it vibrates **es vibriert**
vibration **die Vibration(en)**
wave **die Welle(n)**
  long wave **die Langwelle(n)**
  medium/short wave **die Kurzwelle(n)**
wavelength **die Wellenlänge(n)**

Electricity

alternating current **der Wechselstrom**
battery **die Batterie(n)**
charge **die Ladung(en)**
I charge the battery **ich lade die Batterie auf***
circuit **der Stromkreis(e)**
current **der Strom(-e), die Strömung(en)**
direct current **der Gleichstrom**
electrical **elektrisch**
electricity **die Elektrizität**
electrode **die Elektrode(n)**
electron **das Elektron(en)**
electronic **elektronisch**
electronics **die Elektronik**
positive **positiv**
negative **negativ**
voltage **die Spannung(en)**

Nuclear physics

atom **das Atom(e)**
atomic **atomar, Atom-**
fission **die Spaltung(en)**
fusion **die Verschmelzung(en)**
molecular **molekular**
molecule **das Molekül(e)**
neutron **das Neutron(en)**
nuclear **Nuklear-, Kern-**
nuclear energy **die Nuklearenergie**
nuclear reactor **der Kernreaktor(en)**
nucleus **der Nukleus, der Kern(e)**
particle **das Partikel(-)**
proton **das Proton(en)**
quantum theory **die Quantentheorie(n)**
radiation **die (Aus)strahlung(en)**

Water has a boiling point of 100 degrees centigrade.	**Der Siedepunkt des Wassers liegt bei 100 Grad Celsius.**
What is the wattage of this appliance?	**Wieviel Watt hat dieses Gerät?**

➤ MEASURING 4b; DESCRIBING THINGS 5c; ENERGY 23c

23c The earth & space

Energy & fuels

coal **die Kohle(n)**
concentration **die Konzentration(en)**
coolant **das Kühlmittel(-)**
energy **die Energie(n)**
energy conservation **die Energiesparmaßnahmen** *(pl)*
energy consumption **der Energieverbrauch**
energy crisis **die Energiekrise(n)**
energy needs **der Energiebedarf**
energy source **die Energiequelle(n)**
energy waste **die Energieverschwendung**
fossil fuel **der fossile Brennstoff(e)**
fuel **der Treibstoff**
fuel consumption **der Kraftstoffverbrauch**
it generates **es erzeugt**
geothermal energy **die geothermische Energie**
global warming **die globale Erwärmung**
greenhouse effect **der Treibhauseffekt**
hole in the ozone layer **das Ozonloch(-̈er)**
hydro-electric dam **der hydro-elektrische Damm(-̈e)**
hydro-electric power **die Wasserkraft**
insulation **die Isolation**
natural gas **das Erdgas(e)**
nuclear energy **die Atomenergie, die Kernkraft**
nuclear power station **das Kernkraftwerk(e)**
oil **das Öl(e)**
oil production **die Ölherstellung**
oil-producing country **das Ölförderland(-̈er)**
ozone layer **die Ozonschicht**

petroleum **das Petroleum, das Erdöl(e)**
propellant *(rocket fuel)* **der Raketentreibstoff(e)**
raw materials **der Rohstoff(e)**
solar cell **die Solarzelle(n)**
solar energy **die Solarenergie**
thermal energy **die Wärmeenergie**
wave power **die Wellenkraft**
tidal power station **das Gezeitenkraftwerk**
wind energy/power **die Windenergie**

Geology

carbon-dating **die Kohlenstoffdatierung**
I excavate **ich grabe aus***
geologist **der Geologe(n)** *(wk)*
gemstone **der Edelstein(e)**
layer **die Schicht(en)**
loam **der Lehm**
mine **das Bergwerk(e)**
I mine (for) **ich grabe (nach +dat)**
ore **das Erz(e)**
quarry **der Steinbruch(-̈e)**
sand **der Sand(e)**
sediment **das Sediment(e), die Ablagerung(en)**
soil **das Erdreich**
stalactite **der Stalaktit(en)** *(wk)*
stalagmite **der Stalagmit(en)** *(wk)*

Space

asteroid **der Asteroid(en)**
eclipse **die Finsternis(se)**
it eclipses **es verfinstert**
galactic **galaktisch**
galaxy **das Sternsystem(e)**
light year **das Lichtjahr(e)**
meteorite **der Meteorit(en)** *(wk)*
moon **der Mond(e)**
full moon **der Vollmond**
new moon **der Neumond**
orbit **der Orbit(s), die**

➤ COMPOUNDS, MINERALS App.23b; POLLUTION 24e

Planetenbahn(en)
planet   **der Planet(en)**
shooting-star   **die Sternschnuppe(n)**
solar system   **das Sonnensystem(e)**
solstice   **die Sonnenwende(n)**
space   **der Raum, das Weltall**
star   **der Stern(e)**
sun   **die Sonne(n)**
sunspot   **der Sonnenfleck(en)**
the heavens   **der Himmel(-)**
universe   **das Universum (-en), das Weltall**

Space research & travel

antenna   **die Antenne(n)**
astrologer   **der Astrolog(en)** *(wk)*
astronomer   **der Astronom(en)** *(wk)*
astronaut   **der Astronaut(en)** *(wk)*
big-bang theory   **die Urknalltheorie**
cosmonaut   **der Kosmonaut(en)** *(wk)*
dish antenna   **die Parabolantenne(n)**
gravitational pull   **die Anziehungskraft**
launch   **der Raketenabschuß (-sse)**
launch pad   **die Abschußrampe(n)**
space module   **die Raumkapsel(n)**
moon-buggy   **das**

Mondfahrzeug(e)
moon-landing   **die Mondlandung(en)**
observatory   **das Observatorium (-ien)**
orbit   **der Orbit(s)**
planetarium   **das Planetarium (-ien)**
it re-enters   **es tritt wieder ein***
relativity   **die Relativität**
rocket   **die Rakete(n)**
rocket fuel   **der Raketenkraftstoff(e)**
satellite   **der Satellit(en)** *(wk)*
   communications   **der Kommunikationssatellit(en)**
   spy   **der Spionagesatellit(en)**
   weather   **der Wettersatellit(en)**
sky lab   **das Observatorium (-ien)**
space   **der Weltraum**
space flight   **der Weltraumflug(-e)**
space probe   **die Weltraumsonde(n)**
space shuttle   **die Raumfähre(n)**
space walk   **der Weltraumspaziergang(-e)**
spacecraft   **das Raumschiff(e)**
spacesuit   **der Raumanzug(-e)**
stratosphere   **die Stratosphäre**
telescope   **das Teleskop(e)**
time-warp   **die Zeitverzerrung**
touchdow   **die Landung(en), das Aufsetzen**
zodiac   **der Tierkreis(e)**

By studying the light received from stars many millions of light years away, scientists hope to discover the origins of the universe.

Durch die Untersuchung des Lichtes, welches von Sternen empfangen wird, die viele Lichtjahre entfernt sind, hoffen die Wissenschaftler, den Ursprung des Universums zu entdecken/ergründen.

The earth orbits the sun.

Die Erde umkreist die Sonne.

➤ PLANETS & STARS, SIGNS OF THE ZODIAC App.23c

The Environment: the natural world

24a Geography

area **das Gebiet(e), die Gegend(en)**
bottom **der Fuß(-̈sse), der Grund(-̈e)**
clean **sauber**
continent **der Kontinent(e)**
country **das Land(-̈er), das Gelände(-)**
   in the country **auf dem Land(e)**
countryside **die Landschaft(en)**
dangerous **gefährlich**
deep **tief**
dirty **schmutzig**
earth tremor **die Erschütterung(en)**
earthquake **das Erdbeben(-)**
equator **der Äquator**
equatorial **äquatorial**
eruption **der Ausbruch(-̈e)**
it erupts **es bricht aus*** *(brechen)*
flat **flach, glatt**
it floods **es läuft über*** *(laufen)*, **es überschwemmt**

it flows **es fließt**
friendly **freundlich, angenehm**
geographical **geographisch**
geography **die Geographie**
gradient **die Steigung(en), das Gefälle(-)**
hemisphere **die Hemisphäre(n), die Halbkugel(n)**
high **hoch**
hill **der Hügel(-), der Berg(e)**
incline/slope **der Abhang(-̈e)**
it is situated **es ist gelegen, es liegt**
lake **der See(n)**
land **das Land(-̈er)**
   land *(property/real estate)* **der Grund und Boden**
it is located **es ist gelegen, es liegt**
location **die Lage(n)**
map **die Karte(n)**
mountain **der Berg(e)**
national park **der Nationalpark(s)**
nature **die Natur**

Germany extends from the mountains of the Alps to the North and Baltic Seas. There are no natural frontiers to the west and east.

The Zugspitze is the highest mountain in the Bavarian Alps.

In the central mountain area one finds plateaux, hills, volcanic mountains and valleys.

Deutschland reicht vom Hochgebirge der Alpen bis zur Nord- und Ostsee. Es gibt keine natürliche Abgrenzung nach Westen und Osten.

Die Zugspitze ist der höchste Berg in den Bayerischen Alpen.

In der Mittelgebirgszone findet man Hochflächen, Berglandschaften, vulkanische Formen und Tallandschaften.

nature conservancy **der Naturschutz**
nature trail **der Naturlehrpfad(e)**
peaceful **ruhig, friedlich, still**
pleasant **angenehm**
pole **der Pol(e)**
province **die Provinz(en)**
region **die Region(en), das Gebiet(e)**
regional **regional**
river **der Fluß (-̈sse)**
sand **der Sand(e)**
scenery **die Landschaft(en)**
sea **die See(n), das Meer(e)**
  shallow sea **das Wattenmeer**
by the seaside **am Meer**
spring **die Quelle(n)**
steep **steil**
tall **hoch**
territory **das Gebiet(e)**
top **die Spitze(n), der Gipfel(-)**
the tropics **die Tropen** *(pl)*
unfriendly **unfreundlich**
water **das Wasser(-)**
  fresh water **das Süßwasser**
  salt water **das Salzwasser**
wood **der Wald(-̈er)**
zenith **der Zenit** *(no pl)*
zone **die Zone(n)**

Man-made features

aqueduct **das Aquädukt(e)**
bridge **die Brücke(n)**
canal **der Kanal(-̈e)**
capital (city) **die Hauptstadt(-̈e)**
city **die Großstadt(-̈e)**
country road **die Landstraße(n)**
dam **der Damm(-̈e), der Stausee(n)**
embankment **die Böschung(en)**
factory **die Fabrik(en), das Werk(e)**
farm **der Bauernhof(-̈e), das Gut(-̈er)**
farmland **der Acker(-̈), das Ackerland**
field **das Feld(er)**
hamlet **das kleine Dorf(-̈er)**
harbour **der Hafen(-̈)**
industry **die Industrie(n)**
marina **der Yachthafen(-̈)**
oasis **die Oase(n)**
reclaimed land **das gewonnene Land**
reservoir **das Reservoir(s), der Speicher(-)**
town **die Stadt(-̈e)**
track **der Feldweg(e)**
village **das Dorf(-̈er)**
well **der Brunnen(-)**

The surface of the North German plain was formed by the glaciers of the ice ages.

Die Oberfläche des Norddeutschen Tieflandes wurde von den Gletschern der Eiszeiten geformt.

The North Sea has very high and low tides. Many islands and half islands rise out of the shallow coastal waters.

Die Nordsee hat ausgeprägte Gezeiten (Ebbe - Flut). Vor der Küste erheben sich aus dem Wattenmeer viele Inseln und Halligen.

The bog was drained by ditches and reclaimed.

Das Moor wurde durch Kanäle entwässert und urbar gemacht.

➤ GEOGRAPHICAL FEATURES App.24a; DIRECTIONS 2b; COUNTRIES App.20a

24b The animal world

Animals

animal **das Tier(e)**
it barks **es bellt**
it bites **es beißt**
it bounds **es springt**
it breeds **es vermehrt sich**
budgerigar **der Wellensittich(e)**
burrow **der (Kaninchen)bau(e)**
cage **der Käfig(e)**
carnivore **der Fleischfresser(-)**
cat **die Katze(n)**
it crawls **es kriecht**
den **die Höhle(n), das Versteck(e)**
dog **der Hund(e)**
I feed **ich füttere**
it feeds **es frißt (fressen)**
food **das Futter**
gerbil **die Wüstenspringmaus(⁼e)**
goldfish **der Goldfisch(e)**
guinea pig **das Meerschweinchen(-)**
habitat **der Lebensraum(⁼e)**
hamster **der Hamster(-)**
herbivore **der Pflanzenfresser(-)**
it hibernates **es hält den Winterschlaf**
it howls **es heult**
hut/hutch **der Stall(⁼e)**
I keep a cat **ich halte eine Katze**
kitten **das Kätzchen(-)**
lair **das Lager(-), die Höhle(n)**
it leaps **es springt**
litter **der Wurf(⁼e)**
mammal **das Säugetier(e)**
it miaows **es miaut**
mouse **die Maus(⁼e)**
omnivore **der Allesfresser(-)**
pack **das Rudel(-)**
pet **das Haustier(e)**
predator **das Raubtier(e)**
prey **die Beute, das Beutetier(e)**
puppy **das Hündchen(-)**
rabbit **das Kaninchen(-)**

rabies **die Tollwut**
reptile **das Reptil(ien)**
it roars **es brüllt**
safari park **der Safaripark(s)**
it squeaks **es piept, es quiekt**
I stroke **ich streich(e)le**
tortoise **die Schildkröte(n)**
I walk (the dog) **ich führe ... aus***
wildlife park **das Wildreservat(e), das Wildschutzgebiet(e)**
zoo **der Zoo(s), der Tiergarten(⁼)**

Birds

claw **die Klaue(n)**
it crows **es kräht**
it flies **es fliegt**
flock **die Schar(en), der Schwarm(⁼e)**
it hovers **es schwebt, es steht**
it migrates **es zieht nach Süden**
migratory bird **der Zugvogel(⁼)**
nest **das Nest(er)**
it nests **es nistet**
it pecks at **es pickt**
it sings **es singt**

Sealife/Waterlife

alligator **der Alligator(en)**
anemone **die Seeanemone(n)**
angling **das Angeln**
coral **die Koralle(n)**
crab **der Krebs(e)**
crocodile **das Krokodil(e)**
dolphin **der Delphin(e)**
fish **der Fisch(e)**
I fish **ich fische**
harpoon **die Harpune(n)**
hook **der Haken(-)**
marine **Meeres-, See-**
mollusc **die Molluske(n)**
net **das Netz(e)**
octopus **der Tintenfisch(e), der Krake(n) (wk)**
plankton **das Plankton (no pl)**

➤ WILD ANIMALS, ANIMAL BODY PARTS App.24b; FARM ANIMALS 24c

rod   die Rute(n)
seal   der Seehund(e)
shark   der Hai(e)
shoal   der Schwarm(¨e)
shrimp   die Krabbe(n)
starfish   der Seestern(e)
it swims   es schwimmt
turtle   die Wasserschildkröte(n)
whale   der Wal(e)
whaling   der Walfang *(no pl)*

Insects

ant   die Ameise(n)
bee   die Biene(n)
   queen bee   die
      Bienenkönigin(nen)
   worker bee   die
      Arbeiterbiene(n)
bedbug   die Wanze(n)
beetle   der Käfer(-)
bug   das Insekt(en) *(wk)*
butterfly   der Schmetterling(e)
it buzzes   es summt
caterpiller   die Raupe(n)
cocoon   der Kokon(s)
cockroach   die Kakerlake(n)
cricket   die Grille(n)
dragonfly   die Libelle(n)

flea   der Floh(¨e)
fly   die Fliege(n)
hive   der Bienenkorb(¨e)
insect   das Insekt(en)
invertebrate   wirbellos
ladybird/lady bug   der
      Marienkäfer(-)
larva   die Larve(n)
locust   die Heuschrecke(n)
it metamorphoses   es verwandelt
      sich
mosquito   die Steckmücke(n), der
      Moskito(s)
moth   die Motte(n)
scorpion   der Skorpion(e)
silkworm   die Seidenraupe(n)
slug   die Nacktschnecke(n)
snail   die Schnecke(n)
spider   die Spinne(n)
it spins (a web)   es spinnt (ein
      Netz)
it stings   es sticht
termite   die Termite(n)
tick   die Zecke(n)
web   das Spinnengewebe(-)
wasp   die Wespe(n)
worm   der Wurm(¨er)

The half islands are important as a resting and migration area for northern birds of passage.	**Die Hallig ist wichtig als Rast und Durchzugszone für nordische Zugvögel.**
The state recognises the value of the area for flora and birds.	**Der Wert des Gebiets für die Pflanzen- und Vogelwelt wird staatlich anerkannt.**
Many animals are threatened with extinction.	**Viele Tiere werden vom Aussterben bedroht.**
They are scattered, rare or endangered.	**Sie sind zerstreut, selten oder gefährdet.**
Seals get caught in the remains of nets.	**Seehunde verfangen sich in Netzenresten.**

➤ BIRDS App.24b; FISH & SEA FOOD 10b, POULTRY 10c

24c Farming & gardening

Farm animals

bull   **der Bulle(n)** *(wk)*
cattle   **das Vieh** *(no pl)*, **die Rinder**
   (pl)
chicken   **das Huhn(¨-er)**
cock   **der Hahn(¨-e)**
cow   **die Kuh(¨-e)**
it crows   **es kräht**
dairy *(adj)*   **Milch-**
duck   **die Ente(n)**
it eats   **es frißt** *(fressen)*
feed   **das Futter** *(no pl)*
it feeds   **es frißt** *(fressen)*
foal   **das Fohlen(-)**
fodder   **das Futter**
food   **die Nahrung**
it gallops   **es galoppiert**
goat   **die Ziege(n)**
goose   **die Gans(¨-e)**
it grazes   **es grast, es weidet**
I groom   **ich striegle, ich putze**
it grunts   **es grunzt**
horse   **das Pferd(e)**
horseshoe   **das Hufeisen(-)**
it kicks   **es tritt** *(treten)*
kid   **das Zicklein(-)**
I milk   **ich melke**
it moos   **es muht**
it neighs   **es wiehert**
ox   **der Ochse(n)**
pasture   **die Weide(n)**
it pecks   **es pickt**
pig   **das Schwein(e)**

pony   **das Pony(s)**
poultry   **das Geflügel** *(no pl)*
produce   **das Produkt(e)**
it quacks   **es quakt**
I ride (a horse)   **ich reite (ein Pferd)**
rooster   **der Hahn(¨-e), das**
   Hähnchen(-)
I shear   **ich schere**
sheep   **das Schaf(e)**
sheep dog   **der Schäferhund(e)**
I slaughter   **ich schlachte**
stallion   **der Zuchthengst(e)**
it trots   **es trabt**

On the farm

agricultural   **landwirtschaftlich**
agriculture   **die Landwirtschaft**
arable land   **das Ackerland** *(no pl)*
barn   **die Scheune(n), der**
   Scheuer(-)
combine harvester   **der**
   Mähdrescher(-)
crop   **die Ernte(n)**
dairy   **die Molkerei(en)**
farm   **der Bauernhof(¨-e)**
farmhouse   **das Bauernhaus(¨-er)**
farm labourer/laborer   **der**
   Landarbeiter(-)
farmyard   **der Hof(¨-e)**
fence   **der Zaun(¨-e)**
harvest   **die Ernte(n)**
I harvest   **ich ernte**
hay   **das Heu**

The most important cereal crops
are wheat and rye. Besides
cereals, fruit, vegetables and wine
are cultivated.

The common agricultural policy
has as its aim to increase
agricultural productivity and to
stabilise the markets.

**Die wichtigsten Getreidearten
sind Weizen und Roggen. Neben
Getreide werden Obst, Gemüse
und Wein angebaut.**

**Die gemeinsame Agrarpolitik hat
als Ziel, die Produktivität der
Landwirtschaft zu steigern und
die Märkte zu stabilisieren.**

haystack **der Heuschober(-)**
irrigate **ich bewässere**
milk churn **die Milchkanne(n)**
milking machine **die Melkmaschine(n)**
orchard **der Obstgarten(-)**
pen **der Pferch(e), die Hürde(n)**
pigsty **der Schweinestall(-e)**
silage **die Silage** *(no pl)*
slaughterhouse **der Schlachthof(-e)**
stable **der Stall(-e)**
stud farm **das Gestüt(e)**
tractor **der Traktor(en)**

Agriculture & gardening

acorn **die Eichel(n)**
allotment **der Schrebergarten(-)**
barley **die Gerste**
it blooms **es blüht**
bloom **die Blüte(n)**
bouquet **der Strauß(-e)**
bud **die Knospe(n)**
bulb **die Zwiebel(n), die Knolle(n)**
bush **der Busch(-e), der Strauch(-e)**
compost **der Kompost(e)**
corn **das Getreide(-), das Korn(-er)**
corn *(US)* **der Mais**
I cultivate **ich kultiviere**
I dig **ich grabe**
flower **die Blume(n), die Blüte(n)**
it flowers **es blüht**
flower bed **das Blumenbeet(e)**
flower pot **der Blumentopf(-e)**
foliage **das Laub, die Blätter**
forestry **die Forstwirtschaft**
garden/yard *(US)* **der Garten(-)**
I garden/work in the yard **ich arbeite im Garten**
gardening **die Gartenarbeit(en)**
I gather **ich ernte, ich sammle**
grain **das Getreide(-), das Korn(-er)**
grass **das Gras(-er)**
I grow **ich ziehe, ich baue ... an***

it grows **es wächst** *(wachsen)*
hedge **die Hecke(n), der Zaun(-e)**
horticulture **der Gartenbau**
house plant **die Zimmerpflanze(n)**
lawn **der Rasen(-)**
leaf **das Blatt(-er)**
maize **der Mais**
market gardening **der Gemüsebau**
I mow **ich mähe**
oats **der Hafer**
petal **das Blütenblatt(-er)**
I pick **ich pflücke**
I plant **ich pflanze**
plant **die Pflanze(n)**
pollen **der Pollen(-)**
I reap **ich schneide, ich mähe**
ripe **reif**
it ripens **es reift**
rockery **der Steingarten(-)**
root **die Wurzel(n)**
rotten **faul, morsch, verdorben**
rye **der Roggen**
sap **der Saft(-e)**
seed **der Samen(-)**
species **die Art(en)**
stem **der Stiel(e), der Stamm(-e)**
thorn **der Dornenbusch(-e)**
I trim *(hedge)* **ich stutze**
I transplant **ich verpflanze, ich pflanze ... um***
tree **der Baum(-e)**
tuber **die Knolle(n)**
undergrowth **das Unterholz(-er), das Gebüsch, das Gestrüpp**
vegetable(s) **das Gemüse** *(no pl)*
vegetable garden **der Gemüsegarten(-)**
vegetation **die Vegetation(en)**
vine **die Weinrebe(n)**
vineyard **der Weinberg(e)**
I water **ich bewässere, ich gieße**
weed **das Unkraut(-er)**
I weed **ich jäte**
wheat **der Weizen**
it wilts **es welkt**
wine cultivation **der Wein(an)bau**

➤ FLOWERS & WEEDS, TREES App.24c; TOOLS App.8b

24d Weather

anticyclone **die Antizyklone(n)**
avalanche **die Lawine(n)**
average temperature **die Durchschnittstemperatur(en)**
bad weather **das Schlechtwetter**
bright **heiter**
bright period **die Aufheiterung(en)**
centigrade **das Grad Celsius**
changeable **veränderlich**
clear skies **der klare Himmel**
climate **das Klima(te/s)**
climatic **klimatisch**
cloud **die Wolke(n)**
clouded over **bewölkt**
cloudless **wolkenlos**
cloudy **wolkig**
cold **kalt**
it is cold **es ist kalt**
cold front **die Kaltfront(en)**
it is cool **es ist kühl/frisch**
cyclone **die Zyklone(n)**
daily temperature **die Tagestemperatur(en)**
damp **feucht**
degree **das Grad(e)**
  above zero **über Null**
  below zero **unter Null**
depression **das Tiefdruckgebiet(e)**

drizzle **der Nieselregen(-), der Sprühregen(-)**
drought **die Dürre**
dry **trocken**
dull **trüb, grau, verhangen**
earth tremor **das Erdzittern, die Erschütterung(en)**
earthquake **das Erdbeben(-)**
it's fine **es ist schön**
flash **der Blitz(e)**
fog **der Nebel(-)**
it is foggy **es ist nebelig**
it's freezing **es ist eisig, es friert**
freezing fog **der gefrierende Nebel**
frost **der Frost(¨e)**
frosty **frostig**
gale **der Sturm(¨e)**
gale warning **die Sturmwarnung(en)**
it's hailing **es hagelt**
hailstone **das Hagelkorn(¨er)**
  soft hail **die Graupel(n)**
heat **die Hitze**
heatwave **die Hitzewelle(n)**
high pressure **der Hochdruck**
highest temperature **die Höchsttemperatur(en)**
it's hot **es ist heiß/warm**

The forecast is for strong winds and icy polar air. Thick snow caused 90 kilometre/kilometer long traffic jams.

Die Vorhersage meldet starken Wind und eisige Polarluft. Dicker Schnee verursachte 90 Kilometer lange Staus.

Further outlook: bright to start with, then overcast with stormy showers. Highest temperatures around 9°C.

Weitere Aussichten: anfangs aufgeheitert, sonst stark bewölkt mit gewittrigen Schauern. Die Höchstwerte liegen um/bei 9 Grad.

A stormy low pressure trough is moving east.

Der Ausläufer eines Sturmtiefs zieht nach Osten.

hurricane **der Orkan(e)**
ice **das Eis**
Indian summer **der**
  Altweibersommer
lightning **der Blitz(e)**
low pressure **der Tiefdruck**
lowest temperature **die**
  Tiefsttemperatur(en)
mild **mild**
mist **der Dunst**
misty **dunstig**
meteorology **die Wetterkunde**
monsoon **der Monsun(e)**
moon **der Mond(e)**
overcast **bedeckt**
it pours **es gießt in Strömen**
rain **der Regen(-)**
it's raining **es regnet**
rainy **regnerisch**
shade **der Schatten(-)**
it shines **es scheint**
shower **der Schauer(-)**
snow **der Schnee**
snowball **der Schneeball(¨e)**
snowdrift **die Schneewehe(n)**
snowfall **der Schneefall(¨e)**
snowflake **die Schneeflocke(n)**
snowman **der Schneemann(¨er)**
snow conditions **die**
  Schneeverhältnisse (pl)
it's snowing **es schneit**

snowstorm **der Schneesturm(¨e)**
storm **der Sturm(¨e)**
stormy **stürmig**
sultry **schwül**
sun/sunshine **der Sonnenschein**
sunny **sonnig**
thunder **der Donner(-)**
it's thunder and lightning **es blitzt**
  und donnert
thunderbolt **der Blitz(e)**
thunderstorm **das Gewitter(-)**
torrent **der Sturzbach(¨e), die**
  Flut(en)
torrential **sintflutartig**
tropical **tropisch**
trough **der Ausläufer(-)**
typhoon **der Taifun(e)**
warm **warm**
warm front **die Warmfront(en)**
weather **das Wetter**
weather conditions **die**
  Witterungsbedingungen
weather forecast **die**
  Wettervorhersage(n)
weather report **der**
  Wetterbericht(e)
wet **nass**
wind **der Wind(e)**
windy **windig**
wonderful **wunderschön,**
  wunderbar

What foul weather! In this weather
we stay at home.

Was für Mistwetter! Bei diesem
Wetter bleiben wir zu Hause.

Germany belongs to the temperate
zone with rainfall at all seasons.

Deutschland gehört der
kühlgemäßigten Zone an, mit
Niederschlägen zu allen
Jahreszeiten.

The average temperature in
summer is 17-21° Centigrade.

Die durchschnittlichen
Temperaturen im Hochsommer
liegen zwischen 17° und 20°C.

24e Pollution

balance of nature **das Gleichgewicht der Erde**
it becomes extinct **es stirbt aus* (sterben)**
conservation **der Umweltschutz**
conservationist **der Umweltschützer(-)**
I conserve **ich konserviere, ich erhalte**
I consume **ich verbrauche**
consumption **der Verbrauch** (no pl)
corrosion **die Korrosion**
I damage **ich beschädige**
damaging **schädlich**
danger (to) **die Gefahr** (+acc)
I destroy **ich zerstöre**
disaster **das Unglück(e)**
disposable **Einweg-, Wegwerf-**
disposal **die Beseitigung(en)**
I dispose of **ich beseitige**
I do without **ich komme ohne aus***
ecology **die Ökologie**
ecosystem **das Ökosystem(e)**
environment **die Umwelt**
environmentally friendly **umweltfreundlich**
harmful substance **der Schadstoff(e)**
I improve **ich verbessere**
I insulate **ich isoliere**
litter **die Abfälle** (pl), **der Müll** (no pl)

natural resources **die Bodenschätze** (pl)
nuclear reprocessing plant **die Atom(müll)wiederaufberei- tungsanlage(n)**
nuclear waste **der Atommüll**
ozone **das Ozon**
poison **das Gift(e)**
I poison **ich vergifte**
pollutant **der Schadstoff(e)**
I pollute **ich verschmutze**
pollution **die (Umwelt)verschmutzung**
I predict **ich sage voraus***
I protect **ich beschütze**
recyclable **wiederverwertbar**
I recycle **ich verwerte wieder***
recycled paper **das Recyclingpapier**
recycling skip **der Recyclingcontainer(-)**
refuse **der Müll** (no pl)
residue **der Rückstand(¨e), der Rest(e)**
it runs out **es geht aus*, es wird verbraucht**
scrap metal **der Schrott**
solar power **der Solarstrom**
I throw away **ich werfe weg***
waste (domestic) **der Abfall(¨e), der Müll**
waste disposal **die Abfallbeseitigung(en)**

Chemical solvents can cause headaches and allergies.

Chemische Lösemittel können Kopfschmerzen und Allergien verursachen.

Artificial fertilizers and insecticides poison the soil and ground water.

Kunstdünger und Gifte gegen Schädlinge verseuchen Boden und Grundwasser.

Young people are committed to environmental causes.

Junge Leute engagieren sich für den Umwelt- und Naturschutz.

waste disposal unit **der Müllschlucker**
waste product **das Abfallprodukt(e)**
wind power **die Windenergie**

On the earth

artificial fertilizer **der Künstdünger(-)**
bio-degradable **biologisch abbaubar**
deforestation **die Abholzung(en)**
destruction of forests **die Zerstörung der Wälder**
nature reserve **das Naturschutzgebiet(e)**
nitrate **das Nitrat(e)**
pesticide **das Pestizid(e)**
radioactive **radioaktiv**
rain forest **der Regenwald(¨er)**
rubbish/garbage dump **die Abfalldeponie(n)**
soil erosion **die Bodenerosion**
weedkiller **das Unkrautvertilgungsmittel(-)**

In the atmosphere

acid rain **der saure Regen**
aerosol(system) **das Aerosol(e)**
aerosol can **die Spraydose(n)**
air pollution **die Luftverschmutzung(en)**
catalytic convertor **der Katalysator(en)** *(wk)*
CFCs **der FCKW**
emission (of gas) **die Emission(en), das Ausströmen**
it emits **es gibt ab*, es strahlt aus***
exhaust pipe **das Auspuffrohr(e)**
hole in the ozone layer **das Ozonloch(¨er)**
incinerator **der Verbrennungsofen(¨)**
lead-free/unleaded petrol/gasoline **das bleifreie Benzin**
skin cancer **der Hautkrebs**
I spray **ich spritze**
waste gases **die Abgase** *(pl)*

In rivers & seas

drainage **die Kanalisation, die Entwässerung**
drought **die Dürre(n)**
effluent **das Abwasser(¨)**
flooding **die Überschwemmung(en)**
ground water **das Grundwasser**
oil slick **der Ölteppich(e)**
phosphate **das Phosphat(e)**
sewage **das Abwasser(¨)**
sewage treatment **die Abwasserbehandlung(en)**
water consumption **der Wasserverbrauch**
water level **der Wasserstand**
water pollution **die Wasserverschmutzung**
water supply *(to town)* **die Wasserversorgung**

The development of harmful ozone must be prevented.	**Die Entwicklung des schädlichen Bodenozons muß bekämpft werden.**
People talk a lot about natural farming, alternative energy sources and recycling.	**Man spricht viel von ökologischem Landbau, alternativen Energien und Recycling.**
Rubbish is recycled.	**Der Müll wird wiederverarbeitet.**

➤ NUCLEAR PHYSICS 23b

Government & politics

25a Political life

I abolish **ich schaffe ab***
act (of parliament) **das Gesetz(e)**
administration **die Administration(en)**
I appoint **ich berufe, ich ernenne**
appointment **die Berufung(en)**
asylum-seeker **der Asylbewerber(-)**
it becomes law **es wird (zum) Gesetz**
bill **der Gesetzentwurf(ẅe)**
I bring down (government) **ich bringe zu Fall**
citizen **der Bürger(-) [-in]**
civil disobedience **der zivile Ungehorsam, die Unruhe(n)**
civil servant **der/die Beamte** (adj/n) **[-in]**
civil war **der Bürgerkrieg(e)**
coalition **die Koalition(en)**
it comes into effect **es tritt in Kraft**
common **gemeinsam**
constitution **das Grundgesetz(e), die Verfassung(en)**
co-operation **die Kooperation(en)**
corruption **die Korruption(en)**
county **die Grafschaft(en)**
coup **der Staatsstreich(e)**
crisis **die Krise(n)**
debate **die Debatte(n)**
decree **der Erlaß (-sse)**
delegate **der/die Delegierte** (adj/n)
I demonstrate **ich demonstriere**
demonstration **die Demonstration(en)**
I discuss **ich diskutiere, ich bespreche**
discussion **die Diskussion(en)**
I dismiss **ich entlasse**
I dissolve **ich löse auf***

district **der Kreis(e), der Bezirk(e)**
I draw up (a bill) **ich setze auf***, **ich entwerfe**
duty **die Pflicht(en)**
Easterner (fam) **der Ossi(s)**
I emigrate **ich emigriere**
equality **die Gleichheit(en)**
executive **die Exekutive**
executive (government) **exekutiv**
foreign policy **die Auslandspolitik** (no pl)
I form a pact with **ich schließe einen Pakt mit jdm.**
freedom **die Freiheit(en)**
freedom of speech **die Redefreiheit(en)**
federal state **das Bundesland(ẅer)**
I govern **ich regiere**
government **die Regierung(en)**
human right **das Menschenrecht(-)**
I introduce (a bill) **ich bringe ein***
judiciary **die Gerichtsbehörden** (pl)
law **das Gesetz(e)**
I lead **ich leite, ich führe**
legislation **die Gesetzgebung(en)**
legislature **die Legislative**
liberty **die Freiheit(en)**
local affairs/politics **die Kommunalpolitik**
local government **die Kreis-/Stadtverwaltung(en)**
long-term **langfristig**
majority **die Mehrheit(en)**
meeting **dis Sitzung(en)**
middle-class **der Mittelstand** (no pl)
middle-class (person) **der Vertreter der Mittelklasse**

ministry **das Ministerium (-ien)**
minority **die Minderheit(en)**
moderate **der/die Gemäßigte** *(adj/n)*
moderate *(adj)* **mäßig**
nation **die Nation(en), das Volk(¨er)**
national **national**
national flag **die Nationalflagge(en)**
I nationalize **ich verstaatliche**
I oppose **ich bekämpfe**
opposition **die Opposition(en)**
I organize **ich organisiere**
I overthrow **ich stürze**
pact **der Pakt(e)**
I pass (a bill) **ich verabschiede (ein Gesetz)**
policy **die Politik**
political **politisch**
political group **die Fraktion(en)**
politician **der Politiker(-) [-in]**
politics **die Politik**
power **die Macht(¨e)**
I privatize **ich privatisiere**
I protest **ich protestiere**
public **die Öffentlichkeit**
public *(adj)* **öffentlich**
public good **das öffentliche Interesse, das Gemeinwohl**
public opinion **die öffentliche Meinung(en)**
I ratify **ich fertige aus***
reactionary **reaktionär**
I reform **ich reformiere**

reform **die Reform(en)**
I reject **ich lehne ab***
I repeal *(an act)* **ich hebe auf***
I represent **ich vertrete**
I repress **ich unterdrücke**
I resign **ich trete zurück***
responsible **verantwortlich**
responsiblity **die Verantwortlichkeit(en)**
reunification **die Wiederver-einigung(en), die Wende** *(fam)*
I rule **ich herrsche**
sanction **die Sanktion(en)**
seat **der Sitz(e)**
solidarity **die Solidarität**
speech **die Rede(n)**
state **der Staat(en)**
statesman **der Staatsmann(¨er)**
I support **ich unterstütze**
I take power **ich ergreife die Macht**
term of office **die Wahlperiode(n)**
I throw out a bill **ich lehne ein Gesetz ab***
unconstitutional **verfassungswidrig**
unilateral **einseitig**
unity **die Einheit**
veto **das Veto(s)**
I veto **ich lege ein Veto ein***
Westerner *(fam)* **der Wessi(s)**
working class **die Arbeiterklasse(n)**
working-class *(person)* **der Arbeiter(-) [-in]**

The wall between east and west was opened in 1989. The totalitarian communist regime was removed.

German unity was completed in 1990, when the first free elections for the whole of Germany took place.

Die Mauer zwischen Ost und West wurde 1989 geöffnet. Das totalitäre, kommunistische Regime wurde beseitigt.

Die deutsche Einheit wurde 1990 vollendet, als die erste freie gesamtdeutsche Wahl stattfand.

➤ WAR 27a; SOCIAL ISSUES 12; THE ECONOMY 14e

25b Elections & political ideology

Elections

ballot **die Abstimmung(en)**
ballot box **die Wahlurne(n)**
ballot paper **der Wahlzettel(-)**
by-election **die Nachwahl(en)**
campaign **der Wahlkampf(¨e)**
candidate **der Kandidat(en)** *(wk)*
constituency **der Wahlkreis(e)**
I count **ich zähle**
I elect **ich wähle**
election **die Wahl(en)**
electorate **die Wähler** *(pl)*
enfranchised **wahlberechtigt**
entitled to vote **wahlberechtigt**
floating voter **der Wechselwähler(-)**
general election **allgemeine Wahlen**
I go to the polls **ich gehe zur Abstimmung/Wahl**
I hold an election **ich halte eine Wahl ab***
opinion poll **die Meinungsumfrage(n)**
poll **die Abstimmung(en)**
I recount **ich zähle nach***
referendum **das Referendum (-en)**
right to vote **das Wahlrecht(e)**

I stand for election **ich stelle mich zur Wahl**
suffrage **das Stimmrecht(e)**
swing **der Meinungsumschwung(¨e)**
term of office **die Regierungszeit(en)**
universal suffrage **das allgemeine Wahlrecht**
vote **die Stimme(n)**
I vote (for X) **ich stimme (für X)**
voter **der Wähler(-) [-in]**

Political ideology

anarchist **der Anarchist(en)** *(wk)* **[-in]**
anarchy **die Anarchie(n)**
anti-Semitic **antisemitisch**
anti-Semitism **der Antisemitismus**
aristocracy **die Aristokratie**
aristocrat **der Aristokrat(en)** *(wk)* **[-in]**
aristocratic **aristokratisch**
capitalism **der Kapitalismus**
capitalist **der Kapitalist(en)** *(wk)*
centre/center ground **die Mitte**
communism **der Kommunismus**
communist **der Kommunist(en)**

The members of parliament are elected for four years. The 5% clause means that a party must get 5% of votes before it gets a seat in parliament.

Die Mitglieder des Bundestages werden auf vier Jahren gewählt. Die "Fünf-Prozent-Klausel" bedeutet, daß eine Partei fünf Prozent der Stimmen bekommen muß, bevor sie einen Sitz im Parlament bekommt.

– How do you vote? – I have always voted Christian-Democrat.

– Wie wählst du? – Ich wähle seit jeher die Christdemokraten.

Since reunification we can freely visit the West.

Seit der Wende können wir den Westen frei besuchen.

(wk) [-in]
conservatism **der Konservatismus**
conservative **konservativ**
democracy **die Demokratie(n)**
democrat **der Demokrat(en)** *(wk)* [-in]
democratic **demokratisch**
duke **der Herzog(¨e)** [-in]
empire **das Reich(e)**
emperor/empress **der Kaiser(-)** [-in]
extremist **der Extremist(en)** *(wk)* [-in]
far left **linksradikal/-extrem**
far right **rechtsradikal/-extrem**
fascism **der Faschismus**
fascist **der Faschist(en)** [-in]
I gain independence **ich erlange die Unabhängigkeit**
ideology **die Ideologie(n)**
imperialism **der Imperialismus**
imperialist **der Imperialist(en)** *(wk)*
independence **die Unabhängigkeit**
independent **unabhängig**
king **der König(e)**
Labour party *(UK)* **die Labour Partei**
left **links**
left-wing **der linke Flügel**

liberal **liberal**
Liberal Democrat **der Liberaldemokrat(en)** *(wk)* [-in]
liberalism **der Liberalismus**
Liberals **die Liberalen** *(pl)*
marxism **der Marxismus**
marxist **der Marxist(en)** *(wk)*
monarchy **die Monarchie(n)**
nationalism **der Nationalismus**
nationalist **der Nationalist(en)** *(wk)*
Nazi **der Nazi(s)**
patriotic **patriotisch**
patriotism **der Patriotismus**
prince **der Prinz(en)** *(wk)*
princess **die Prinzessin(nen)**
queen **die Königin(nen)**
radicalism **der Radikalismus**
radical **radikal**
republic **die Republik(en)**
republican **der Republikaner(-)** [-in]
    republican *(adj)* **republikanisch**
republicanism **der Republikanismus**
revolutionary **revolutionär**
right **rechts**
right-wing **recht(s)**
royal **königlich**
royalist **royalistisch**
socialism **der Sozialismus**
Socialist **der Sozialist(en)**
    socialist *(adj)* **sozialistisch**

Young Germans are not very interested in politics. Those who belong to the Green Party or to the extreme left parties are politically active.

The chancellor is elected by Parliament. In the 12th Parliament the CDU/CSU/FDP coalition was in power.

Deutsche Jugendliche sind politisch nicht stark engagiert. Anhänger der Grünen oder der linksextremen Parteien sind politisch aktiv.

Der Bundeskanzler wird vom Bundestag gewählt. Im 12. Deutschen Bundestag stand die CDU/CSU/FDP Koalition an der Macht.

▶ POLITICAL INSTITUTIONS, POLITICIANS App.25b

Crime & justice

26a Crime

accomplice **der Komplize(n)** *(wk)* **[-in]**

alias **der Deckname(n)** *(wk)*

armed **bewaffnet**

arson **die Brandstiftung**

assault **der Überfall(⁻e)**

assault and battery **die Körperverletzung**

attack **das Attentat(e)**

battered baby **das mißhandelte Baby**

bomb attack **der Bombenanschlag(⁻e)**

fire bomb attack **der Brandanschlag(⁻e)**

bribery **die Bestechung**

burglar **der Einbrecher(-) [-in]**

burglary **der Einbruch(⁻e)**

I burgle/burglarize **ich breche ein***

car theft **der Autodiebstahl(⁻e)**

child abuse **die Kindesmißhandlung**

I come to blows **ich schlage mich (mit** +dat)

I commit **ich begehe**

crime **das Verbrechen(-)**

crime rate **die Kriminalitätsrate(n)**

crime wave **die Verbrechenswelle(n)**

criminal **der Verbrecher(-) [-in]**

I deceive **ich täusche**

delinquency **die Kriminalität**

drug abuse **der Drogenmißbrauch**

drug addict **der/die Drogenabhängige** *(adj/n)*

drug barons **der Drogenbaron(e)**

drug dealer **der Drogenhändler(-)**

drug pusher **der Dealer(-)**

drugs **die Drogen**

drug-trafficking **der Drogenhandel**

I embezzle **ich unterschlage**

embezzlement **die Unterschlagung(en)**

espionage **die Spionage**

extortion **die Erpressung(en)**

I fight **ich streite, ich kämpfe**

fight **der Streit(e), der Kampf(⁻e)**

firearm **die Schußwaffe(n)**

I forge **ich fälsche**

forged **gefälscht**

forgery **die Fälschung(en)**

fraud **der Betrug(⁻e)**

gang **die Bande(n)**

gang warfare **der Bandenkrieg(e)**

grievous bodily harm (GBH) **die schwere Körperverletzung(en)**

gun **die Schußwaffe(n)**

Carlos the Jackal was captured in the Sudan. He was the internationally most wanted top terrorist.
He had many aliases. He was on the run. He confessed to one bomb attack.

Carlos, der Schakal, wurde im Sudan festgenommen. Er war der international meistgesuchte Top-Terrorist.
Er trug viele Decknamen. Er war auf der Flucht. Er bekannte sich zu einem Bombenanschlag.

---

handbag snatching **der Taschendiebstahl(¨e)**
handcuffs **die Handschellen** *(pl)*
Help! **Hilfe!**
I hi-jack **ich entführe**
hi-jacker **der Entführer(-)**
hold-up **die Überfall(¨e)**
hooker **die Nutte(n)**
hostage **die Geisel(n)**
illegal **illegal**
I importune **ich belästige**
I injure/wound **ich verletze**
I joy ride **ich joy-ride**
joy riding **das Joy-Riding**
I kidnap **ich entführe, ich kidnappe**
kidnapper **der Entführer(-), der Kidnapper(-)**
kidnapping **die Entführung, das Kidnapping**
I kill **ich töte, ich ermorde**
killer **der Mörder(-) [-in]**
knife **das Messer(-)**
I knife **ich ersteche**
knifing **die Messerstecherei(en)**
legal **legal**
living off immoral earnings **die Zuhälterei**
mafia **die Mafia**
I mug **ich raube ... aus*, ich überfalle**
mugger **der Straßenräuber(-)**
mugging **der Straßenraub** *(no pl)*
murder **der Mord(e)**
I murder **ich ermorde**
murderer **der Mörder(-)**
I offend **ich werde straffällig**

pickpocket **der Taschendieb(e)**
pickpocketing **der Taschendiebstahl(¨e)**
pimp **der Zuhälter(-)**
pimping **die Zuhälterei**
poison **das Gift(e)**
I poison **ich vergifte**
I procure **ich beschaffe**
prostitute **der/die Prostituierte** *(adj/n)*
prostitution **die Prostitution**
I rape **ich vergewaltige**
rape **die Vergewaltigung(en)**
receiver **der Hehler(-) [-in]**
reprisals **die Vergeltung(en)**
I shoot at **ich beschieße**
shop-lifting **der Ladendiebstahl(¨e)**
slander **die Verleumdung(en)**
I smuggle **ich schmuggle**
spy **der Spion(e) [-in]**
I steal **ich stehle**
stolen goods **das Diebesgut**
tax evasion **die Steuerhinterziehung(en)**
terrorist **der Terrorist(en)** *(wk)*
torture **die Folter(n)**
I torture **ich foltere**
theft **der Diebstahl(¨e)**
thief **der Dieb(e)**
traffic offence/violation **der Verkehrsverstoß (-e)**
I traffick **ich schiebe**
underworld **die Unterwelt(en)**
vandalism **der Vandalismus**
victim **das Opfer(-)**

Plutonium smugglers demand millions of dollars.	**Plutonium-Schmuggler verlangen Millionen von Dollars.**
They were caught red-handed.	**Sie wurden auf frischer Tat ertappt.**
We went to the police.	**Wir sind zur Polizei gegangen.**

➤ WEAPONS 27b; ADDICTION & VIOLENCE 12d

26b Trial

accusation **die Anklage(n)**
I accuse **ich klage ... an***
accused person **der/die Angeklagte** *(adj/n)*
I acquit **ich spreche jdn. frei***
appeal **der Einspruch(-̈e)**
I appeal **ich erhebe Einspruch**
I appear in court **ich erscheine vor Gericht**
case **der Fall(-̈e)**
compensation **die Entschädigung(en)**
confession **das Geständnis(se)**
I confess **ich gestehe**
I convince **ich überzeuge**
costs **die Kosten** *(pl)*
counsel for the defendant/defense **der Verteidiger(-) [-in]**
court **das Gericht(e)**
court of appeal **das Berufungsgericht(e)**
courtroom **der Gerichtssaal (-säle)**
I cross-question **ich verhöre**
I debate **ich debattiere**
defence/defense **die Verteidigung**
I defend (myself) **ich verteidige (mich)**
defendant **der/die Angeklagte** *(adj/n)*
diminished responsibility **verminderte Zurechnungsfähigkeit**
I disagree **ich stimme nicht überein***
I discuss **ich diskutiere**

dock **die Anklagebank(-̈e)**
I enquire **ich untersuche**
evidence **die Aussage(n), der Beweis(e)**
examining magistrate **der Untersuchungsrichter(-)**
extenuating circumstances **mildernde Umstände** *(pl)*
I extradite **ich liefere aus***
eye-witness **der Augenzeuge(n)** *(wk)* **[-in]**
I find guilty **ich befinde für schuldig, ich spreche jdn. schuldig**
I give evidence **ich bezeuge**
I give evidence **ich sage für jdn. aus***
guilt **die Schuld**
guilty **schuldig**
high court of appeal **die höchste Berufungsinstanz(en)**
I impeach **ich klage an***
impeachment **die Anfechtung(en), die Anklage(n)**
indictment **die Anklageschrift(en)**
innocence **die Unschuld**
innocent **unschuldig**
judge **der Richter(-) [-in]**
juror **der/die Geschworene** *(adj/n)*
jury **die Geschworenen** *(pl)*
jury-box **die Geschworenenbank(-̈e)**
justice **die Gerechtigkeit**
lawsuit **der Prozeß (-sse)**
lawyer **der Rechtsanwalt(-̈e)**

What's the case for the prosecution?

Worauf stützt sich die Anklage?

We haven't enough evidence.

Wir haben unzureichende Beweise.

The police search was without result.

Die Polizeifahndung blieb ohne Erfolg.

leniency **die Nachsichtigkeit(en)**
life imprisonment **die lebenslängliche Haft** *(no pl)*
litigation **der Prozeß (-sse)**
magistrate **der (Friedens)richter(-) [-in]**
magistrate's court **das Gericht(e)**
mercy **die Gnade**
minor offence **das leichte Vergehen(-)**
miscarriage of justice **das Fehlurteil(e)**
motive **das Motiv(e)**
not guilty **nicht schuldig**
oath **der Eid(e), der Schwur(-e)**
offence **die Straftat(en), das Vergehen(-)**
on remand **in Untersuchungshaft**
I pass judgement **ich fälle das Urteil**
perjury **der Meineid** *(no pl)*
plea **das Plädoyer(s)**
plea bargaining **die Verhandlung(en)**
I plead guilty/not guilty **ich bekenne mich schuldig/ unschuldig**
premeditation **der Vorsatz**
I prosecute **ich verfolge**
prosecution **die strafrechtliche Verfolgung**
public prosecutor **der Staatsanwalt(-e)**
district attorney **der Bezirksstaatsanwalt(-e)**
public prosecutor's office **die Staatsanwaltskanzlei**

I question **ich befrage**
I interrogate **ich verhöre**
retrial **die Wiederaufnahme des Verfahrens**
I rescue **ich rette**
I reward **ich belohne**
speech for the defence/defense **die Verteidigung**
I stand accused **ich stehe angeklagt**
I stand bail (for someone) **ich bürge (für jdn.)**
statement **die Aussage(n)**
I sue/I take to court **ich verklage, ich bringe vor Gericht**
I sue for divorce **ich reiche die Scheidung ein***
summons **die Vorladung(en)**
I suspect **ich verdächtige**
suspect **der/die Verdächtige** *(adj/n)*
Supreme Court **der Oberste Gerichtshof**
sustained! **stattgegeben!**
I swear **ich schwöre**
I take legal proceedings **ich bringe vor Gericht**
I take prisoner **ich nehme gefangen**
trial **das Verfahren(-)**
unanimous **einstimmig**
verdict **das Urteil(e)**
I witness **ich bezeuge**
witness **der Zeuge(n)** *(wk)* **[-in]**
witness box **der Zeugenstand**
writ **der Haftbefehl(e)**

- They've caught her. She pleaded guilty.
- What was the verdict?
- She went to prison. She got life.

- Will she have to serve that long?

- Sie wurde erwischt/gefaßt. Sie hat sich schuldig bekannt.
- Wie lautete das Urteil?
- Sie kam ins Gefängnis. Sie hat lebenslänglich bekommen.
- Wird sie so lange absitzen müssen?

➤ PUNISHMENT 26c

26c Punishment & crime prevention

Punishment

confinement **die Haft**
 in solitary confinement **die Einzelhaft**
I convict **ich erkläre jdn. für schuldig**
convict **der Sträfling(e)**
death penalty **die Todesstrafe(n)**
I deport **ich weise aus***
I escape **ich fliehe aus** +dat, **ich entkomme** +dat
fine **die Geldstrafe(n)**
I fine **ich belege mit einer Geldstrafe**
he was fined **er mußte eine Strafe bezahlen**
I free **ich spreche frei***
hard labour/labor **die Zwangsarbeit**
I imprison **ich inhaftiere**
jail sentence **die Gefängnisstrafe(n)**
prison **das Gefängnis(se)**
prisoner **der/die Gefangene** *(adj/n)*
I punish **ich bestrafe**
punishment **die Bestrafung(en), die Strafe(n)**
I release on bail **ich lasse jdn. gegen Kaution frei***
I reprieve **ich begnadige**
I sentence to death **ich verurteile zum Tode**
I serve a sentence **ich sitze eine Strafe ab***
sentence **die Strafe(n)**
severity **die Strenge**
suspended sentence **(zur Bewährung) ausgesetztes Urteil**

Crime prevention

alarm **der Alarm(e), die Sicherung(en)**
 burglar alarm **die Alarmanlage(n)**
 car alarm **die Autosicherung(en)**
autopsy **die Autopsie(n)**
arrest **die Verhaftung(en)**
I arrest **ich verhafte, ich stelle**
baton **der Knüppel(-)**
(hearing) in camera **hinter verschlossenen Türen**
I break the law **ich breche das Gesetz**
I catch **ich ertappe, ich fange**
chief of police **der Polizeichef(s)**
civil law **das Zivilrecht**
clue **die Spur(en)**
crime prevention **die Verbrechensverhütung**
criminal law **das Strafgesetz(e)**
I have a criminal record **ich bin vorbestraft**
customs **der Zoll** *(no pl)*
customs officer **der Zollbeamte(n)** *(adj/n)* **[-in]**

He has no previous convictions. He was given a fine.	**Er ist nicht vorbestraft. Er wurde zu einer Geldstrafe verurteilt.**
His friend is on probation.	**Sein Freund steht unter Polizeiaufsicht.**
He's been inside.	**Er hat gesessen.**

deportation **die Abschiebung(en)**
detective **der Detektiv(e) [-in]**
drugs raid **die Drogenrazzia (-ien)**
drugs squad **die Drogenfahndungsbehörde(n)**
enquiry **die Untersuchung(en), die Nachforschung(en)**
error **der Fehler(-)**
escape **die Flucht(en)**
I escape (from) **ich flüchte (vor +dat)**
examination **das Verhör(e)**
I examine **ich verhöre**
extradition **die Auslieferung(en)**
fingerprint **der Fingerabdruck(ˉe)**
fugitive **der Flüchtling(e)**
guard dog **der Wachhund(e)**
handcuff **die Handschelle(n)**
I handcuff **ich lege die Handschellen an***
identikit/photofit picture **das Phantombild(er)**
I inform the police **ich verständige die Polizei**
informer **der Informant** *(wk)* **[-in]**
interview **die Befragung(en)**
I interview **ich befrage**
I investigate **ich untersuche**
investigation **die Ermittlungen** *(pl)*
investigator **der Ermittler**
private investigator **der Privatdetektiv(e)**
key **der Schlüssel(-)**
law **das Gesetz(e)**

law and order **die öffentliche Ordnung**
lock **das Schloß (ˉsser)**
I lock **ich schließe ab***
padlock **das Vorhängeschloß (ˉsser)**
plain-clothes police **der Polizist** *(wk)* **in Zivil**
police **die Polizei**
police headquarters **das Polizeihauptquartier(e)**
police informer **der Polizei-spitzel(-)**
police station **das Polizeirevier(e)**
policeman **der Polizist(en)** *(wk)*
policewoman **die Polizistin(nen)**
I question **ich vernehme**
ransom **das Lösegeld(er)**
reward **die Belohnung(en)**
riot police **das Überfallkommando(s)**
search **die Fahndung(en)**
secret service **der Geheimdienst(e)**
security **die Sicherheit**
security firm **der Sicherheitsdienst(e)**
speed trap **die Radarfalle(n)**
station **das Revier(e)**
traffic police **die Verkehrspolizei**
traffic warden **die Politesse(n)**
truncheon **der Polizeiknüppel(-)**
warrant **der Haftbefehl(e)**
search warrant **der Durchsuchungsbefehl(e)**

He was declared guilty and given a suspended sentence of two years. | **Er wurde schuldig gesprochen und zu zwei Jahren Gefängnis mit Bewährung verurteilt.**

The witness is under police protection. | **Der Zeuge steht unter Polizeischutz.**

There's a reward for the finder. | **Es gibt einen Finderlohn.**

War & peace

27a War

I abduct	**ich entführe**
aggression	**die Aggression(en)**
air force	**die Luftwaffe(n)**
airlift	**die Luftbrücke(n)**
air-raid	**der Luftangriff(e)**
air-raid shelter	**der Luftschutzbunker(-)**
air-raid warning	**der Luftschutzalarm(e)**
ambush	**der Hinterhalt(e)**
anti-aircraft	**die Flugabwehr**
army	**die Armee(n), das Heer(e)**
I assassinate	**ich ermorde**
assault	**der Angriff(e)**
atomic	**Atom-**
I attack	**ich greife an***
attack	**der Angriff(e)**
barracks	**die Kaserne(n)**
battle	**die Schlacht(en)**
battlefield	**das Schlachtfeld(er)**
blast	**die Explosion(en)**
I blockade	**ich blockiere**
blockade	**die Blockade(n)**
I blow up	**ich sprenge**
brave	**mutig**
war breaks out	**der Krieg bricht aus***
I call up	**ich berufe ein***
camp	**das Lager(-)**
campaign	**der Feldzug(¨e)**
I capture	**ich nehme gefangen***
cause	**die Ursache(n)**
I claim responsibility for	**ich erkläre mich für verantwortlich**
I commit	**ich begehe**
conflict	**der Konflikt(e)**
confrontation	**die Konfrontation(en)**
conquest	**die Eroberung(en)**
I contaminate	**ich verseuche**

conventional (weapon)	**konventionell (Waffen)**
court-marshal	**das Kriegsgericht(e)**
cowardly	**feige**
the plane crashes	**das Flugzeug stürzt ab***
I crush (opposition)	**ich vernichte (den Gegner)**
I declare (war)	**ich erkläre (den Krieg)**
defeat	**die Niederlage(n)**
I defeat	**ich schlage**
defence/defense	**die Verteidigung(en)**
I defend	**ich verteidige**
I destroy	**ich zerstöre**
I detain	**ich verhafte**
I detect	**ich entdecke**
devastating	**verheerend**
enemy	**der Feind(e)**
espionage	**die Spionage(n)**
ethnic cleansing	**die ethnische Säuberung(en)**
I evacuate	**ich evakuiere**
evacuation	**die Evakuierung(en)**
I fight a battle	**ich führe einen Kampf**
I fight off	**ich wehre ab***
I flee (from)	**ich fliehe (vor** +dat**)**
front	**die Front(en)**
guerrilla warfare	**der Guerrillakrieg(e)**
harmful	**schädlich**
headquarters	**das Hauptquartier(e)**
hostilities	**die Feindseligkeiten** *(pl)*
I interrogate	**ich verhöre**
interrogation	**das Verhör(e)**
I intervene	**ich schreite ein***

intervention **das Eingreifen**
intimidation **die Einschüchterung(en)**
I invade **ich überfalle**
invasion **die Invasion(en)**
I issue an ultimatum **ich stelle ein Ultimatum**
manoeuvres/maneuvers **das Manöver(-)**
massacre **das Massaker(-)**
missing in action **vermißt**
military service **der Kriegsdienst(e)**
mobilization **die Mobilmachung(en)**
I mobilize **ich mobilisiere**
morale **die Moral**
multilateral **multilateral**
navy **die Kriegsmarine(n)**
nuclear **Kern-**
occupation **die Besetzung(en)**
I occupy **ich besetzte**
offensive **die Offensive(n)**
I patrol **ich patrouilliere**
peace **der Frieden**
propaganda **die Propaganda**
I protect (from) **ich schütze (vor +dat)**
I provoke **ich provoziere**
it rages **es tobt**
raid **der Angriff(e)**
reinforcements **die Verstärkung(en)**
reprisals **die Repressalie(n)**
I resist **ich leiste Widerstand**
resistance **der Widerstand(¨e)**

retreat **der Rückzug(¨e)**
review **die Parade(n)**
I revolt **ich rebelliere**
revolution **die Revolution(en)**
riot **der Aufruhr(e)**
rubble **die Trümmer** *(pl)*
security check **die Sicherheitskontrolle(n)**
shelter **die Sicherheit**
siege **die Belagerung(en)**
skirmish **das Gefecht(e)**
I spy **ich spioniere**
I start a war **ich fange einen Krieg an***
strategy **die Strategie(n)**
strike power **die Schlagkraft(¨e)**
the vessel submerges/surfaces **das Schiff taucht unter*/auf***
survival **das Überleben**
tactics **die Taktik** *(no pl)*
terrorist attack **der Terroranschlag(¨e)**
I threaten **ich vedrohe, ich drohe +dat**
trench **der Schützengraben(¨)**
underground **die Untergrundbewegung(en)**
victory **der Sieg(e)**
war-mongering **die Kriegshetze**
I win **ich gewinne**
wound **die Wunde(n)**
I wound **ich verwunde, ich verletze**

The event which has most marked the twentieth century is the Second World War. Hitler invaded Poland on September 1, 1939.

Two days later, Britain and France declared war on Germany.

Der 2. Weltkrieg war das markierendste Ereignis des 20. Jahrhunderts. Hitler überfiel Polen am 1. September 1939.

Zwei Tage später erklärten Großbritannien und Frankreich Deutschland den Krieg.

27b Military personnel & weaponry

Military personnel

aggressor **der Aggressor(en)**
ally **der/die Verbündete** *(adj/n)*
Allies **die Alliierten** *(pl)*
archer **der Bogenschütze(n)** *(wk)*
assassin **der Mörder(-) [-in]**
casualty *(dead)* **das Opfer(-)**
cavalry **die Kavallerie(n)**
civilian **der Zivilist(en)** *(wk)*
commandos **die Kommandos** *(pl)*
conscientious objector **der
Kriegsdienstverweigerer(-)**
conscript **der/die Wehrpflichtige**
(adj/n)
convoy **der Konvoi(s)**
deserter **der Deserteur(e)**
division **die Division(en)**
foot soldier **der Infanterist(en)**
(wk)
general **der General(-̈e)**
guard **die Wache(n)**
guerrilla **der Guerrilla(s), der
Freischärler(-)**
hostage **die Geisel(n)**
infantry **die Infanterie(n)**
intelligence officer **der
Nachrichtenoffizier(e)**
marine(s) **die Marine(n)**
NCO **der Unteroffizier(e)**
orderly **der Sanitäter(-)**
parachutist **der
Fallschirmspringer(-) [-in]**
prisoner of war **der/die
Kriegsgefangene** *(adj/n)*
rank **der Rang(-̈e)**
rebel **der Rebell(en)** *(wk)*
recruit **der Rekrut(e)** *(wk)*
regiment **das Regiment(e)**
seaman/sailor **der Seemann
(-leute)**
Secretary of War **der
Kriegsminister(-)**
secret agent **der Geheimagent(en)**
(wk)

sentry **der Wachposten(-)**
sniper **der Scharfschütze(n)** *(wk)*
soldier **der Soldat(en)** *(wk)*
spy **der Spion(e) [-in]**
squadron **das Schwadron(e)**
staff **das Personal, der Stab(-̈e)**
terrorist **der Terrorist(en)** *(wk)*
traitor **der Verräter(-) [-in]**
troop **die Truppe(n)**
victor **der Sieger(-)**
War Minister **der Kriegs-
minister(-)**

Weaponry

I aim (at) **ich ziele (auf +acc)**
aircraft carrier **der
Flugzeugträger(-)**
ammunition **die Munition(en)**
armaments **die Ausrüstung(en)**
armoured/armored car **der
Panzerwagen(-)**
arms **die Waffen** *(pl)*
arms trade **der Waffenhandel**
arms race **das Wettrüsten**
artillery **die Artillerie(n)**
bacteriological **bakteriologisch**
barbed wire **der Stacheldraht(-̈e)**
bayonet **das Bajonett(e)**
aerial bombing **der Luftangriff(e)**
I bomb(ard) **ich bombardiere**
bomb **die Bombe(n)**
bomb alert **der Bombenalarm(e)**
bombardment **die
Bombardierung(en)**
bomber *(aircraft)* **der Bomber(-)**
bullet **die Kugel(n)**
car bomb **die Autobombe(n)**
chemical warfare **die chemische
Kriegsführung**
chemical weapon **die chemische
Waffe(n)**
crossbow **die (Stand)armbrust(-̈e)**
destroyer *(ship)* **der Zerstörer(-)**
I execute **ich richte hin***

I explode a bomb   **ich bringe eine Bombe zur Explosion**
explosive   **der Sprengstoff(e)**
   explosive *(adj)*   **explosiv**
fall-out   **der Ausfall** *(no pl)*
fighter plane   **das Jagdflugzeug(e)**
I fire (at)   **ich feure (auf** +acc)**, ich verschieße**
frigate   **die Fregatte(n)**
gas   **das Gas(e)**
gas attack   **der Gasangriff(e)**
gun   **die Schußwaffe(n)**
hand-grenade   **die Handgranate(n)**
H-bomb   **die Wasserstoffbombe(n)**
I hit   **ich treffe**
jet *(plane)*   **der Jet(s)**
I kill   **ich töte, ich bringe ums Leben**
knife   **das Messer(-)**
laser   **der Laser(-)**
letter-bomb   **die Briefbombe(n)**
machine-gun   **das Maschinengewehr(e)**
minefield   **das Minenfeld(er)**
mine-sweeper   **das Minensuchboot(e)**
missile   **die Rakete(n)**
missile launcher   **der Raketenwerfer(-)**
mortar   **der Minenwerfer(-)**
neutron bomb   **die Neutronenbombe(n)**
nuclear warfare   **der Atomkrieg(e)**
nuclear warhead   **der Nuklearsprengkopf(ᵁe)**

pistol   **die Pistole(n)**
poison gas   **das Giftgas(e)**
radar   **der Radar** *(no pl)*
radar screen   **der Radarschirm(e)**
radiation   **die Strahlung(en)**
radiation sickness   **die Strahlenkrankheit(en)**
radio-active   **radioaktiv**
revolver   **der Revolver(-)**
rifle   **das Gewehr(e)**
rocket   **die Rakete(n)**
rocket attack   **der Raketenangriff(e)**
I sabotage   **ich sabotiere**
shell   **die Granate(n)**
I shoot at   **ich beschieße**
I shoot dead   **ich erschieße**
shotgun   **die Schrotflinte(n)**
shrapnel   **das Schrapnell** *(no pl)*
I sink the ship   **ich versenke das Schiff**
the ship sinks   **das Schiff sinkt**
I stock-pile   **ich lege Vorräte an***
submachine-gun   **die Maschinenpistole(n)**
submarine   **das U-Boot(e)**
tank   **der Panzer(-)**
target   **das Ziel(e)**
I test   **ich prüfe, ich teste**
torpedo   **der Torpedo(s)**
torpedo attack   **der Torpedoangriff(e)**
I torpedo   **ich torpediere**
warship   **das Kriegsschiff(e)**
weapon   **die Waffe(n)**

War is waged on the civil population.

Der Krieg wird gegen die Zivilbevölkerung geführt.

Conventional weapons do not deter.

Konventionelle Waffen schrecken nicht ab.

Six people were wounded when a shell landed in the old town.

Sechs Leute wurden verwundet, als eine Granate in die Altstadt einschlug.

➤ CRIME 26a

27c Peace & international relations

Peace

I ban **ich verbiete**
cease-fire **der Waffenstillstand(¨e)**
control **die Kontrolle(n)**
I demobilize **ich demobilisiere**
deterrent **das Abschreckungsmittel(-)**
I diminish tension **ich entspanne die Lage**
disarmament **die Abrüstung(en)**
exchanges of information **der Informationsaustausch(e)**
free **frei**
I free **ich befreie**
freedom **die Freiheit(en)**
human rights **die Menschenrechte** *(pl)*
I make peace **ich schließe den Frieden**
I mediate **ich vermittle**
national service **der Bundeswehrdienst**
I negotiate **ich verhandle**
negotiation **die Verhandlung(en)**
neutral **neutral**
neutrality **die Neutralität**
pacifist **der Pazifist(en)** *(wk)*
pacifism **der Pazifismus**

peace plan **der Friedensplan(¨e)**
peace protester **der Friedensdemonstrant(en)** *(wk)*
peace talks **die Friedensverhandlung(en)**
peace-keeping force **die Friedenstruppen** *(pl)*
I ratify *(treaty)* **ich ratifiziere**
surrender **die Kapitulation(en)**
I surrender **ich kapituliere**
test ban **der Teststopp(s)**
treaty **der Vertrag(¨e), das Abkommen(-)**
uncommitted **nicht verpflichtet/ungebunden**
victory **der Sieg(e)**

International relations

aid **die (Entwicklungs)hilfe**
ambassador **der Botschafter(-) [-in]**
arms limitation **die Rüstungsbegrenzung**
attaché **der Attaché(s)**
citizen **der Staatsbürger(-) [-in]**
citizenship **die Staatsbürgerschaft**
consul **der Konsul(n) [-in]**
consulate **das Konsulat(e)**
developing country **das**

We are looking for a compromise.	**Wir suchen nach einem Kompromiß.**
The conditions in the ultimatum must be respected.	**Die Bedingungen des Ultimatums müssen beachtet werden.**
The areas which had been annexed had to be given back.	**Die Gebiete, die erobert worden waren, mußten zurückgegeben werden.**
The use of UNO forces is demanded.	**Man verlangt den Einsatz der UNO-Truppen.**

Entwicklungsland(-̈er)
diplomacy **die Diplomatie**
diplomat **der Diplomat(en)** *(wk)*
diplomatic immunity **die Immunität**
embassy **die Botschaft(en)**
emergency aid **die Nothilfe**
envoy **der/die Gesandte** *(adj/n)*
famine **die Hungersnot(-̈e)**
foreign affairs **die Außenpolitik**
foreign aid **die Auslandshilfe**
foreigner **der Ausländer(-) [-in]**
I join *(organization)* **ich trete** +dat
    bei*
national security **die**
    Staatssicherheit
non-aligned **blockfrei**
overseas **in Übersee**
relief organization **die**
    Hilfsorganisation(en)
relief supplies **die Hilfsgüter** *(pl)*
I represent **ich vertrete**
sanctions **die Sanktion(en)**
summit meeting **die**
    Gipfelkonferenz(en)
Third World **die Dritte Welt**

Trade

agricultural policy **die Agrarpolitik**
balance of payments **die**
    Zahlungsbilanz(en)

balance of trade **die**
    Handelsbilanz(en)
Common market **die EG, der**
    Binnenmarkt(-̈e)
currency **die Währung(en)**
customs **der Einfuhrzoll(-̈e)**
customs union **die Zollunion(en)**
exchange rate **der Wechselkurs(e)**
exports **die Ausfuhr** *(no pl)*
floating currency **die freigegebene**
    Währung(en)
it floats **es schwebt, es variiert**
foreign exchange **die Devisen** *(pl)*
foreign investment **die**
    ausländischen Investition(en)
free-trade zone **die Freie**
    Handelszone(n)
gap between rich and poor **der**
    Unterschied(e) zwischen Arm
    und Reich
GNP (gross national product) **das**
    Bruttosozialprodukt(e)
import control **die Importkontrolle(n)**
import **die Einfuhr** *(no pl)*
tariff barriers **die Tarifschranken**
    (pl)
tariff **der (Zoll)tarif(e)**
trade gap *(negative)* **die**
    Handelsspanne(n)

An intervention by NATO could
bring peace closer or extend the
war.

Eine Intervention der Nato
könnte den Frieden näher
bringen oder den Krieg
verlängern.

There is no foreign exchange to
pay for German goods.

Die Devisen fehlen, um
deutsche Lieferungen zu
bezahlen.

Trade with the East is to be
encouraged.

Der Osthandel soll gefördert
werden.

GATT (General Agreement on
Tariffs and Trade)

das Allgemeine Zoll- und
Handelsabkommen.

C
APPENDICES

Appendices

3b Clocks & watches*

alarm clock **der Wecker(-)**
clock **die Uhr(en)**
cuckoo clock **die Kuckucksuhr(en)**
dial **das Zifferblatt(⁻er)**
digital watch **die Digitaluhr(en)**
egg-timer **die Sanduhr(en)**
grandfather clock **die Standuhr(en)**
hand (of a clock) **der Zeiger(-)**
    hour hand **der kleine Zeiger(-)**
    minute hand **der Minutenzeiger(-)**
    second hand **der Sekundenzeiger(-)**
hour-glass **die Sanduhr(en)**
pendulum **der Pendel(-)**
stop-watch **die Stoppuhr(en)**
sundial **die Sonnenuhr(en)**
timer (on cooker) **der Zeitmesser(-)**
watch **die Armbanduhr(en)**
    watch strap **das Uhrarmband(⁻er)**
I wind up **ich ziehe ... auf***

4d Mathematical & geometrical terms

acute **spitz**
algebra **die Algebra**
algebraic **algebräisch**
Arabic numerals **arabische Ziffern** *(pl)*
arithmetic **das Rechnen**
arithmetical **Rechnen-**
average **der Durchschnitt(e)**
    average *(adj)* **durchschnittlich**
axis **die Achse(n)**
calculus **die Infinitesimalrechnung**
circumference **der Umfang(⁻e)**
complex **komplex**
constant **die Konstante(n)**
cube **die dritte Potenz**
cube root **die Kubikwurzel(n)**
cubed **hoch drei**
cubic **Kubik-**
decimal **die Dezimalzahl(en)**
    decimal *(adj)* **dezimal**
decimal point **das Komma(s)**
equality **die Gleichheit**
factor **der Faktor(en)**
I factorize **ich zerlege in Faktoren**
fraction **der Bruch(⁻e)**
function **die Funktion(en)**
geometry **die Geometrie**
geometry set **das Reißzeug(e)**
geometrical **geometrisch**
imaginary number **die imaginäre Zahl(en)**
integer **die ganze Zahl(en)**
irrational **irrational**
logarithm **der Logarithmus**
mean **der Mittelwert(e)**
median **der Zentralwert(e)**
multiple **das Vielfache**
natural **natürlich**
nine is to three as ... **neun verhält sich zu drei wie ...**
numerical **numerisch**
obtuse **stumpf**
prime number **die Primzahl(en)**
probability **die Wahrscheinlichkeit(en)**
product **das Produkt(e)**
quotient **der Quotient(en)**
I raise to a power **ich erhebe in die zweite Potenz**
    2 to the power of 2 **2 hoch 2**
    to the *n*th power **die n-te Potenz**
radius **der Halbmesser(-)**
ratio **das Verhältnis(se)**
rational **rational**
real **reell**
reciprocal **der reziproke Wert(e)**
Roman numeral **die römische Ziffer(n)**
set **die Reihe(n), die Menge(n)**
square **die Quadratzahl(en)**
    the square of 2 **die zweite Potenz zu zwei**
square root **die Quadratwurzel(n)**
symmetry **die Symmetrie(n)**
symmetrical (a-) **(a)symmetrisch**

* Appendices are numbered by most relevant Vocabulary.

table *(multiplication)* **das Einmaleins**
  I say my three times table **ich sage das Einmal-Drei auf***
tangent **die Tangente(n)**
trigonometry **die Trigonometrie**
variable **die Variable(n)**
vector **der Vektor(en)**

5b Parts of the body

---

ankle **der Knöchel(-), das Fußgelenk(e)**
appendix **der Blinddarm(¨e)**
arm **der Arm(e)**
artery **die Arterie(n)**
back **der Rücken(-)**
backbone **das Rückgrat(e)**
bladder **die Blase(n)**
blood **das Blut** *(no pl)*
blood pressure **der Blutdruck(¨e)**
body **der Körper(-)**
bone **der Knochen(-)**
bowel **der Darm(¨e)**
brain **das Gehirn(e)**
breast **die Brust(¨e)**
buttocks **das Gesäß(e)**
cheek **die Backe(n)**
chest **der Brustkorb(¨e)**
chin **das Kinn(e)**
ear **das Ohr(en)**
elbow **der Ellbogen(¨/)**
eye **das Auge(n)**
eyeball **der Augapfel(¨)**
eyebrow **die Augenbraue(n)**
eyelash **die Augenwimper(n)**
eyelid **das Augenlid(er)**
face **das Gesicht(er)**
finger **der Finger(-)**
fingernail **der Fingernagel(¨)**
foot **der Fuß(¨e)**
forehead **die Stirn(en)**
genitalia **die Genitalien** *(pl)*
gland **die Drüse(n)**
hair **das Haar(e)**
hand **die Hand(¨e)**
head **der Kopf(¨e)**
heart **das Herz(en)**
hip **die Hüfte(n)**
hormone **das Hormon(e)**

index finger **der Zeigefinger(-)**
jaw **der Kiefer(-)**
kidney **die Niere(n)**
knee **das Knie(-)**
knuckle **der (Finger)knöchel(-)**
leg **das Bein(e)**
lip **die Lippe(n)**
liver **die Leber(n)**
lung **die Lunge(n)**
mouth **der Mund(¨er)**
muscle **der Muskel(n)**
nape of neck **der Nacken(-)**
neck **der Hals(¨e)**
nerve **der Nerv(en)**
nervous system **das Nervensystem(e)**
nose **die Nase(n)**
nostril **das Nasenloch(¨er)**
organ **das Organ(e)**
penis **der Penis(se/Penes)**
rib **die Rippe(n)**
shoulder **die Schulter(n)**
skin **die Haut(¨e)**
stomach **der Magen(/ ¨)**
thigh **der Schenkel(-)**
throat **der Hals(¨e)**
thumb **der Daumen(-)**
toe **die Zehe(n)**
tongue **die Zunge(n)**
tonsil **die Mandel(n)**
tooth **der Zahn(¨e)**
vagina **die Scheide(n)**
vein **die Vene(n)**
waist **die Taille(n)**
womb **die Gebärmutter(¨)**
wrist **das Handgelenk(e)**

6a Human characteristics*

---

absentminded(ness) **zerstreut, die Zerstreutheit**
active **aktiv**
adaptable **anpassungsfähig**
adaptability **die Anpassungsfähigkeit**
affectionate **liebevoll**
aggression **die Aggression**
aggressive **aggressiv**
ambition **der Ehrgeiz, die Ambition(en)**

---

* German negative forms are indicated where possible by **(in)** or **(un)**.

6a Human characteristics (cont.)

ambitious **ehrgeizig**
amusing **amüsant, lustig**
anxious **ängstlich**
anxiety **die Ängstlichkeit**
arrogance **die Arroganz**
arrogant **arrogant**
artistic **künstlerisch**
attractive **attraktiv**
bad/evil **böse**
bad-tempered **schlechtgelaunt**
boring **langweilig**
brave **mutig, tapfer**
care **die Sorge(n)**
careful **sorgfältig**
careless(ness) **unvorsichtig, die Unvorsichtigkeit**
caution **die Vorsichtigkeit**
cautious **vorsichtig**
charm **der Charme** *(no pl)*
charming **charmant**
cheek **die Unverschämtheit(en)**
cheeky **frech**
cheerful **vergnügt**
clever **begabt**
cold **kalt**
comic **lustig**
confidence **das Selbstvertrauen**
confident **selbstsicher**
conscientious **gewissenhaft**
courage **der Mut**
courteous **höflich**
courtesy **die Höflichkeit**
cowardly **feig, feige**
creative (-ity) **kreativ, die Kreativität**
critical **kritisch**
cruel(ty) **grausam, die Grausamkeit**
cultured **gebildet**
cunning **schlau, die Schlauheit**
curious **neugierig**
curiosity **die Neugierde**
decisive (in-) **(un)entschlossen**
demanding **anspruchsvoll**
dependent (in-) **(un)abhängig**
dependence (in-) **die (Un)abhängigkeit**
diligence **der Fleiß**
distrust **das Mißtrauen**

distrustful **mißtrauisch**
eccentric **exzentrisch**
energetic **energisch**
energy **die Energie**
envy (-ious) **der Neid, neidisch**
extroverted **extravertiert**
extrovertion **die Extravertiertheit**
faithful (un-) **(un)treu**
faithfulness **die Treue**
friendly (un-) **(un)freundlich**
friendliness (un-) **die (Un)freundlichkeit**
frivolous **leichtsinnig**
generocity **die Großzügigkeit**
generous **großzügig**
gentle **sanft(mütig)**
gentleness **die Sanftmut**
good-tempered **gutmütig**
greed(y) **die Habgier, habgierig**
hard-working **fleißig**
helpful **hilfsbereit**
honest (dis-) **(un)ehrlich**
honesty (dis-) **die (Un)ehrlichkeit**
honour **die Ehre**
humane (in-) **(in)human**
humble **bescheiden**
humour/humor **der Humor**
humourous/humorous **humorvoll**
hypocritical **heuchlerisch**
idealistic **idealistisch**
imagination **die Phantasie(n)**
imaginative **phantasievoll**
independent **selbstständig**
individualistic **individuell**
innocence **die Unschuld**
innocent **unschuldig**
inquisitive **neugierig**
intelligence **die Intelligenz**
intelligent **intelligent**
introverted **introvertiert**
introvertion **die Introvertiertheit**
ironic **ironisch**
kind **nett, lieb**
kindness **die Freundichkeit, die Liebenswürdigkeit**
lazy (-iness) **faul, die Faulheit**
liberal **liberal**
likeable **sympathisch**

lively **lebhaft**
lonely (-iness) **einsam, die Einsamkeit**
loveable **liebenswürdig**
mad(ness) **verrückt, die Verrücktheit**
malicious(ness) **boshaft, die Boshaftigkeit**
mature (im-) **(un)reif**
mean/stingy **knauserig**
modest(y) **bescheiden, die Bescheidenheit**
mood **die Laune(n)**
moody **launenhaft**
moral (im-) **(un)moralisch**
naive(ty) **naiv, die Naivität**
natural **natürlich**
nervous(ness) **ängstlich, die Ängstlichkeit**
nice(ness) **freundlich, die Freundlichkeit**
obedience (dis-) **der (Un)gehorsam**
obedient (dis-) **(un)gehorsam**
open(ness) **offen, die Offenheit**
optimistic **optimistisch**
original **originell**
originality **die Originalität**
patience (im-) **die (Un)geduld**
patient (im-) **(un)geduldig**
pessimistic **pessimistisch**
pleasant **angenehm, nett**
polite (im-) **(un)höflich**
politeness (im-) **die (Un)höflichkeit**
possessive **gebieterisch**
prejudiced (un-) **(un)voreingenommen gegen** +acc
pride **der Stolz**
proud **stolz**
reason **die Vernunft**
reasonable (un-) **(un)vernünftig**
rebellious **rebellisch**
reserve **die Zurückhaltung**
reserved **zurückhaltend**
respect(ful) **der Respekt, respektvoll**
respectable **angesehen, anständig**
responsible (ir-) **(un)zuverlässig**
rude **grob, unhöflich**
rudeness **die Unhöflichkeit(en)**
sad(ness) **traurig, die Traurigkeit**

sarcasm **der Sarkasmus (-en)**
sarcastic **sarkastisch**
scorn **der Spott**
scornful **spöttisch**
self-confident **selbstsicher, selbstbewußt**
self-confidence **die Selbstbewußtsein**
self-esteem **die Selbstachtung**
selfish **selbstsüchtig**
selfishness **der Egoismus**
self-sufficient **selbstständig**
self-sufficiency **die Selbstständigkeit**
sensible (not) **(un)vernünftig**
sensitive (in-) **(un)empfindlich**
sensitivity (in-) **die (Un)empfindlichkeit**
serious **ernst**
shy **schüchtern**
shyness **die Schüchternheit**
silent **schweigsam**
silly **dumm, doof**
sincere **aufrichtig**
sincerity **die Aufrichtigkeit**
skilful **geschickt**
skill/skillfulness **die Geschicktheit**
sociable (un-) **(un)gesellig**
sociability (un-) **die (Un)geselligkeit**
strange(ness) **fremd, die Fremdheit**
strict(ness) **streng, die Strenge**
stubborn(ness) **eigensinnig, die Eigensinnigkeit**
stupid(ity) **dumm, die Dummheit**
suspicious **mißtrauisch**
sweet **süß, lieb**
sympathetic (un-) **(un)verständnisvoll**
sympathy **das Mitgefühl**
tact(ful/less) **der Takt, taktvoll, taktlos**
talented **begabt**
talkative **gesprächig**
temperamental **temperamentvoll**
thoughtful **rücksichtsvoll**
thoughtless **rücksichtslos**
tidy (un-) **(un)ordentlich**
tolerance (in-) **die (In)toleranz**
tolerant (in-) **(in)tolerant**
traditional **traditionell**
trust **das Vertrauen**
trusting **vertrauensvoll**

unselfish(ness) **selbstlos, die Selbstlosigkeit**

vain **eitel, eingebildet**

vanity **die Eitelkeit(en)**

violent (-ence) **brutal, die Brutalität**

virtuous **tugendhaft**

warm **warmherzig**

well-adjusted **ausgeglichen**

well-behaved **wohlerzogen**

wisdom **die Klugheit**

wise **klug, weise**

wit **der Witz**

witty **geistreich**

7a Relatives

distant relative **der/die entfernte Verwandte** *(adj/n)*

distantly related **entfernt miteinander verwandt**

godchild **das Patenkind(er)**

goddaughter **die Patentochter(̈)**

godfather **der Pate(n)** *(wk)*

godson **der Patensohn(̈e)**

great-aunt **die Großtante(n)**

great grandchild **der Großenkel(-)**

great-grandfather **der Urgroßvater(̈)**

great-grandmother **die Urgroßmutter(̈)**

great-nephew **der Großneffe(n)** *(wk)*

great-niece **die Großnichte(n)**

great-uncle **der Großonkel(-)**

8b Tools

axe/ax **die Axt(̈e)**

bit **der Bohreinsatz(̈e)**

blade **die Klinge(n)**

bolt **der Bolzen(-)**

bucket **der Eimer(-)**

chisel **der Meißel(-), der Beitel(-)**

crowbar **das Brecheisen** *(no pl)*

drill **der Bohrer(-)**

file **die Feile(n)**

garden glove **der Gartenhandschuh(e)**

garden shears **die Heckenschere(n)**

hammer **der Hammer(̈)**

hedge clippers **die Heckenschere(n)**

hoe **die Hacke(n)**

hose **der Schlauch(̈e)**

ladder **die Leiter(n)**

lawn-mower **der Rasenmäher(-)**

mallet **der Holzhammer(̈)**

nail **der Nagel(̈)**

nut **die (Schrauben)mutter(n)**

paint **die Farbe(n), der Lack(e)**

paint brush **der Pinsel(-)**

pickaxe/ax **die Spitzhacke(n)**

plane **der Hobel(-)**

pliers **die (Kombi)zange(n)**

rake **die Harke(n)**

roller **die Walze(n)**

  roller *(for paint)* **die Rolle(n)**

sandpaper **das Schmirgelpapier** *(no pl)*

saw **die Säge(n)**

screw **die Schraube(n)**

screwdriver **der Schraubenzieher(-)**

shovel **die Schaufel(n), die Schippe(n)**

spade **der Spaten(-)**

spanner/wrench *(adjustable)* **der Schraubenschlüssel(-)**

spirit level **die Wasserwaage(n)**

step-ladder **die Stufenleiter(n)**

tool **das Werkzeug(e)**

  gardening tool **das (Garten)gerät(e)**

toolbox **der Werkzeugkasten(̈)**

trowel **die Kelle(n)**

varnish **der Lack(e)**

vice/vise **der Schraubstock(̈e)**

9a Shops, stores & services

antique shop/store **der Antiquitätenladen(̈)**

art shop/store **der Kunstladen(̈)**

baker's/bakery **die Bäckerei(en)**

bank **die Bank(en)**

betting shop/bookmaker's **das Wettbüro(s)**

bookshop/store **die Bücherei(en)**

boutique **die Boutique(n)**

butcher's **die Metzgerei(en), die Fleischerei(en)**

cakeshop/store **die Konditorei(en)**

car accessory/spares shop/store **der Laden für Autozubehör**

charity shop/store **der Karitasladen(̈e)**

chemist's/drugstore **die Apotheke(n),
die Drogerie(n)**
clothes shop/store **das
Kleidergeschäft(e)**
cobbler's **der Schuhmacher(-)**
cosmetics shop/store **der
Kosmetikladen(⁼)**
covered market **der überdachte
Markt(⁼e)**
dairy **die Molkerei(en)**
delicatessen **der Delikatessenladen(⁼)**
department store **das Warenhaus(⁼er)**
drugstore **die Drogerie(n)**
dry-cleaners **die chemische
Reinigung(en)**
electrical shop/store **der Elektroladen(⁼)**
fast-food shop/store **der
Schnellimbiß(laden(⁼))**
fishmonger's **der Fischladen(⁼)**
fishstall **der Fischstand(⁼e)**
florist's **das Blumengeschäft(e)**
furniture shop/store **das
Möbelgeschäft(e)**
garden centre/center **das
Gartencenter(-), die Gärtnerei(en)**
greengrocer's **der Obst- und
Gemüseladen(⁼)**
grocer's **der Lebensmittelladen(⁼)**
hairdresser's **der Friseur(salon)**
hardware shop/store **der
Eisenwarenladen(⁼)**
health-food shop/store **das
Reformhaus(⁼er)**
hypermarket **der Verbrauchermarkt(⁼e)**
indoor market **der Hallenmarkt(⁼e)**
jeweller/jeweler **der Juwelier(e)**
jeweller's/jewelry store **das
Schmuckwarengeschäft(e)**
kiosk **der Kiosk(e)**
launderette **der Waschsalon(s)**
lottery kiosk **der Lotteriekiosk(e)**
market **der Markt(⁼e)**
menswear shop/store **das Geschäft für
Männerbekleidung**
music shop/store **der Musikladen(⁼)**
newsagent's/newsstand **der
Zeitungshändler/-stand(⁼e)**

newspaper kiosk **der Zeitungskiosk(e)**
open-air/outdoor market **der Markt(⁼e)**
optician's **der Optiker(-) [-in]**
petshop/pet store **die
Tierhandlung(en)**
pharmacy **die Apotheke(n)**
photographic shop/store **der
Fotoladen(⁼)**
post-office **die Post** *(no pl)*, **das
Postamt(⁼er)**
pottery shop/store **das
Töpferwarengeschäft(e)**
shoe repair shop/store **die
Schuhreparatur(en), die
Schusterei(en)**
shoeshop/store **das Schuhgeschäft(e)**
shop/store **das Geschäft(e), der
Laden(⁼)**
shopping arcade **die
Einkaufspassage(n)**
shopping centre/mall **das
Einkaufszentrum (-en)**
souvenir shop/store **der
Souvenirladen(⁼)**
sports shop/store **das Sportgeschäft(e)**
stationer's/stationery store **das
Schreibwarengeschäft(e)**
store **das Warenhaus(⁼er)**
superstore **das Kaufhaus(⁼er)**
supermarket **der Supermarkt(⁼e)**
sweetshop/candy store **der
Süßwarenladen(⁼)**
take-away food shop/store **der
Schnellimbiß (-bisse)**
tobacconist's/tobacco store **der
Tabakwarenladen(⁼)**
toyshop/store **das
Spielwarengeschäft(e)**
travel agent's/store **das Reisebüro(s)**
vendor **der Verkäufer(-) [-in]**
vending machine **der Automat(en)**
video-shop/store **der Videoladen(⁼)**

9a Currencies

Austrian shilling **der Schilling(e)**
dollar **der Dollar(s)**
franc **der Franc(s)**

guilder **der Gulden(-)**
lira **die Lira (-e)**
German mark **die D(eutsche)-Mark(en)**
peseta **die Peseta(s/-en)**
pound sterling **das Pfund(-)**
rouble **der Rubel(-)**
Swiss franc **der Schweizer Franken(-)**
yen **der Yen(s)**

9c Jeweller/Jewelry

bangle **der Armreif(e)**
chain bracelet **das Gliederarmband(-er)**
brooch **die Brosche(n)**
carat **das Karat(e)**
chain **die Kette(n)**
charm **das Amulett(e)**
crown **die Krone(n)**
crown jewels **die Kronjuwelen** *(pl)*
cuff links **die Manschettenknöpfe** *(pl)*
earring **der Ohrring(e)**
engagement ring **der Verlobungsring(e)**
eternity ring **der Erinnerungsring(e)**
jewel **das Juwel(en), der Edelstein(e)**
jewel box **das Schmuckkästchen(-)**
jewellery/jewelry **der Schmuck** *(no pl)*
medal **die Medaille(n)**
medallion **das Medaillon(s)**
necklace **die Halskette(n)**
pendant **der Anhänger(-)**
precious stone/gem **der Edelstein(e)**
real **echt**
ring **der Ring(e)**
semi-precious stone **der Halbedelstein(e)**
signet ring **der Siegelring(e)**
tiara **das Diadem(e)**
tie pin **die Krawattennadel(n)**
wedding ring **der Ehering(e)**

9c Precious stones & metals

agate **der Achat(e)**
amber **der Bernstein** *(no pl)*
amethyst **der Amethyst(e)**
chrome **das Chrom** *(no pl)*
copper **das Kupfer** *(no pl)*

coral **die Koralle(n)**
crystal **das Kristall** *(no pl)*
diamond **der Diamant(en)**
emerald **der Smaragd(e)**
gold **das Gold** *(no pl)*
gold plate **vergoldet**
ivory **das Elfenbein(e)**
jade **der/die Jade** *(no pl)*
mother of pearl **das Perlmutt** *(no pl)*
onyx **der Onyx(e)**
pearl **die Perle(n)**
pewter **das Zinn** *(no pl)*
platinum **das Platin** *(no pl)*
quartz **der Quarz(e)**
ruby **der Rubin(e)**
sapphire **der Saphir(e)**
silver plate **versilbert**
silver **das Silber** *(no pl)*
topaz **der Topas(e)**
turquoise **der Türkis(e)**

10c Herbs & spices

aniseed **der Anis(e)**
basil **das Basilikum** *(no pl)*
bay leaf **das Lorbeerblatt(-er)**
caraway **der Kümmel** *(no pl)*
chives **der Schnittlauch** *(no pl)*
cinnamon **der Zimt(e)**
clove **die Nelke(n)**
dill **der Dill(e)**
garlic **der Knoblauch** *(no pl)*
ginger **der Ingwer** *(no pl)*
horseradish **der Meerrettich(e), der Kren** *(no pl)*
juniper **der Wacholder** *(no pl)*
marjoram **der Majoran(e)**
mint **die Minz(e)**
mixed herbs **die Kräuter** *(pl)*
nutmeg **die Muskatnuß (-sse)**
oregano **der Origano** *(no pl)*
parsley **die Petersilie** *(no pl)*
pepper **der Pfeffer(-)**
rosemary **der Rosmarin** *(no pl)*
saffron **der Safran(e)**
sage **der Salbei** *(no pl)*
tarragon **der Estragon** *(no pl)*
thyme **der Thymian(e)**

10d Cooking utensils

alumin(i)um foil **die Aluminiumfolie(n)**
baking tray **das Kuchenblech(e)**
cake tin **die Springform(en)**
carving knife **das Tranchiermesser(-)**
colander **der Seiher(-)**
food processor **die Küchenmaschine(n)**
fork **die Gabel(n)**
frying pan/fry-pan **die Bratpfanne(n)**
grater **die Reibe(n)**
greaseproof/wax paper **das Pergamentpapier** *(no pl)*
grill **der Grill(s)**
kettle **der Kessel(-)**
knife **das Messer(-)**
lid **der Deckel(-)**
pot **der Topf(-̈e)**
rolling pin **das Nudelholz(-̈er)**
saucepan/casserole dish **der Kochtopf(-̈e)**
scales **die Waage(n)**
sieve **das Sieb(e)**
skewer **der Spieß(e)**
spatula **der Teigschaber(-)**
spoon **der Löffel(-)**
tablespoon(ful) **der Eßlöffel(voll)**
teaspoon(ful) **der Teelöffel(voll)**
tenderizer **der Fleischklopfer(-)**
tin/can-opener **der Büchsenöffner(-)**

11c Illnesses & diseases

AIDS **AIDS**
angina **die Angina**
appendicitis **die Blinddarmentzündung(en)**
arthritis **die Arthritis**
asthma **das Asthma**
bronchitis **die Bronchitis**
bubonic plague **die Beulenpest**
cancer **der Krebs**
chickenpox **die Windpocken** *(pl)*
cholera **die Cholera**
colic **die Kolik**
cold **die Erkältung(en), der Schnupfen(-)**
constipation **die Verstopfung(en)**

dermatitis **die Hautentzündung(en)**
diabetes **die Diabetes, die Zuckerkrankheit**
diarrhoea **der Durchfall**
diphtheria **die Diphtherie(n)**
eczema **das Ekzem(e), der Hautausschlag(-̈e)**
epilepsy **die Epilepsie(n)**
fever **das Fieber(-)**
fit **der epileptische Anfall(-̈e)**
flu **die Grippe(n)**
food-poisoning **die Lebensmittelvergiftung(en)**
gall-stone **der Gallenstein(e)**
German measles **die Röteln** *(pl)*
gingivitis **die Zahnfleischentzündung(en)**
gonorrhoea **der Tripper**
haemorrhoid **die Hämorrhoide(n)**
heart attack **der Herzanfall(-̈e)**
hepatitis **die Hepatitis**
hernia **der Bruch(-̈e)**
HIV-positive **HIV-positiv**
incontinence **die Inkontinenz**
influenza **die Grippe(n)**
jaundice **die Gelbsucht**
leukaemia **die Leukämie**
malaria **die Malaria**
measles **die Masern** *(pl)*
meningitis **die Hirnhautentzündung(en)**
mumps **der Mumps** *(no pl)*
pile **die Hämorrhoide(n)**
pneumonia **die Lungenentzündung(en)**
polio **die Kinderlähmung**
rabies **die Tollwut**
salmonella **die Salmonellen** *(pl)*
scabies **die Krätze**
seasickness **die Seekrankheit(en)**
sickness **die Übelkeit**
smallpox **die Pocken** *(pl)*
stroke **der Schlaganfall(-̈e)**
syphilis **die Syphilis**
temperature **das Fieber**
tetanus **der Tetanus, der Wundstarrkrampf**
thrombosis **die Thrombose(n)**

tonsillitis **die Mandelentzündung(en)**
toothache **die Zahnschmerzen** *(pl)*
tuberculosis **die Tuberkulose(n)**
ulcer **das Geschwür(e)**
urinary infection **die Harnwegsinfektion(en)**
venereal disease **die Geschlechtskrankheit(en)**
whooping cough **der Keuchhusten**
yellow fever **das Gelbfieber**

13b Holidays & religious festivals

All Saints (Nov 1) **das Allerheiligen**
All Souls (Nov 2) **das Allerseelen**
Ascension Day **der Himmelfahrtstag(e)**
Ash Wednesday **der Aschermittwoch(e)**
Assumption Day (Aug 15) **die Mariä Himmelfahrt**
Candlemas **das Mariä Lichtmeß**
Christmas **das Weihnachten**
Christmas Day **der erste Weihnachtstag**
Christmas Eve **der Heiligabend(e)**
Corpus Christi **der Fronleichnam**
Easter **das Osterfest(e)**
Easter Monday **der Ostermontag(e)**
Easter Sunday **der Ostersonntag(e)**
Good Friday **der Karfreitag(e)**
Labour/Labor Day **der Tag der Arbeit**
Lent **die Fastenzeit(en)**
New Year's Day **der Neujahrstag(e)**
New Year's Eve **das Silvester**
Palm Sunday **der Palmsonntag(e)**
Passover **das Passah**
Ramadan **der Ramadan**
Sabbath **der Sabbat**
Shrove Tuesday **der Faschingsdienstag(e)**
Whitsun **das Pfingstfest(e)**

14b Professions & jobs

The arts

actor/actress **der Schauspieler(-) [-in]**
announcer **der Ansager(-) [-in]**
architect **der Architekt(en)** *(wk)* **[-in]**

artist **der Künstler(-) [-in]**
book-seller **der Buchhändler(-) [-in]**
cameraman **der Kameramann(¨er) [-frau]**
editor **der Herausgeber(-) [-in]**
film/movie director **der Filmdirektor(en) (wk) [-in]**
film/movie star **der Filmstar(s)**
journalist **der Journalist(en)** *(wk)* **[-in]**
musician **der Musiker(-) [-in]**
painter *(artist)* **der Maler(-) [-in]**
photographer **der Fotograph(en)** *(wk)* **[-in]**
poet **der Dichter(-) [-in]**
printer **der Drucker(-) [-in]**
producer *(theatre/theater)* **der Regisseur(e) [-in]**
publisher **der Verleger(-) [-in]**
reporter **der Reporter(-) [-in]**
sculptor **der Bildhauer(-) [-in]**
singer **der Sänger(-) [-in]**
TV announcer **der Fernsehansager(-) [-in]**
writer **der Schriftsteller(-) [-in]**

Education & research

headteacher/principal **der Direktor(en) (wk) [-in], der Schulleiter(-) [-in]**
lecturer **der Dozent(en)** *(wk)* **[-in]**
primary teacher **der Grundschullehrer(-) [-in]**
researcher **der Forscher(-) [-in]**
scientist **der Wissenschaftler(-) [-in]**
secondary teacher **der Gymnasial/Realschullehrer(-) [-in]**
student **der Student(en)** *(wk)* **[-in]**
technician **der Techniker(-) [-in]**

Food & retail

baker **der Bäcker(-) [-in]**
brewer **der Brauer(-)**
butcher **der Fleischer(-) [-in], der Metzger(-) [-in]**
buyer **der Käufer(-) [-in]**
caterer *(supplying meals)* **der Lieferant(en)** *(wk)*
chemist/drugist **der Apotheker(-) [-in],**

der Drogist(en) *(wk)* [-in]
cook   der Koch(-e) [-in]
farmer   der Bauer(n), die Bäuerin(nen)
fisherman   der Fischer(-)
fishmonger   der Fischhändler(-) [-in]
florist   der Florist(en) *(wk)* [-in]
greengrocer   der Obst- und
   Gemüsehändler(-) [-in]
grocer   der Lebensmittelhändler(-)
   [-in]
jeweller/jeweler   der Juwelier(e)
pharmacist   der Apotheker(-)[-in]
pork-butcher   der Fleischer(-) [-in]
representative   der Vertreter(-) [-in]
shop assistant   der Verkäufer(-) [-in]
shopkeeper/storekeeper   der
   Ladenbesitzer(-) [-in]
tobacconist   der Tabakhändler(-) [-in]
waiter   der Kellner(-) [-in]
wine-grower   der Weinbauer(n)
   [-bäuerin(nen)]

Government service

civil-servant   der Beamte *(adj/n)*, die
   Beamtin(nen)
clerk   der Angestellte(n) *(adj/n)*
customs officer   der Zollbeamte(n)
   (adj/n)
fireman   der Feuerwehrmann(-er)
judge   der Richter(-) [-in]
member of Parliament/senator   der/die
   Abgeordnete *(adj/n)*, der
   Senator(en) [-in]
minister   der Minister(-) [-in]
officer   der Offizier(e)
policeman/woman   der Polizist(en) *(wk)*
   [-in]
politician   der Politiker(-) [-in]
sailor   der Matrose(n) *(wk)*
secret agent   der Geheimagent(en)
   (wk) [-in]
serviceman   der Soldat(en) *(wk)*
soldier   der Soldat(en) *(wk)*

Health care

dentist   der Zahnarzt(-e) [-in]
doctor (Dr)   der Arzt(-e) [-in]

midwife   die Hebamme(n)
nurse   die Krankenschwester(n)
optician   der Optiker(-) [-in]
psychiatrist   der Psychiater(-) [-in]
psychologist   der Psychologe(n) *(wk)*
   [-in]
surgeon   der Chirurg(en) *(wk)* [-in]
vet   der Tierarzt(-e) [-in]

In manufacturing & construction

bricklayer   der Maurer(-)
builder   der Bauunternehmer(-)
carpenter   der Zimmermann
   (-leute)
engineer   der Ingenieur(e) [-in]
foreman   der Vorarbeiter(-) [-in]
glazier   der Glaser(-)
industrialist   der/die Industrielle *(adj/n)*
labourer/laborer   der Arbeiter(-) [-in]
manufacturer   der Hersteller(-) [-in]
mechanic   der Mechaniker(-) [-in]
metalworker   der Metallarbeiter(-) [-in]
miner   der Bergarbeiter(-) [-in]
plasterer   der Gipser(-) [-in]
stonemason   der Steinmetz(en) *(wk)*

Services

accountant   der Buchhalter(-) [-in]
actuary   der Vertreter(-) [-in]
agent   der Agent(en) *(wk)* [-in]
bank-manager   der Bankmanager(-)
   [-in]
businessman   der Geschäftsmann
   (-leute)
businesswoman   die Geschäftsfrau(en)
careers adviser   der Berufsberater(-)
   [-in]
caretaker   der Hausmeister(-) [-in]
cleaner   die Putzfrau(en)
computer programmer   der
   Computerprogrammierer(-) [-in]
counsellor   der Berater(-) [-in]
draughtsman   der technische
   Zeichner(-) [-in]
dustman/garbageman   der
   Müllmann(-er/-leute)
electrician   der Elektriker(-) [-in]

estate/real estate agent **der Grundstücksmakler(-) [-in]**
furniture remover **der Spediteur(e)**
gardener **der Gärtner(-) [-in]**
gasman **der Gasmann(¨er)**
guide **der (Stadt-/Reise)führer(-) [-in]**
hairdresser **der Friseur(e) [-euse]**
insurance agent/broker **der Versicherungsvertreter(-) [-in]**
interpreter **der Dolmetscher(-) [-in]**
lawyer **der Anwalt(¨e) [¨-in]**
librarian **der Bibliothekar(e) [-in]**
office worker **der Büroarbeiter(-) [-in]**
painter & decorator **der Anstreicher(-) [-in]**
plumber **der Klempner(-) [-in]**
postman **der Briefträger(-) [-in]**
priest **der Priester(-) [-in]**
receptionist **der Empfangschef(s) [-dame(n)]**
servant **der Diener(-) [-in]**
social worker **der Sozialarbeiter(-) [-in]**
solicitor **der Rechtsanwalt(¨e) [¨-in]**
stockbroker **der Börsenmakler(-) [-in]**
surveyor **der Landvermesser(-) [-in]**
tax inspector **der Steuerbeamte** *(adj/n)* **[-beamtin]**
trade-unionist **der Gewerkschafter(-) [-in]**
translator **der Übersetzer(-) [-in]**
travel agent **der Reisebürokaufmann (-kaufleute)**
typist **die Schreibkraft(¨e)**
undertaker **der Leichenbestatter(-) [-in]**

Transport

airstewardess **die Stewardeß (-ssen)**
bus driver **der Busfahrer(-) [-in]**
driver **der Fahrer(-) [-in]**
driving instructor **der Fahrlehrer(-) [-in]**
lorry/truck driver **der LKW-Fahrer(-) [-in]**
pilot **der Pilot(en)** *(wk)* **[-in]**
taxi driver **der Taxifahrer(-) [-in]**
ticket inspector **der Fahrkartenkontrolleur(e)**

14b Places of work

blast furnace **der Hochofen(¨)**
branch office **die Zweigstelle(n)**
brewery **die Brauerei(en)**
business park **der Industriepark(s)**
construction site **die Baustelle(n)**
distillery **die Schnapsbrennerei(en)**
factory **die Fabrik(en)**
farm **der Bauernhof(¨e)**
foundry **die Gießerei(en)**
head office **die Hauptgeschäftsstelle(n)**
hospital **das Krankenhaus(¨er)**
mill **die Mühle(n)**
    paper mill **die Papierfabrik(en)**
    rolling mill **das Walzwerk(e)**
    sawmill **die Sägemühle(n)**
    spinning mill **die Spinnerei(en)**
    steel mill **das Stahlwerk(e)**
    weaving mill **die Weberei(en)**
mine **das Bergwerk(e)**
office **das Büro(s)**
plant **die Fabrik(en)**
shop/store **der Laden(¨e), das Kaufhaus(¨er)**
steelworks/steel plant **das Stahlwerk(e)**
theme park **der Freizeitpark(s)**
vineyard/winery **der Weinberg(e)**
warehouse **das Lagerhaus(¨er)**
workshop **die Werkstatt(¨en), die Werkstätte(n)**

14b Company personnel & deparments

accounts department **die Buchhaltung(en)**
apprentice **der Lehrling(e)**
assistant **der Assistent(en)** *(wk)* **[-in]**
associate **der Kollege(n)** *(wk)*, **die Kollegin(nen)**
board of directors **der Vorstand(¨e)**
boss **der Chef(s) [-in]**
colleague **der Kollege(n)** *(wk)*
department **die Abteilung(en)**
director **der Direktor(en) [-in]**
division **die Abteilung(en)**
employee **der/die Angestellte** *(adj/n)*

employer **der Arbeitgeber(-) [-in]**
executive **der Manager(-) [-in]**
foreman **der Vorarbeiter(-) [-in]**
labourer/laborer **der Arbeiter(-) [-in]**
line manager **der/die Vorgesetzte**
  (adj/n)
management **das Management(s)**
manager/ess **der Manager(-) [-in]**
managing director/CEO **der**
  Geschäftsführer(-) [-in]
marketing department **die**
  Marketingabteilung(en)
personal assistant **der persönliche**
  Assistent(en) *(wk)* **[-in]**
president **der Präsident(en)** *(wk)*
production department **die**
  Produktionsabteilung(en)
sales department **die**
  Verkaufsabteilung(en)
secretary **der Sekretär(e) [-in]**
specialist **der Spezialist(en)** *(wk)* **[-in]**
staff/personnel **das Personal**
team **das Team(s)**
trainee **der Praktikant(en)** *(wk)* **[-in]**
vice president **der Vizepräsident(en)**
  (wk) **[-in]**

15e Letter writing formulae

Dear Mr. & Mrs. ... **Sehr geehrter Herr**
  ..., sehr geehrte Frau ...
Dear Hans **Lieber Hans**
Dear Anja **Liebe Anja**
Dear Anja and Hans **Liebe Anja, lieber**
  Hans
Dear Sir **Sehr geehrter Herr**
  Personalmanager!
Dear Madam **Sehr geehrte Frau**
  Doktor ...
Dear Sirs **Sehr geehrte Herren, Sehr**
  geehrte Damen und Herren
Dear colleague **Lieber Kollege, liebe**
  Kollegin
My dear friends **Liebe Freunde**
I am pleased **ich bin erfreut**
I enclose **ich füge bei***
All the best **Alles Gute**
Greetings from **Grüße aus/von**

Love from **Viele liebe Grüße von** +dat,
  alles Liebe
With best wishes **mit den besten**
  Wünschen
With kind regards **mit freundlichen**
  Grüßen
With greetings from **Es grüßt Sie ...,**
  Herzliche Grüße von Deinem ...,
  Viele Grüße an Euch beide ...
Yours faithfully **hochachtungsvoll**
Yours sincerely **mit freundlichen**
  Grüßen

15f Computer hardware

adaptor **der Adapter(-)**
battery **die Batterie(n)**
brightness **die Helligkeit**
CD-ROM **die CD-ROM**
central processing unit **der zentrale**
  Prozessor(en)
charger **das Ladegerät(e)**
chip **der Chip(s)**
compatibility **die Vereinbarkeit(en)**
compatible **vereinbar, kompatibel**
computer **der Computer(-)**
computer system **das**
  Computersystem(e)
continuous paper **das Endlospapier**
cursor **der Cursor(s)**
daisy wheel **der Typenraddrucker(-)**
disc/disk drive **das Laufwerk(e)**
disc/disk **die Festplatte(n)**
diskette **die Diskette(n)**
display **die Anzeige(n)**
dot matrix **der Nadeldrucker(-)**
double density disc/disk **die DD**
  Diskette (doppelte Dichte)
drive **das Laufwerk(e)**
floppy disc/disk **die Diskette(n)**
floppy drive **das Diskettenlaufwerk(e)**
function key **die Funktionstaste(n)**
hard copy **der Ausdruck(¨e)**
hard disc/disk **die Festplatte(n)**
hardware **die Hardware**
high density disc/disk **die High-**
  Density-Diskette(n)
IBM-compatible **IBM-kompatibel**

incompatible **inkompatibel**
ink cartridge **die Patrone(n)**
inkjet **der Tintenstrahldrucker(-)**
input **die Eingabe(n)**
integrated circuit **die integrierte Schaltung(en)**
interface **die Schnittstelle(n)**
keyboard **die Tastatur(en)**
lap-top **der Laptop(s)**
laser printer **der Laserdrucker(-)**
liquid crystal display **die Flüssigkristallanzeige(n)**
low/high density **niedrige/hohe Dichte(n)**
main-frame computer **der Großrechner(-)**
microprocessor **der Mikroprozessor(en)** *(wk)*
mini computer **der Minicomputer(-)**
memory **der Arbeitsspeicher(-), die Speicherkapazität(en)**
modem **das Modem(s)**
mouse **die Maus(-̈e)**
network **das Netz(werk)(e)**
note book **das Notebook(s)**
on line **angeschlossen, online**
package **das Paket(e)**
personal computer/PC **der Personalcomputer(-), der PC(s)**
plug-in drive **das externe Diskettenlaufwerk(e)**
port **der Anschluß (-̈sse), die Schnittstelle(n)**
printer **der Drucker(-)**
processor **der Prozessor(en), der Rechner(-)**
RAM **der RAM-Chip(s)**
ribbon **das Band(-̈er)**
screen **der Bildschirm(e)**
server **der Server(-)**
socket/port **der Anschluß (-̈sse)**
storage **die Speicherung(en)**
terminal **das Terminal(s)**
toner **der Toner(-)**
VDU **das VDU**
viewdata system **das Bfx-System(e)**
visual display unit **das Datensichtgerät(e)**

15f Computer software

algebraic **algebräisch**
algorithm **der Algorithmus (-en)**
application **die Anwendung(en)**
bug **die Wanze(n)**
byte **das Byte(s)**
coding **das Kodieren**
command **der Befehl(e)**
computer aided design (CAD) **das rechnergestützte Konstruieren**
computer aided learning (CAL) **das computergestützte Lernen**
computer language **die Computersprache(n)**
copy **die Kopie(n)**
data **die Daten** *(pl)*
data capture **das Datenerfassen**
data logging **das Dateneintragen**
databank **die Datenbank(en)**
data processing **die Datenverarbeitung(en)**
database **das Datenbankprogramm(e)**
default option **der Default(s)**
directory **das Verzeichnis(se)**
double clicking **das Doppelklicken**
escape **die Escapetaste**
field **das Feld(er)**
file **die Datei(en)**
flow chart **das Flußdiagramm(e)**
format **das Format(e)**
function **die Funktion(en)**
grahical **graphisch, Grafik-**
graphical application **das Grafikprogamm(e)**
graphics **die Graphiken** *(pl)*
help **die Hilfe(n)**
help menu **das Hilfsprogramm(e)**
language **die Sprache(n)**
logic circuit **die Logik-Schaltung(en)**
logic gate **das Logikgatter(-)**
macro **der Makro(s)**
memory **der Arbeitsspeicher(-)**
menu **das Menü(s)**
operating system **das Betriebssystem(e)**
output **die Ausgabe(n)**

password **das Passwort(-̈er)**
program(me) **das Programm(e)**
programmable **programmierbar**
programmer **der Programmierer(-) [-in]**
programming **das Programmieren**
pull-down menu **das Hilfefenster(-)**
reference archive **das
    Nachschlagearchiv(e)**
return **die Eingabetaste(n)**
software **die Software**
software package **das
    Softwarepaket(e)**
space bar **die Leertaste(n)**
spreadsheet **die Bildschirmtabelle(n)**
statistics package **das
    Statistikpaket(e)**
text system **das Textprogramm(e)**
virus **der Virus (-en)**

16a Hobbies

angling **das Angeln**
birdwatching **das Vögelbeobachten**
archeology **die Archäologie**
ballroom dancing **die
    Gesellschaftstänze** (pl)
carpentry **das Tischlern**
chess **das Schach**
collecting antiques **Antiquitäten
    sammeln**
collecting stamps **Briefmarken
    sammeln**
dancing **das Tanzen**
DIY/do it yourself **das Basteln**
fishing **das Fischen, das Angeln**
gardening **die Gartenarbeit**
gambling **das Glückspiel(e)**
going to the cinema/movies **ins Kino
    gehen**
listening to music **Musik hören**
knitting **das Stricken**
photography **das Fotografieren**
reading **das Lesen**
sewing **das Nähen**
spinning **das Spinnen**
walking **das Spazierengehen, das
    Wandern**
watching television **das Fernsehen**

16c Photography

automatic **automatisch**
camera **die Kamera(s)**
camera case **die Fototasche(n)**
I develop **ich entwickle**
developing/processing **die
    Entwicklung**
I enlarge **ich vergrößere**
exposure counter **der Zähler(-)**
film **der Film(e)**
    black and white film **der
        Schwarzweißfilm(e)**
    colour/color film **der Farbfilm(e)**
filter **das/der Filter(-)**
flash **der Blitz(e)**
flash attachment **das Blitzlicht(er)**
home movie **das Heimvideo(s)**
I focus the camera **ich stelle ein***
    in focus **scharf (eingestellt)**
    out of focus **unscharf**
it is jammed **es klemmt**
lens **das Objektiv(e)**
    telephoto lens **das Teleobjektiv(e)**
    wide-angle lens **das
        Weitwinkelobjektiv(e)**
lens cap **die Schutzkappe(n)**
light **das Licht, die Beleuchtung**
    daylight **das Tageslicht**
light meter **der Belichtungsmesser(-)**
movie camera **die Filmcamera(s)**
negative **das Negativ(e)**
over-exposed **überbelichtet**
over-exposure **die Überbelichtung**
picture **das Bild(er)**
photogenic **fotogen**
photo(graph) **das Foto(s), die
    Fotografie(n)**
    holiday/vacation photo **die
        Aufnahme(n)**
    passport photo **das Paßfoto(s)**
photograph album **das
    Fotoalbum(s/-en)**
shutter **der Verschluß (-̈sse)**
slide **das Dia(s), das Diapositiv(e)**
snap **der Schnappschuß (-̈sse)**
I take (photos) **ich nehme auf***

video camera **die Videokamera(s)**
video cassette **die Videokassette(n)**
I wind on **ich spule weiter***

17a Artistic styles & periods

Art Nouveau **der Jugendstil**
Baroque **der Barock**
baroque **barock**
Bauhaus **das Bauhaus**
Byzantine **byzantinisch**
Celtic **keltisch**
classical **klassisch**
classical artist/writer **der Klassiker(-)**
Classical period **die Klassik**
Cubism **der Kubismus**
Dada **der Dadaismus**
Expressionism **der Expressionismus**
expressionist **der Expressionist(en)**
  (wk)
expressionistic **expressionistisch**
Flemish **flämisch**
Germanic **germanisch**
Gothic art **die Gotik**
Gothic **gotisch**
Greek **griechisch**
Impressionism **der Impressionismus**
Impressionist **der Impressionist(en)**
  (wk)
Impressionist **impressionistisch**
Naturalism **der Naturalismus**
naturalistic **naturalistisch**
Neo-classical **der Klassizismus**
Neo-gothic **die Neugotik**
New Objectivity **die Neue Sachlichkeit**
Norman **romanisch**
pop art **die Pop-Art**
Realism **der Realismus**
realist **der Realist(en)** *(wk)*
realistic **realistisch**
Renaissance **die Renaissance**
Rococo **das Rokoko**
Roman **römisch**
Romanesque **romanisch**
Romantic age **die Romantik**
Romantic **der Romantiker(-)**
romantic **romantisch**
Storm and Stress **der Sturm und**

Drang
Surrealism **der Surrealismus**
Surrealist **der Surrealist(en)** *(wk)*
surrealistic **surrealistisch**
Venetian **venezianisch**

17b Architectural features

aisle **das Seitenschiff(e)**
arch **der Bogen(¨)**
bas relief **das Basrelief(s)**
battlement **die Zinnen** *(pl)*
buttress **der Strebepfeiler**
capital **das Kapitell(e)**
choir **der Chor(e/¨e)**
colonnade **der Säulengang(¨e)**
column **die Säule(n)**
  corinthian **korinthisch**
  doric **dorisch**
  ionic **ionisch**
crossing **die Vierung(en)**
crypt **die Krypta (-en)**
cupola **die Kuppel(n)**
drawbridge **die Zugbrücke(n)**
eave **der Dachvorsprung(¨e)**
façade **die Fassade(n)**
gable **der Giebel(-)**
gargoyle **der Wasserspeier(-)**
gothic arch **der Spitzbogen(¨)**
half-timbered **das Holzfachwerk**
half-timbered house **das**
  Fachwerkhaus(¨er)
headstone **der Grabstein(e)**
nave **das Schiff(e)**
overhanging **vorstehend**
pagoda **die Pagode(n)**
pilaster **der Halbpfeiler(-)**
porch **die Vorhalle(n)**
portico **der Portikus (-en)**
relief **das Relief(s)**
roof **das Dach(¨er)**
sacristy **die Sakristei(en)**
spire/steeple **der Kirchturm(¨e)**
stucco **der Stuck**
transept **das Querschiff(e)**
triumphal arch **der Triumphbogen(¨)**
vault **das Gewölbe(-)**
vaulted **gewölbt**

17c Publishing

abridged version   **die gekürzte Ausgabe(n)**

acknowledgements to   **mein/unser Dank gilt** +dat

appendix   **der Anhang(-̈e)**

author   **der Autor(en) [-in], der Verfasser(-) [-in]**

best-seller   **der Bestseller(-)**

bibliography   **die Bibliographie(n)**

book fair   **die Buchmesse(n)**

catalogue/catalog   **der Katalog(e)**

chapter   **das Kapitel(-)**

contents   **der Inhalt(e)**

  table of contents   **das Inhaltsverzeichnis(se)**

contract   **der Vertrag(-̈e)**

copy   **das Exemplar(e)**

copyright   **das Copyright**

cover *(of book)*   **der Buchumschlag(-̈e)**

deadline   **der Fristablauf(-̈e)**

dedicated to   **gewidmet** +dat/**an** +acc

edition   **die Ausgabe(n)**

  first edition   **die Erstausgabe(n)**

  latest edition   **die neueste Ausgabe**

editor   **der Redakteur(e), der Herausgeber(-)**

  desk editor   **der Lektor(en) [-in]**

  general editor   **der Chefredakteur(e) [-in]**

footnotes   **die Fußnote(n)**

illustrations   **die Illustration(en)**

manuscript   **das Manuskript(e)**

out of print   **vergriffen**

paperback   **das Taschenbuch(-̈er)**

preface   **das Vorwort(e)**

I print   **ich drucke**

proof-reading   **das Korrekturlesen**

publication date   **das Erscheinungsdatum (-en)**

I publish   **ich bringe heraus*, ich veröffentliche**

just published   **neu erschienen**

publisher   **der Verleger(-)**

publishing   **das Verlagswesen(-)**

publishing house   **das Verlagshaus(-̈er)**

translation   **die Übersetzung(en), die Übertragung(en)**

version   **die Fassung(en)**

with a forward by   **mit einem Vorwort von** +dat

17d Musicians & instruments

accompanist   **der Begleiter(-) [-in]**

accordion   **das Akkordeon(s)**

alto   **der Alt(e), die Altstimme(n)**

bagpipe   **der Dudelsack(-̈e)**

band leader   **der Kapellmeister(-)**

baritone   **der Bariton**

bass (singer)   **der Bassist(en)**

bassoon   **das Fagott(e)**

bells   **die Glocke(n)**

busker   **der Straßenmusikant(en)** *(wk)* **[-in]**

castanets   **die Kastagnietten** *(pl)*

cellist   **der Cellist(en) [-in]**

cello   **das Cello(s/-i)**

cembalo   **das Cembalo(s)**

chorister   **der Chorknabe(n)** *(wk)*

clarinet   **die Klarinette(n)**

classical guitar   **die klassische Gitarre(n)**

clavichord   **das Klavichord(e)**

conductor   **der Dirigent(en)** *(wk)* **[-in]**

contralto   **der Alt(e), die Altstimme(n)**

cymbal   **das Becken(-)**

double bass   **der Kontrabaß (-̈sse)**

drum   **das Schlagzeug(e)**

flautist   **der Flötist(en)** *(wk)* **[-in]**

flute   **die Querflöte(n)**

French horn   **das Waldhorn(-̈er)**

grand piano   **der Flügel(-)**

guitar   **die Gitarre(n)** *(wk)* **[-in]**

guitarist   **der Gitarrist(en)**

harmonium   **das Harmonium (-ien)**

harp   **die Harfe(n)**

harpist   **der Harfenspieler(-) [-in]**

harpsichord   **das Cembalo(s)**

horn   **das Horn(-̈er)**

hurdy-gurdy   **der Leierkasten(-̈)**

jews' harp   **die Maultrommel(n)**

lyre   **die Leier(n)**

mandolin   **die Mandoline(n)**

mezzo-soprano **der Mezzosopran(e)**
mouth-organ **die Mundharmonika(s)**
oboe **die Oboe(n)**
orchestra leader **der Konzertmeister(-)
[-in]**
orchestra player **das
Orchestermitglied(er)**
organ **die Orgel(n)**
organist **der Organist(en) [-in]**
percussion **das Schlagzeug** *(no pl)*
percussionist **der Schlagzeuger(-) [-in]**
pianist *(professional)* **der Pianist(en)
[-in]**
piano **das Klavier(e)**
pipe **die Flöte(n)**
recorder **die Blockflöte(n)**
saxophone **das Saxophon(e)**
soprano **der Sopran(e)**
spinet **das Spinett(e)**
squeeze-box **die Ziehharmonika(s)**
steel drum **das (Stahl)schlagzeug** *(no
pl)*
synthesizer **der Synthesizer(-)**
tenor **der Tenor(̈e)**
timpani **die Timpani** *(pl)*, **die
Kesselpauken**
triangle **der/das Triangel(-)**
trombone **die Posaune(n)**
trumpet **die Trompete(n)**
tuba **die Tuba(s)**
viol **die Viola (-en)**
viola **die Bratsche(n)**
viola player **der Bratschenspieler(-)
[-in]**
violin **die Violine(n)**
violinist **der Violinist(en)** *(wk)* **[-in]**
violoncello **das Violoncello (-i)**
vocalist **der Sänger(-) [-in]**
xylophone **das Xylophon(e)**

17d Musical forms

aria **die Arie(n)**
ballad **die Ballade(n)**
cantata **die Kantate(n)**
canzonetta **die Kanzonette(n)**
chamber music **die Kammermusik** *(no
pl)*

choral music **die Chormusik** *(no pl)*
chorale **der Choral(̈e)**
concerto **das Konzert(e), das
Concerto (-i)**
  piano concerto **das
Klavierkonzert(e)**
duet **das Duett(e)**
fugue **die Fuge(n)**
madrigal **das Madrigal(e)**
march **die Marschmusik, der
Marsch(̈e)**
music drama **das Musikdrama (-en)**
musical *(comedy)* **das Musical(s)**
nocturne **die Nokturne(n)**
octet **das Oktett(e)**
opera **die Oper(n)**
operetta **die Operette(n)**
oratorio **das Oratorium (-ia/-ien)**
overture **die Ouvertüre(n)**
prelude **das Präludium (-ia/-ien)**
quartet **das Quartett(e)**
quintet **das Quintett(e)**
recitative **das Rezitativ(e)**
requiem Mass **die Totenmesse(n)**
rondo **das Rondo(s)**
sacred music **die geistliche Musik**
septet **das Septett(e)**
serenade **die Serenade(n)**
sextet **das Sextett(e)**
sonata **die Sonate(n)**
song-cycle **der Liederzyklus (-en)**
string quartet **das Streichquartett(e)**
suite **die Suite(n)**
symphonietta **die Sinfonietta (-en)**
symphony **die Symphonie(n)**
trio **das Trio(s)**
  piano trio **das Klaviertrio(s)**

17d Musical terms

accompaniment **die Begleitung(en)**
arpeggio **die Arpeggio(s)**
bar **der Takt(e)**
beat **der Schlag(̈e)**
bow **der Bogen(̈)**
bowing **die Bogenführung**
cadence **die Kadenz(en)**
chord **der Akkord(e)**

clef **der Notenschlüssel(-)**
   bass **der F-Schlüssel**
   treble **der Violinschlüssel**
conductor **der Dirigent(en)** *(wk)* **[-in]**
I conduct **ich dirigiere**
discord **die Disharmonie(n)**
first violin **die erste Geige(n)**
harmony **die Harmonie(n)**
improvisation **die Improvisation(en)**
key **der Notenschlüssel(-)**
   major **das Dur** *(no pl)*
   minor **das Moll** *(no pl)*
note **der Ton(¨e), die Note(n)**
   breve **die ganze Note(n)**
   minim/half note **die Halbe(n)**
   crotchet/quarter note **das Viertel(-)**
   quaver/eighth note **das Achtel(-)**
   semibreve **die ganze Taktnote(n)**
   semiquaver/sixteenth note **das Sechszehntel(-)**
   semitone **der Halbton(¨e)**
   tone **der Ton(¨e)**
mute **der Dämpfer(-)**
reed **das Rohrblattinstrument(e)**
scale **die Tonleiter(n)**
score **die Partitur(en)**
sheet *(of music)* **das Notenblatt(¨er)**
triplet **die Triole(n)**

Notes & keys

C, C sharp, C flat **das C, Cis, Ces**
D, D sharp, D flat **das D, Dis, Des**
E, E sharp, E flat **das E, Eis, Es**
F, F sharp, F flat **das F, Fis, Fes**
G, G sharp, G flat **das G, Gis, Ges**
A, A sharp, A flat **das A, Ais, As**
B, B sharp **das H, His**
B flat **B**
B-minor **H-Moll**
B flat minor **B-Moll**
C double sharp, etc. **Cisis, usw.**
C double flat, etc. **Ceses, usw.**
B double flat, etc. **Bes, usw.**
flat sign **das Be**
sharp sign **das Kreuz(e)**
natural sign **das Auflösungszeichen(-)**

17e Film/Movie genres

adventure **der Abenteuerfilm(e)**
animation **der Trickfilm(e)**
black and white **schwarz-weiß**
black comedy **der schwarze (Galgen)humor**
B-movie **das B-Movie(s)**
cartoons **der Trickfilm(e)**
comedy **die Komödie(n)**
documentary **der Dokumentarfilm(e)**
feature film/movie **der Spielfilm(e)**
horror **der Horrorfilm(e)**
low-budget **der Film mit kleinem Budget**
sci-fi **Science-Fiction**
short film/movie **der Kurzfilm(e)**
silent film/movie **der Stummfilm(e)**
thriller **der Thriller(-), der Krimi(s)**
video-clip **der Videoclip(s)**
war film/movie **der Kriegsfilm(e)**
western **der Western(-)**
weepie **der Schmachtfetzen(-)**

19c Parts of the car

alternator **die Lichtmaschine(n)**
automatic gear **die Getriebeautomatik**
back wheel **das Hinterrad(¨er)**
battery **die Batterie(n)**
bodywork **die Karosserie(n)**
bonnet/hood **die Motorhaube(n)**
boot/trunk **der Kofferraum(¨e)**
brake **die Bremse(n)**
bumper **die Stoßstange(n)**
carburettor **der Vergaser(-)**
catalytic converter **der Katalysator(-)**
choke **der Choke(s)**
clutch **die Kupplung(en)**
dashboard **das Armaturenbrett(er)**
door **die Tür(en)**
   front door **die Vordertür(en)**
   passenger door **die Beifahrertür(en)**
engine/motor **der Motor(en)**
exhaust **der Auspuff**
front seat **der Vordersitz(e)**
front wheel **das Vorderrad(¨er)**

gearbox **das Getriebe(-)**
headlight **der Scheinwerfer(-)**
horn **die Hupe(n)**
hood **die Haube(n)**
indicator **der Blinker(-)**
lights **die Beleuchtung(en)**
number/license plate **das Nummernschild(er)**
passenger seat **der Beifahrersitz(e)**
pedal **das Pedal(e)**
    accelerator **das Gaspedal(e)**
    brake **das Bremspedal(e)**
    clutch **das Kupplungspedal(e)**
plug **die Zündkerze(n)**
rear-view mirror **der Rückspiegel(-)**
registration number **die Registrationsnummer(n)**
roof **das Dach(-er)**
roof-rack **der Dachgepäckträger(-)**
safety belt **der Sicherheitsgurt(e)**
spare **Ersatz-**
    spare part **das Ersatzteil(e)**
    spare wheel **das Ersatzrad(-er)**
speedometer **der Tachometer(-)**
starter **der Anlasser(-)**
steering wheel **das Steuer(rad)(-er)**
tank **der Tank(s)**
tyre/tire **der Reifen(-)**
    back tyre/tire **der Hinterreifen(-)**
    front tyre/tire **der Vorderreifen(-)**
    spare tyre/tire **der Ersatzreifen(-)**
tyre/tire pressure **der Reifendruck(-e)**
wheel **das Rad(-er)**
windscreen/windshield **die Windschutzscheibe(n)**
windscreen/windshield wiper **der Scheibenwischer(-)**

19c Road signs

Danger! **Gefahr!, Vorsicht!**
Diversion **Umleitung**
End of diversion **Ende der Umleitung**
Entry **Einfahrt**
Exit **Ausfahrt**
Free parking **Parken gebührenfrei**
Keep clear **Halteverbot, Ausfahrt freihalten**

Maximum speed **die Höchstgeschwindigkeit(en)**
Men at work! **Achtung, Baustelle!**
Motorway/Expressway entrance **die Autobahnauffahrt(en)**
Motorway/Expressway junction **das Kreuz**
No entry **Kein Zugang, Keine Zufahrt**
No overtaking/passing **Überholverbot**
No parking **Parken verboten, Parkverbot**
One way **Einbahnstraße**
Pedestrians crossing **der Fußgängerübergang**
Pedestrian zone **die Fußgängerzone**
Residents only **Anlieger frei**
Road closed **Straße gesperrt**
Roadworks **Straßenbau**
Stop **Halt!, Stop!**
Toll **gebührenpflichtige Straße**

20a Tourist sights

abbey **die Abtei(en)**
amusement park **der Vergnügungspark(s)**
amphitheatre/amphitheater **das Amphitheater(-)**
aquarium **das Aquarium (-ien)**
art gallery **die Kunstgalerie(n)**
battle field **das Schlachtfeld(er)**
battlements **die Zinnen** *(pl)*
boulevard **der Boulevard(s)**
casino **das (Spiel)kasino(s)**
castle **das Schloß (-sser)**
catacombs **die Katakomben** *(pl)*
cathedral **die Kathedrale(n), der Dom(e)**
cave **die Höhle(n)**
cemetery **der Friedhof(-e)**
circus **der Zirkus(se)**
city **der Stadt(-e)**
city wall **die Stadtmauer(n)**
chapel **die Kapelle(n)**
church **die Kirche(n)**
concert hall **die Konzerthalle(n)**
convent **das Kloster(-)**
exhibition **die Ausstellung(en)**

fortress   die Festung(en)
fountain   der (Spring)brunnen(-)
gardens   der Botanische Garten(-)
harbour/harbor   der Hafen(-)
library   die Bibliothek(en)
mansion   das Herrenhaus(-er)
market   der Markt(-e)
monastery   das Kloster(-)
monument   das Denkmal(-er)
museum   das Museum (Museen)
opera house   das Opernhaus(-er)
palace   der Palast(-e), das Schloß
   (-sser)
parliament building   das
   Parlamentsgebäude(-)
pier   der Anleger(-)
planetarium   das Planetarium (-ien)
ruin   die Ruine(n)
shopping area   das Geschäftsviertel(-)
square   der Platz(-e)
stadium   das Stadion (-ien)
statue   die Statue(n)
temple   der Tempel(-)
theatre/theater   das Theater(-)
tomb   das Grab(-er)
tower   der Turm(-e)
town centre/downtown   die Stadtmitte(n)
town hall   das Rathaus(-er)
university   die Universität(en)
wall   die Mauer(-)
zoo   der Zoo(s)

20a On the beach

bathing hut/cabana   die Badekabine(n)
beach   der Strand(-e)
beach ball   der Wasserball(-e)
bucket and spade/pail and shovel   der
   Eimer(-) und die Schaufel(-)
deck-chair   der Liegestuhl(-e)
I dive   ich springe, ich tauche
diver   der Taucher(-) [-in]
sand   der Sand (no pl)
   grain of sand   das Sandkorn(-er)
sandcastle   die Sandburg(en)
sandy beach   der Sandstrand(-e)
scuba diving   das Sporttauchen
sea   das Meer(e)

sea shore   der Strand(-e)
snorkel   das Schnorchel(-)
I go snorkelling   ich gehe schnorcheln
sun-tan lotion   das Sonnenöl(e)
sunshade   der Sonnenschirm(e)
I surf   ich surfe
surfboard   das Surfbrett(er)
surfboarder   der Surfer(-) [-in], der
   Wellenreiter(-) [-in]
surfing   das Surfen, das Surfing
I swim   ich schwimme
water-skiing   das Wasserskilaufen
windbreak   der Windschutz (no pl)
windsurfing/sailboarding   das
   Windsurfen
I go windsurfing   ich windsurfe

20a Countries/Regions
–adjectives–inhabitants

All countries are neuter unless otherwise
shown. Where an article is shown, it should
always be used with the name of the country.
   The adjective is normally used as a neuter
noun to form the language, e,g. **Englisch**
(sometimes **das Englische**). When used as an
adjective it always starts with a lower case letter, e,g, **englisch**.
   The inhabitants are shown in the masculine
singular. They fall into the following groups:
– those ending in **-r** have no plural ending,
and form the feminine by adding **-in(nen)**;
– those ending in **-e** are weak masculine
nouns with an **-n** ending in every case except
the nominative; the feminine is formed by
dropping the **-e** and adding **-in(nen)**.
Note **der Franzose** fem. **die Französin**; **der
Schwabe** fem. **die Schwäbin**.
– **der Deutsche** (**ein Deutscher**, fem. **die/eine
Deutsche**) is an adjectival noun.

Africa   **Afrika, afrikanisch, Afrikaner**
Alsace   **Elsaß, elsässisch, Elsässer**
America   **Amerika, amerikanisch,
   Amerikaner**
Arabia   **Arabien, arabisch, Araber**
Argentina   **Argentinien, argentinisch,
   Argentinier**
Asia   **Asien, asiatisch, Asiat(en)** (wk)
Australia   **Australien, australisch, der
   Australier**

Austria **Österreich, österreichisch, der Österreicher**

Bavaria **Bayern, bayrisch, Bayer**

Belgium **Belgien, belgisch, Belgier**

Bosnia **Bosnien, bosnisch, Bosnier**

Brazil **Brasilien, brasilianisch, Brasilianer**

Bulgaria **Bulgarien, bulgarisch, Bulgare**

Canada **Kanada, kanadisch, Kanadier**

China **China, chinesisch, Chinese**

Czech Republic **die Tschechische Republik, tschechisch, Tscheche**

Denmark **Dänemark, dänisch, Däne**

Egypt **Ägypten, ägyptisch, Ägypter**

England **England, englisch, Engländer**

Europe **Europa, europäisch, Europäer**

Finland **Finnland, finnisch, Finne**

France **Frankreich, französisch, Franzose**

Germany **Deutschland, deutsch, Deutsche** *(adj/n)*

Great Britain **Großbritannien, britisch, Brite**

Greece **Griechenland, griechisch, Grieche**

Holland **Holland, holländisch, Holländer**

Hungary **Ungarn, ungarisch, Ungar**

Iceland **Island, isländisch, Isländer**

India **Indien, indisch, Inder**

Iran **der Iran, iranisch, Iraner**

Iraq **der Iraq, irakisch, Iraker**

Ireland **Irland, irisch, Ire**

Israel **Israel, hebräisch, Israeli(s)**

Italy **Italien, italienisch, Italiener**

Japan **Japan, japanisch, Japaner**

Lebanon **der Libanon, libanesisch, Libanese**

Lorraine **Lothringen, lothringisch, Lothringer**

Luxemburg **Luxemburg, luxemburgisch, Luxemburger**

Morocco **Marokko, marokkanisch, Marokkaner**

Netherlands **die Niederlande, niederländisch, Niederländer**

New Zealand **Neuseeland, neuseeländisch, Neuseeländer**

Northern Ireland **Nordirland, nordirisch, Nordire**

Norway **Norwegen, norwegisch, Norweger**

Pakistan **Pakistan, pakistanisch, Pakistaner**

Palestine **Palästina, palästinensisch, Palästinenser**

Poland **Polen, polnisch, Pole**

Portugal **Portugal, portugiesisch, Portugiese**

Romania **Rumänien, rumänisch, Rumäne**

Russia **Rußland, russisch, Russe**

Saudi Arabia **Saudi-Arabien, saudiarabisch, Saudi(s)**

Scandinavia **Skandinavien, skandinavisch, Skandinavier**

Scotland **Schottland, schottisch, Schotte**

Slovakia **die Slowakei, slowakisch, Slowake**

South Africa **Südafrika, südafrikanisch, Südafrikaner**

South America **Südamerika, südamerikanisch, Südamerikaner**

Spain **Spanien, spanisch, Spanier**

Sudan **der Sudan, sudanesisch, Sudanese**

Swabia **Schwaben, schwäbisch, Schwabe**

Sweden **Schweden, schwedisch, Schwede**

Switzerland **die Schweiz, schweizerisch, Schweizer**

Turkey **die Türkei, türkisch, Türke**

Wales **Wales, walisisch, Waliser**

The East German states **die neuen Bundesländer**

European Community **die Europäische Gemeinschaft**

European Union **die Europäische Union**

The Far East **der Ferne Osten**
The Near East **der Nahe Osten**
United Kingdom **das Vereinigte Königreich**
United States **die Vereinigten Staaten, die USA** *(pl)*

Former countries

Czechoslovakia **die Tschechoslowakei**
East Germany **die DDR (Deutsche Demokratische Republik)**
Jugoslavia **Jugoslawien**
West Germany **die BRD (die Bundesrepublik Deutschland)**
Soviet Union **die Sowjetunion**
Soviet *(adj)* **sowjetisch**
USSR **die UdSSR** *(pl)*

20a Some towns

The adjectives are formed in most cases by adding **-er**. The capital letter is retained, e.g. **der Kölner Dom**.
Note: **Basler, hannoverisch, mailändisch, Münchner, römisch**.
The inhabitant ends in **-er**, fem. **-erin**. Note: **Hannoveraner, Mailänder, Münchner, Römer**.

Aix -la-Chapelle **Aachen**
Antwerp **Antwerpen**
Athens **Athen**
Basle **Basel**
Belgrade **Belgrad**
Bruges **Brügge**
Brussels **Brüssel**
Cairo **Kairo**
Cologne **Köln**
Dunkirk **Dünkirchen**
Edinburgh **Edinburg**
Geneva **Genf**
the Hague **Den Haag**
Hanover **Hannover**
Liege **Lüttich**
Lisbon **Lissabon**
Milan **Mailand**
Moscow **Moskau**
Mulhouse **Mülhausen**
Munich **München**
Naples **Neapel**

Nice **Nizza**
Nuremberg **Nürnberg**
Prague **Prag**
Rome **Rom**
Strasbourg **Straßburg**
Venice **Venedig**
Vienna **Wien**
Warsaw **Warschau**
Zurich **Zürich**

20a Rivers, lakes, mountains

Alps **die Alpen**
Antarctic **die Antarktis**
Antarctic Circle **der südliche Polarkreis**
Antartic Ocean **das Südpolarmeer**
Arctic **die Arktis**
Arctic Circle **der nördliche Polarkreis**
Arctic Ocean **das Nordpolarmeer**
Atlantic **der Atlantik**
Baltic **die Ostsee**
Caspian Sea **das Kaspische Meer**
Danube **die Donau**
Dead Sea **das Tote Meer**
Everest **der Mount Everest**
Himalayas **der Himalaja**
Lake Constance **der Bodensee**
Mediterranean **das Mittelmeer**
Moselle **die Mosel**
North Pole **der Nordpol**
North See **die Nordsee**
Pacific **der Pazifik, der Stille Ozean**
Pyrenees **die Pyrenäen**
Red Sea **das Rote Meer**
Rhine **der Rhein**
South Pole **der Südpol**
Thames **die Themse**
Vesuvius **der Vesuv**
Volga **die Wolga**

21a Languages*

Afrikaans **Afrikaans**
Basque **Baskisch**
Celtic *(adj)* **keltisch**
Flemish **Flämisch**
Gaelic **Gälisch**
Germanic *(adj)* **germanisch**

* For other languages ➤App.20a Countries/Regions-adjectives-inhabitants

Hindi **Hindi**
Indo-European *(adj)* **indoeuropäisch**
Indo-Germanic *(adj)* **indogermanisch**
Latin **Latein, Lateinische**
Low German **Plattdeutsch**
Romance *(adj)* **romanisch**
Slavonic *(adj)* **slawisch**
Swiss German **Schweizerdeutsch**
Urdu **Urdu**

21b Grammar

accusative **der Akkusativ**
   accusative *(adj)* **Akkusativ-**
adjective **das Adjektiv(e)**
adverb **das Adverb(ien)**
agreement **die Übereinstimmung(en)**
it agrees with **es stimmt mit +dat**
   überein*
article **der Artikel(-)**
case **der Fall(-̈e)**
case ending **die Endung(en)**
clause **der Satz(-̈e)**
comparative **der Komparativ**
conjunction **die Konjunktion(en)**
dative **der Dativ**
declension **die Deklination(en)**
definite **bestimmt**
demonstrative **Demonstrativ-**
direct object **das direkte Objekt(e)**
exception **die Ausnahme(n)**
feminine **weiblich**
gender **das Geschlecht(er)**
genitive **der Genitiv**
indefinite **unbestimmt**
indirect object **das indirekte Objekt(e)**
interrogative **der Interrogativ**
masculine **männlich**
negative **negativ**
neuter **sächlich**
nominative **der Nominativ**
noun **das Substantiv(e), das Nomen(-)**
object **das Objekt(e)**
phrase **die Phrase(n)**
plural **der Plural, die Mehrzahl**
possessive **Possessiv-**
prefix **die Vorsilbe(n)**
preposition **die Präposition(en)**

pronoun **das Pronomen (-a)**
   interrogative **das**
   Interrrogativpronomen
   personal **das Personalpronomen**
   relative **das Relativpronomen**
reflexive **Reflexiv-**
rule **die Regel(n)**
sequence (of words) **die Wortfolge(n)**
singular **die Einzahl, der Singular**
suffix **die Nachsilbe(n)**
superlative **der Superlativ(e)**
subject **das Subjekt(e)**
syntax **die Syntax**
word order **die Wortstellung(en)**

Verbs

active voice **das Aktiv**
auxiliary **das Hilfsverb(en)**
compound **zusammengesetzt**
conditional **der Konditional**
formation **die Bildung(en)**
future **das Futur**
gerund **das Gerundium**
imperative **der Imperativ**
imperfect **das Imperfekt**
impersonal **unpersönlich**
infinitive **der Infinitiv**
intransitive **intransitiv**
irregular **unregelmäßig**
passive voice **das Passiv**
participle **das Partizip**
   past participle **das Partizip Perfekt**
past **die Vergangenheit**
   past *(adj)* **vergangen**
perfect **das Perfekt**
person **die Person(en)**
   first person singular **erste Person**
   Singular
present **das Präsens**
reflexive **das Reflexiv**
   reflexive *(adj)* **reflexiv**
regular **regelmäßig**
sequence (of verbs) **die Zeitenfolge(n)**
simple **einfach**
stem **der Stamm(-̈e)**
strong **stark**
subjunctive **der Konjunktiv**

system **das System(e)**
tense **die Zeitform(en)**
transitive **transitiv**
use **der Gebrauch**
verb **das Verb(en)**
weak **schwach**

21b Punctuation

apostrophe **der Apostroph(e)**
asterisk **das Sternchen(-)**
bracket **die Klammer(n)**
colon **der Doppelpunkt(e)**
comma **das Komma(s)**
dash **der Bindestrich(e)**
decimal point **das Komma(s)**
exclamation mark **das Ausrufezeichen(-)**
full stop/period **der Punkt(e)**
inverted comma **das Anführungszeichen(-)**
parentheses **die Klammer(n)**
question mark **das Fragezeichen(-)**
semicolon **das Semikolon(s), der Strichpunkt(e)**

22b The class in Germany

die Vorklasse(n) reception class
die Grundstufe(n) primary phase
die erste Klasse Class 1 (age 6/7)
die zweite Klasse Class 2 (age 7/8)
die dritte Klasse Class 3 (age 8/9)
die vierte Klasse Class 4 (age 9/10)
die Orientierungsstufe(n) transition phase
die fünfte Klasse Class 5 (age 10/11)
die sechste Klasse Class 6 (age 11/12)
die Sekundarstufe(n) secondary phase
die siebte Klasse Class 7 (age 12/13)
die achte Klasse Class 8 (age 13/14)
die neunte Klasse Class 9 (age 14/15)
die zehnte Klasse Class 10 (age 15/16)
die Oberstufe(n) sixth form/final years
in der Oberstufe in the sixth form/final years
die Einführungsphase Class 11 (age 16/17)
die elfte Klasse Class 11 (age 16/17)

die zwölfte Klasse (die Unterprima) Class 12 (age 17/18)
die dreizehnte Klasse (die Oberprima) Class 13 (age 18/19)

22b Stationery

adhesive tape **der Tesafilm**
ball-point **der Kugelschreiber(-)**
biro **der Kuli(s)**
boardrubber/eraser **der Schwamm(ⁱe)**
carbon paper **das Kohlepapier**
card index **die Kartei(en)**
chalk **die Kreide(n)**
clip board **das Klemmbrett(er)**
compasses **der Zirkel(-)**
correction fluid **die Korrekkurflüssigkeit(en)**
diary/datebook **der Terminkalender(-)**
drawing pin **die Reißzwecke(n)**
envelope **der Briefumschlag(ⁱe)**
exercise book **das Heft(e)**
felt-tip **der Filzstift(e)**
fiber/fiber-tip **der Faserschreiber(-)**
file **die Akte(n)**
filing cabinet **der Aktenschrank(ⁱe)**
fountain pen **der Füllfederhalter(-)**
glue **der Klebstoff(e)**
guillotine **die Schneidemaschine**
highlighter **der Textmarker(-)**
hole punch **der Locher(-)**
ink **die Tinte(n)**
ink refill **die Nachfüllpatrone(n)**
in-tray/out-tray **die Ablage für Eingänge/Ausgänge**
label **das Etikett(e)**
marker **der Stift(e), der Marker(-)**
note book **das Notizbuch(ⁱer)**
note paper **das Briefpapier(e)**
OHP **der Overheadprojector**
paper **das Papier(e)**
paper clip **die Büroklammer(n)**
pen **der Stift(e)**
pencil **der Bleistift(e)**
photocopier **der Kopierer(-)**
pocket calculator **der Taschenrechner(-)**
protractor **der Winkelmesser(-)**
ring binder **der Ringordner(-)**

rubber band/elastic band **der Gummiband(⁻er)**
rubber/eraser **der Radiergummi(s)**
ruler **das Lineal(e)**
scissors **die Schere(n)**
screen **der Bildschirm(e)**
set square **das Zeichendreieck(e)**
sheet of paper **das Blatt(⁻er)**
shredder **der Papierwolf(⁻e)**
stamp **der Stempel(-)**
stapler **der Bürohefter(-)**
staple remover **der Heftklammerentferner(-)**
text-book **das Lehrbuch(⁻er)**
typewriter **die Schreibmaschine(n)**
typewriter ribbon **das Farbband(⁻er)**
transparency **das Transparent(e), die Folie(n)**
waste-paper basket **der Abfalleimer(-), der Papierkorb(⁻e)**
whiteboard **die Weißwand(⁻e)**

23a Scientific disciplines

applied sciences **die angewandten Wissenschaft(en)**
anthropology **die Anthropologie(n)**
astronomy **die Astronomie**
biochemistry **die Biochemie**
biology **die Biologie**
botany **die Botanik**
chemistry **die Chemie**
geology **die Geologie**
medicine **die Medizin**
microbiology **die Mikrobiologie**
physics **die Physik**
physical sciences **die Naturwissenschaft(en)**
physiology **die Physiologie**
psychology **die Psychologie**
social sciences **die Sozialwissenschaft(en)**
technology **die Technologie(n)**
zoology **die Zoologie**

23b Chemical elements

aluminium/aluminum **das Aluminium**
arsenic **das Arsenik**

calcium **das Kalzium**
carbon **der Kohlenstoff**
chlorine **das Chlor**
copper **das Kupfer**
gold **das Gold**
hydrogen **der Wasserstoff**
iodine **das Jod**
iron **das Eisen**
lead **das Blei**
magnesium **das Magnesium**
mercury **das Quecksilber**
nitrogen **der Stickstoff**
oxygen **der Sauerstoff**
phosphorus **der Phosphor**
platinum **das Platin**
plutonium **das Plutonium**
potassium **das Kalium**
silver **das Silber**
sodium **das Natrium**
sulphur **der Schwefel**
uranium **das Uran**
zinc **das Zink**

23b Minerals, compounds & alloys

acetic acid **die Essigsäure(n)**
alloy **die Metallegierung(en)**
ammonia **das Ammoniak**
asbestos **der Asbest**
bauxite **der Bauxit**
brass **das Messing**
carbon dioxide **das Kohlendioxid(e)**
carbon monoxide **das Kohlenmonoxid(e)**
chalk **die Kreide(n)**
chalky **kalkhaltig**
clay **der Lehm**
copper oxide **das Kupferoxid(e)**
diamond **der Diamant(en)** *(wk)*
granite **der Granit(e)**
graphite **der Graphit(e)**
hydrochloric acid **die Salzsäure(n)**
iron oxide **das Eisenoxid(e)**
lead oxide **das Bleioxid(e)**
lime **der Kalk(e)**
limestone **der Kalkstein(e)**
loam **der Lehm**
marble **der Marmor**

nickel   der Nickel
nitric acid   die Salpetersäure(n)
it oxidizes   es oxydiert
ore   das Erz(e)
ozone   das Ozon
propane   das Propan
quartz   der Quarz(e)
sand   der Sand
sandstone   der Sandstein(e)
silica   die Kieselerde
silver nitrate   das Silbernitrat(e)
slate   der Schiefer
sodium bicarbonate   das Natron
sodium carbonate   das Natriumkarbonat(e)
sodium chloride   das Natriumchlorid(e)
sulphuric acid   die Schwefelsäure(n)
tin   das Zinn

23c The zodiac

Aries   der Widder(-)
Taurus   der Stier(e)
Gemini   die Zwillinge (pl)
Cancer   der Krebs(e)
Leo   der Löwe(n)
Virgo   die Jungfrau(en)
Libra   die Waage(n)
Scorpio   der Skorpion(e)
Sagittarius   der Schütze(n)
Capricorn   der Steinbock(-e)
Aquarius   der Wassermann(-er)
Pisces   die Fische (pl)

23c Planets & stars

Earth   die Erde
Venus   die Venus
Mercury   der Merkur
Pluto   der Pluto
Mars   der Mars
Jupiter   der Jupiter
Saturn   der Saturn
Uranus   der Uranus
Neptune   der Neptun
Pole star   der Polarstern
Halley's comet   der Halleysche Komet
Southern cross   das Kreuz des Südens
Great Bear   der Große Bär (wk)

24a Geographical features

archipelago   der Archipel(e)
bank (river)   das Ufer(-)
bay   die Bucht(en)
beach   der Strand(-e)
canyon   der Cañon(s)
cliff   die Klippe(n)
coast(line)   die Küste(n)
creek   die Bucht(en)
current   die Strömung(en), der Strom
delta   das Delta(s)
desert   die Wüste(n)
escarpment   der Steilhang(-e), die Böschung(en)
estuary   die (Fluß)mündung(en)
fjord   der Fjord(e)
foothills   die Gebirgsausläufer (pl)
forest   der Wald(-er)
    coniferous forest   der Nadelwald(-er)
    deciduous forest   der Laubwald(-er)
geyser   der Geysir(e)
heath   die Heide
hill   der Hügel(-), der Berg(e)
island   die Insel(n), die Hallig(en)
jungle   der Dschungel(-), der Urwald(-er)
lake   der See(n)
marsh   der Sumpf(-e)
meadow   die Wiese(n)
moor   das Hochmoor(e)
mountain   der Berg(e)
    mountains   das Gebirge(-)
mountain range   die Bergkette(n), die Gebirgskette(n)
mudflat   das Watt
ocean   der Ozean(e), das Meer(e)
ocean floor   der Meeresboden(-)
peak   der Gipfel(-), die Bergspitze(n)
peninsula   die Halbinsel(n)
plateau   das Plateau(s), die Hochebene(n)
reef   das Riff(e)
ridge   der Rücken
river   der Fluß (-sse)
    river (major)   der Strom(-e)

riverbed **das Flußbett(en)**
rockpool **die Vertiefung in einer Felsplatte**
sea **die See(n), das Meer(e)**
  shallow sea **das Wattenmeer**
by the seaside **am Meer**
shore **das Ufer(-), der Strand(ˉe)**
spring **die Quelle(n)**
steppe **die Steppe(n)**
stream **der Bach(ˉe), die Strömung(en)**
tundra **die Tundra (-en)**
valley **das Tal(ˉer)**
volcano **der Vulkan(e)**
waterfall **der Wasserfall(ˉe)**
wood **der Wald(ˉer)**
woodland **das Waldland(ˉer)**

24b Wild animals

badger **der Dachs(e)**
bear **der Bär(en)** *(wk)*
beaver **der Biber(-)**
bison/buffalo **der Büffel(-)**
coyote **der Kojote(n)** *(wk)*
deer **der Hirsch(e)**
elephant **der Elefant(en)** *(wk)*
elk **der Elch(e)**
fox **der Fuchs(ˉe)**
frog **der Frosch(ˉe)**
grizzly bear **der Grizzlybär(en)** *(wk)*
hare **der Hase(n)**
hedgehog **der Igel(-)**
lion **der Löwe(n)** *(wk)*
lizard **die Eidechse(n)**
mole **der Maulwurf(ˉe)**
monkey **der Affe(n)** *(wk)*
moose **der Elch(e)**
mouse **die Maus(ˉe)**
otter **der Otter(-)**
rat **die Ratte(n)**
reindeer **das Ren(e)**
snake **die Schlange(n)**
tiger **der Tiger(-)**
toad **die Kröte(n)**
whale **der Wal(e)**
wildcat **die Wildkatze(n)**
wolf **der Wolf(ˉe)**

24b Birds

albatross **der Albatros(se)**
blackbird **die Amsel(n)**
bluetit **die Blaumeise(n)**
budgerigar **der Wellensittich(e)**
buzzard **der Bussard(e)**
chaffinch **der Buchfink(en)**
crow **die Krähe(n)**
dove **die Taube(n)**
eagle **der Adler(-)**
  golden eagle **der Steinadler(-)**
emu **der Emu(s)**
hawk/falcon **der Falke(n)** *(wk)*, **der Habicht(e)**
heron **der Reiher(-)**
hummingbird **der Kolibri(s)**
kingfisher **der Eisvogel(ˉ)**
magpie **die Elster(n)**
ostrich **der Strauß(e)**
owl **die Eule(n)**
parrot **der Papagei(en)**
peacock **der Pfau(e)**
pelican **der Pelikan(e)**
penguin **der Pinguin(e)**
robin **das Rotkehlchen(-)**
seagull **die Möwe(n)**
sparrow **der Sperling(e), der Spatz(en)**
starling **der Star(e)**
swallow **die Schwalbe(n)**
swan **der Schwan(ˉe)**
swift **der Mauersegler(-)**
thrush **die Drossel(n)**
woodpecker **der Specht(e)**
wren **der Zaunkönig(e)**

24b Parts of the animal body

beak **der Schnabel(ˉ)**
claw **die Kralle(n)**
comb **der Kamm(ˉe)**
feather **die Feder(n)**
fin **die Flosse(n)**
fleece **das Schaffell(e)**
fur **der Pelz(e)**
gills **die Kieme(n)**
hide **das Fell(e)**
hoof **der Huf(e)**

mane   die Mähne(n)
paw   die Pfote(n), die Tatze(n)
pelt   der Pelz(e), das Fell(e)
scale   die Schuppe(n)
shell   die Schale(n)
tail   der Schwanz(-̈e)
trunk   der Rüssel(-)
tusk   der Stoßzahn(-̈e)
udder   das Euter(-)
wing   der Flügel(-)

24c Trees

apple tree   der Apfelbaum(-̈e)
ash   die Esche(n)
beech   die Buche(n)
cherry tree   der Kirschbaum(-̈e)
chestnut   der Kastanienbaum(-̈e)
cypress   die Zypresse(n)
eucalyptus   der Eukalyptusbaum(-̈e)
fig tree   der Feigenbaum(-̈e)
fir tree   die Tanne(n), die Fichte(n)
fruit tree   der Obstbaum(-̈e)
holly   die Stechpalme(n)
maple   der Ahornbaum(-̈e)
oak   die Eiche(n)
olive tree   der Olivenbaum(-̈e)
palm   die Palme(n)
peach tree   der Pfirsichbaum(-̈e)
pear tree   der Birnbaum(-̈e)
pine   die Kiefer(n)
plum tree   der Pflaumenbaum(-̈e)
poplar   die Pappel(n)
rhododendron   der Rhododendron (-en)
walnut tree   der Walnußbaum(-̈e)
willow   die Weide(n)
yew   die Eibe(n)

24c Flowers & weeds

azalea   die Azalee(n)
cactus   der Kaktus (-een)
carnation   die Nelke(n)
chrysanthemum   die Chrysantheme(n)
clover   der Klee
crocus   der Krokus(se)
daffodil   die Osterglocke(n)
dahlia   die Dahlie(n)

daisy   das Gänseblümchen(-)
dandelion   der Löwenzahn(-̈e)
foxglove   der Fingerhut(-̈e)
fern   der Farn(e), das Farnkraut(-̈er)
geranium   die Geranie(n)
hydrangea   die Hortensie(n)
lily   die Seerose(n), die Lilie(n)
lily of the valley   das Maiglöckchen(-)
nettle (stinging)   die Nessel(n)
orchid   die Orchidee(n)
pansy   das Stiefmütterchen(-)
poppy   der Mohn
primrose   die Erdschlüsselblume(n)
rose   die Rose(n)
snowdrop   das Schneeglöckchen(-)
sunflower   die Sonnenblume(n)
thistle   die Distel(n)
tulip   die Tulpe(n)
violet   das Veilchen(-)

25b Political institutions

assembly   die Versammlung(en)
association   der Verein(e), der Verband(-̈e)
cabinet   das Kabinett(e)
   shadow cabinet *(UK)*   das Schattenkabinett
confederation   der Bund(-̈e)
congress   der Kongreß (-sse)
council   der (Stadt)rat(-̈e)
federal council   der Bundesrat(-̈e)
federal government   der Bundestag(e)
federation   der Staatenbund(-̈e)
House of Representatives   das Repräsentantenhaus
local authority   die Behörde(n)
Lower Chamber/House   das Unterhaus(-̈er)
parliament *(UK)*   das Parlament(e)
party   die Partei(en), die Fraktion(en)
Senate   der Senat(e)
state parliament   der Landtag(e)
town council   der Stadtrat(-̈e)
town hall   das Rathaus(-̈er)
Upper House/Chamber   das Oberhaus(-̈er)

25b Representatives & politicians

Chancellor **der Kanzler(-) [-in]**
   federal chancellor **der**
   Bundeskanzler(-)
congressman/woman **der/die**
   Kongreßabgeordnete *(adj/n)*
Foreign Minister/Secretary of State **der**
   Außenminister(-) [-in]
head of state **das Staatsoberhaupt(-̈er)**
leader **der Fraktionschef(s) [-in]**
leader of the party/party leader **der/die**
   Parteivorsitzende *(adj/n)*
mayor **der Bürgermeister(-) [-in]**
member of parliament **der/die**
   Abgeordnete *(adj/n)*
minister **der Minister(-) [-in]**
Home Secretary/Minister of the Interior
   der Innenminister(-) [-in]
politician **der Politiker(-) [-in]**
President **der Präsident(en)** *(wk)* **[-in]**
   federal president **der**
   Bundespräsident(en) *(wk)* **[-in]**
Prime Minister **der Premierminister(-)**
   [-in]
representative **der/die Abgeordnete**
   (adj/n)
senator **der Senator(en)**
Speaker **der (Regierungs)sprecher(-)**
   [-in], der/die Vorsitzende *(adj/n)*

German political parties

BRD/Bundesrepublik Deutschlands
   German Federal Republic
DDR/Deutsche Demokratische
   Republik German Democratic
   Republic
FDP/Freie Demokratische Partei Free
   Democratic party (centre)
die Grünen/Bündnis 90 Green parties
Linke Liste 15 far left
SED/Sozialistische Einheitspartei
   Deutschlands Socialist Party of
   unity (left)
CDU/Christlich-Demokratische Union
   Christian Democratic Union (right)
CSU/Christlich-Soziale Union
   Christian-Social Union (right)
PDS/Partei des Demokratischen
   Sozialismus Democratic Socialism
   Party (left)
KPD/Kommunistische Partei
   Deutschlands Communist Party
SDP Sozialdemokratische Partei
   Deutschlands Social Democratic
   Party (left)

27b Military ranks

admiral **der Admiral(e/-̈e)**
air marshal **der Marschall(-̈e) der**
   Luftstreitkräfte
brigadier **der Brigadegeneral(e)**
captain **der Hauptmann(-̈er) (-leute)**
commodore **der Flotillenadmiral(e/-̈e)**
corporal **der Obergefreite** *(adj/n)*
fieldmarshal **der Feldmarschall(-̈e)**
general **der General(e)**
lieutenant **der Leutnant(s)**
major **der Major(e)**
private **der einfache Soldat(en)** *(wk)*
rear-admiral **der Konteradmiral(e/-̈e)**
sergeant **der Feldwebel(-)**
sergeant-major **der Oberfeldwebel(-)**

27c International organizations

Council of Europe **der Europarat**
Council of Ministers **der Ministerrat**
EC/European Community **die**
   Europäische Gemeinschaft, EG
EU/European Union **die Europäische**
   Union, EU
NATO/North Atlantic Treaty Organization
   die Nato
OECD/Organization for Economic
   Cooperation and Development **die**
   OECD
Security Council **der Sicherheitsrat**
UNO/United Nations Organization **die**
   Vereinten Nationen, die UNO
WHO/World Health Organization **die**
   Weltgesundheitsorganisation, die
   WGO
World Bank **die Weltbank**

D
SUBJECT INDEX

Subject index

References are to Vocabularies